Shakespeare's
ROMEO & JULIET

THE MANGA EDITION

D1016869

Shakespeare's
ROMEO & JULIET

THE MANGA EDITION

Adam Sexton • Yali Lin

WILEY

Wiley Publishing, Inc.

Published by Wiley Publishing, Inc., Hoboken, New Jersey

For general information on our other products and services or to obtain technical support please contact our Customer Care Department within the U.S. at (800) 762-2974, outside the U.S. at (317) 572-3993 or fax (317) 572-4002.

Wiley also publishes its books in a variety of electronic formats. Some content that appears in print may not be available in electronic books. For more information about Wiley products, please visit our web site at www.wiley.com.

Library of Congress Control Number: 2007940644

ISBN: 978-0-470-09758-8

Printed in the United States of America

10 9 8 7 6 5

Book design by Elizabeth Brooks
Book production by Wiley Publishing, Inc. Composition Services

CONTENTS

Adam Sexton is author of *Master Class in Fiction Writing* and editor of the anthologies *Love Stories, Rap on Rap,* and *Desperately Seeking Madonna.* He has written on art and entertainment for *The New York Times* and *The Village Voice,* and he teaches fiction writing and literature at New York University and critical reading and writing at Parsons School of Design. A graduate of Columbia University and the University of Pennsylvania, he lives in Brooklyn with his wife and son.

Yali Lin was born in Guang Dong, southern China. She started drawing comics before she knew what they were. At the age of 11, she moved to New York City with her family and read her first comic book in seventh grade. Immediately she fell in love with the endless fantasy worlds one could create in this fast-growing medium. Her influences are found in Japanese manga, mainly Shojo. In May 2006, Yali graduated from the School of Visual Arts with a BFA in cartooning. She is currently drawing her second book and teaches cartooning classes to young children and teens in New York City.

Suiting the Action to the Word: Shakespeare and Manga

by Adam Sexton

> Suit the action to the word, the word to the action...
> —*Hamlet* (Act III, Scene 2)

Four hundred years after the writing of William Shakespeare's plays, it is clear that they are timeless. This is due in part to their infinite adaptability. The plays have been translated into dozens of languages and performed all over the world. Famously creative stage productions have included a version of *Julius Caesar* set in fascist Europe during the 1930s and a so-called "voodoo *Macbeth*." Nor have gender and age proved barriers to casting Shakespeare's characters. The role of Hamlet is occasionally played by a woman—an appropriate reversal, considering that boys acted all the female roles in Shakespeare's day—while the teenaged Romeo and Juliet have been portrayed by couples in their forties and fifties.

It is common knowledge that the plays of Shakespeare transfer especially well to the movie screen. Such has been the case since Thomas Edison made one of the first sound films ever using a scene from *As You Like It*. Recent cinema standouts include *William Shakespeare's Romeo + Juliet*, directed by Baz Luhrmann, and Michael Almereyda's *Hamlet*. Both take place in the present day or near future: Leonardo DiCaprio's Romeo wears a Hawaiian shirt—and Julia Stiles' Ophelia wears a wire, so Claudius and Polonius can eavesdrop on her conversation with Hamlet. Otherwise, these adaptations remain surprisingly faithful to Shakespeare's texts. And both hit the audience as hard as conventional stage productions in which the actors are outfitted with doublets and hose, crossed swords, and what Hamlet calls "a bare bodkin"—his unsheathed dagger (replaced in Almereyda's movie by a gun).

Shakespeare's plays have been set to music as well, in operas and ballets by composers such as Verdi, Tchaikovsky, and Prokofiev. The early comedy *Two Gentlemen of Verona* was adapted for Broadway by the composer of *Hair*, and it won the Tony award for Best Musical the same year that *Grease* was nominated. In the words of theater critic Jan Kott, Shakespeare is indeed "our contemporary."

In short, though some consider the plays of William Shakespeare to be sacrosanct, they have been cut, expanded (it was common in the Victorian era to add songs and even happy endings to the tragedies), and adapted to multiple media, emerging none the worse for wear. Although we cannot be sure of this, it seems likely that the writer, who was a popular artist and a savvy businessman as well as an incomparable poet, would approve.

The graphic novels known as *manga* (Japanese for "whimsical pictures") are a natural medium for Shakespeare's work. Like his tragedies, comedies, histories, and romances, which are thrillingly dynamic if properly staged, manga are of course visual. In fact, a manga is potentially *more* visual than a stage production of one of the plays of Shakespeare. Unbound by the physical realities of the theater, the graphic novel can depict any situation, no matter how fantastical or violent, that its creators are able to pencil, ink, and shade.

Take *Romeo and Juliet*'s famous Queen Mab speech. Even the most creative stage director cannot faithfully present the minuscule fairy described by Mercutio. Manga artists can. The same is true of the drowning of Ophelia in *Hamlet*. It is precisely because these vignettes are unstageable that Shakespeare has his characters describe Queen Mab and the death of Ophelia in such great detail—they must help us imagine them. In its unlimited ability to dramatize, the graphic novel more closely resembles a contemporary film with a colossal special-effects budget than anything produced onstage in the Elizabethan era or since.

At the same time, manga are potentially no less verbal than Shakespeare's spectacularly wordy plays, with this crucial difference: in a production of one of the plays onstage or onscreen, we can hear the words but can't see them. Though Shakespeare is never easy, reading helps. And that is precisely what manga adaptations of the plays allow. Perusing a Shakespeare manga, the reader can linger over speeches, rereading them in part or altogether. Especially in the long and intricate soliloquies typical of Shakespearean tragedy, this allows for an appreciation of the playwright's craft that is difficult if not impossible as those soliloquies move past us during a performance.

Overall, turning the pages of a manga version of one of Shakespeare's plays is something like reading the text of that play while attending a performance, but at one's own pace. Manga is not merely a new medium for the plays of William Shakespeare, but one that is distinctly different from anything to have come before.

A note on authenticity: In order to fit our adaptations into books of less than 200 pages, the writers and editors of *The Manga Editions* have cut words, lines, speeches, even entire scenes from Shakespeare's plays, a practice almost universal among stage and film directors. We have never paraphrased the playwright's language, however, nor have we summarized action. Everything you read in *The Manga Editions* was written by William Shakespeare himself. Finally, footnotes don't interrupt the characters' speeches here, any more than they would in a production of one of Shakespeare's plays onstage or on film.

If the plays of Shakespeare are cinematic, then Romeo and Juliet might be the most cinematic Shakespeare play of all. The screen adaptations of this tragedy directed by Luhrmann and his predecessor Franco Zeffirelli have succeeded at the box office compared not only to other films of Shakespeare's work but to other films in general. As motion pictures and graphic novels resemble one another closely, it follows that Romeo and Juliet and manga are something like a perfect fit.

Most likely it is the close proximity of violent action and romantic love within *Romeo and Juliet* that makes it equally adaptable to movie screen and manga page. The story opens with a riot and concludes following a double suicide, and its turning point is the unintended slaying of one character by another, followed quickly by a revenge killing. Yet the narrative is set into motion by a mutual instance of love at first sight, and *Romeo and Juliet* contains the most famous love scenes in the English language. Unlike productions of Shakespeare's plays on stage, movies allow us to watch action scenes from multiple angles as well as intimate close-ups of kisses. So do manga.

In fact, a single page of manga can present two or more separate scenes simultaneously, a technique the movies rarely utilize. On page 24 of *Shakespeare's Romeo and Juliet: The Manga Edition*, Juliet tells her mother that she will do her best to like Paris, the young man chosen as a suitable husband for her, when they meet at the Capulets' party that evening. On the same page, Romeo reiterates to Mercutio his imagined love for Rosaline, which he says has given him a "soul of lead" that will make dancing with her impossible. In other words, Juliet promises her family to feel something she doesn't, while Romeo insists with his friends on feelings he lacks—a combination that will contrast starkly with the true love both feel when they meet that night.

In dramatizing this story of "two households, both alike in dignity," a manga can show us both households at once.

ACT I

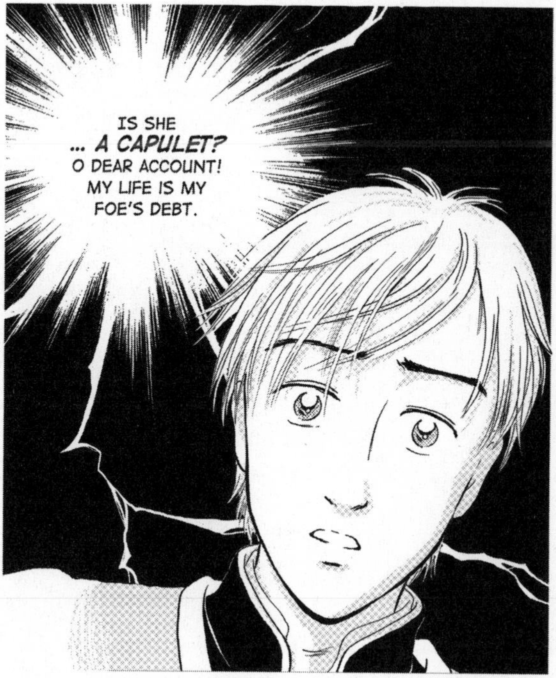
IS SHE
... A CAPULET?
O DEAR ACCOUNT!
MY LIFE IS MY
FOE'S DEBT.

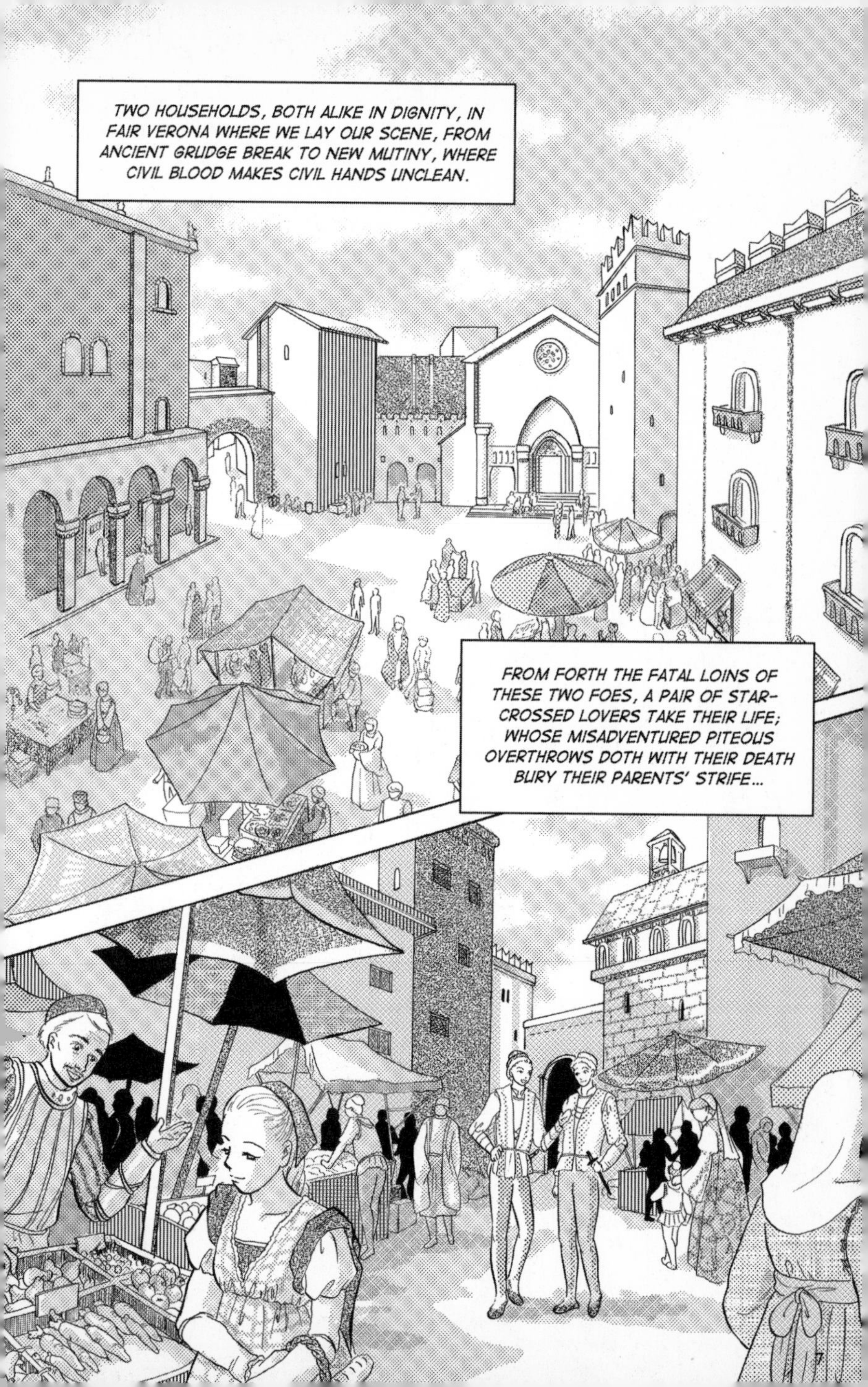
TWO HOUSEHOLDS, BOTH ALIKE IN DIGNITY, IN FAIR VERONA WHERE WE LAY OUR SCENE, FROM ANCIENT GRUDGE BREAK TO NEW MUTINY, WHERE CIVIL BLOOD MAKES CIVIL HANDS UNCLEAN.
FROM FORTH THE FATAL LOINS OF THESE TWO FOES, A PAIR OF STAR-CROSSED LOVERS TAKE THEIR LIFE; WHOSE MISADVENTURED PITEOUS OVERTHROWS DOTH WITH THEIR DEATH BURY THEIR PARENTS' STRIFE...

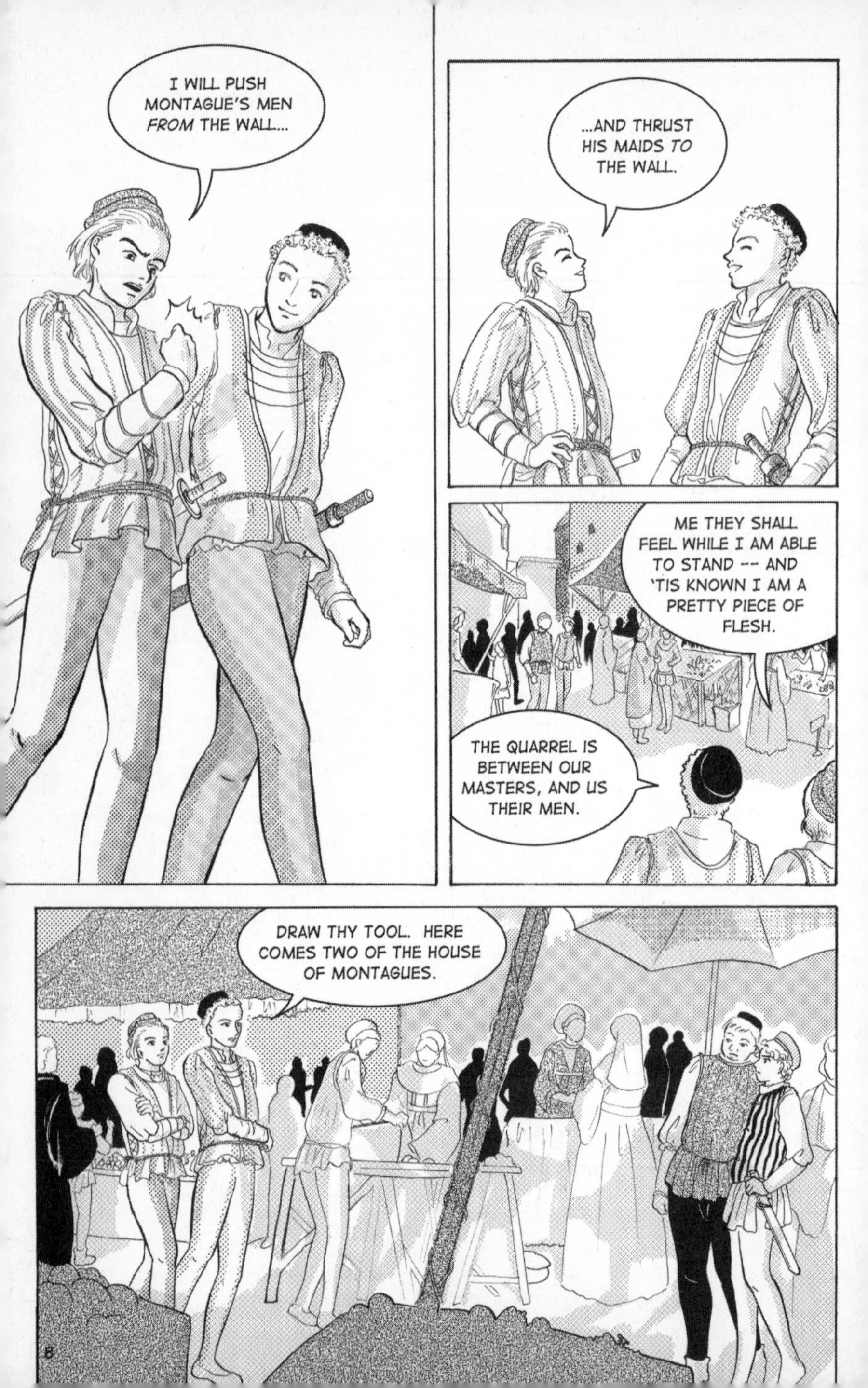
I WILL PUSH MONTAGUE'S MEN *FROM* THE WALL...
...AND THRUST HIS MAIDS *TO* THE WALL.
ME THEY SHALL FEEL WHILE I AM ABLE TO STAND -- AND 'TIS KNOWN I AM A PRETTY PIECE OF FLESH.
THE QUARREL IS BETWEEN OUR MASTERS, AND US THEIR MEN.
DRAW THY TOOL. HERE COMES TWO OF THE HOUSE OF MONTAGUES.

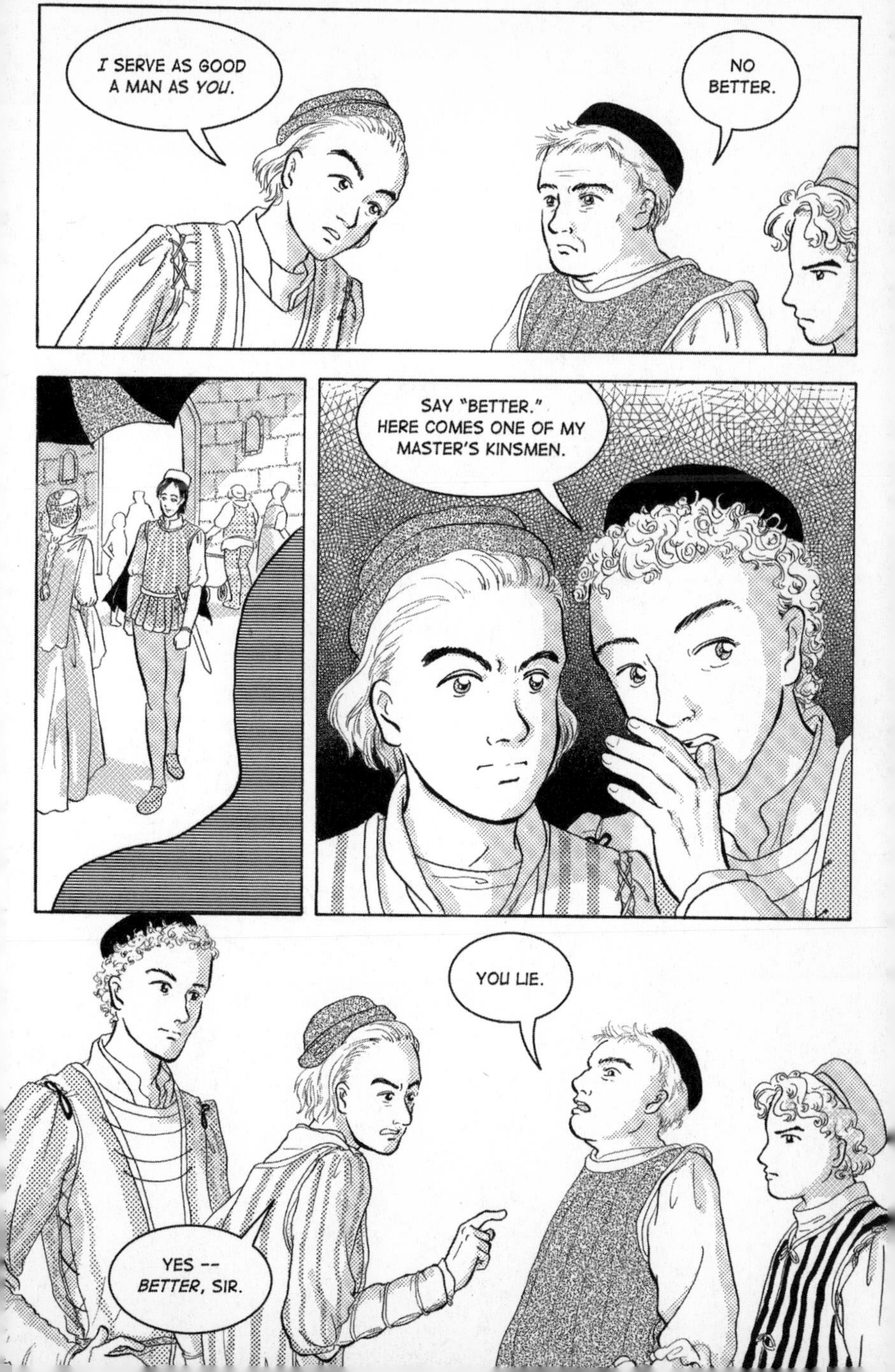
I SERVE AS GOOD A MAN AS *YOU*.
NO BETTER.
SAY "BETTER." HERE COMES ONE OF MY MASTER'S KINSMEN.
YOU LIE.
YES -- *BETTER*, SIR.

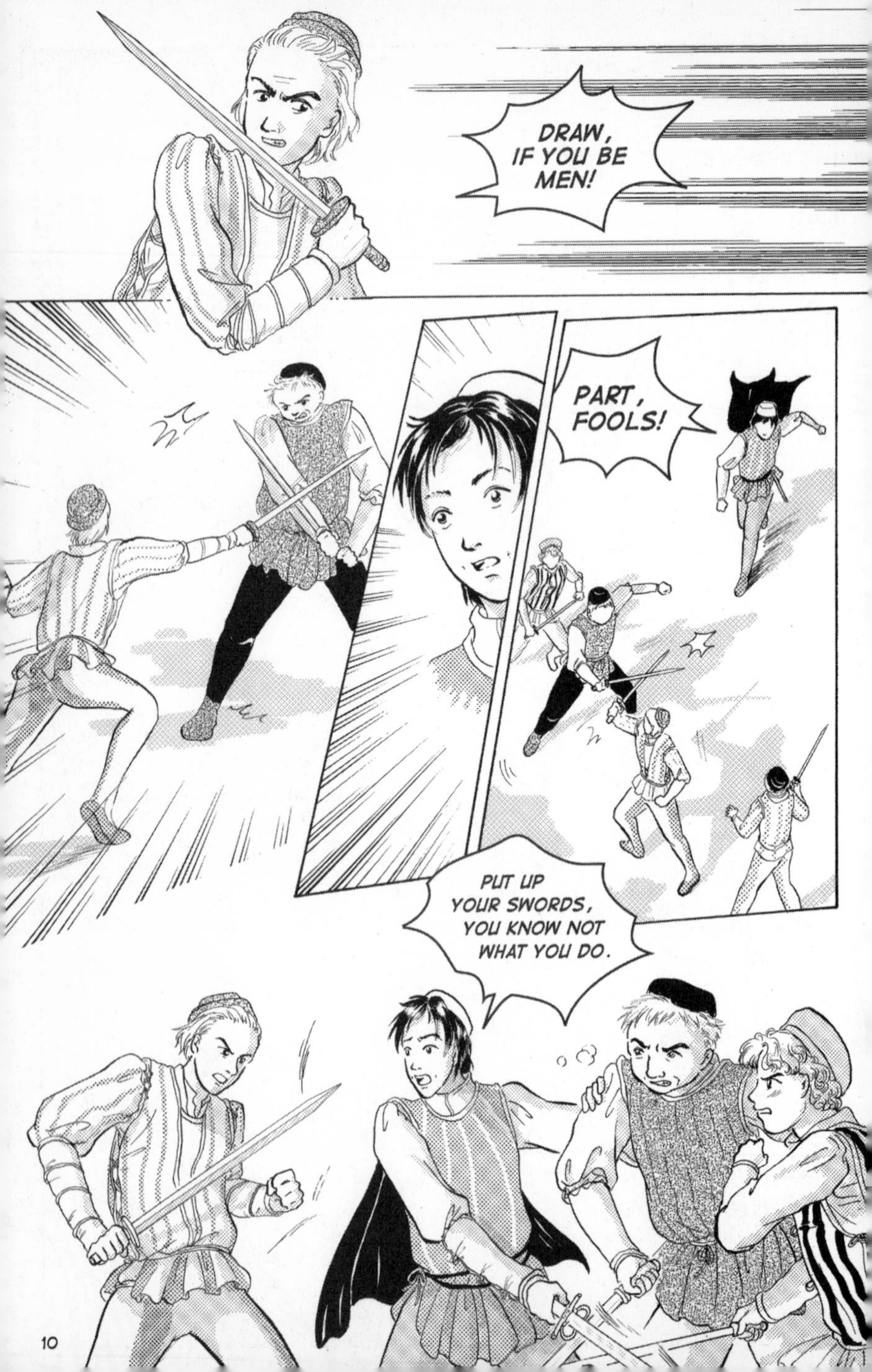
DRAW, IF YOU BE MEN!
PART, FOOLS!
PUT UP YOUR SWORDS, YOU KNOW NOT WHAT YOU DO.

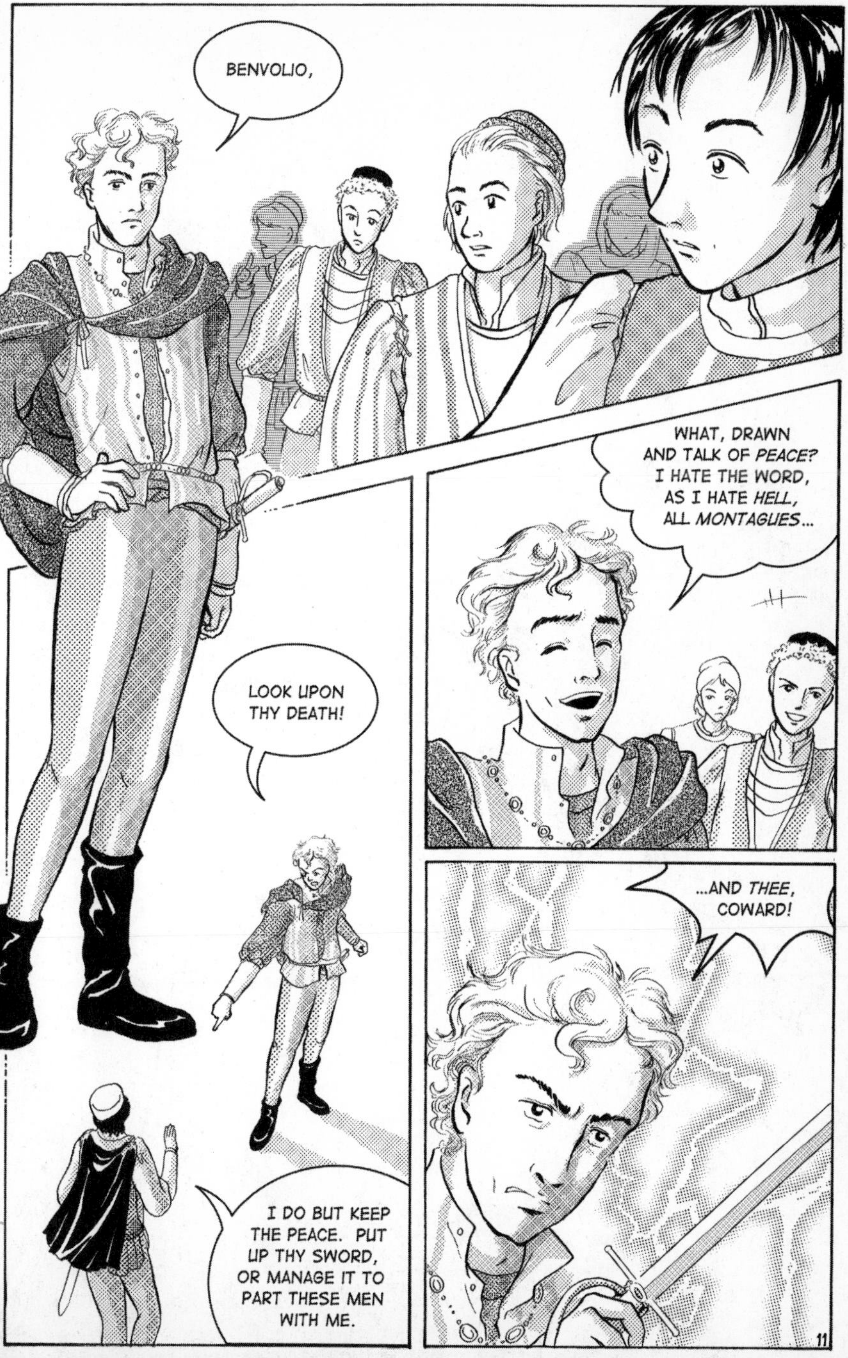
BENVOLIO,
LOOK UPON THY DEATH!
I DO BUT KEEP THE PEACE. PUT UP THY SWORD, OR MANAGE IT TO PART THESE MEN WITH ME.
WHAT, DRAWN AND TALK OF *PEACE?* I HATE THE WORD, AS I HATE *HELL*, ALL *MONTAGUES*...
...AND *THEE*, COWARD!

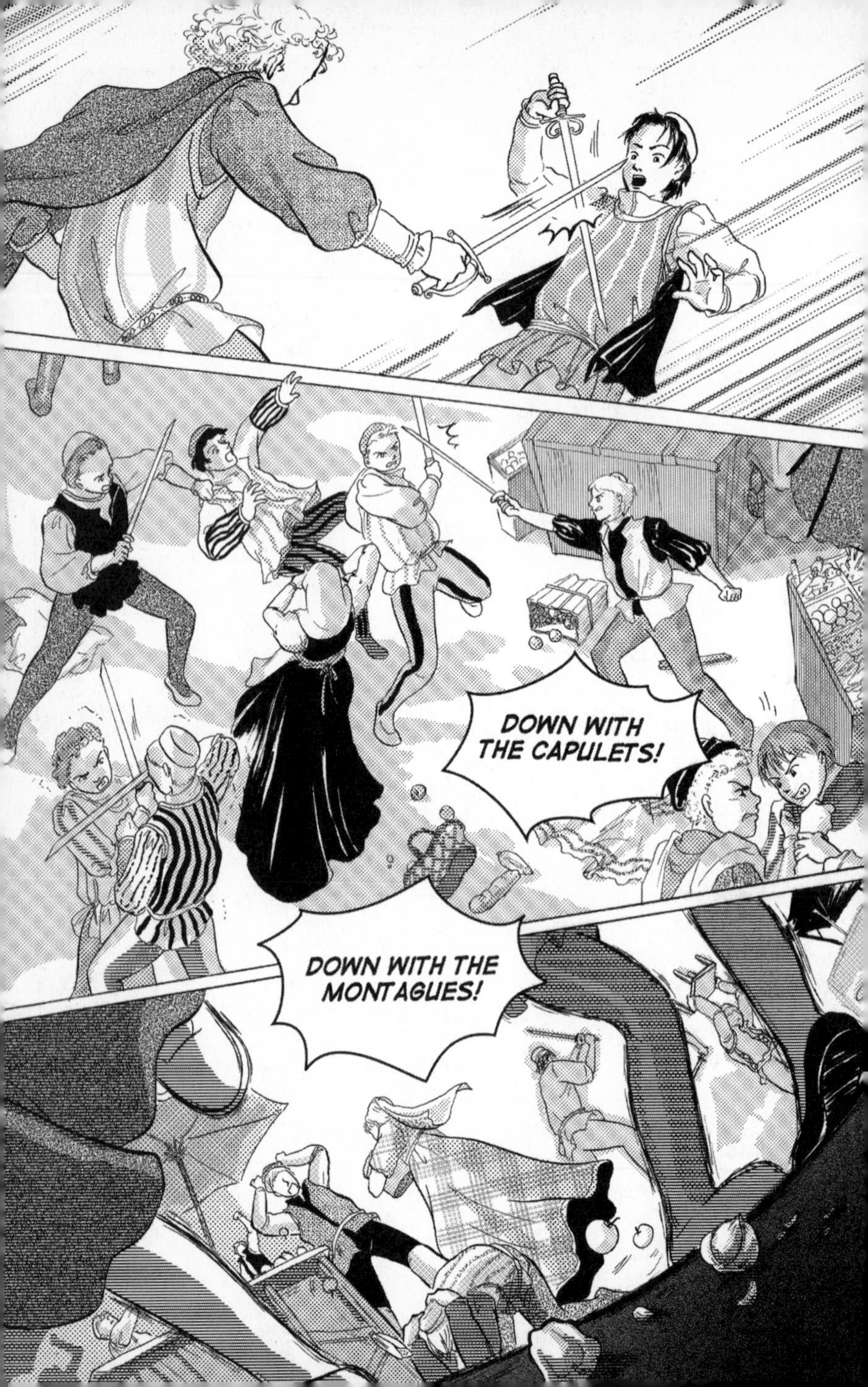
DOWN WITH THE CAPULETS!
DOWN WITH THE MONTAGUES!

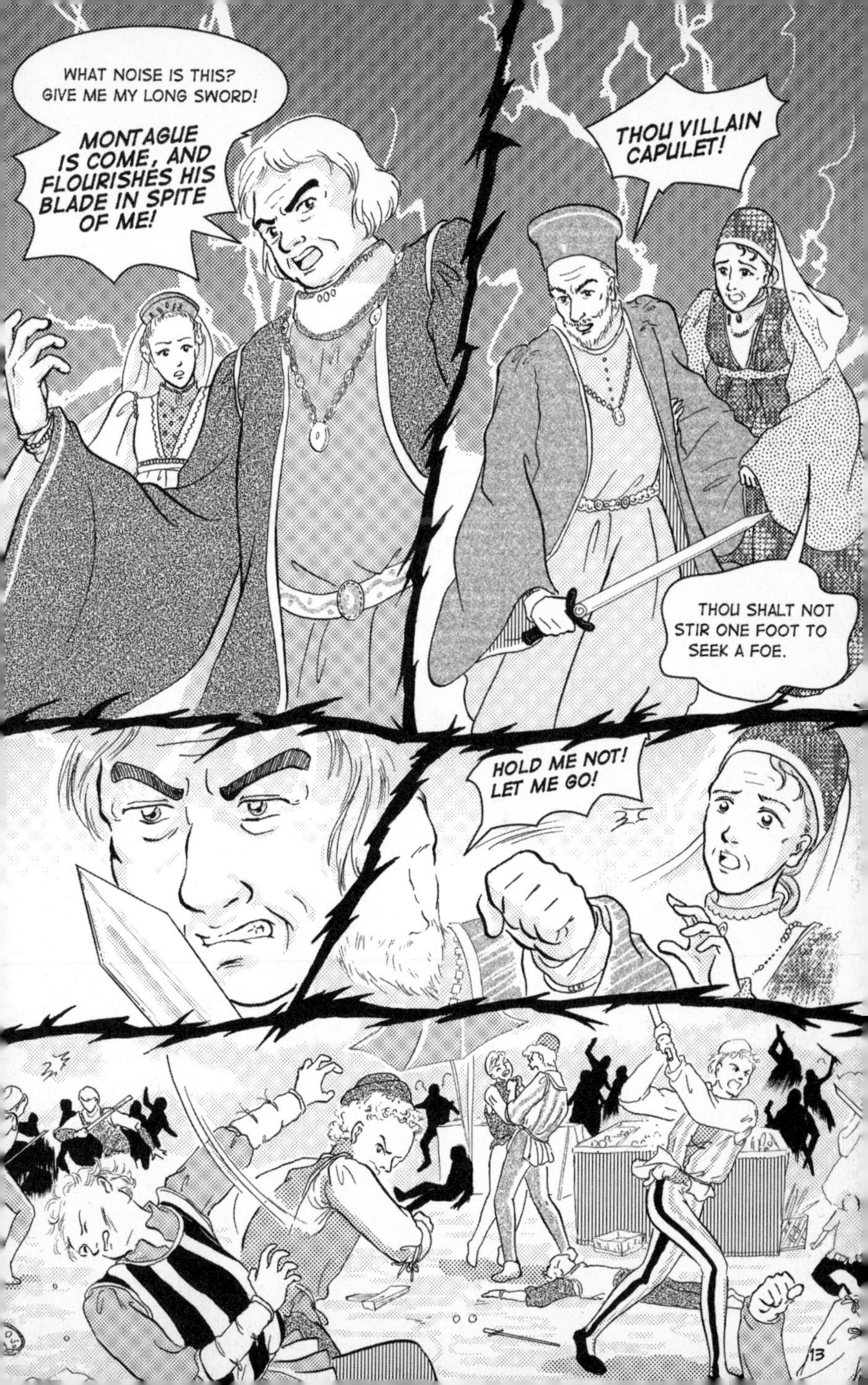
WHAT NOISE IS THIS? GIVE ME MY LONG SWORD!
MONTAGUE IS COME, AND FLOURISHES HIS BLADE IN SPITE OF ME!
THOU VILLAIN CAPULET!
THOU SHALT NOT STIR ONE FOOT TO SEEK A FOE.
HOLD ME NOT! LET ME GO!

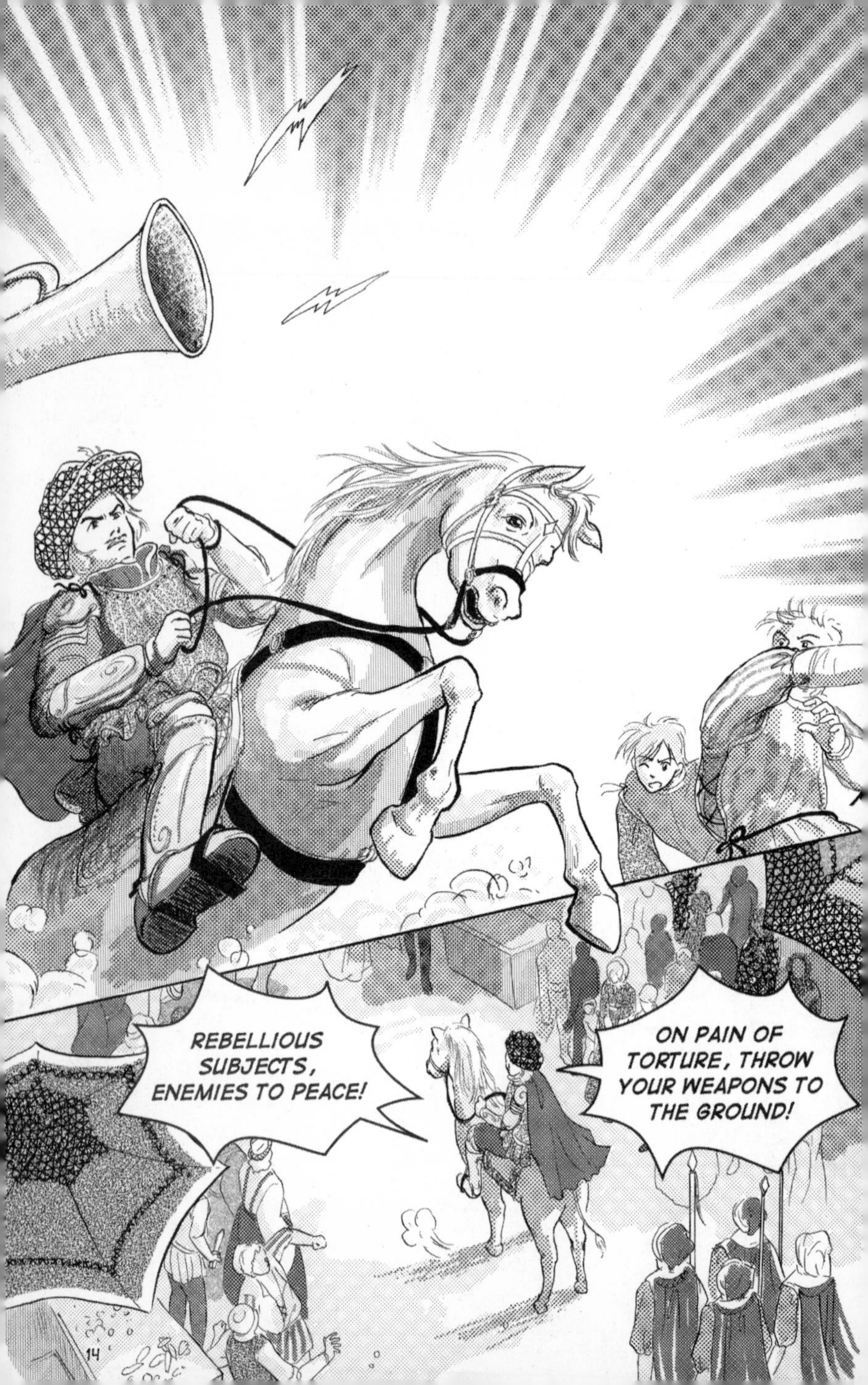
REBELLIOUS SUBJECTS, ENEMIES TO PEACE!
ON PAIN OF TORTURE, THROW YOUR WEAPONS TO THE GROUND!

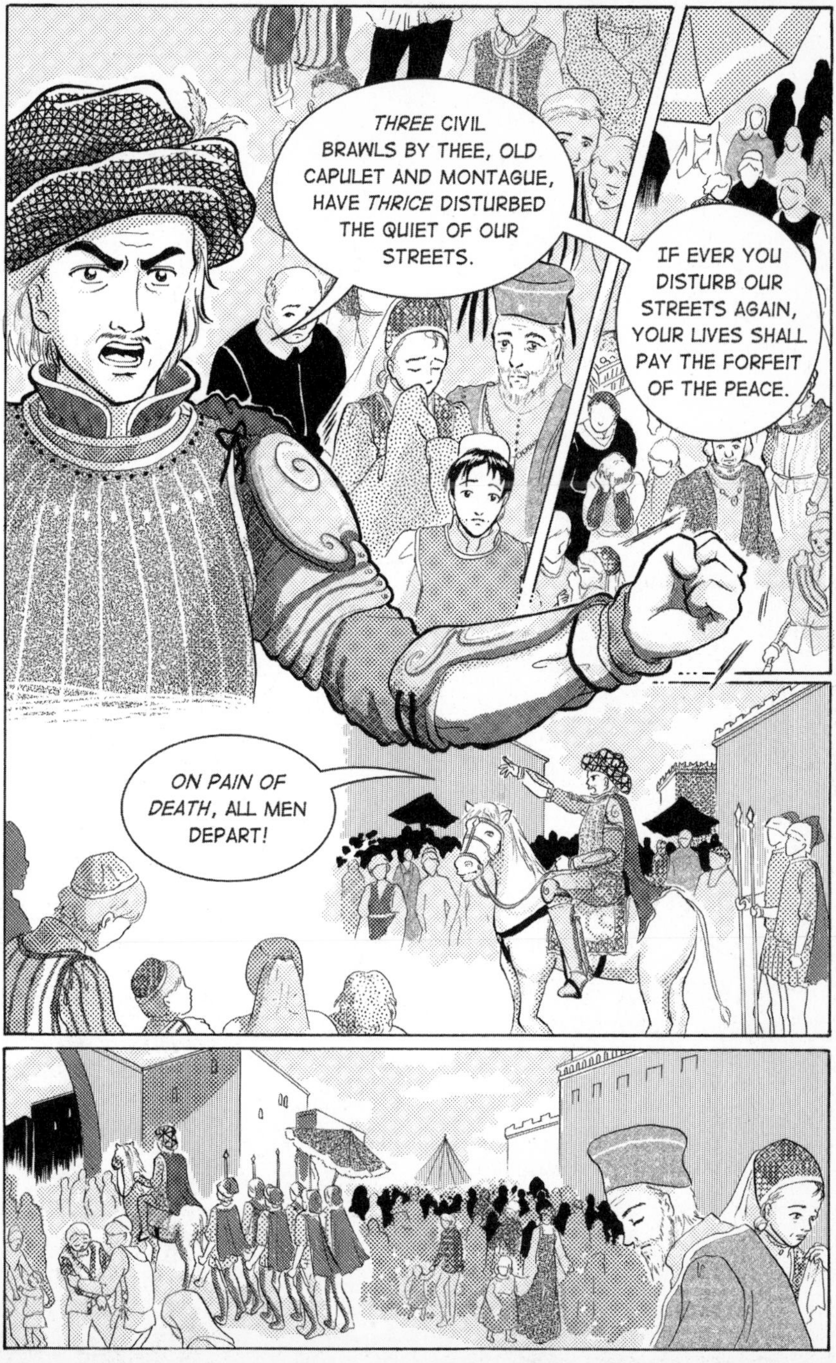
THREE CIVIL BRAWLS BY THEE, OLD CAPULET AND MONTAGUE, HAVE THRICE DISTURBED THE QUIET OF OUR STREETS.
IF EVER YOU DISTURB OUR STREETS AGAIN, YOUR LIVES SHALL PAY THE FORFEIT OF THE PEACE.
ON PAIN OF DEATH, ALL MEN DEPART!

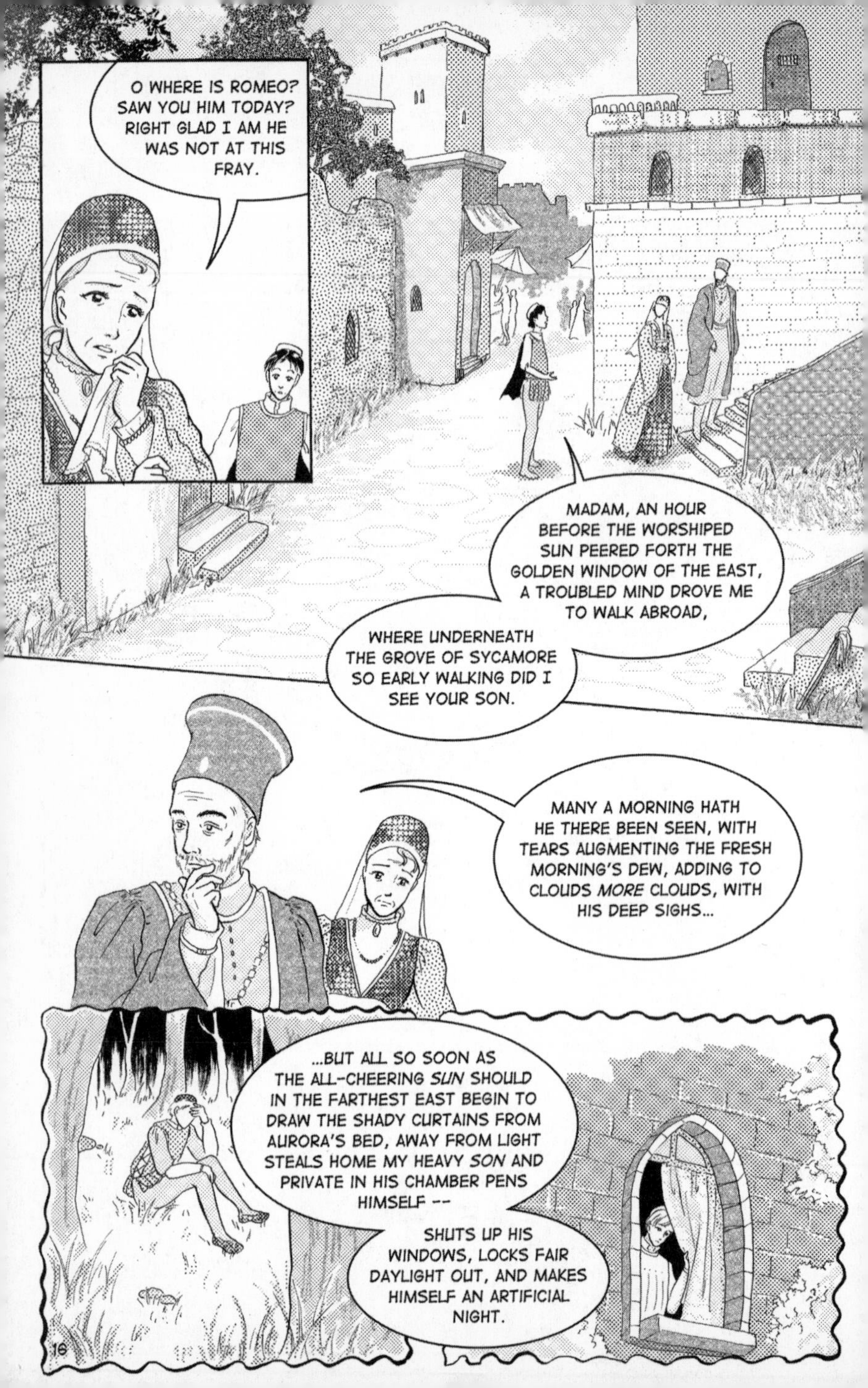
O WHERE IS ROMEO? SAW YOU HIM TODAY? RIGHT GLAD I AM HE WAS NOT AT THIS FRAY.
MADAM, AN HOUR BEFORE THE WORSHIPED SUN PEERED FORTH THE GOLDEN WINDOW OF THE EAST, A TROUBLED MIND DROVE ME TO WALK ABROAD,
WHERE UNDERNEATH THE GROVE OF SYCAMORE SO EARLY WALKING DID I SEE YOUR SON.
MANY A MORNING HATH HE THERE BEEN SEEN, WITH TEARS AUGMENTING THE FRESH MORNING'S DEW, ADDING TO CLOUDS *MORE* CLOUDS, WITH HIS DEEP SIGHS...
...BUT ALL SO SOON AS THE ALL-CHEERING *SUN* SHOULD IN THE FARTHEST EAST BEGIN TO DRAW THE SHADY CURTAINS FROM AURORA'S BED, AWAY FROM LIGHT STEALS HOME MY HEAVY *SON* AND PRIVATE IN HIS CHAMBER PENS HIMSELF --
SHUTS UP HIS WINDOWS, LOCKS FAIR DAYLIGHT OUT, AND MAKES HIMSELF AN ARTIFICIAL NIGHT.

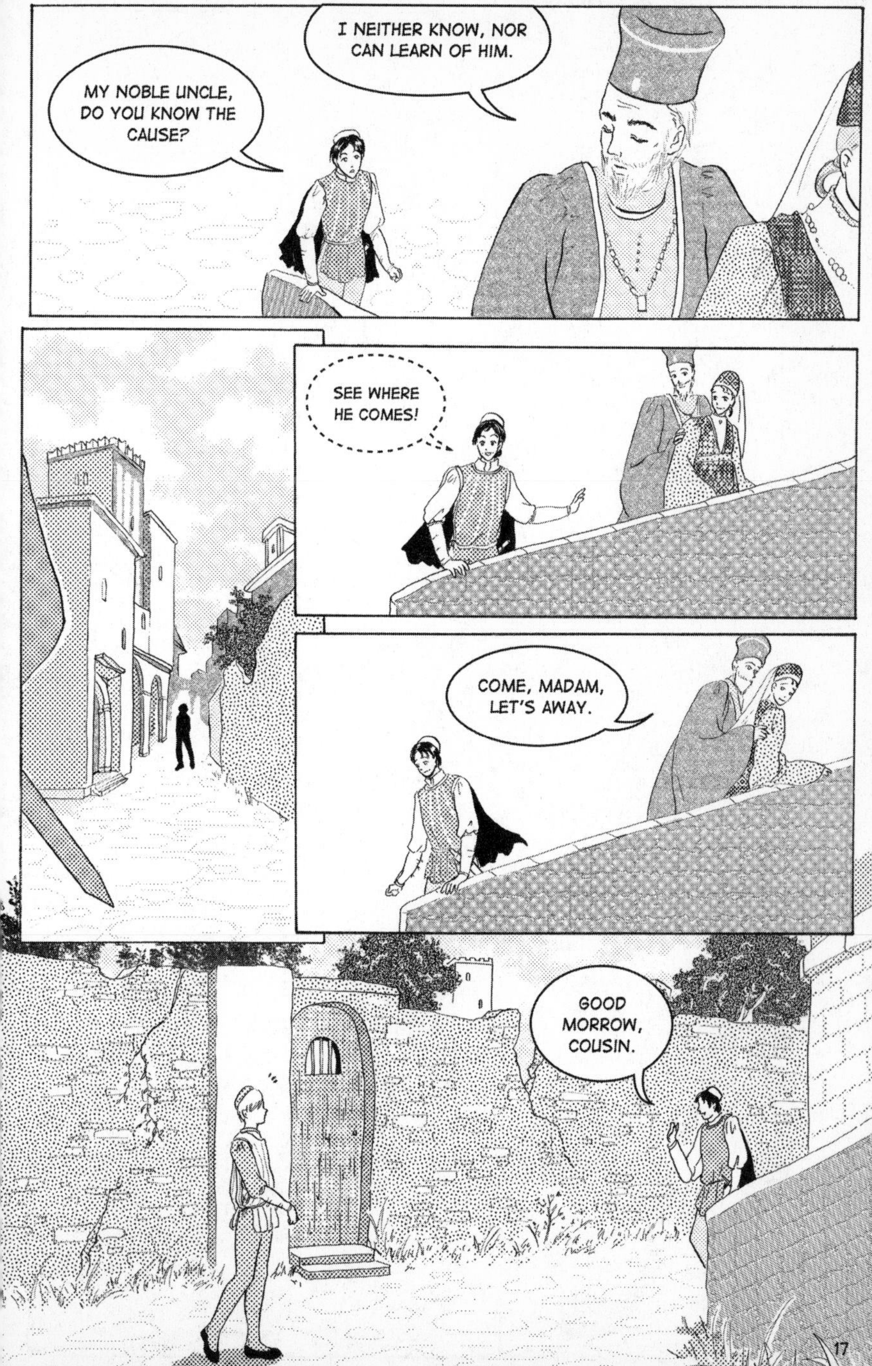
MY NOBLE UNCLE, DO YOU KNOW THE CAUSE?
I NEITHER KNOW, NOR CAN LEARN OF HIM.
SEE WHERE HE COMES!
COME, MADAM, LET'S AWAY.
GOOD MORROW, COUSIN.

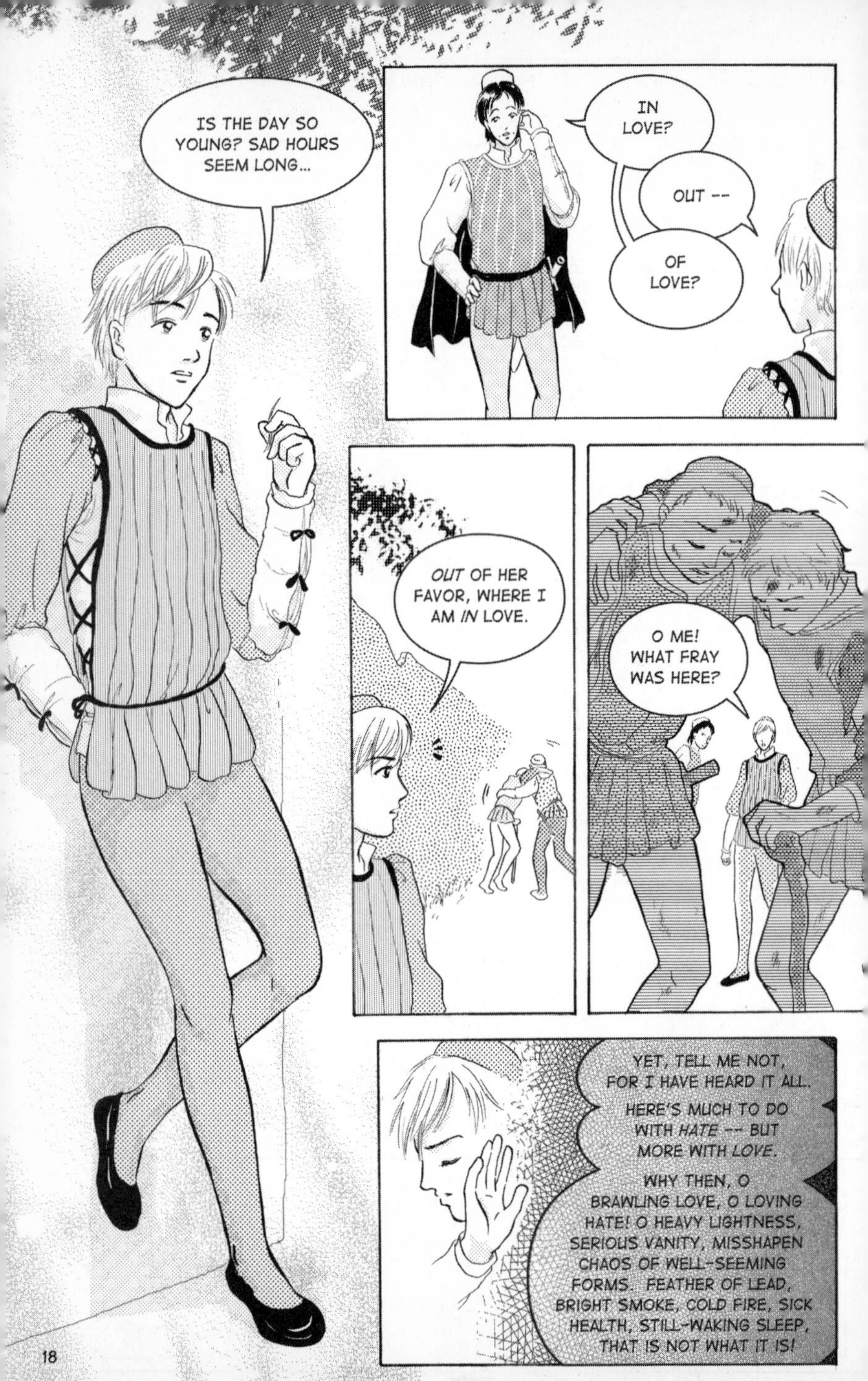
IS THE DAY SO YOUNG? SAD HOURS SEEM LONG...
IN LOVE?
OUT --
OF LOVE?
OUT OF HER FAVOR, WHERE I AM *IN* LOVE.
O ME! WHAT FRAY WAS HERE?
YET, TELL ME NOT, FOR I HAVE HEARD IT ALL.
HERE'S MUCH TO DO WITH *HATE* -- BUT MORE WITH *LOVE*.
WHY THEN, O BRAWLING LOVE, O LOVING HATE! O HEAVY LIGHTNESS, SERIOUS VANITY, MISSHAPEN CHAOS OF WELL-SEEMING FORMS. FEATHER OF LEAD, BRIGHT SMOKE, COLD FIRE, SICK HEALTH, STILL-WAKING SLEEP, THAT IS NOT WHAT IT IS!

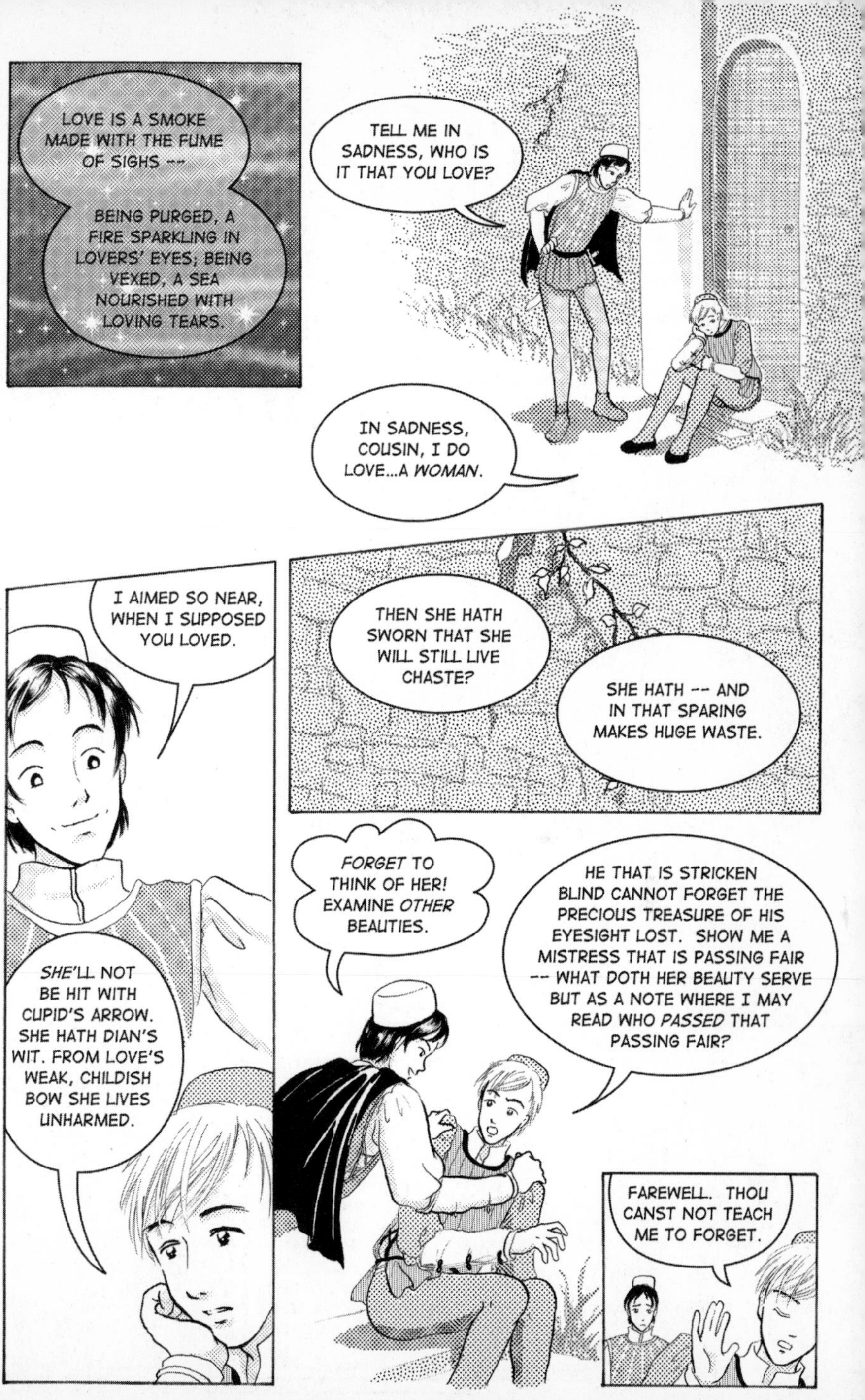
LOVE IS A SMOKE MADE WITH THE FUME OF SIGHS --
BEING PURGED, A FIRE SPARKLING IN LOVERS' EYES; BEING VEXED, A SEA NOURISHED WITH LOVING TEARS.
TELL ME IN SADNESS, WHO IS IT THAT YOU LOVE?
IN SADNESS, COUSIN, I DO LOVE...A *WOMAN*.
I AIMED SO NEAR, WHEN I SUPPOSED YOU LOVED.
SHE'LL NOT BE HIT WITH CUPID'S ARROW. SHE HATH DIAN'S WIT. FROM LOVE'S WEAK, CHILDISH BOW SHE LIVES UNHARMED.
THEN SHE HATH SWORN THAT SHE WILL STILL LIVE CHASTE?
SHE HATH -- AND IN THAT SPARING MAKES HUGE WASTE.
FORGET TO THINK OF HER! EXAMINE *OTHER* BEAUTIES.
HE THAT IS STRICKEN BLIND CANNOT FORGET THE PRECIOUS TREASURE OF HIS EYESIGHT LOST. SHOW ME A MISTRESS THAT IS PASSING FAIR -- WHAT DOTH HER BEAUTY SERVE BUT AS A NOTE WHERE I MAY READ WHO *PASSED* THAT PASSING FAIR?
FAREWELL. THOU CANST NOT TEACH ME TO FORGET.

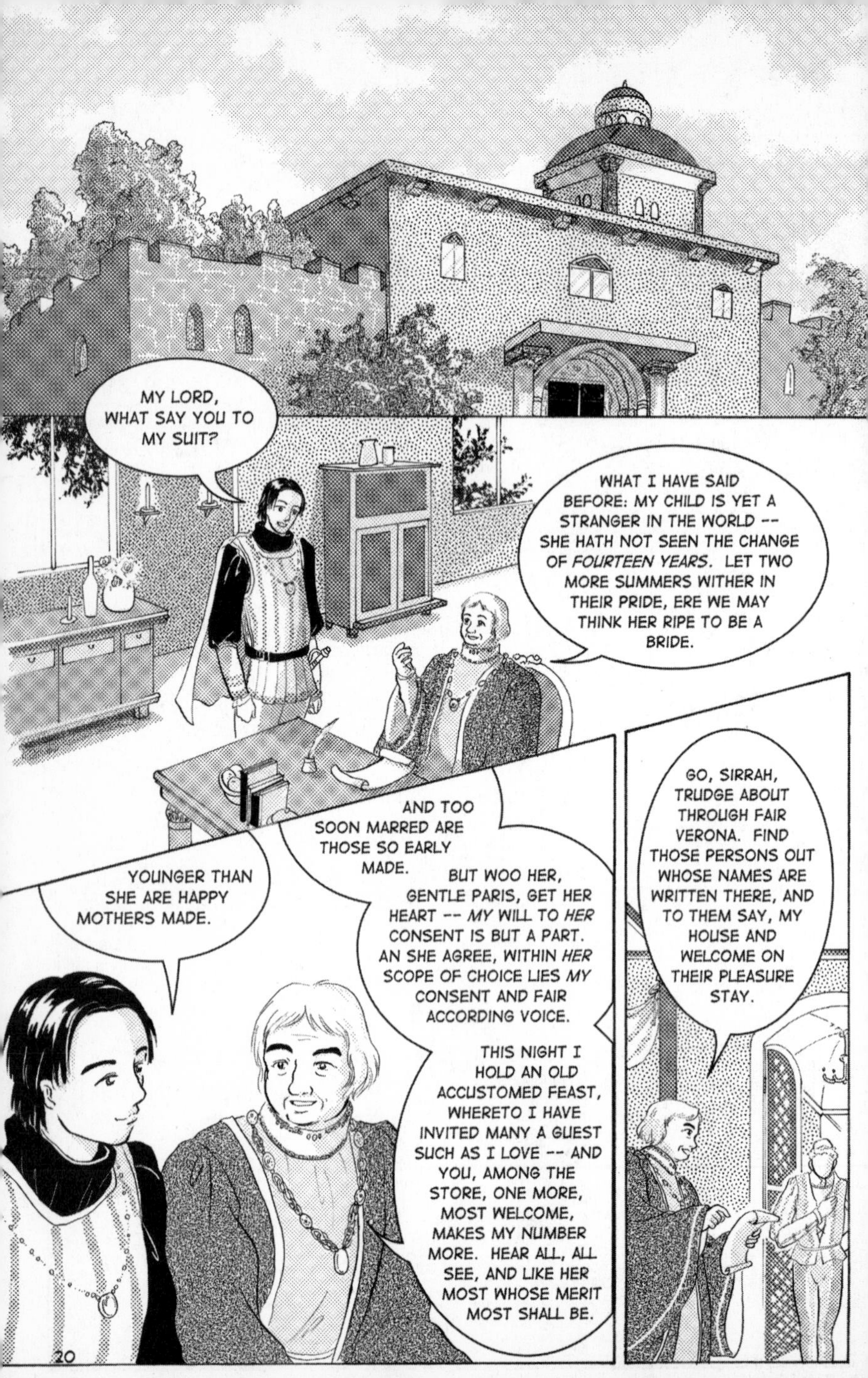
MY LORD, WHAT SAY YOU TO MY SUIT?
WHAT I HAVE SAID BEFORE: MY CHILD IS YET A STRANGER IN THE WORLD -- SHE HATH NOT SEEN THE CHANGE OF *FOURTEEN YEARS*. LET TWO MORE SUMMERS WITHER IN THEIR PRIDE, ERE WE MAY THINK HER RIPE TO BE A BRIDE.
YOUNGER THAN SHE ARE HAPPY MOTHERS MADE.
AND TOO SOON MARRED ARE THOSE SO EARLY MADE.
BUT WOO HER, GENTLE PARIS, GET HER HEART -- *MY* WILL TO *HER* CONSENT IS BUT A PART. AN SHE AGREE, WITHIN *HER* SCOPE OF CHOICE LIES *MY* CONSENT AND FAIR ACCORDING VOICE.
THIS NIGHT I HOLD AN OLD ACCUSTOMED FEAST, WHERETO I HAVE INVITED MANY A GUEST SUCH AS I LOVE -- AND YOU, AMONG THE STORE, ONE MORE, MOST WELCOME, MAKES MY NUMBER MORE. HEAR ALL, ALL SEE, AND LIKE HER MOST WHOSE MERIT MOST SHALL BE.
GO, SIRRAH, TRUDGE ABOUT THROUGH FAIR VERONA. FIND THOSE PERSONS OUT WHOSE NAMES ARE WRITTEN THERE, AND TO THEM SAY, MY HOUSE AND WELCOME ON THEIR PLEASURE STAY.

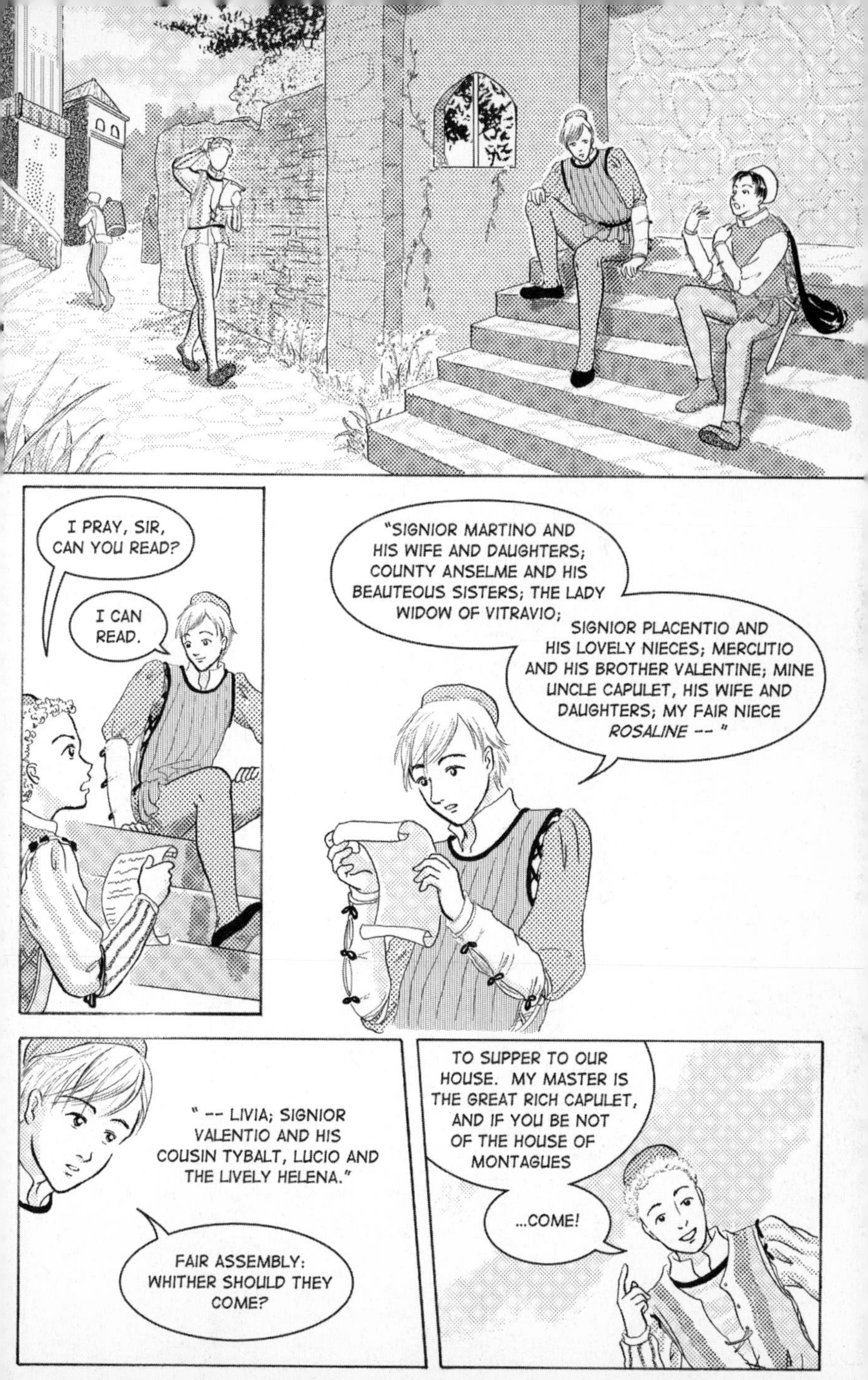
I PRAY, SIR, CAN YOU READ?
I CAN READ.
"SIGNIOR MARTINO AND HIS WIFE AND DAUGHTERS; COUNTY ANSELME AND HIS BEAUTEOUS SISTERS; THE LADY WIDOW OF VITRAVIO;
SIGNIOR PLACENTIO AND HIS LOVELY NIECES; MERCUTIO AND HIS BROTHER VALENTINE; MINE UNCLE CAPULET, HIS WIFE AND DAUGHTERS; MY FAIR NIECE *ROSALINE* -- "
" -- LIVIA; SIGNIOR VALENTIO AND HIS COUSIN TYBALT, LUCIO AND THE LIVELY HELENA."
FAIR ASSEMBLY: WHITHER SHOULD THEY COME?
TO SUPPER TO OUR HOUSE. MY MASTER IS THE GREAT RICH CAPULET, AND IF YOU BE NOT OF THE HOUSE OF MONTAGUES
...COME!

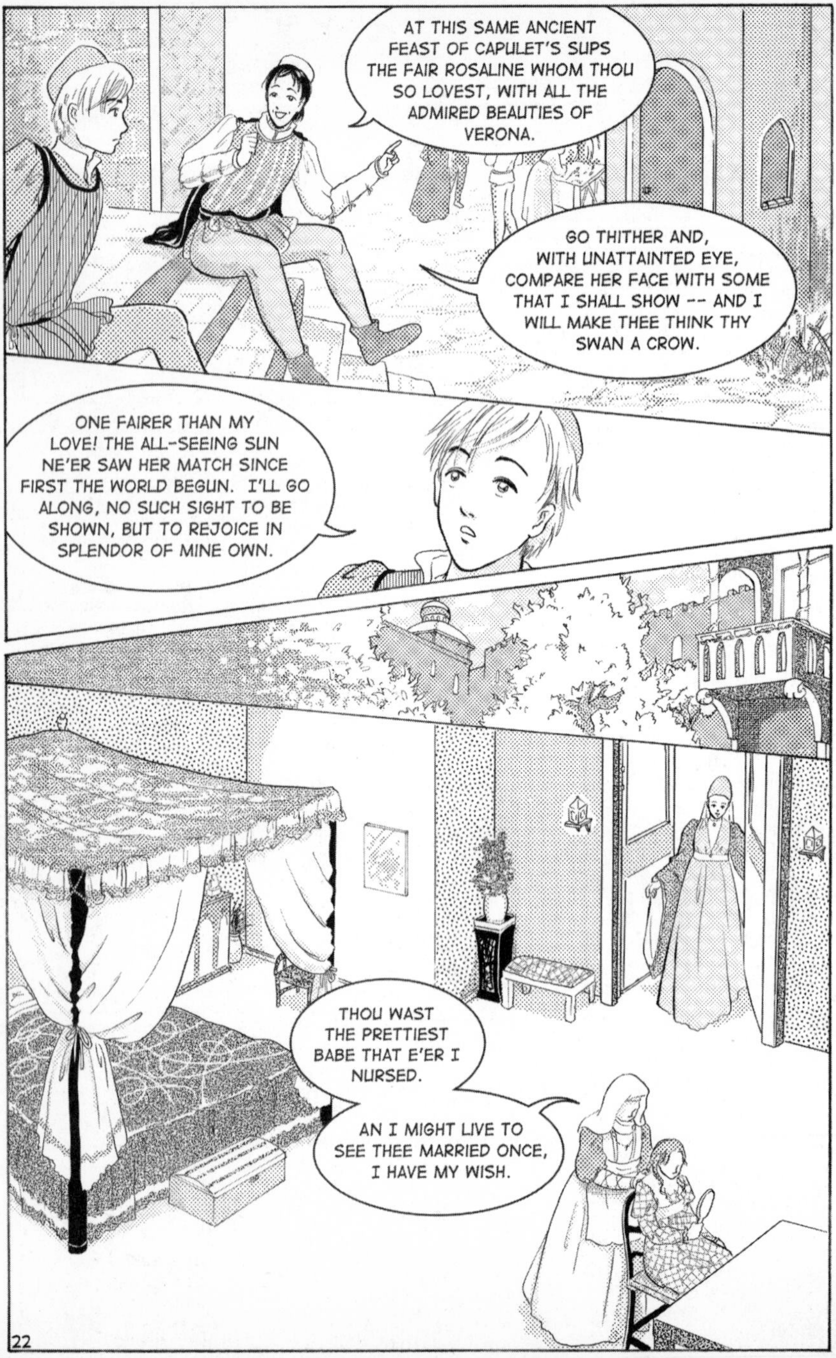
AT THIS SAME ANCIENT FEAST OF CAPULET'S SUPS THE FAIR ROSALINE WHOM THOU SO LOVEST, WITH ALL THE ADMIRED BEAUTIES OF VERONA.
GO THITHER AND, WITH UNATTAINTED EYE, COMPARE HER FACE WITH SOME THAT I SHALL SHOW -- AND I WILL MAKE THEE THINK THY SWAN A CROW.
ONE FAIRER THAN MY LOVE! THE ALL-SEEING SUN NE'ER SAW HER MATCH SINCE FIRST THE WORLD BEGUN. I'LL GO ALONG, NO SUCH SIGHT TO BE SHOWN, BUT TO REJOICE IN SPLENDOR OF MINE OWN.
THOU WAST THE PRETTIEST BABE THAT E'ER I NURSED.
AN I MIGHT LIVE TO SEE THEE MARRIED ONCE, I HAVE MY WISH.

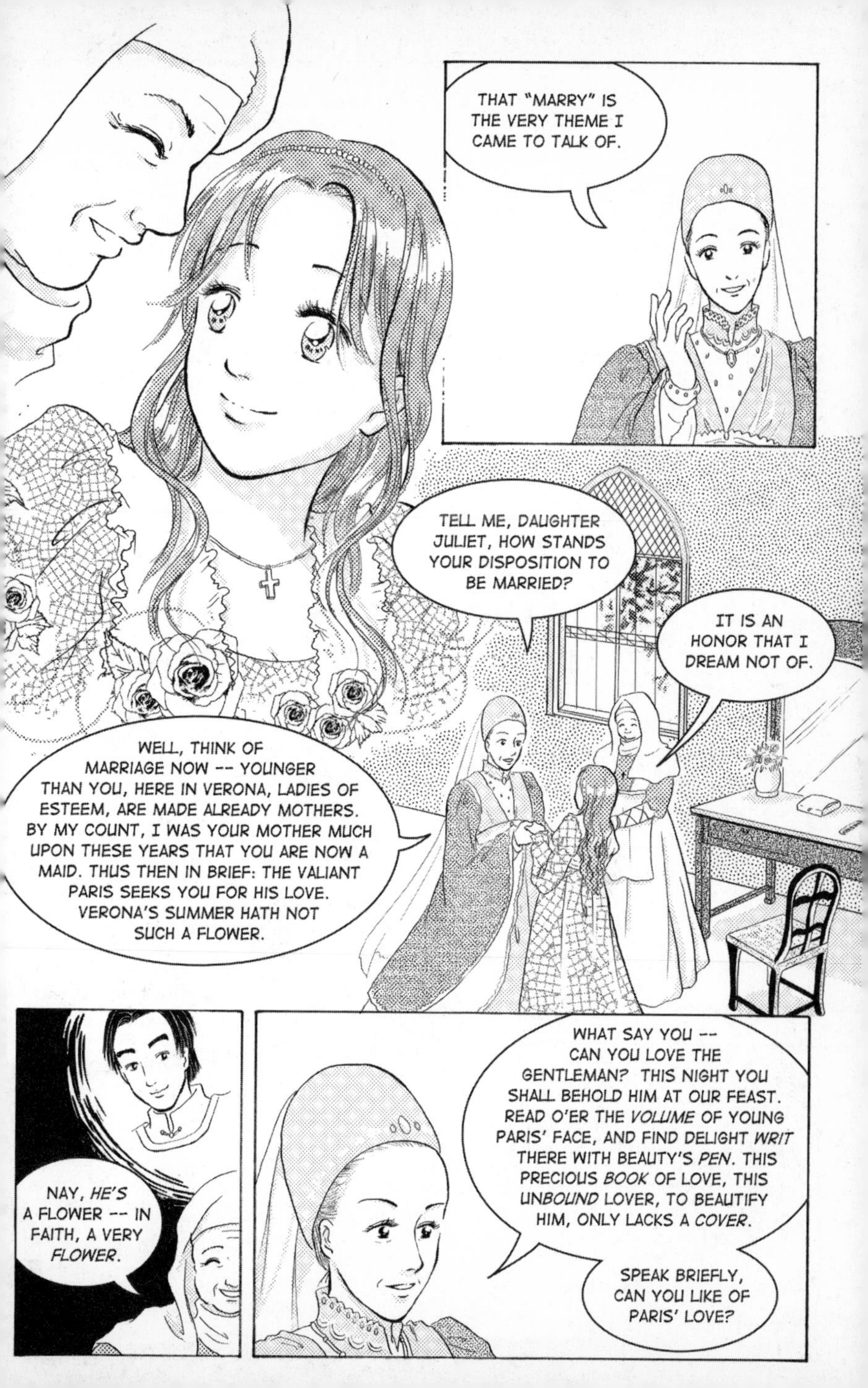
THAT "MARRY" IS THE VERY THEME I CAME TO TALK OF.
TELL ME, DAUGHTER JULIET, HOW STANDS YOUR DISPOSITION TO BE MARRIED?
IT IS AN HONOR THAT I DREAM NOT OF.
WELL, THINK OF MARRIAGE NOW -- YOUNGER THAN YOU, HERE IN VERONA, LADIES OF ESTEEM, ARE MADE ALREADY MOTHERS. BY MY COUNT, I WAS YOUR MOTHER MUCH UPON THESE YEARS THAT YOU ARE NOW A MAID. THUS THEN IN BRIEF: THE VALIANT PARIS SEEKS YOU FOR HIS LOVE. VERONA'S SUMMER HATH NOT SUCH A FLOWER.
NAY, *HE'S* A FLOWER -- IN FAITH, A VERY *FLOWER*.
WHAT SAY YOU -- CAN YOU LOVE THE GENTLEMAN? THIS NIGHT YOU SHALL BEHOLD HIM AT OUR FEAST. READ O'ER THE *VOLUME* OF YOUNG PARIS' FACE, AND FIND DELIGHT *WRIT* THERE WITH BEAUTY'S *PEN*. THIS PRECIOUS *BOOK* OF LOVE, THIS UN*BOUND* LOVER, TO BEAUTIFY HIM, ONLY LACKS A *COVER*.
SPEAK BRIEFLY, CAN YOU LIKE OF PARIS' LOVE?

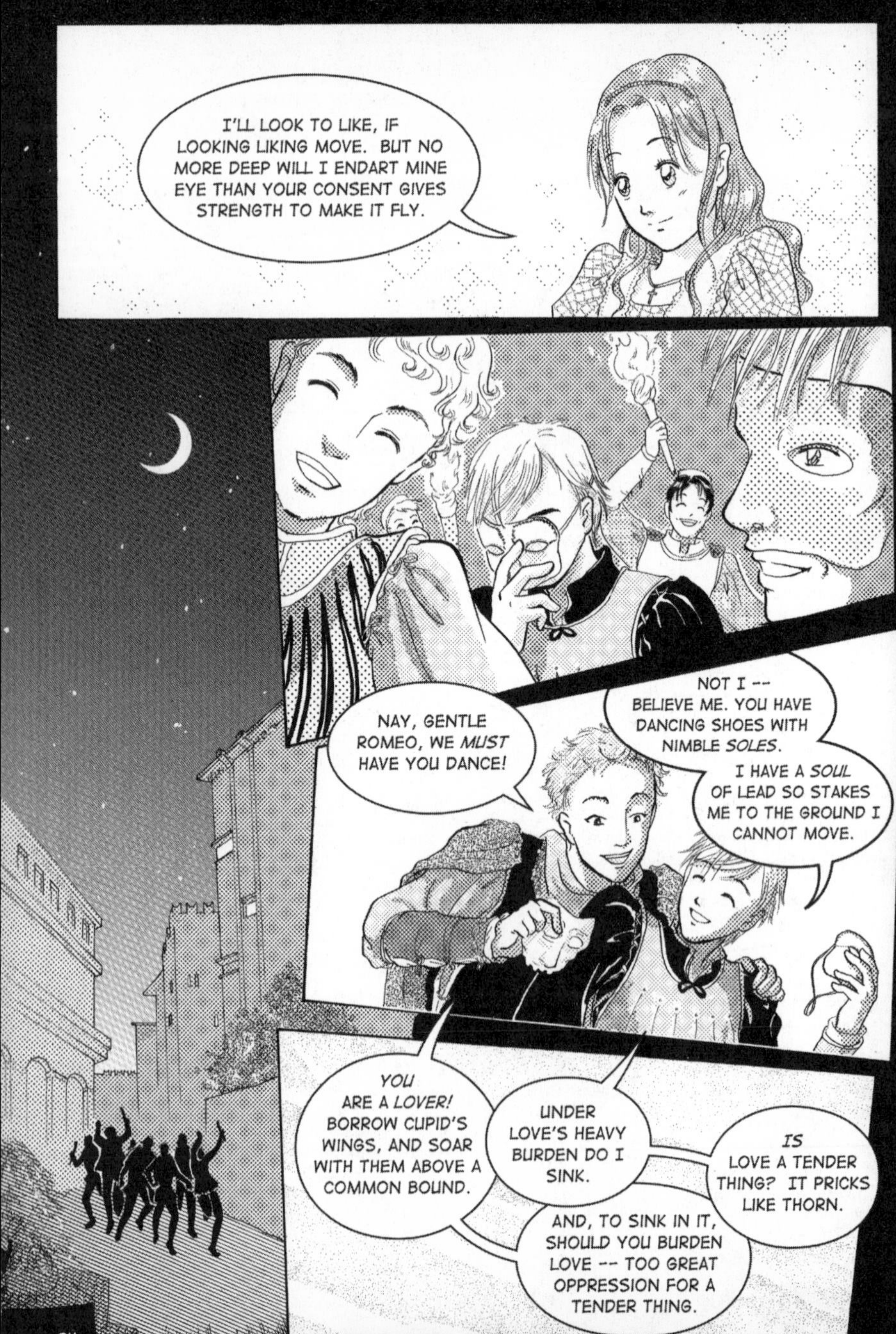
I'LL LOOK TO LIKE, IF LOOKING LIKING MOVE. BUT NO MORE DEEP WILL I ENDART MINE EYE THAN YOUR CONSENT GIVES STRENGTH TO MAKE IT FLY.
NAY, GENTLE ROMEO, WE *MUST* HAVE YOU DANCE!
NOT I -- BELIEVE ME. YOU HAVE DANCING SHOES WITH NIMBLE *SOLES*.
I HAVE A *SOUL* OF LEAD SO STAKES ME TO THE GROUND I CANNOT MOVE.
YOU ARE A *LOVER!* BORROW CUPID'S WINGS, AND SOAR WITH THEM ABOVE A COMMON BOUND.
UNDER LOVE'S HEAVY BURDEN DO I SINK.
AND, TO SINK IN IT, SHOULD YOU BURDEN LOVE -- TOO GREAT OPPRESSION FOR A TENDER THING.
IS LOVE A TENDER THING? IT PRICKS LIKE THORN.

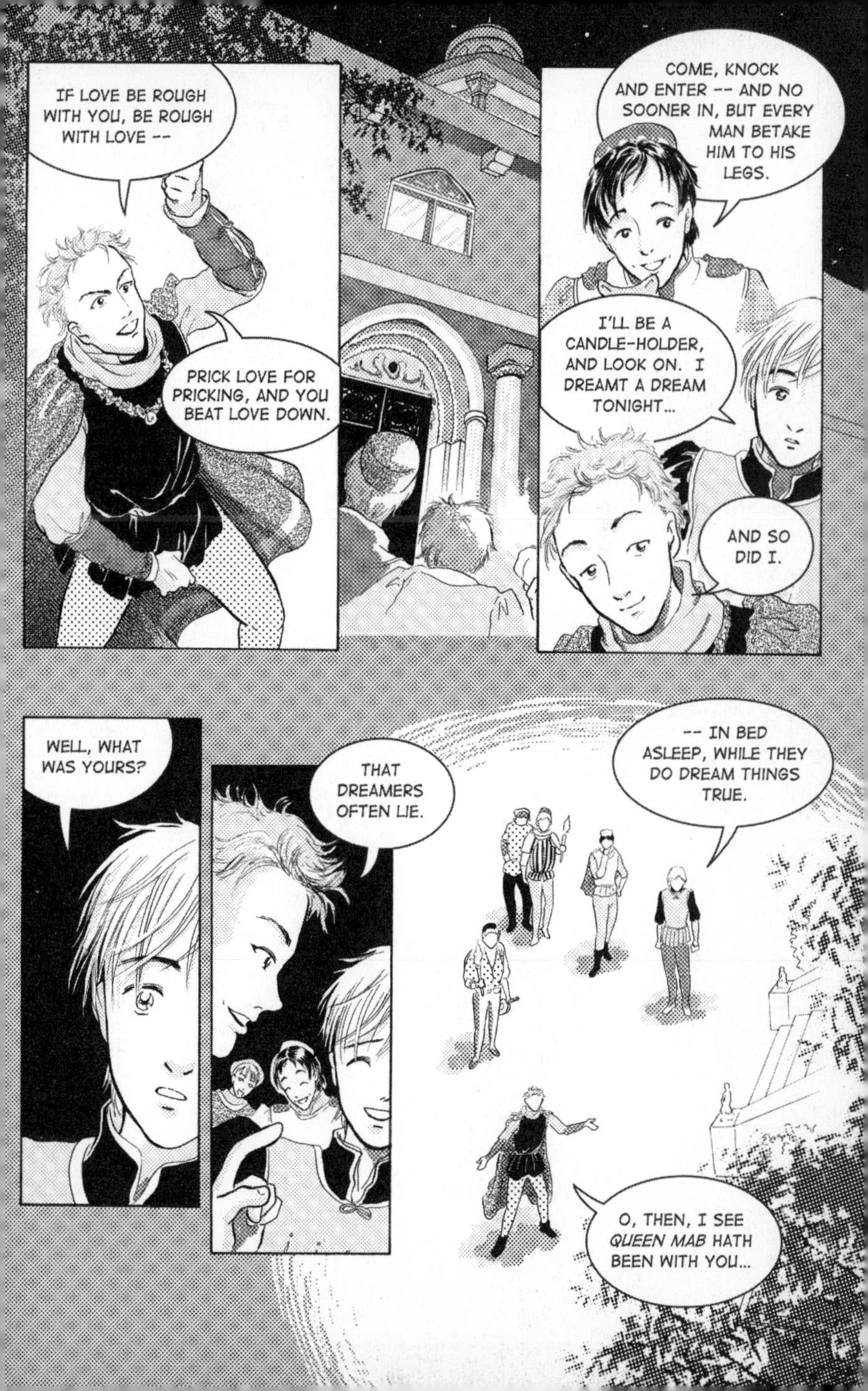
IF LOVE BE ROUGH WITH YOU, BE ROUGH WITH LOVE --
PRICK LOVE FOR PRICKING, AND YOU BEAT LOVE DOWN.
COME, KNOCK AND ENTER -- AND NO SOONER IN, BUT EVERY MAN BETAKE HIM TO HIS LEGS.
I'LL BE A CANDLE-HOLDER, AND LOOK ON. I DREAMT A DREAM TONIGHT...
AND SO DID I.
WELL, WHAT WAS YOURS?
THAT DREAMERS OFTEN LIE.
-- IN BED ASLEEP, WHILE THEY DO DREAM THINGS TRUE.
O, THEN, I SEE *QUEEN MAB* HATH BEEN WITH YOU...

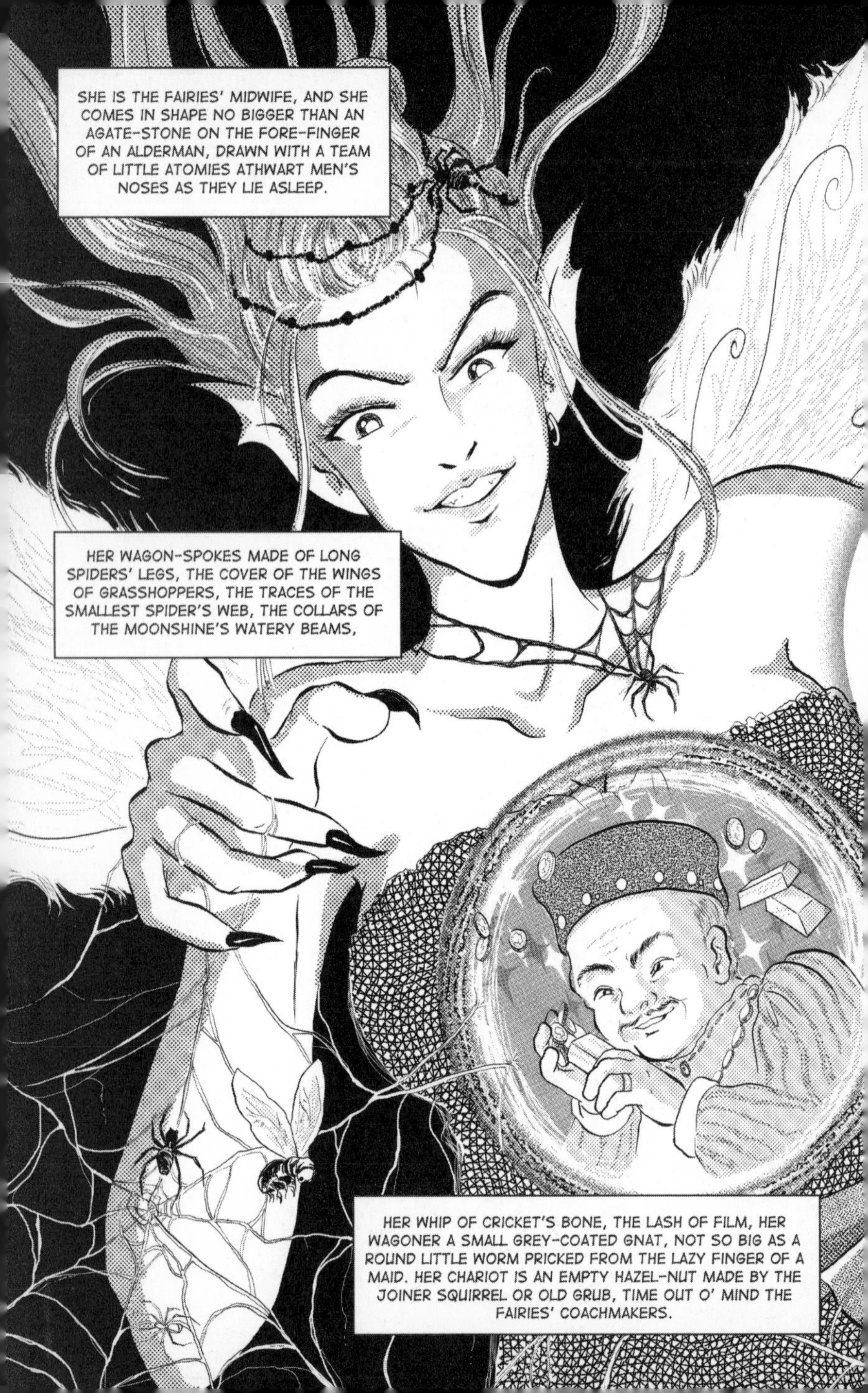
SHE IS THE FAIRIES' MIDWIFE, AND SHE COMES IN SHAPE NO BIGGER THAN AN AGATE-STONE ON THE FORE-FINGER OF AN ALDERMAN, DRAWN WITH A TEAM OF LITTLE ATOMIES ATHWART MEN'S NOSES AS THEY LIE ASLEEP.
HER WAGON-SPOKES MADE OF LONG SPIDERS' LEGS, THE COVER OF THE WINGS OF GRASSHOPPERS, THE TRACES OF THE SMALLEST SPIDER'S WEB, THE COLLARS OF THE MOONSHINE'S WATERY BEAMS,
HER WHIP OF CRICKET'S BONE, THE LASH OF FILM, HER WAGONER A SMALL GREY-COATED GNAT, NOT SO BIG AS A ROUND LITTLE WORM PRICKED FROM THE LAZY FINGER OF A MAID. HER CHARIOT IS AN EMPTY HAZEL-NUT MADE BY THE JOINER SQUIRREL OR OLD GRUB, TIME OUT O' MIND THE FAIRIES' COACHMAKERS.

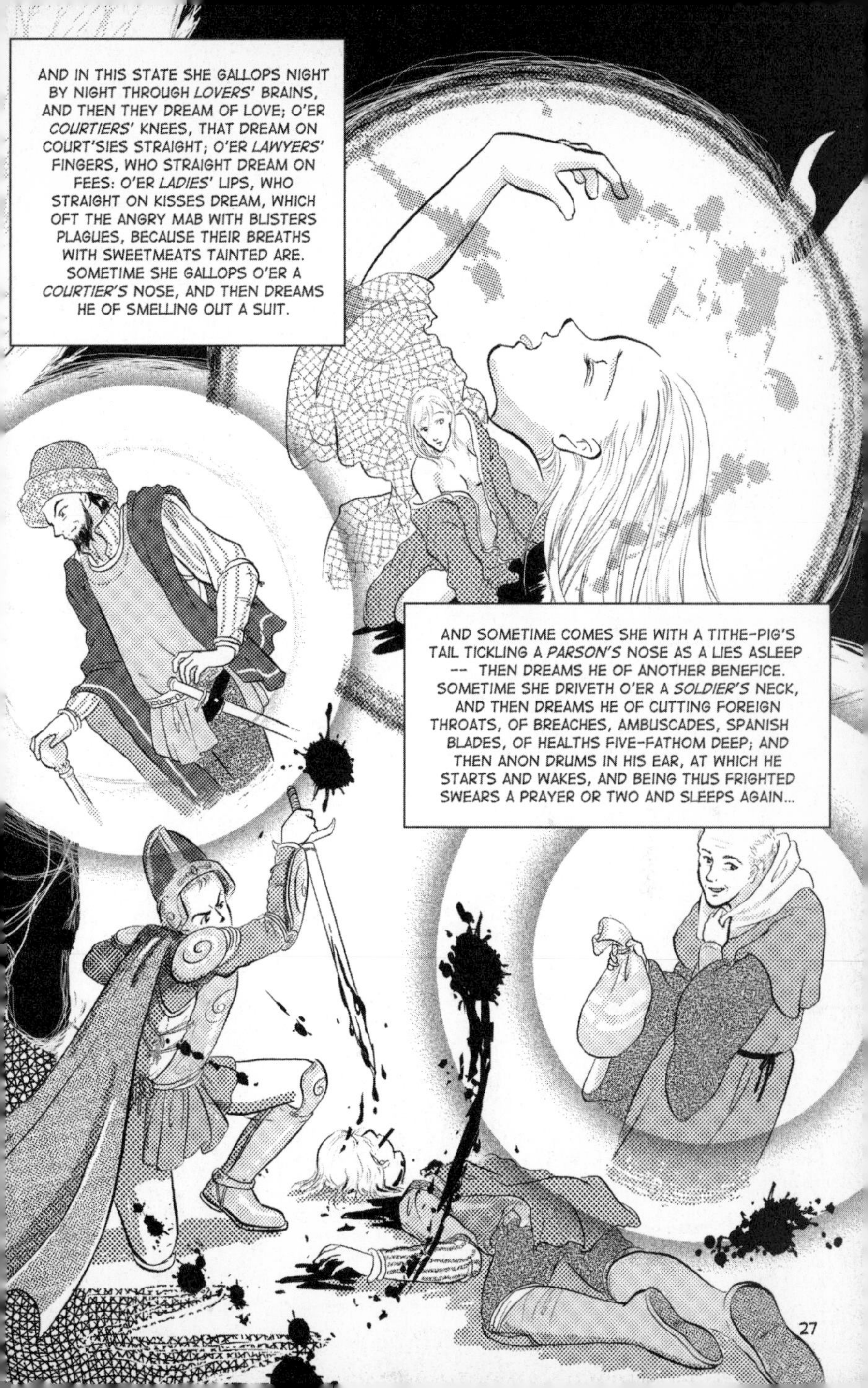
AND IN THIS STATE SHE GALLOPS NIGHT BY NIGHT THROUGH *LOVERS'* BRAINS, AND THEN THEY DREAM OF LOVE; O'ER *COURTIERS'* KNEES, THAT DREAM ON COURT'SIES STRAIGHT; O'ER *LAWYERS'* FINGERS, WHO STRAIGHT DREAM ON FEES: O'ER *LADIES'* LIPS, WHO STRAIGHT ON KISSES DREAM, WHICH OFT THE ANGRY MAB WITH BLISTERS PLAGUES, BECAUSE THEIR BREATHS WITH SWEETMEATS TAINTED ARE. SOMETIME SHE GALLOPS O'ER A *COURTIER'S* NOSE, AND THEN DREAMS HE OF SMELLING OUT A SUIT.
AND SOMETIME COMES SHE WITH A TITHE-PIG'S TAIL TICKLING A *PARSON'S* NOSE AS A LIES ASLEEP -- THEN DREAMS HE OF ANOTHER BENEFICE. SOMETIME SHE DRIVETH O'ER A *SOLDIER'S* NECK, AND THEN DREAMS HE OF CUTTING FOREIGN THROATS, OF BREACHES, AMBUSCADES, SPANISH BLADES, OF HEALTHS FIVE-FATHOM DEEP; AND THEN ANON DRUMS IN HIS EAR, AT WHICH HE STARTS AND WAKES, AND BEING THUS FRIGHTED SWEARS A PRAYER OR TWO AND SLEEPS AGAIN...

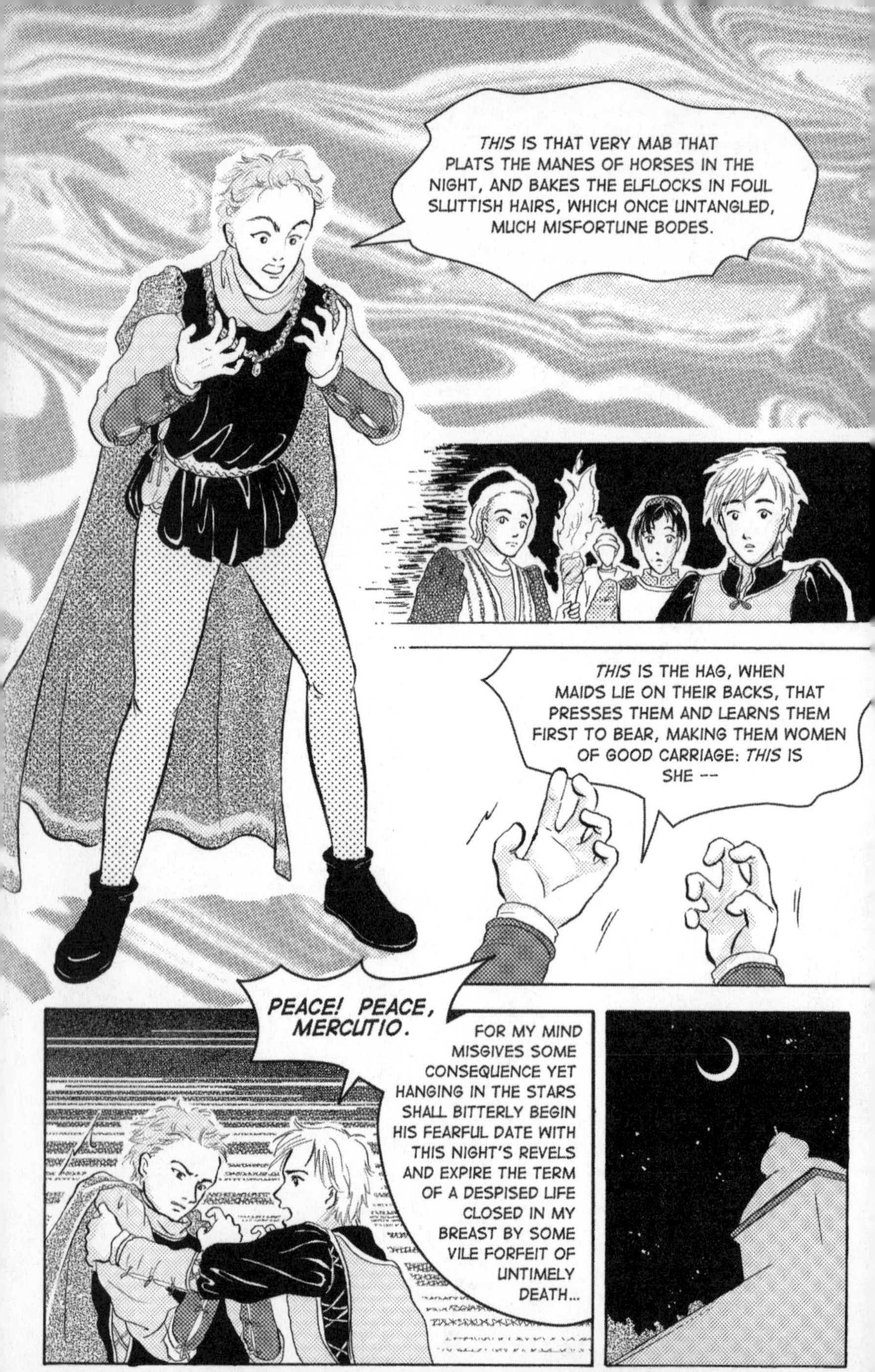
THIS IS THAT VERY MAB THAT PLATS THE MANES OF HORSES IN THE NIGHT, AND BAKES THE ELFLOCKS IN FOUL SLUTTISH HAIRS, WHICH ONCE UNTANGLED, MUCH MISFORTUNE BODES.
THIS IS THE HAG, WHEN MAIDS LIE ON THEIR BACKS, THAT PRESSES THEM AND LEARNS THEM FIRST TO BEAR, MAKING THEM WOMEN OF GOOD CARRIAGE: THIS IS SHE --
PEACE! PEACE, MERCUTIO.
FOR MY MIND MISGIVES SOME CONSEQUENCE YET HANGING IN THE STARS SHALL BITTERLY BEGIN HIS FEARFUL DATE WITH THIS NIGHT'S REVELS AND EXPIRE THE TERM OF A DESPISED LIFE CLOSED IN MY BREAST BY SOME VILE FORFEIT OF UNTIMELY DEATH...

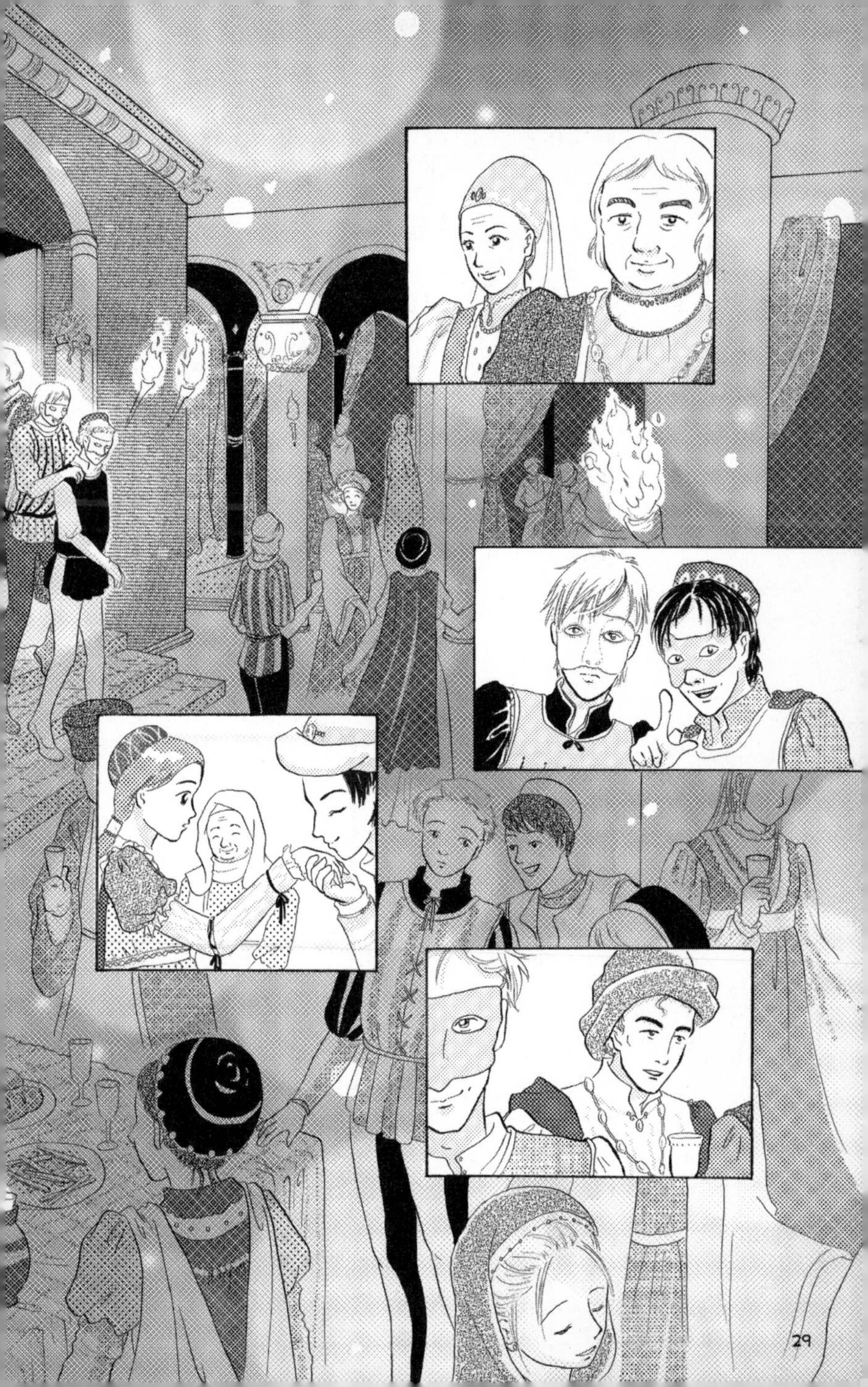

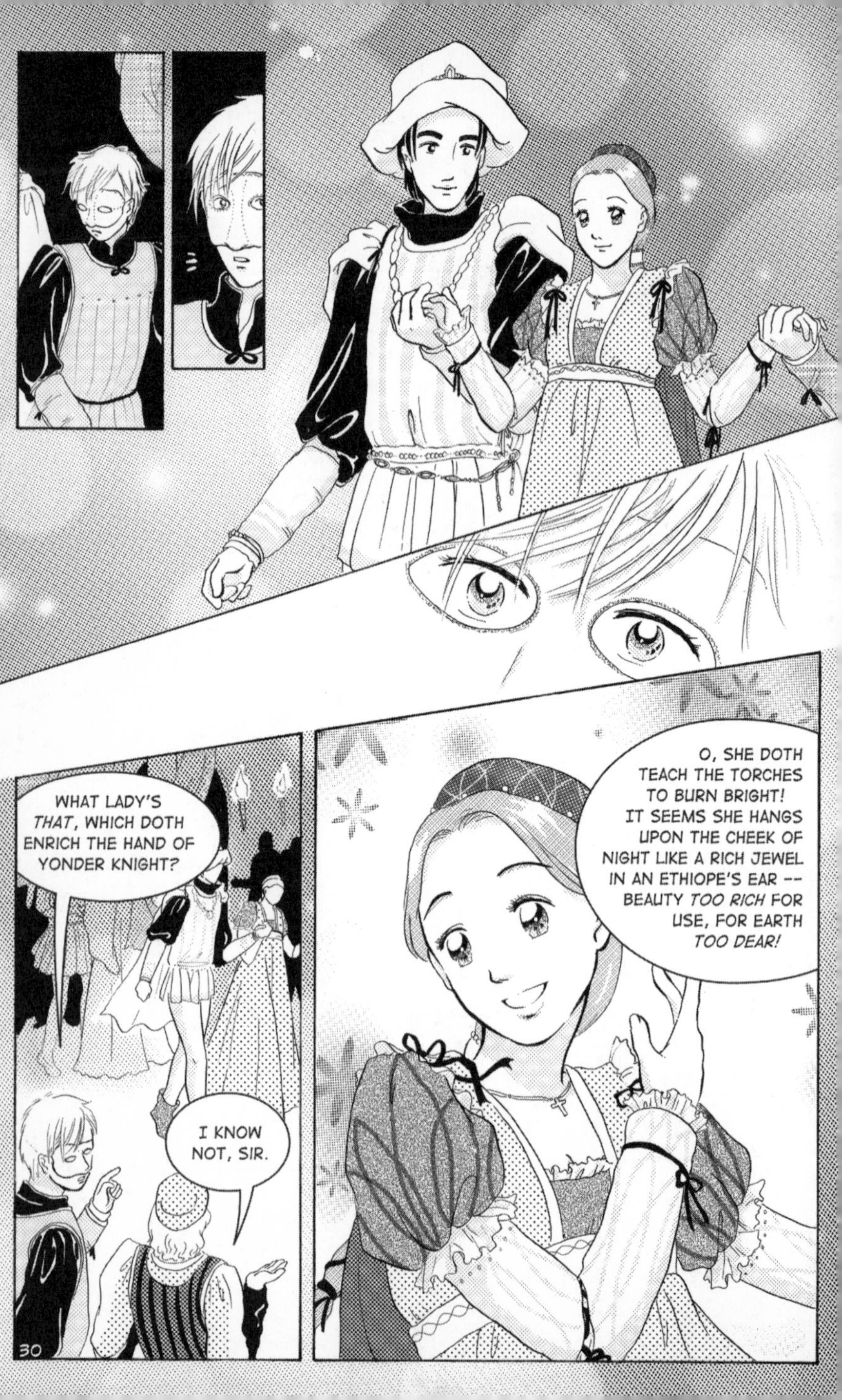
WHAT LADY'S *THAT*, WHICH DOTH ENRICH THE HAND OF YONDER KNIGHT?
I KNOW NOT, SIR.
O, SHE DOTH TEACH THE TORCHES TO BURN BRIGHT! IT SEEMS SHE HANGS UPON THE CHEEK OF NIGHT LIKE A RICH JEWEL IN AN ETHIOPE'S EAR -- BEAUTY *TOO RICH* FOR USE, FOR EARTH *TOO DEAR!*

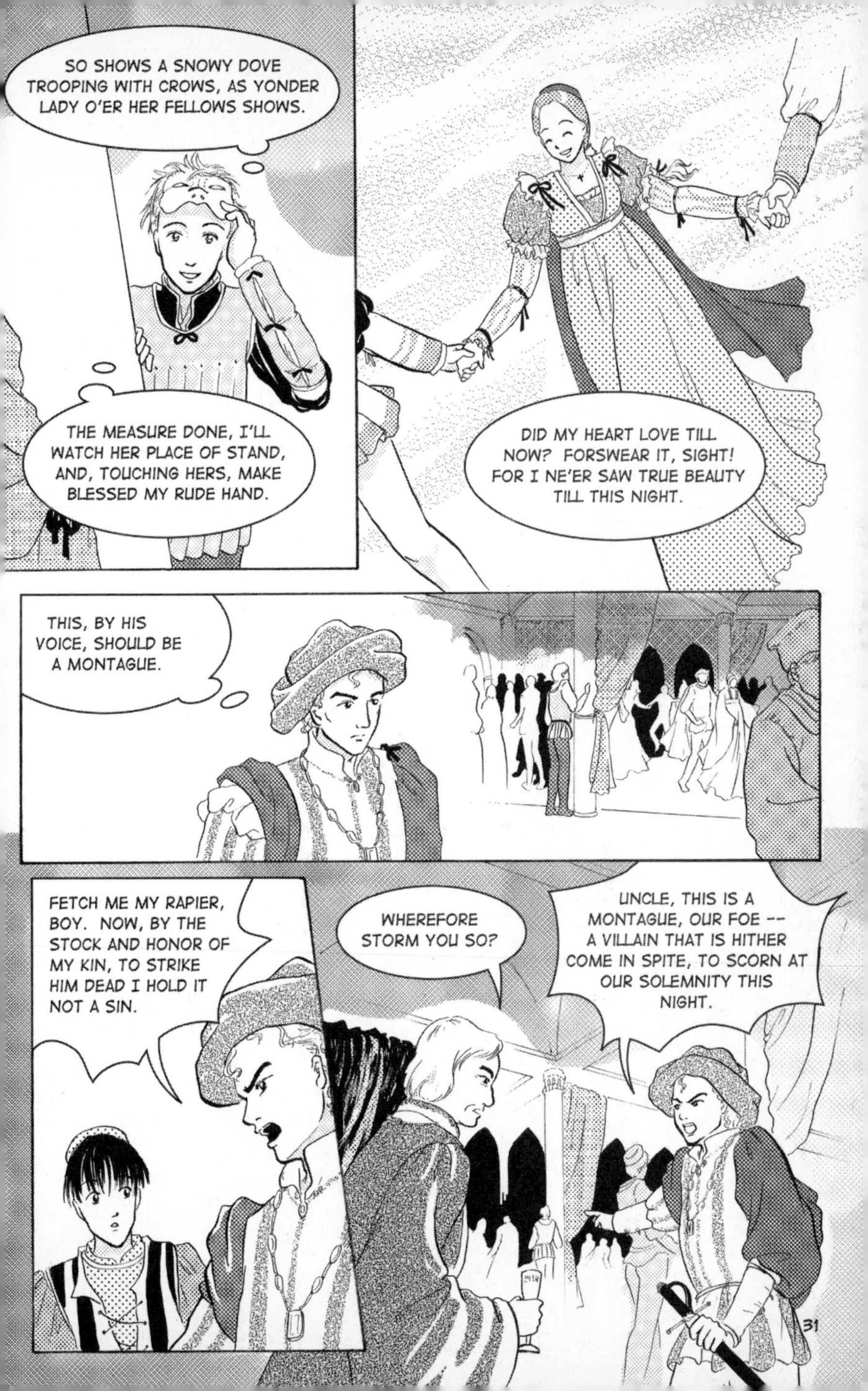
SO SHOWS A SNOWY DOVE TROOPING WITH CROWS, AS YONDER LADY O'ER HER FELLOWS SHOWS.
THE MEASURE DONE, I'LL WATCH HER PLACE OF STAND, AND, TOUCHING HERS, MAKE BLESSED MY RUDE HAND.
DID MY HEART LOVE TILL NOW? FORSWEAR IT, SIGHT! FOR I NE'ER SAW TRUE BEAUTY TILL THIS NIGHT.
THIS, BY HIS VOICE, SHOULD BE A MONTAGUE.
FETCH ME MY RAPIER, BOY. NOW, BY THE STOCK AND HONOR OF MY KIN, TO STRIKE HIM DEAD I HOLD IT NOT A SIN.
WHEREFORE STORM YOU SO?
UNCLE, THIS IS A MONTAGUE, OUR FOE -- A VILLAIN THAT IS HITHER COME IN SPITE, TO SCORN AT OUR SOLEMNITY THIS NIGHT.

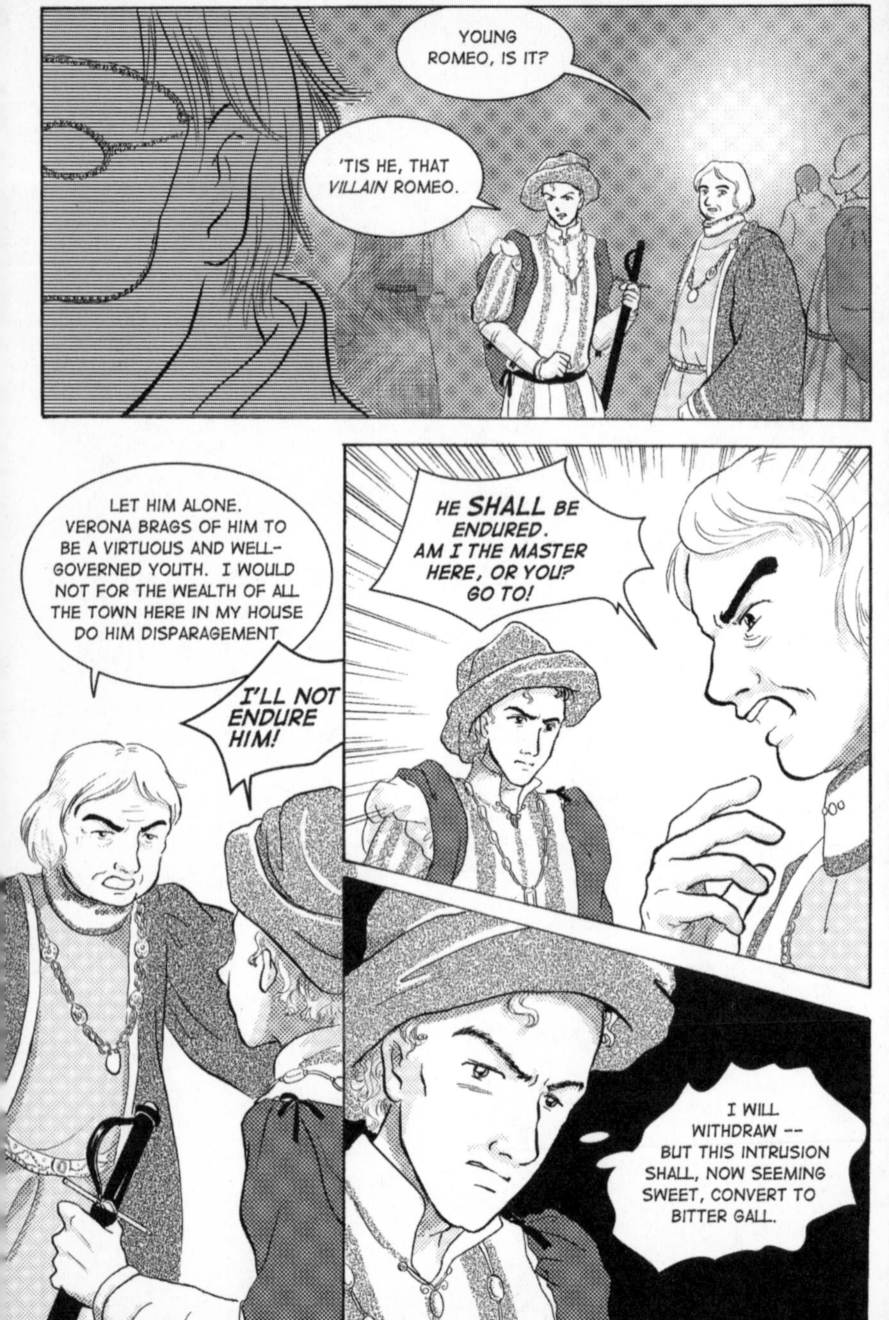
YOUNG ROMEO, IS IT?
'TIS HE, THAT *VILLAIN* ROMEO.
LET HIM ALONE. VERONA BRAGS OF HIM TO BE A VIRTUOUS AND WELL-GOVERNED YOUTH. I WOULD NOT FOR THE WEALTH OF ALL THE TOWN HERE IN MY HOUSE DO HIM DISPARAGEMENT
I'LL NOT ENDURE HIM!
*HE **SHALL** BE ENDURED. AM I THE MASTER HERE, OR YOU? GO TO!*
I WILL WITHDRAW -- BUT THIS INTRUSION SHALL, NOW SEEMING SWEET, CONVERT TO BITTER GALL.

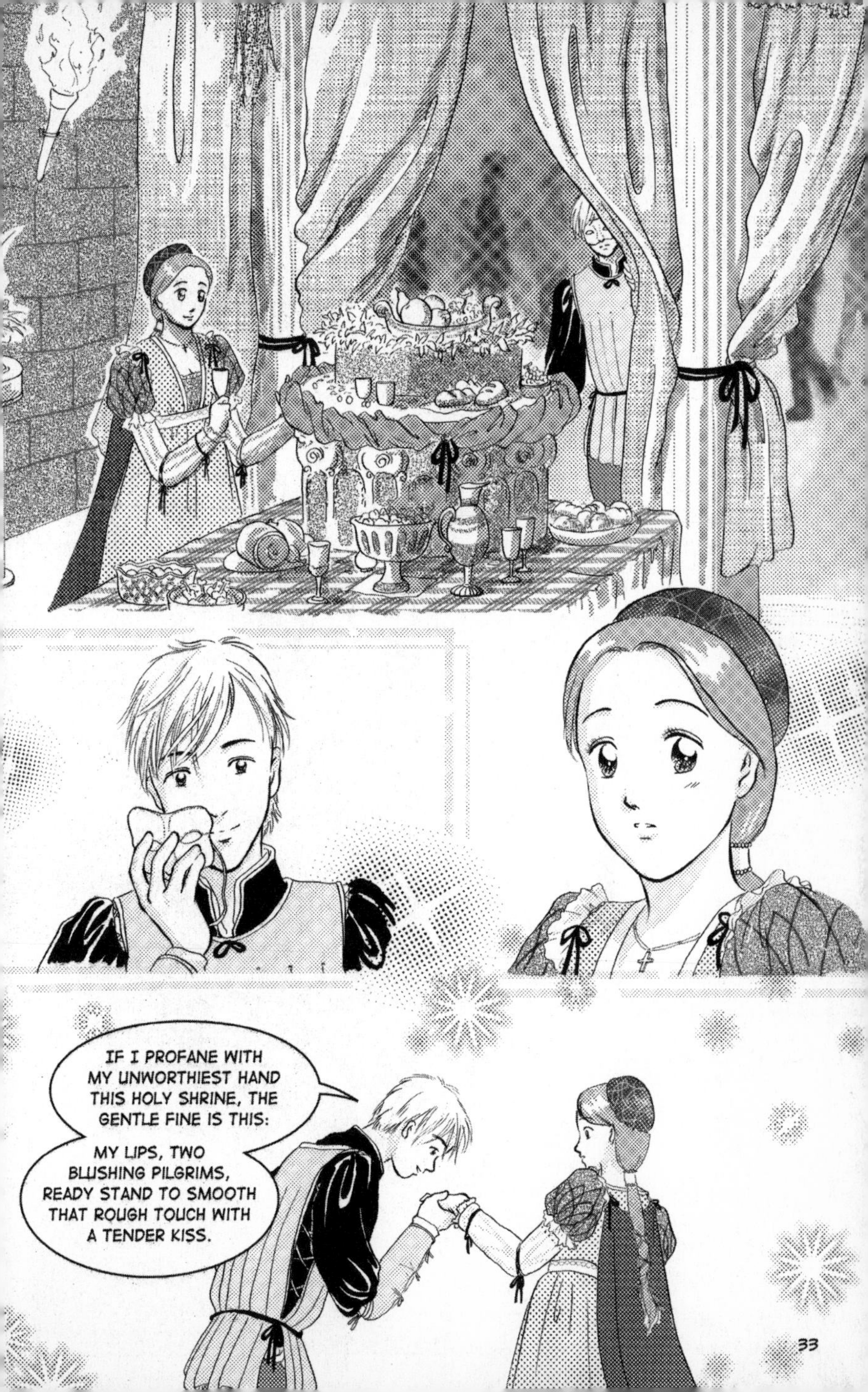
IF I PROFANE WITH MY UNWORTHIEST HAND THIS HOLY SHRINE, THE GENTLE FINE IS THIS:
MY LIPS, TWO BLUSHING PILGRIMS, READY STAND TO SMOOTH THAT ROUGH TOUCH WITH A TENDER KISS.

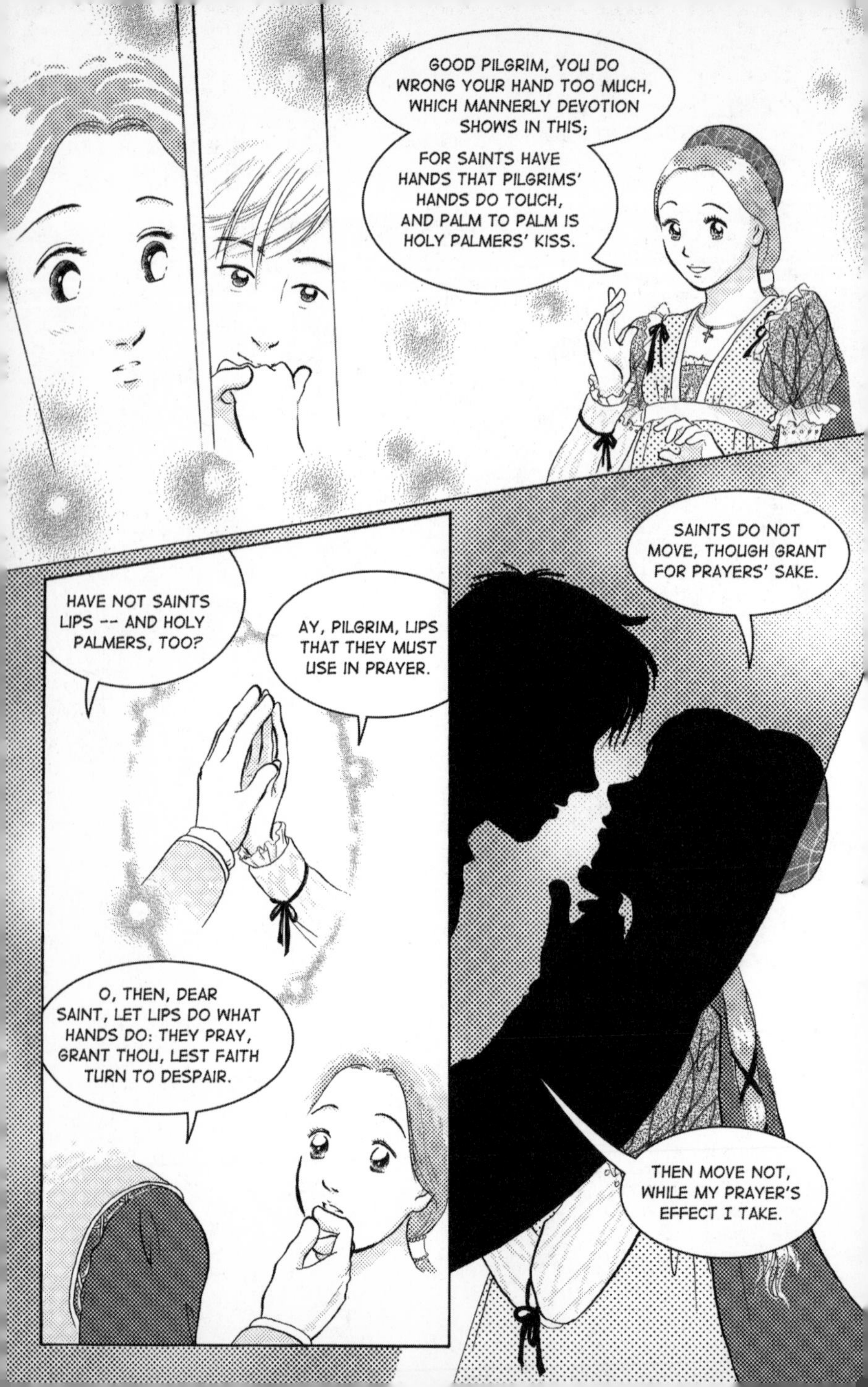
GOOD PILGRIM, YOU DO WRONG YOUR HAND TOO MUCH, WHICH MANNERLY DEVOTION SHOWS IN THIS;
FOR SAINTS HAVE HANDS THAT PILGRIMS' HANDS DO TOUCH, AND PALM TO PALM IS HOLY PALMERS' KISS.
HAVE NOT SAINTS LIPS -- AND HOLY PALMERS, TOO?
AY, PILGRIM, LIPS THAT THEY MUST USE IN PRAYER.
O, THEN, DEAR SAINT, LET LIPS DO WHAT HANDS DO: THEY PRAY, GRANT THOU, LEST FAITH TURN TO DESPAIR.
SAINTS DO NOT MOVE, THOUGH GRANT FOR PRAYERS' SAKE.
THEN MOVE NOT, WHILE MY PRAYER'S EFFECT I TAKE.

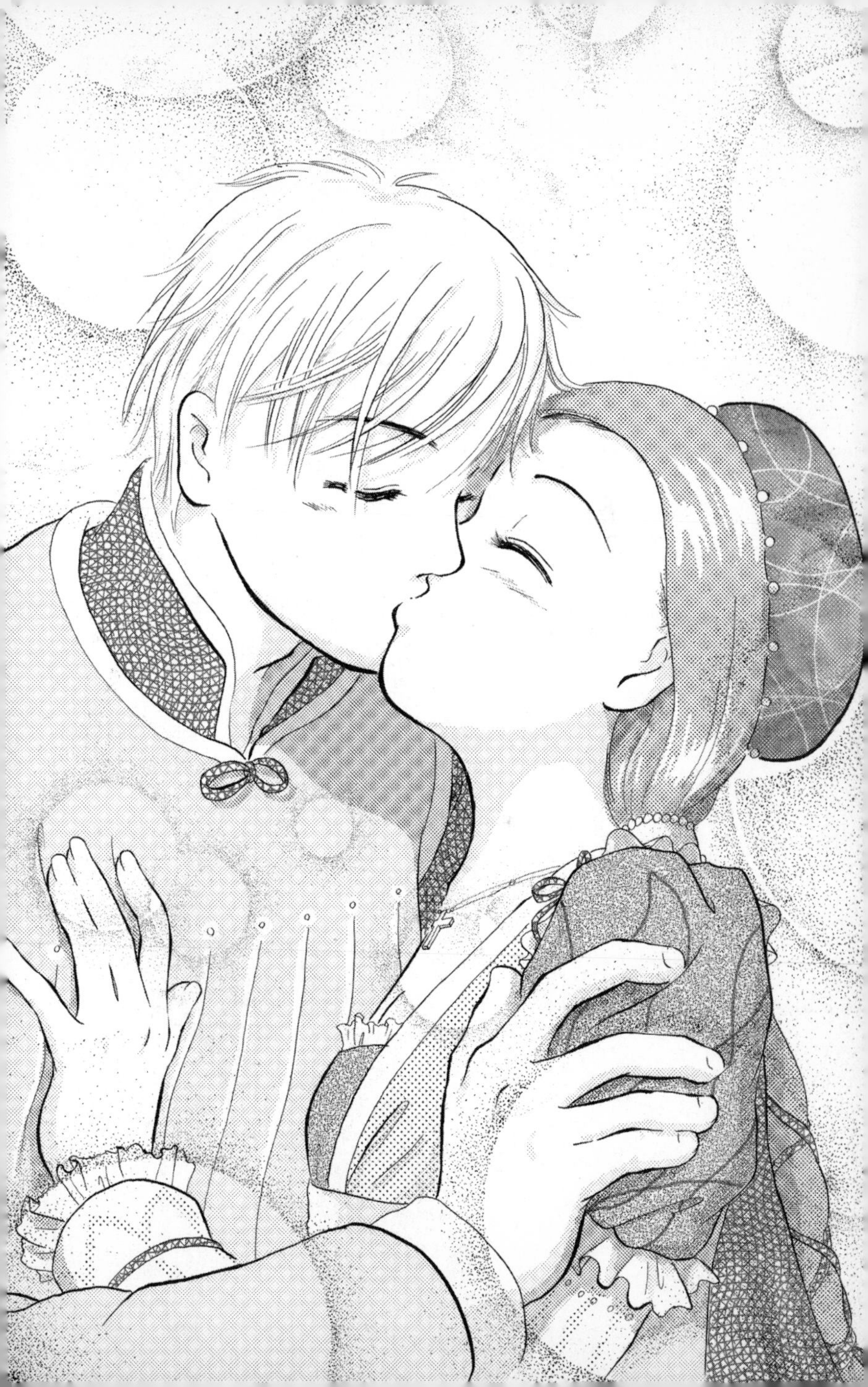

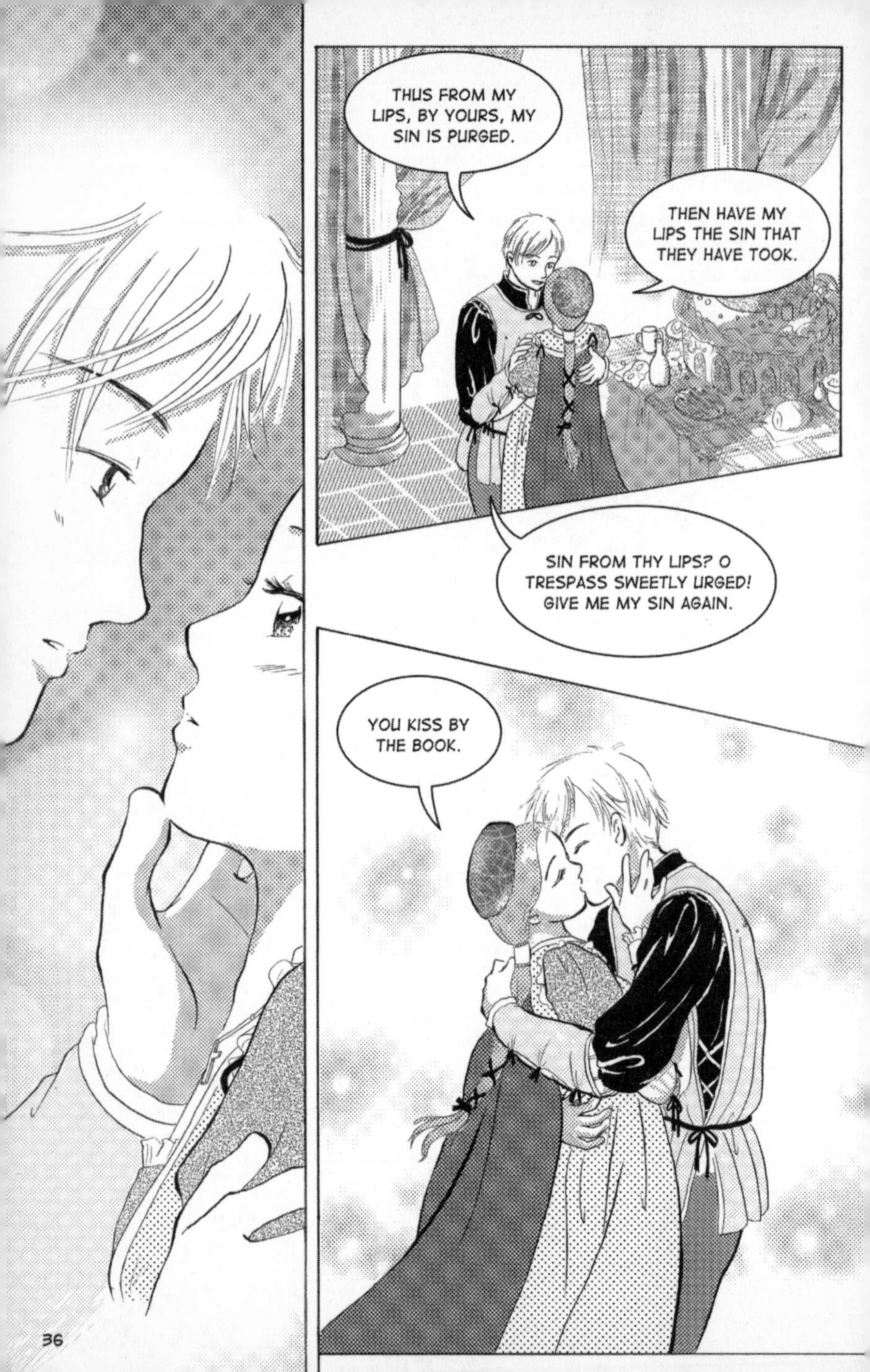
THUS FROM MY LIPS, BY YOURS, MY SIN IS PURGED.
THEN HAVE MY LIPS THE SIN THAT THEY HAVE TOOK.
SIN FROM THY LIPS? O TRESPASS SWEETLY URGED! GIVE ME MY SIN AGAIN.
YOU KISS BY THE BOOK.

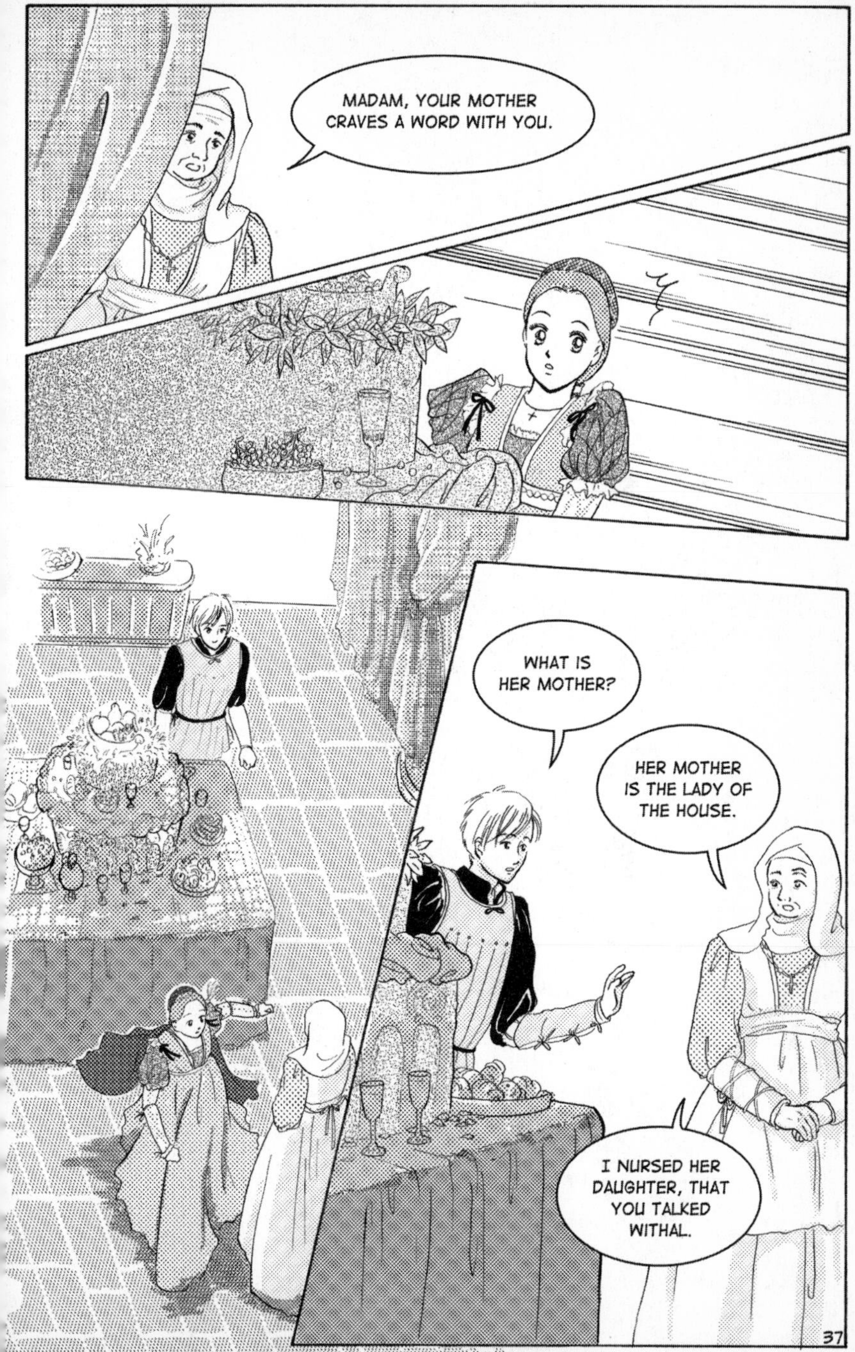
MADAM, YOUR MOTHER CRAVES A WORD WITH YOU.
WHAT IS HER MOTHER?
HER MOTHER IS THE LADY OF THE HOUSE.
I NURSED HER DAUGHTER, THAT YOU TALKED WITHAL.

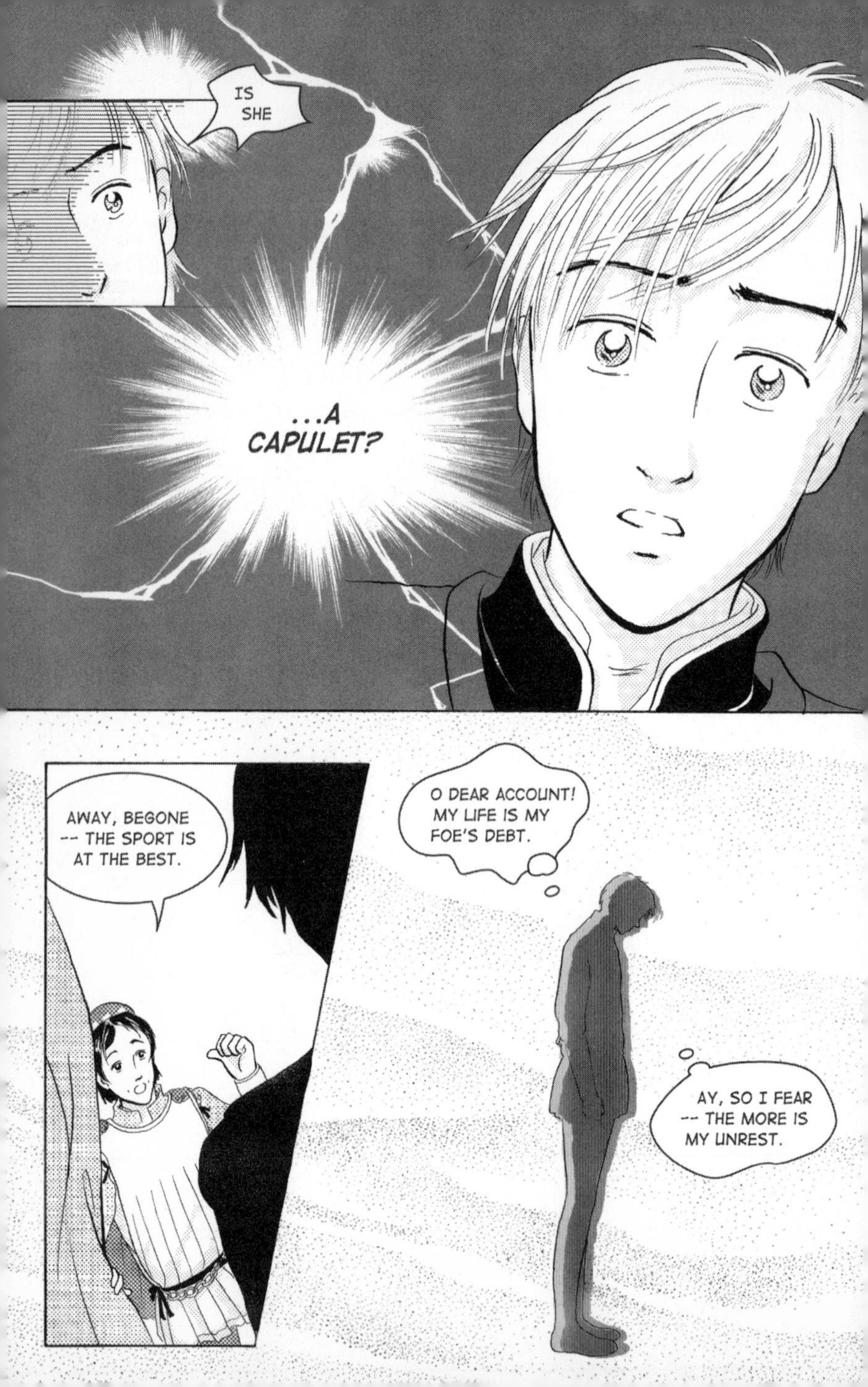
IS SHE
...A CAPULET?
AWAY, BEGONE -- THE SPORT IS AT THE BEST.
O DEAR ACCOUNT! MY LIFE IS MY FOE'S DEBT.
AY, SO I FEAR -- THE MORE IS MY UNREST.

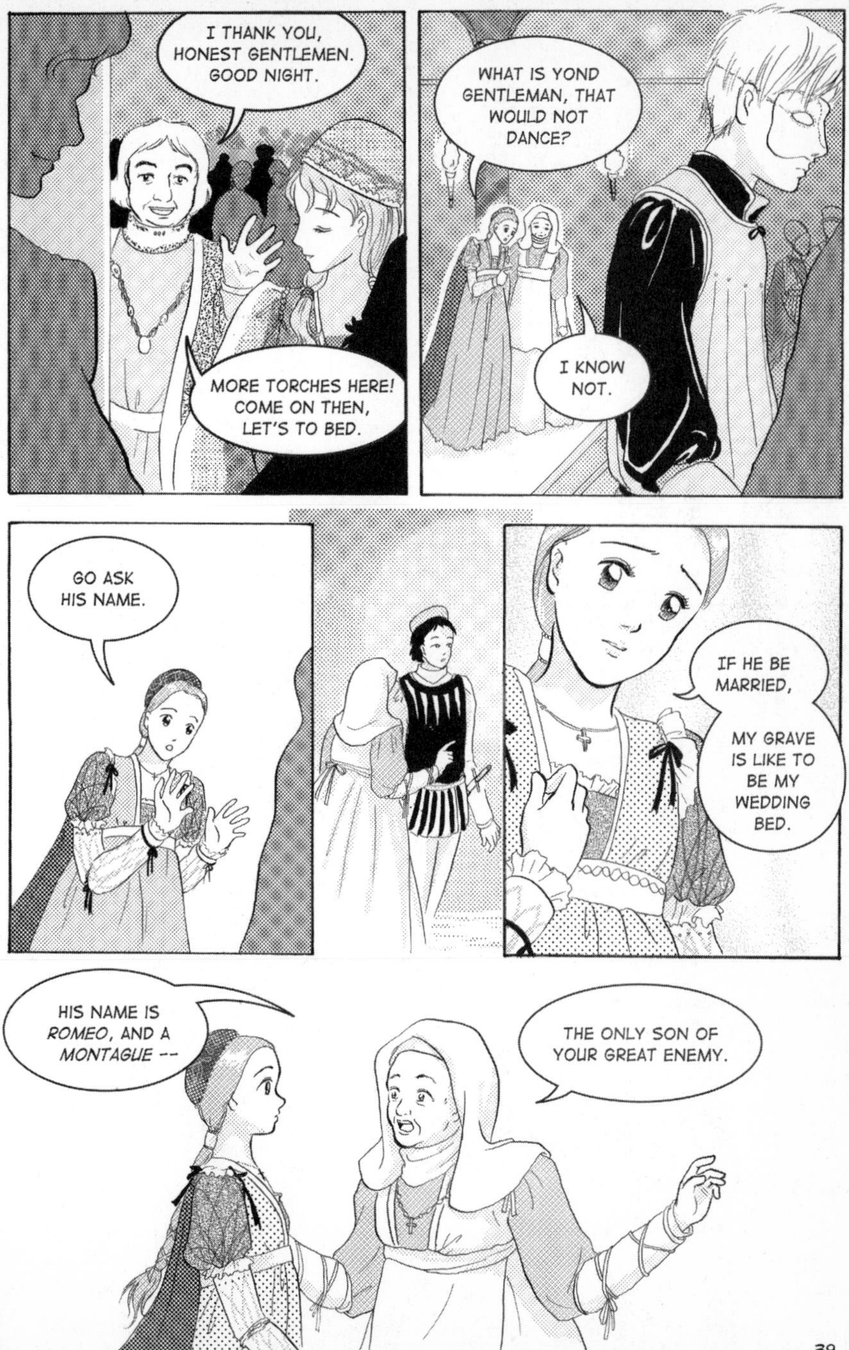
I THANK YOU, HONEST GENTLEMEN. GOOD NIGHT.
MORE TORCHES HERE! COME ON THEN, LET'S TO BED.
WHAT IS YOND GENTLEMAN, THAT WOULD NOT DANCE?
I KNOW NOT.
GO ASK HIS NAME.
IF HE BE MARRIED,
MY GRAVE IS LIKE TO BE MY WEDDING BED.
HIS NAME IS *ROMEO*, AND A *MONTAGUE* --
THE ONLY SON OF YOUR GREAT ENEMY.

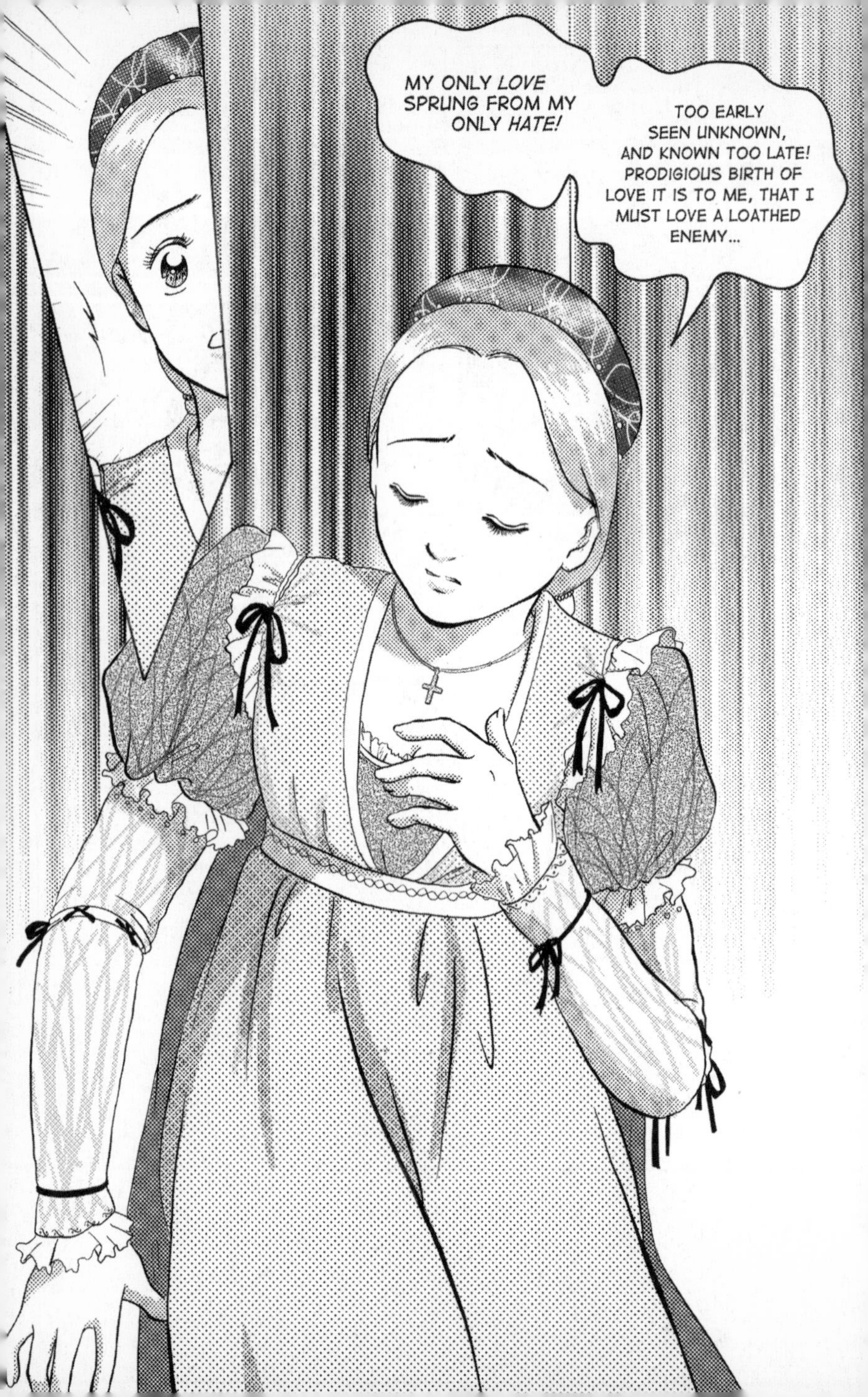
MY ONLY *LOVE* SPRUNG FROM MY ONLY *HATE!*
TOO EARLY SEEN UNKNOWN, AND KNOWN TOO LATE! PRODIGIOUS BIRTH OF LOVE IT IS TO ME, THAT I MUST LOVE A LOATHED ENEMY...

Act II

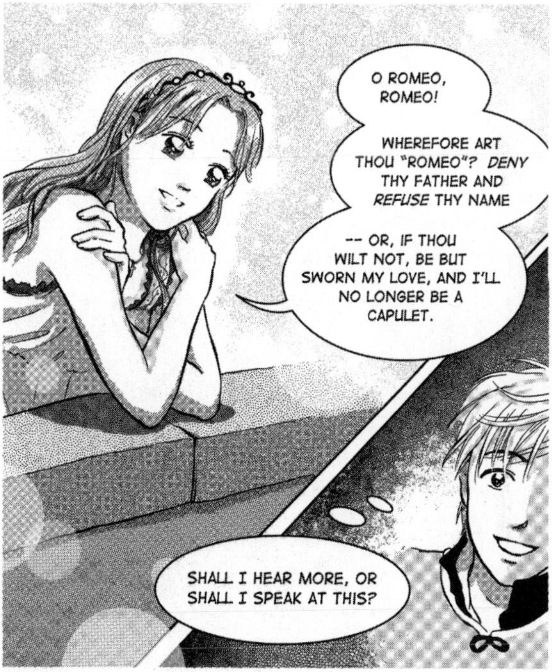
O ROMEO, ROMEO!
WHEREFORE ART THOU "ROMEO"? *DENY* THY FATHER AND *REFUSE* THY NAME
-- OR, IF THOU WILT NOT, BE BUT SWORN MY LOVE, AND I'LL NO LONGER BE A CAPULET.
SHALL I HEAR MORE, OR SHALL I SPEAK AT THIS?

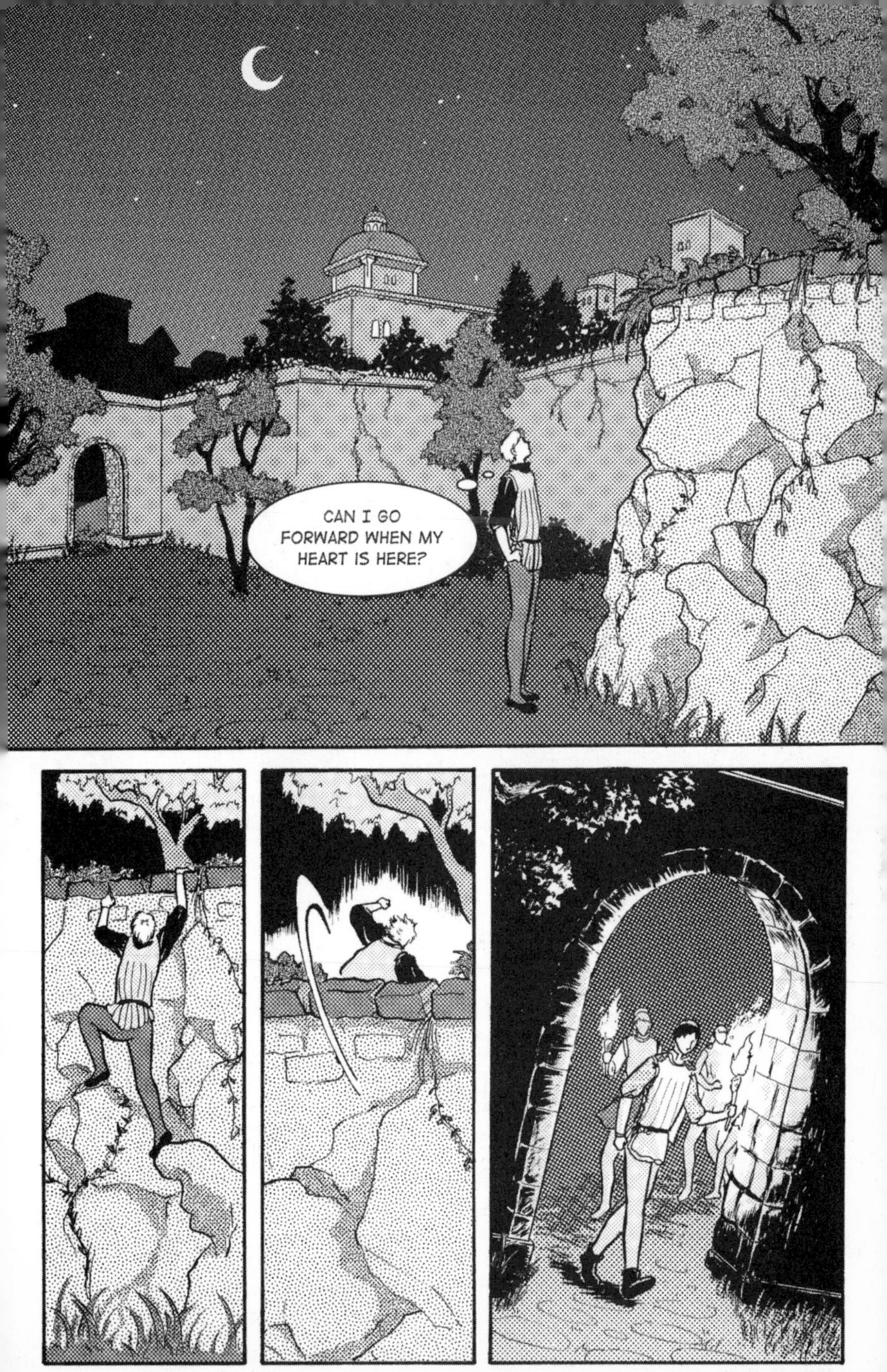
CAN I GO FORWARD WHEN MY HEART IS HERE?

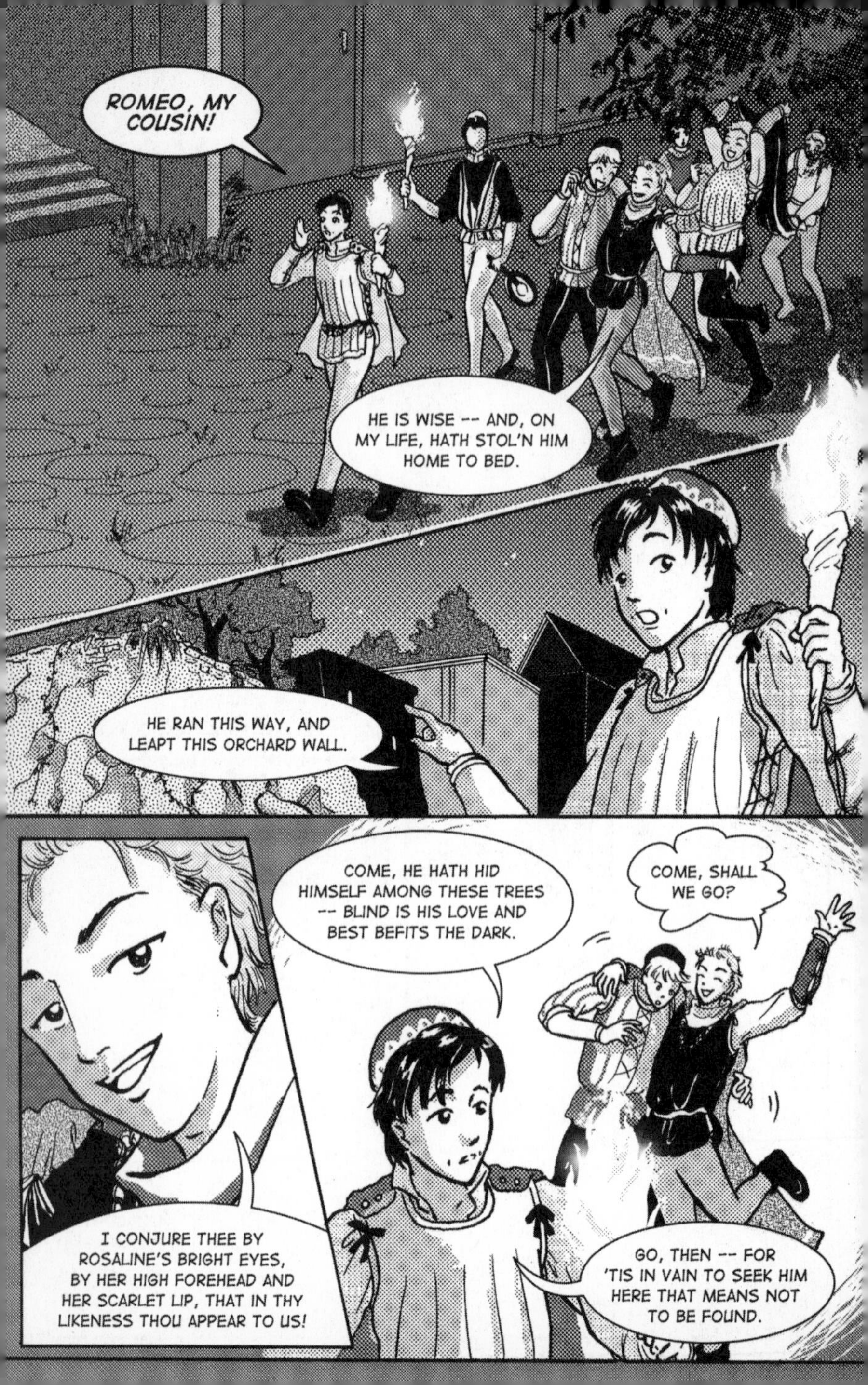
ROMEO, MY COUSIN!
HE IS WISE -- AND, ON MY LIFE, HATH STOL'N HIM HOME TO BED.
HE RAN THIS WAY, AND LEAPT THIS ORCHARD WALL.
I CONJURE THEE BY ROSALINE'S BRIGHT EYES, BY HER HIGH FOREHEAD AND HER SCARLET LIP, THAT IN THY LIKENESS THOU APPEAR TO US!
COME, HE HATH HID HIMSELF AMONG THESE TREES -- BLIND IS HIS LOVE AND BEST BEFITS THE DARK.
COME, SHALL WE GO?
GO, THEN -- FOR 'TIS IN VAIN TO SEEK HIM HERE THAT MEANS NOT TO BE FOUND.

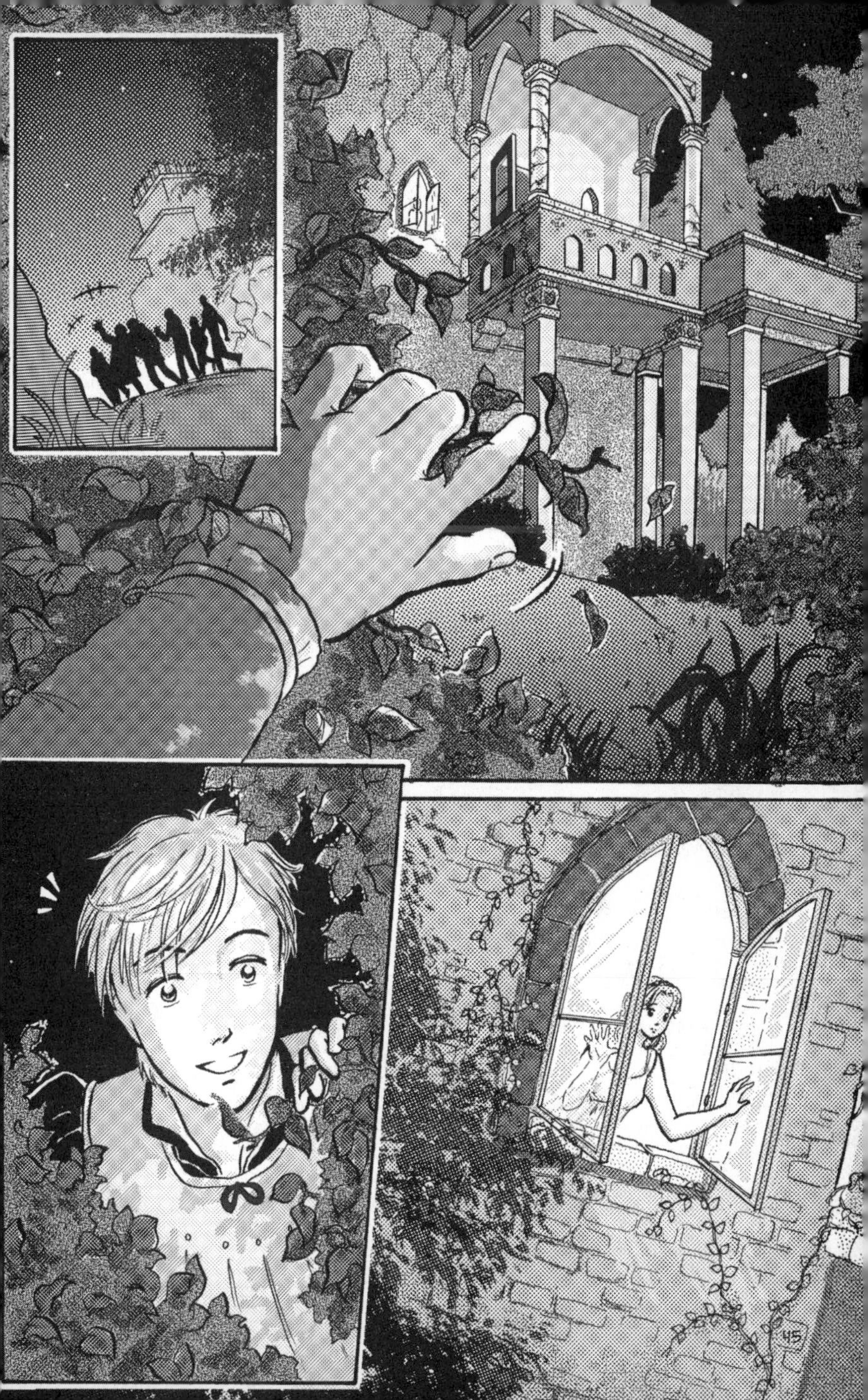

BUT, SOFT! WHAT LIGHT THROUGH YONDER WINDOW BREAKS? IT IS THE EAST, AND JULIET IS THE SUN. ARISE, FAIR SUN, AND KILL THE ENVIOUS MOON, WHO IS ALREADY SICK AND PALE WITH GRIEF THAT THOU, HER MAID, ART FAR MORE FAIR THAN SHE. BE *NOT* HER MAID, SINCE SHE IS ENVIOUS. HER VESTAL LIVERY IS BUT SICK AND GREEN AND NONE BUT FOOLS DO WEAR IT -- CAST IT OFF.

IT IS MY LADY -- O, IT IS MY LOVE! O, THAT SHE *KNEW* SHE WERE! SHE SPEAKS, YET SHE SAYS NOTHING -- WHAT OF THAT? HER EYE DISCOURSES. I WILL ANSWER IT --

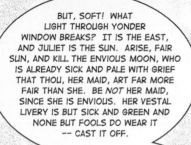

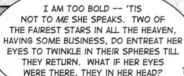

I AM TOO BOLD -- 'TIS NOT TO *ME* SHE SPEAKS. TWO OF THE FAIREST STARS IN ALL THE HEAVEN, HAVING SOME BUSINESS, DO ENTREAT HER EYES TO TWINKLE IN THEIR SPHERES TILL THEY RETURN. WHAT IF HER EYES WERE THERE, THEY IN HER HEAD?

THE BRIGHTNESS OF HER CHEEK WOULD *SHAME* THOSE STARS, AS DAYLIGHT DOTH A LAMP -- HER EYES IN HEAVEN WOULD THROUGH THE AIRY REGION STREAM SO BRIGHT THAT BIRDS WOULD SING AND THINK IT WERE NOT NIGHT.

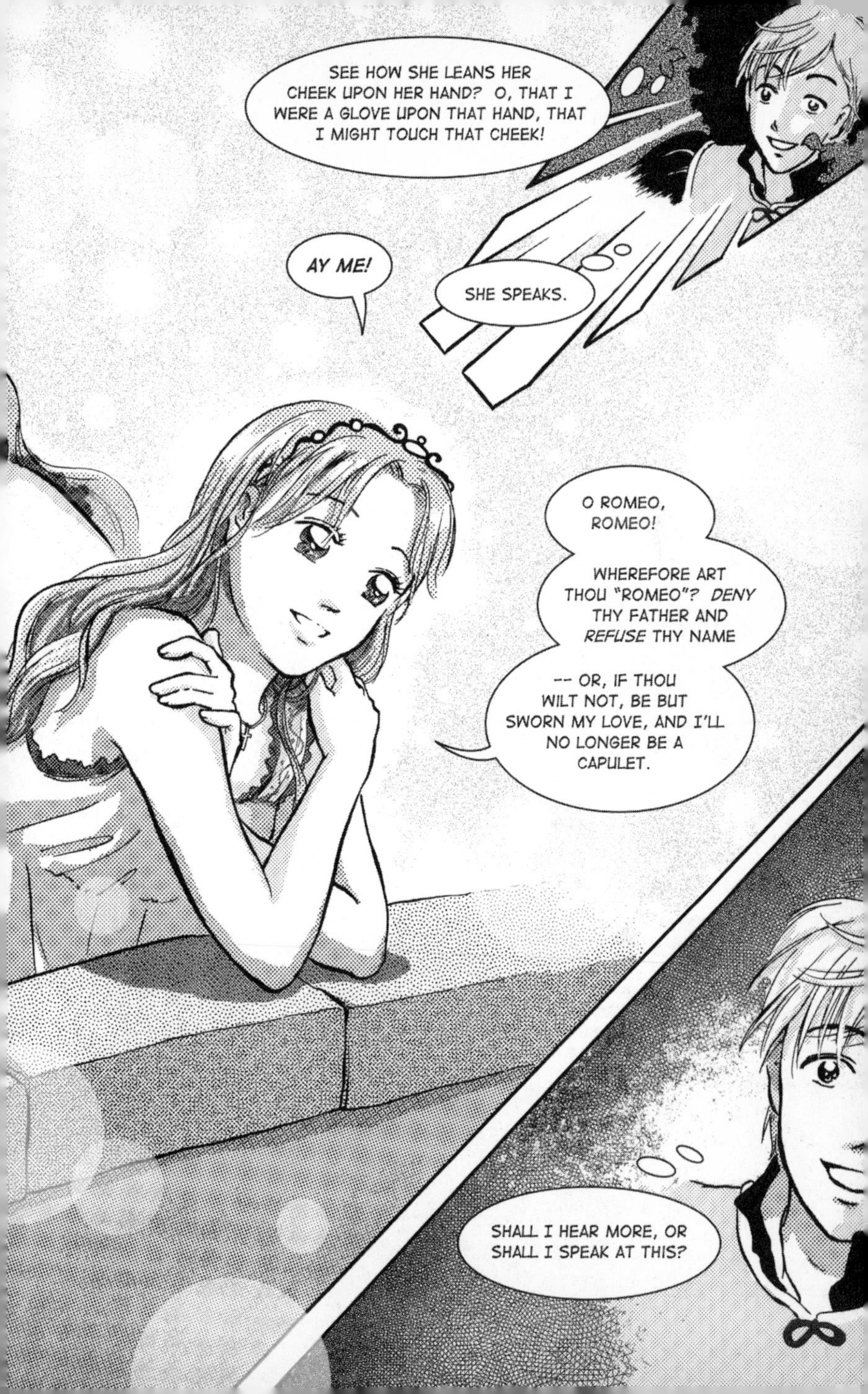
SEE HOW SHE LEANS HER CHEEK UPON HER HAND? O, THAT I WERE A GLOVE UPON THAT HAND, THAT I MIGHT TOUCH THAT CHEEK!
AY ME!
SHE SPEAKS.
O ROMEO, ROMEO!
WHEREFORE ART THOU "ROMEO"? DENY THY FATHER AND REFUSE THY NAME
-- OR, IF THOU WILT NOT, BE BUT SWORN MY LOVE, AND I'LL NO LONGER BE A CAPULET.
SHALL I HEAR MORE, OR SHALL I SPEAK AT THIS?

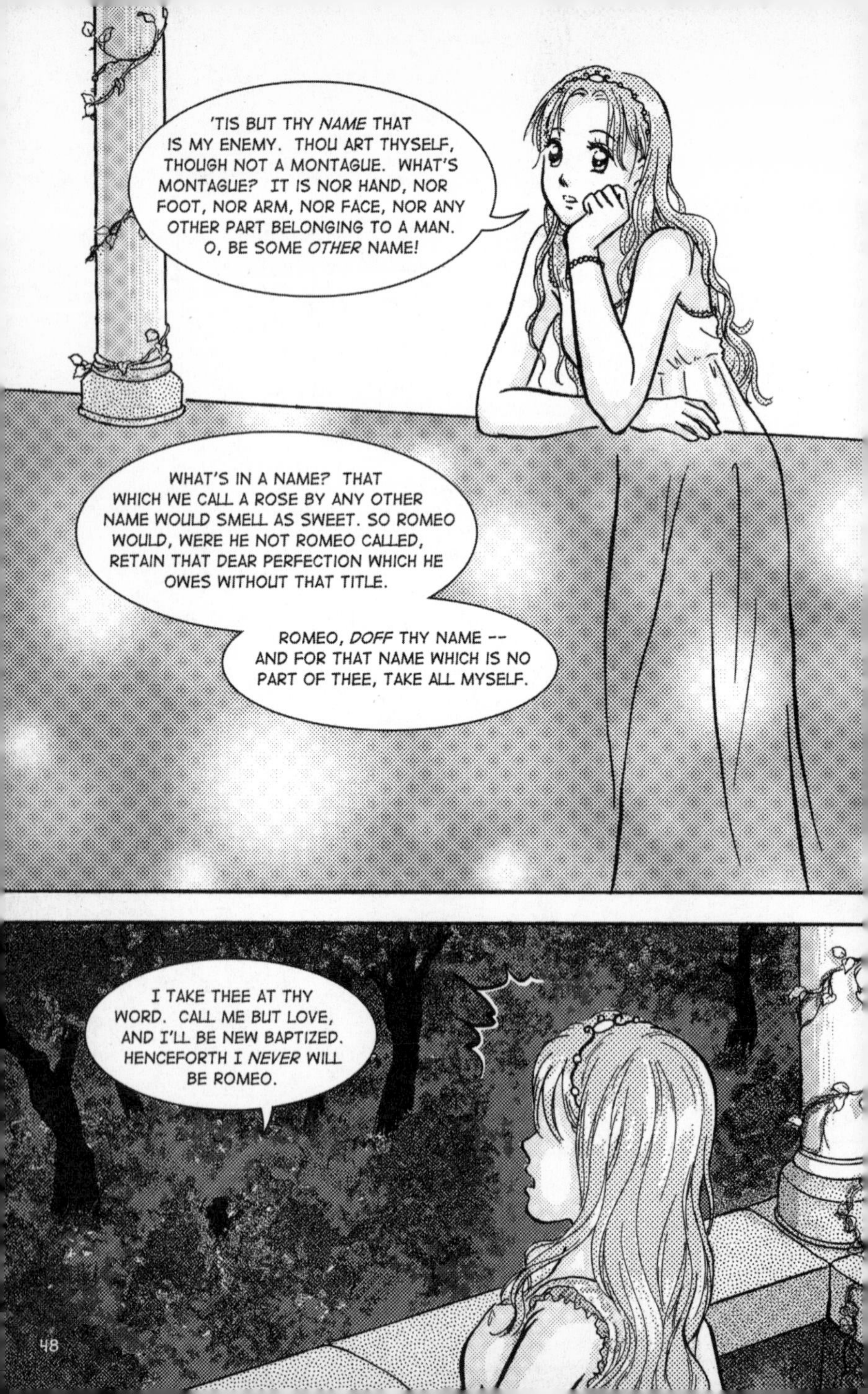
'TIS BUT THY *NAME* THAT IS MY ENEMY. THOU ART THYSELF, THOUGH NOT A MONTAGUE. WHAT'S MONTAGUE? IT IS NOR HAND, NOR FOOT, NOR ARM, NOR FACE, NOR ANY OTHER PART BELONGING TO A MAN. O, BE SOME *OTHER* NAME!
WHAT'S IN A NAME? THAT WHICH WE CALL A ROSE BY ANY OTHER NAME WOULD SMELL AS SWEET. SO ROMEO WOULD, WERE HE NOT ROMEO CALLED, RETAIN THAT DEAR PERFECTION WHICH HE OWES WITHOUT THAT TITLE.
ROMEO, *DOFF* THY NAME -- AND FOR THAT NAME WHICH IS NO PART OF THEE, TAKE ALL MYSELF.
I TAKE THEE AT THY WORD. CALL ME BUT LOVE, AND I'LL BE NEW BAPTIZED. HENCEFORTH I *NEVER* WILL BE ROMEO.

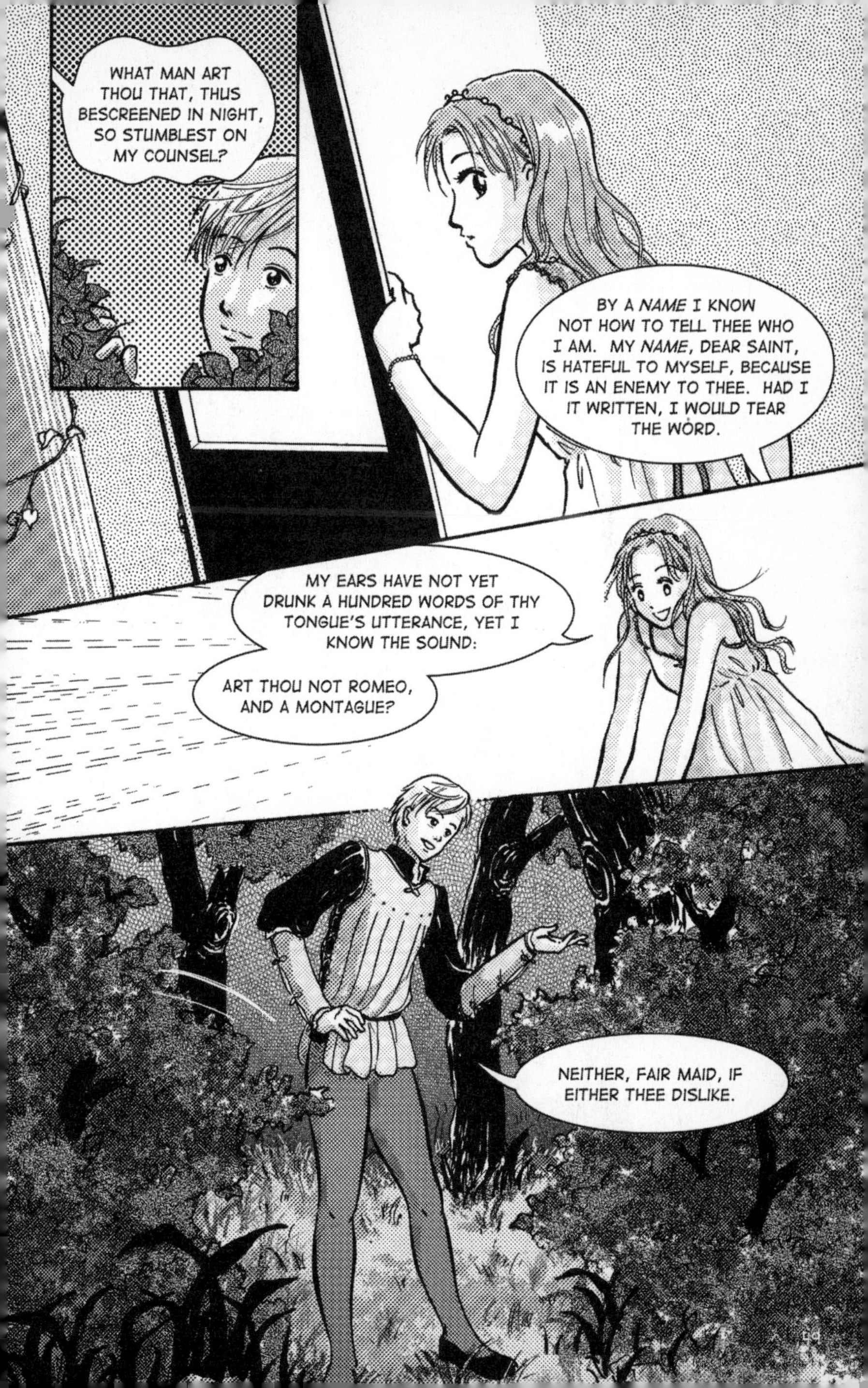

WHAT MAN ART THOU THAT, THUS BESCREENED IN NIGHT, SO STUMBLEST ON MY COUNSEL?
BY A *NAME* I KNOW NOT HOW TO TELL THEE WHO I AM. MY *NAME*, DEAR SAINT, IS HATEFUL TO MYSELF, BECAUSE IT IS AN ENEMY TO THEE. HAD I IT WRITTEN, I WOULD TEAR THE WORD.
MY EARS HAVE NOT YET DRUNK A HUNDRED WORDS OF THY TONGUE'S UTTERANCE, YET I KNOW THE SOUND:
ART THOU NOT ROMEO, AND A MONTAGUE?
NEITHER, FAIR MAID, IF EITHER THEE DISLIKE.

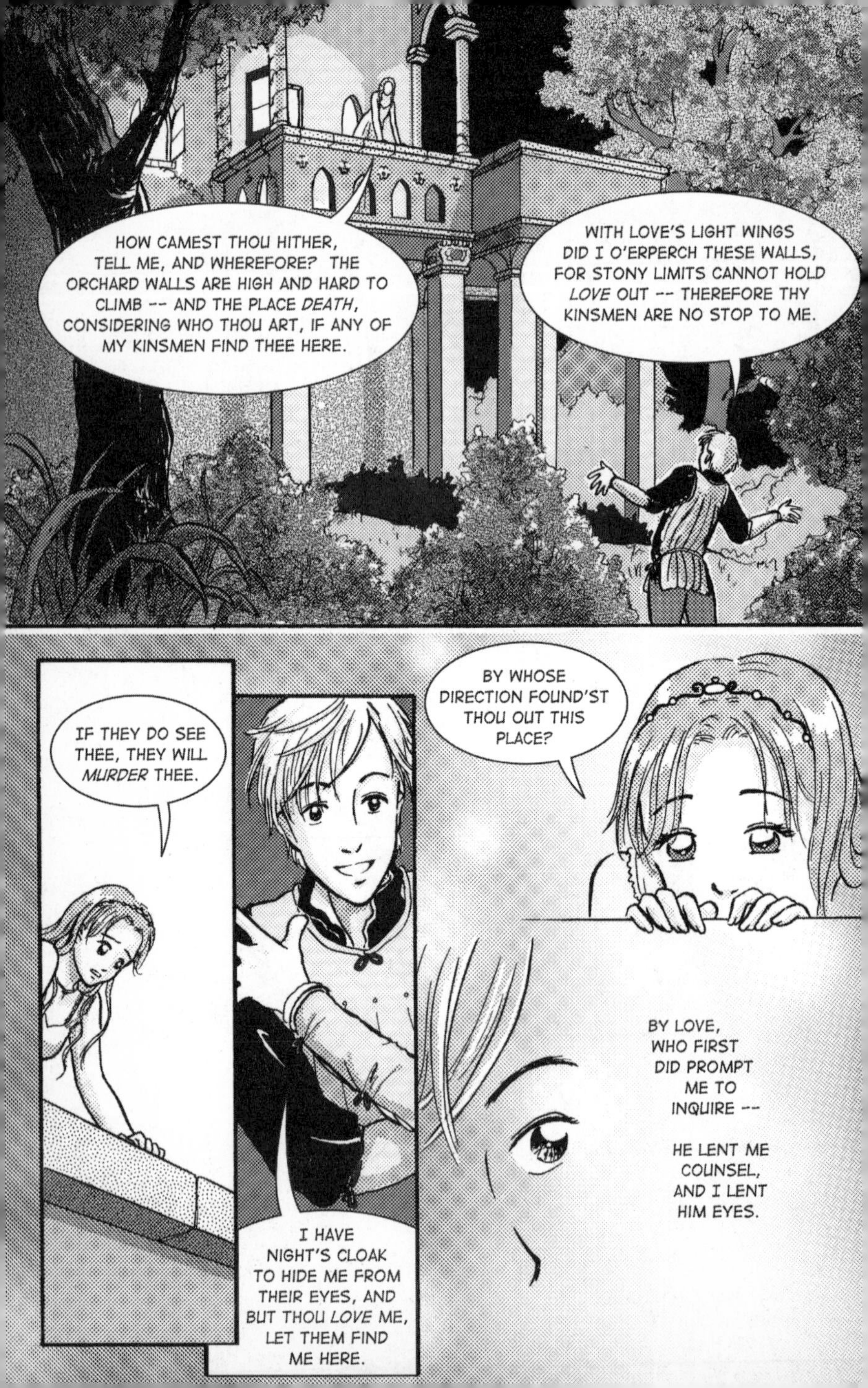
HOW CAMEST THOU HITHER, TELL ME, AND WHEREFORE? THE ORCHARD WALLS ARE HIGH AND HARD TO CLIMB -- AND THE PLACE *DEATH*, CONSIDERING WHO THOU ART, IF ANY OF MY KINSMEN FIND THEE HERE.
WITH LOVE'S LIGHT WINGS DID I O'ERPERCH THESE WALLS, FOR STONY LIMITS CANNOT HOLD *LOVE* OUT -- THEREFORE THY KINSMEN ARE NO STOP TO ME.
IF THEY DO SEE THEE, THEY WILL *MURDER* THEE.
I HAVE NIGHT'S CLOAK TO HIDE ME FROM THEIR EYES, AND BUT THOU *LOVE* ME, LET THEM FIND ME HERE.
BY WHOSE DIRECTION FOUND'ST THOU OUT THIS PLACE?
BY LOVE, WHO FIRST DID PROMPT ME TO INQUIRE --
HE LENT ME COUNSEL, AND I LENT HIM EYES.

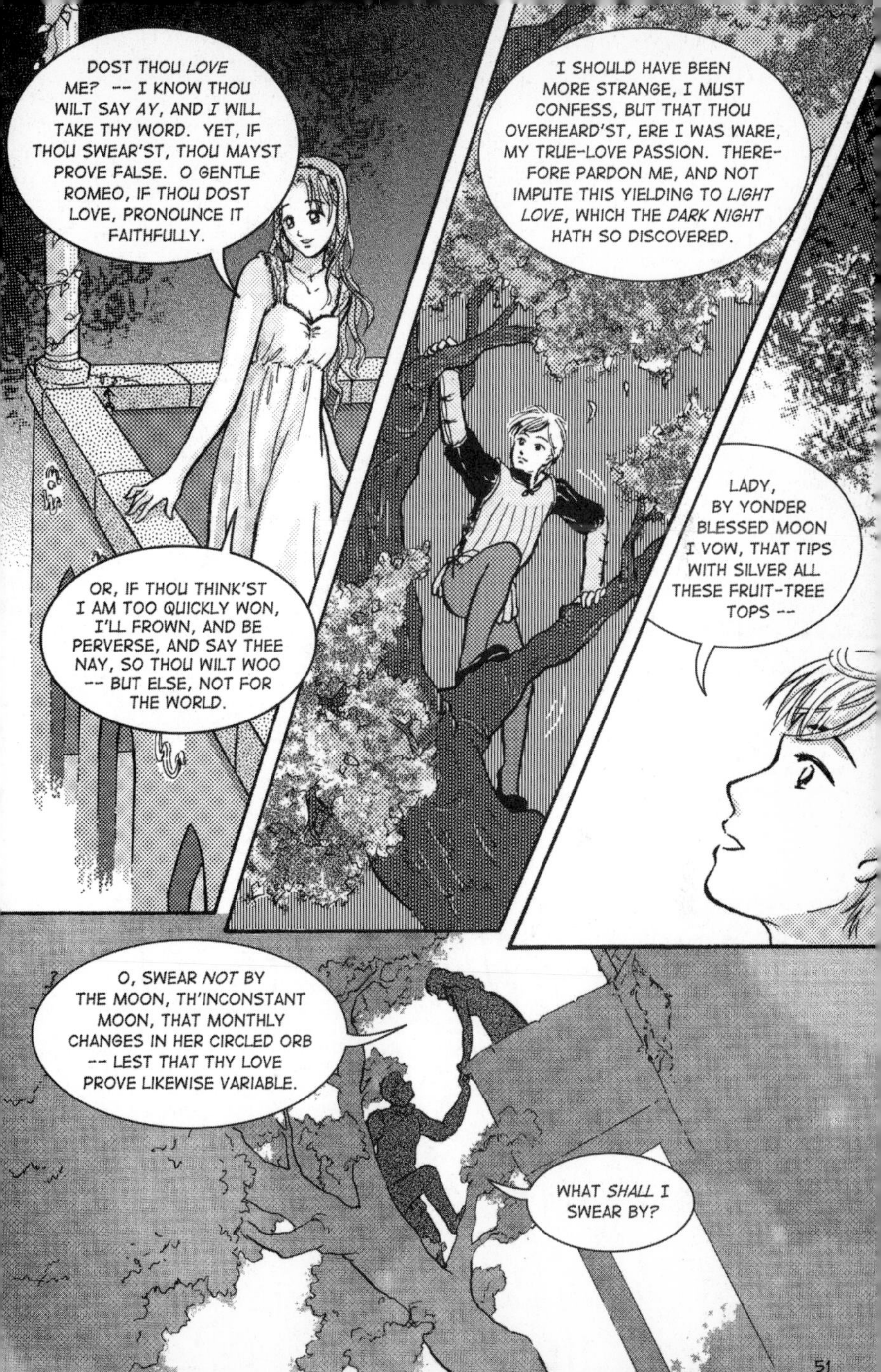
DOST THOU *LOVE* ME? -- I KNOW THOU WILT SAY *AY*, AND *I* WILL TAKE THY WORD. YET, IF THOU SWEAR'ST, THOU MAYST PROVE FALSE. O GENTLE ROMEO, IF THOU DOST LOVE, PRONOUNCE IT FAITHFULLY.
OR, IF THOU THINK'ST I AM TOO QUICKLY WON, I'LL FROWN, AND BE PERVERSE, AND SAY THEE NAY, SO THOU WILT WOO -- BUT ELSE, NOT FOR THE WORLD.
I SHOULD HAVE BEEN MORE STRANGE, I MUST CONFESS, BUT THAT THOU OVERHEARD'ST, ERE I WAS WARE, MY TRUE-LOVE PASSION. THEREFORE PARDON ME, AND NOT IMPUTE THIS YIELDING TO *LIGHT LOVE*, WHICH THE *DARK NIGHT* HATH SO DISCOVERED.
LADY, BY YONDER BLESSED MOON I VOW, THAT TIPS WITH SILVER ALL THESE FRUIT-TREE TOPS --
O, SWEAR *NOT* BY THE MOON, TH'INCONSTANT MOON, THAT MONTHLY CHANGES IN HER CIRCLED ORB -- LEST THAT THY LOVE PROVE LIKEWISE VARIABLE.
WHAT *SHALL* I SWEAR BY?

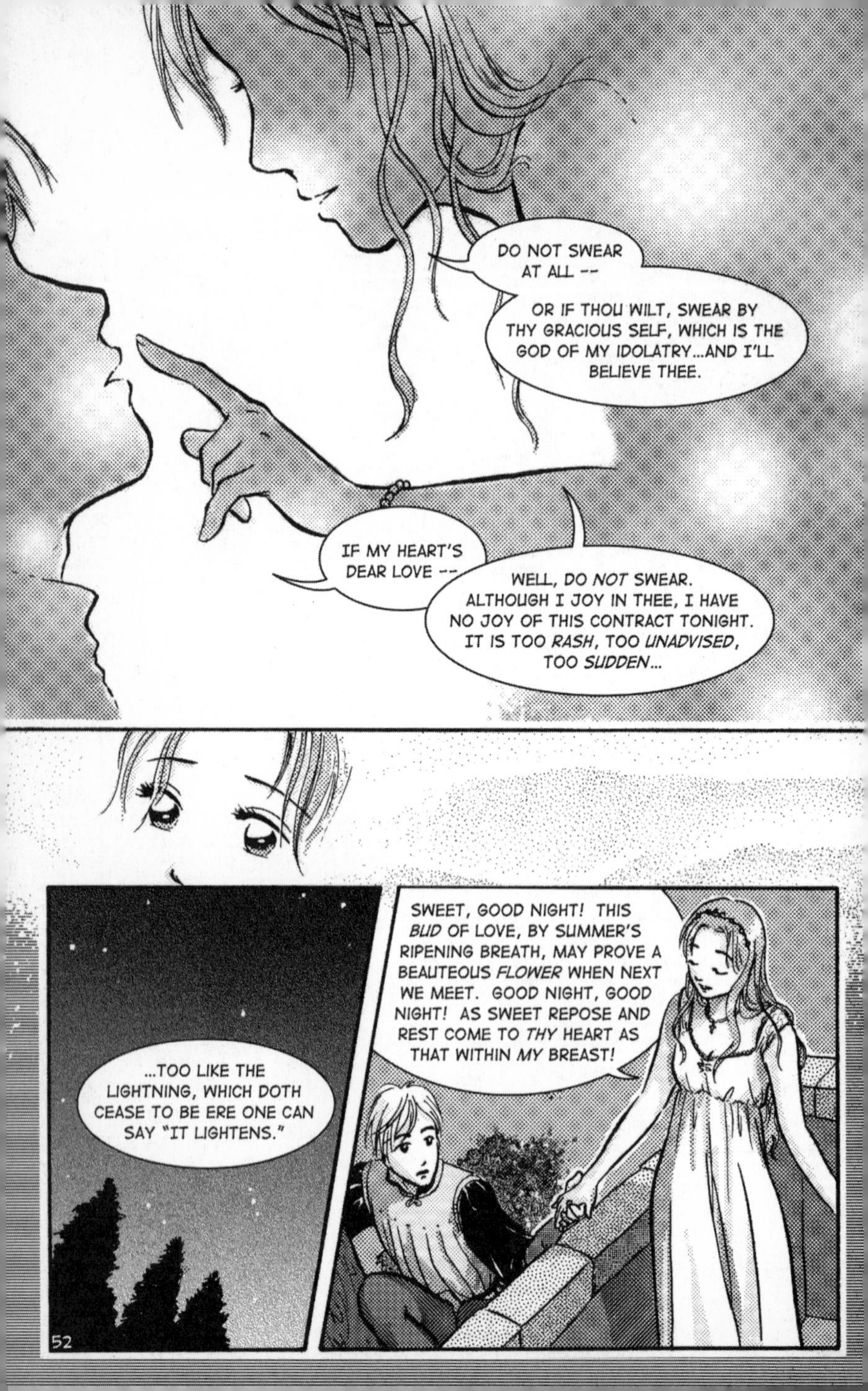
DO NOT SWEAR AT ALL --
OR IF THOU WILT, SWEAR BY THY GRACIOUS SELF, WHICH IS THE GOD OF MY IDOLATRY...AND I'LL BELIEVE THEE.
IF MY HEART'S DEAR LOVE --
WELL, DO *NOT* SWEAR. ALTHOUGH I JOY IN THEE, I HAVE NO JOY OF THIS CONTRACT TONIGHT. IT IS TOO *RASH*, TOO *UNADVISED*, TOO *SUDDEN*...
...TOO LIKE THE LIGHTNING, WHICH DOTH CEASE TO BE ERE ONE CAN SAY "IT LIGHTENS."
SWEET, GOOD NIGHT! THIS *BUD* OF LOVE, BY SUMMER'S RIPENING BREATH, MAY PROVE A BEAUTEOUS *FLOWER* WHEN NEXT WE MEET. GOOD NIGHT, GOOD NIGHT! AS SWEET REPOSE AND REST COME TO *THY* HEART AS THAT WITHIN *MY* BREAST!

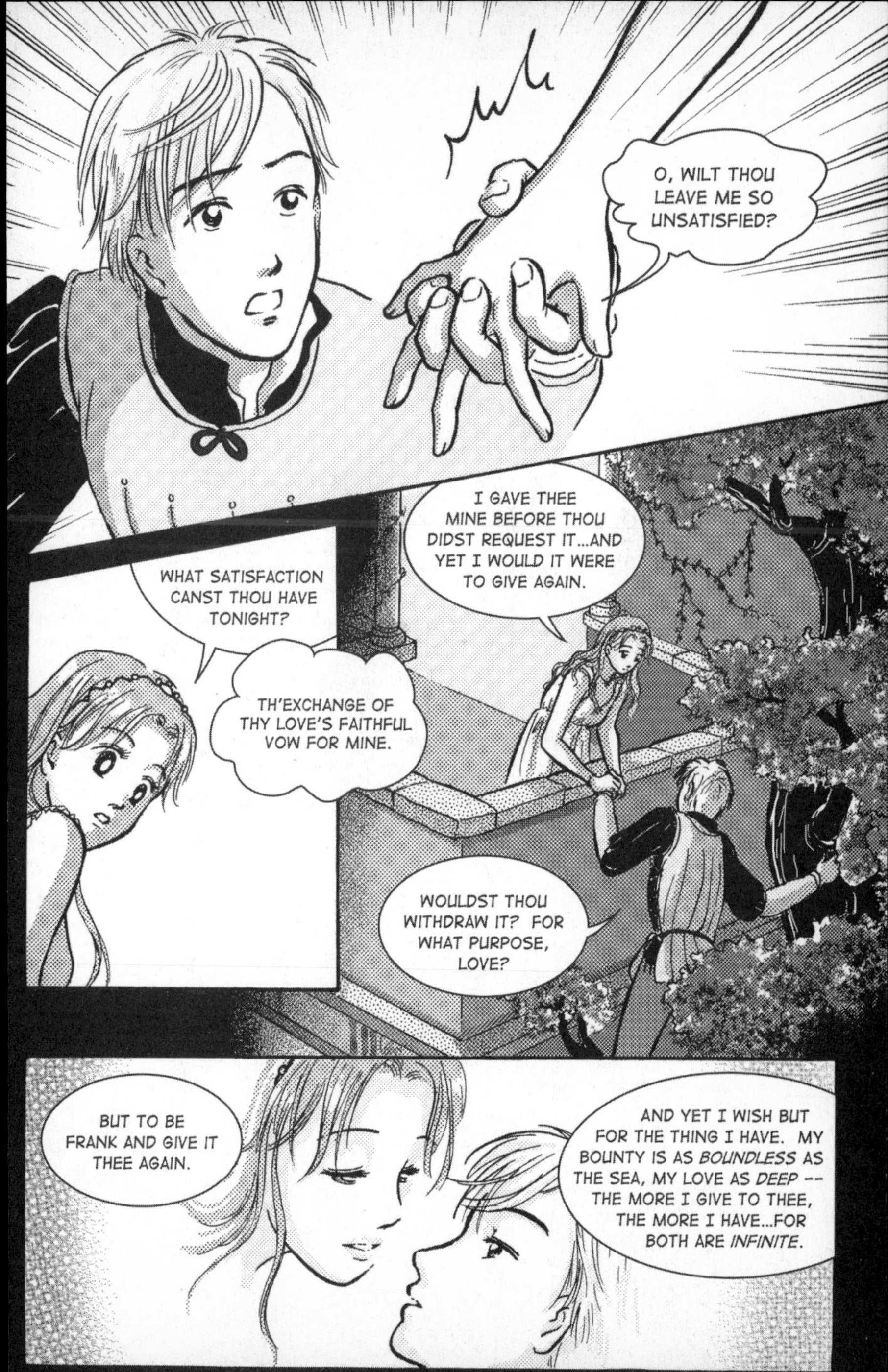
O, WILT THOU LEAVE ME SO UNSATISFIED?
WHAT SATISFACTION CANST THOU HAVE TONIGHT?
TH'EXCHANGE OF THY LOVE'S FAITHFUL VOW FOR MINE.
I GAVE THEE MINE BEFORE THOU DIDST REQUEST IT...AND YET I WOULD IT WERE TO GIVE AGAIN.
WOULDST THOU WITHDRAW IT? FOR WHAT PURPOSE, LOVE?
BUT TO BE FRANK AND GIVE IT THEE AGAIN.
AND YET I WISH BUT FOR THE THING I HAVE. MY BOUNTY IS AS *BOUNDLESS* AS THE SEA, MY LOVE AS *DEEP* -- THE MORE I GIVE TO THEE, THE MORE I HAVE...FOR BOTH ARE *INFINITE*.

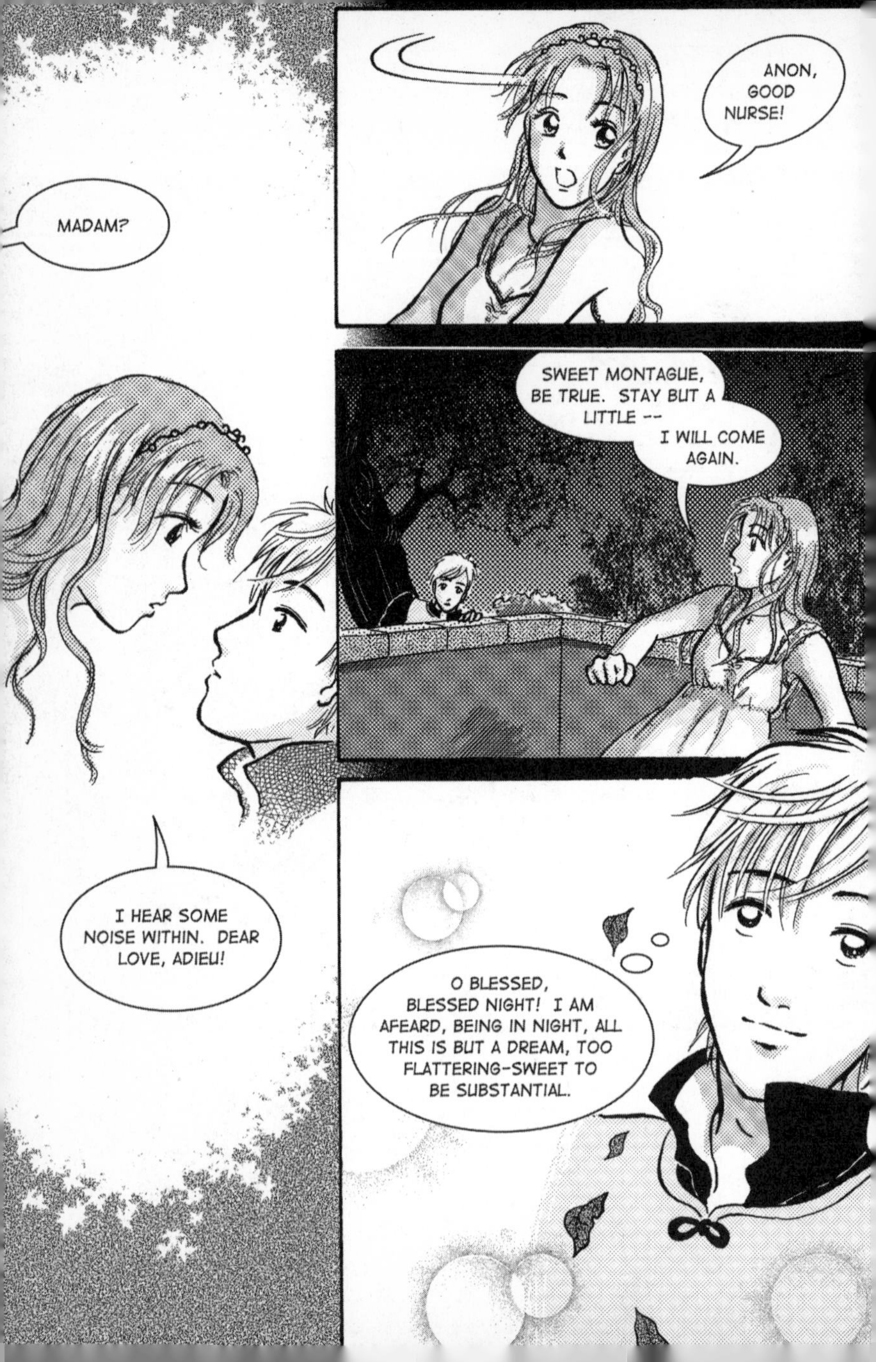
MADAM?
I HEAR SOME NOISE WITHIN. DEAR LOVE, ADIEU!
ANON, GOOD NURSE!
SWEET MONTAGUE, BE TRUE. STAY BUT A LITTLE -- I WILL COME AGAIN.
O BLESSED, BLESSED NIGHT! I AM AFEARD, BEING IN NIGHT, ALL THIS IS BUT A DREAM, TOO FLATTERING-SWEET TO BE SUBSTANTIAL.

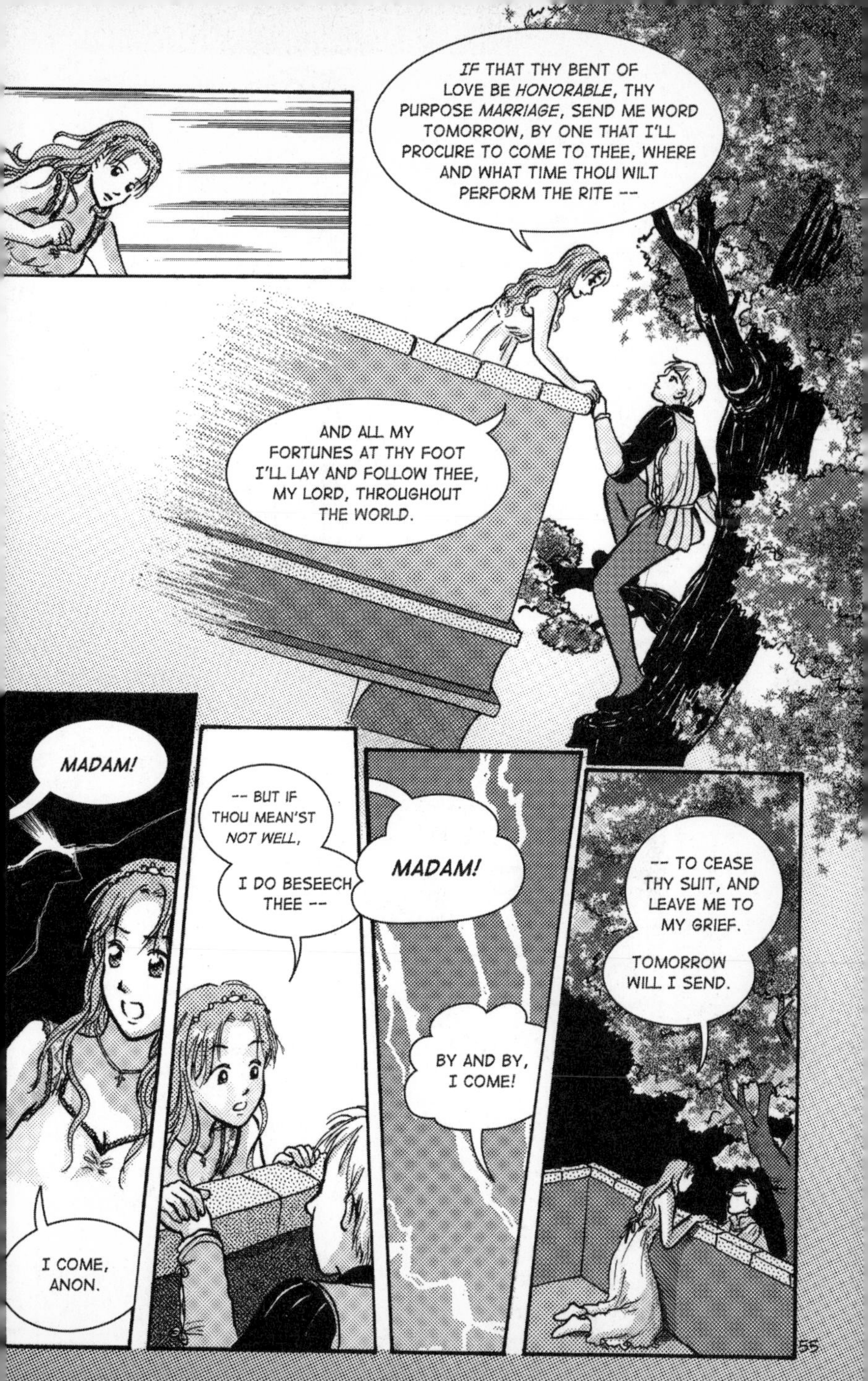

IF THAT THY BENT OF LOVE BE HONORABLE, THY PURPOSE MARRIAGE, SEND ME WORD TOMORROW, BY ONE THAT I'LL PROCURE TO COME TO THEE, WHERE AND WHAT TIME THOU WILT PERFORM THE RITE --
AND ALL MY FORTUNES AT THY FOOT I'LL LAY AND FOLLOW THEE, MY LORD, THROUGHOUT THE WORLD.
MADAM!
I COME, ANON.
-- BUT IF THOU MEAN'ST NOT WELL,
I DO BESEECH THEE --
MADAM!
BY AND BY, I COME!
-- TO CEASE THY SUIT, AND LEAVE ME TO MY GRIEF.
TOMORROW WILL I SEND.

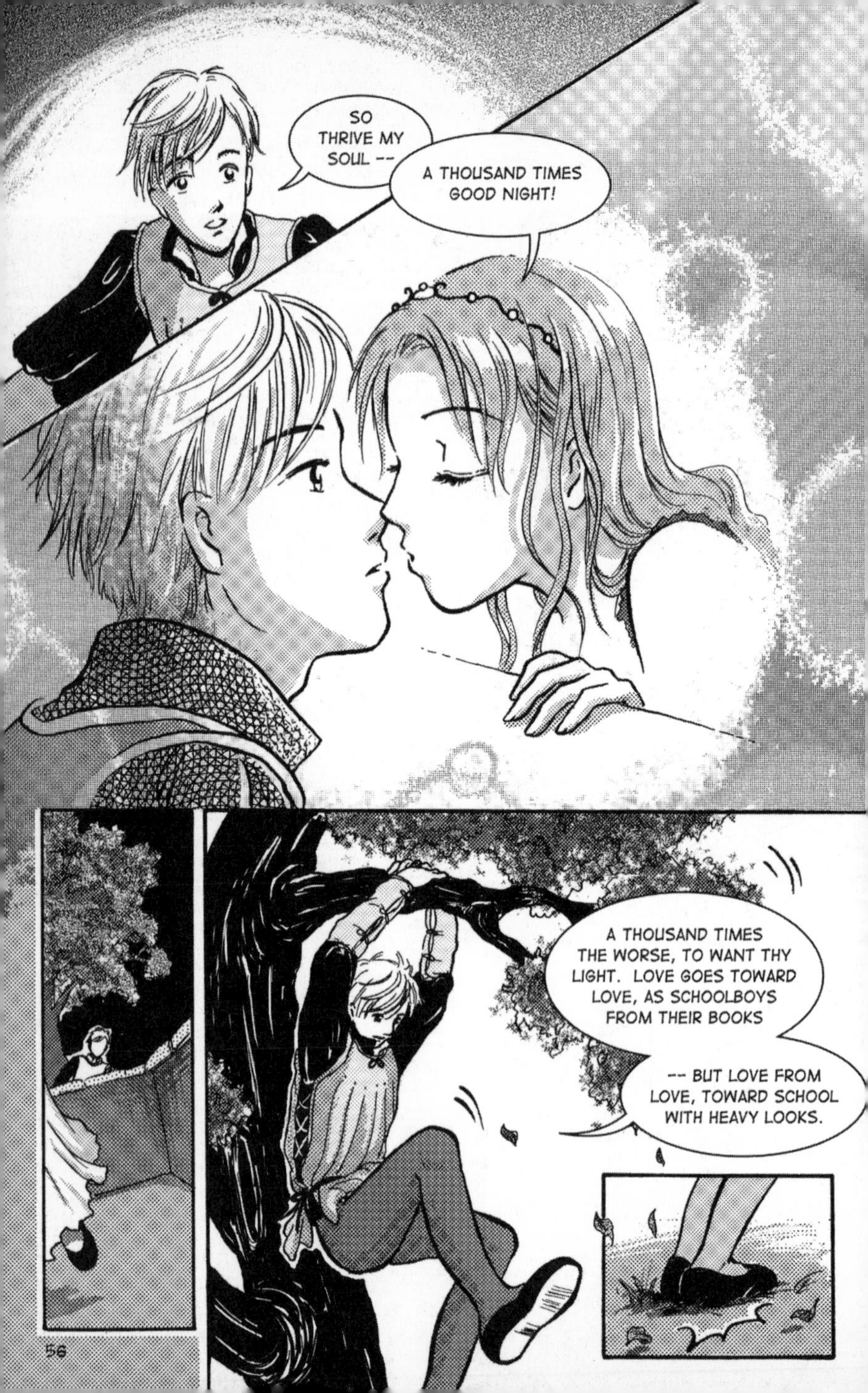
SO THRIVE MY SOUL --
A THOUSAND TIMES GOOD NIGHT!
A THOUSAND TIMES THE WORSE, TO WANT THY LIGHT. LOVE GOES TOWARD LOVE, AS SCHOOLBOYS FROM THEIR BOOKS
-- BUT LOVE FROM LOVE, TOWARD SCHOOL WITH HEAVY LOOKS.

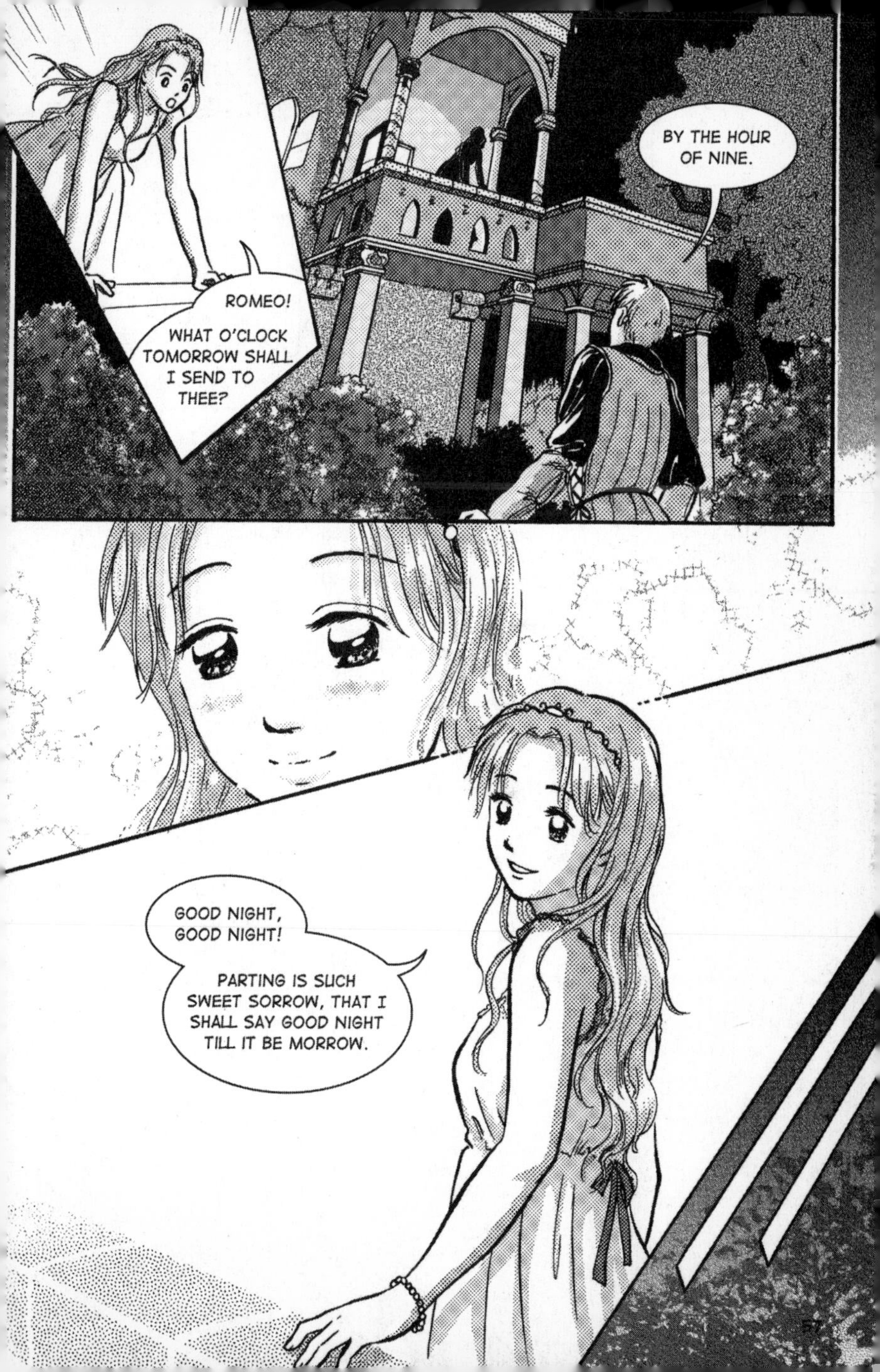
ROMEO!
WHAT O'CLOCK TOMORROW SHALL I SEND TO THEE?
BY THE HOUR OF NINE.
GOOD NIGHT, GOOD NIGHT!
PARTING IS SUCH SWEET SORROW, THAT I SHALL SAY GOOD NIGHT TILL IT BE MORROW.

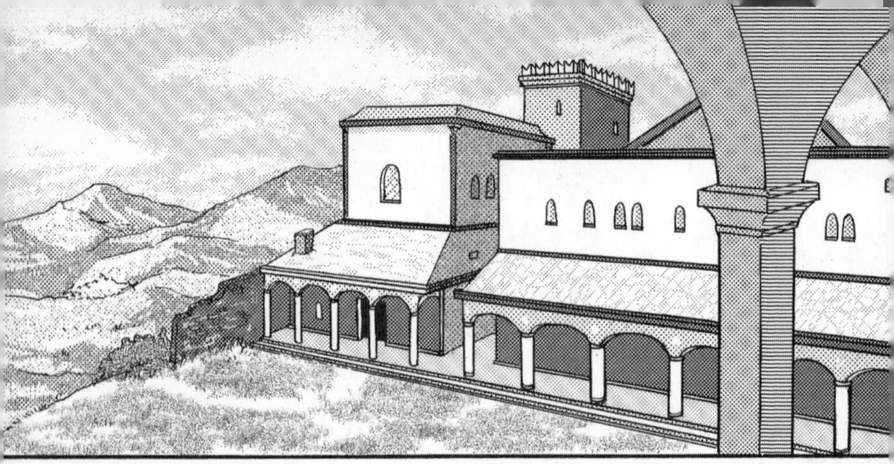

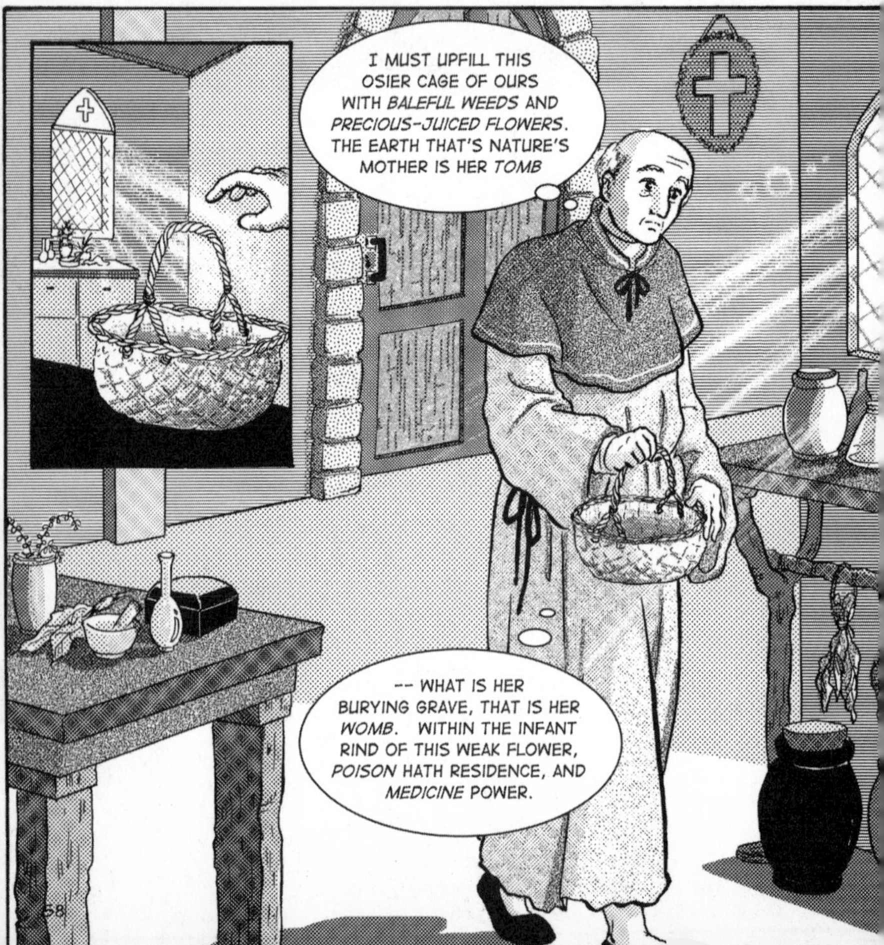
I MUST UPFILL THIS OSIER CAGE OF OURS WITH *BALEFUL WEEDS* AND *PRECIOUS-JUICED FLOWERS*. THE EARTH THAT'S NATURE'S MOTHER IS HER *TOMB*
-- WHAT IS HER BURYING GRAVE, THAT IS HER *WOMB*. WITHIN THE INFANT RIND OF THIS WEAK FLOWER, *POISON* HATH RESIDENCE, AND *MEDICINE* POWER.

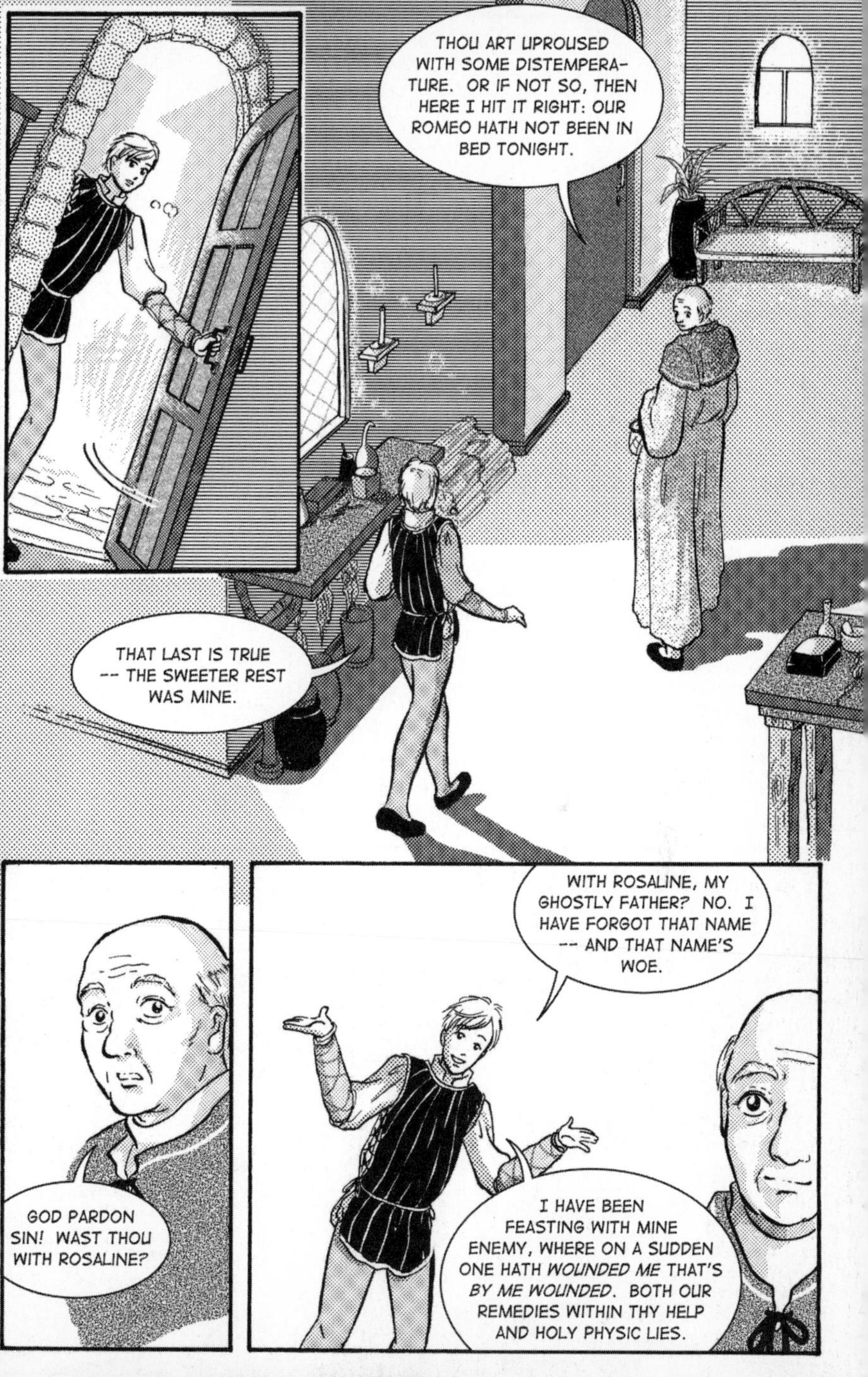
THOU ART UPROUSED WITH SOME DISTEMPERATURE. OR IF NOT SO, THEN HERE I HIT IT RIGHT: OUR ROMEO HATH NOT BEEN IN BED TONIGHT.
THAT LAST IS TRUE -- THE SWEETER REST WAS MINE.
GOD PARDON SIN! WAST THOU WITH ROSALINE?
WITH ROSALINE, MY GHOSTLY FATHER? NO. I HAVE FORGOT THAT NAME -- AND THAT NAME'S WOE.
I HAVE BEEN FEASTING WITH MINE ENEMY, WHERE ON A SUDDEN ONE HATH *WOUNDED ME* THAT'S *BY ME WOUNDED*. BOTH OUR REMEDIES WITHIN THY HELP AND HOLY PHYSIC LIES.

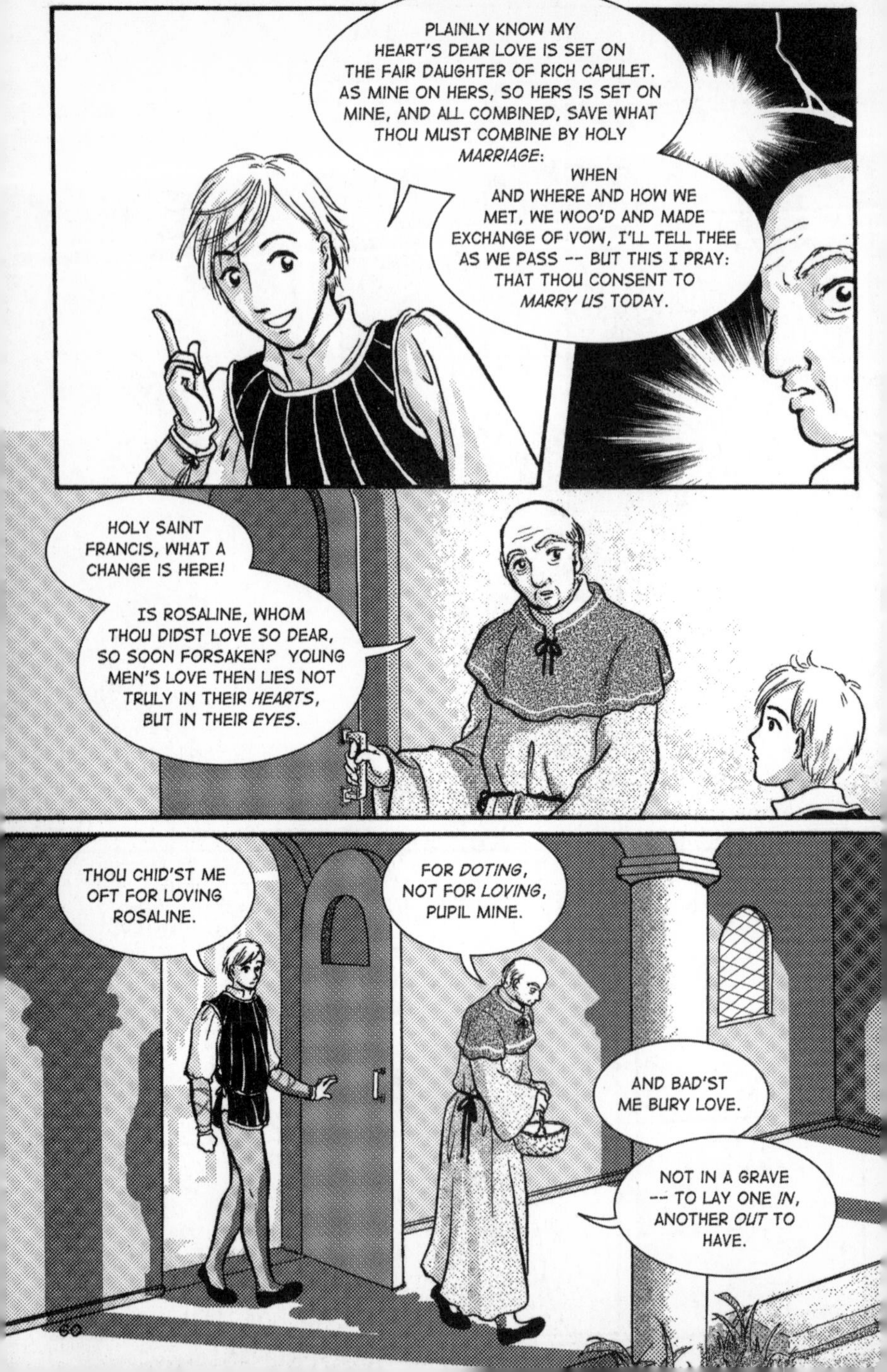
PLAINLY KNOW MY HEART'S DEAR LOVE IS SET ON THE FAIR DAUGHTER OF RICH CAPULET. AS MINE ON HERS, SO HERS IS SET ON MINE, AND ALL COMBINED, SAVE WHAT THOU MUST COMBINE BY HOLY *MARRIAGE*:
WHEN AND WHERE AND HOW WE MET, WE WOO'D AND MADE EXCHANGE OF VOW, I'LL TELL THEE AS WE PASS -- BUT THIS I PRAY: THAT THOU CONSENT TO *MARRY US* TODAY.
HOLY SAINT FRANCIS, WHAT A CHANGE IS HERE!
IS ROSALINE, WHOM THOU DIDST LOVE SO DEAR, SO SOON FORSAKEN? YOUNG MEN'S LOVE THEN LIES NOT TRULY IN THEIR *HEARTS*, BUT IN THEIR *EYES*.
THOU CHID'ST ME OFT FOR LOVING ROSALINE.
FOR *DOTING*, NOT FOR *LOVING*, PUPIL MINE.
AND BAD'ST ME BURY LOVE.
NOT IN A GRAVE -- TO LAY ONE *IN*, ANOTHER *OUT* TO HAVE.

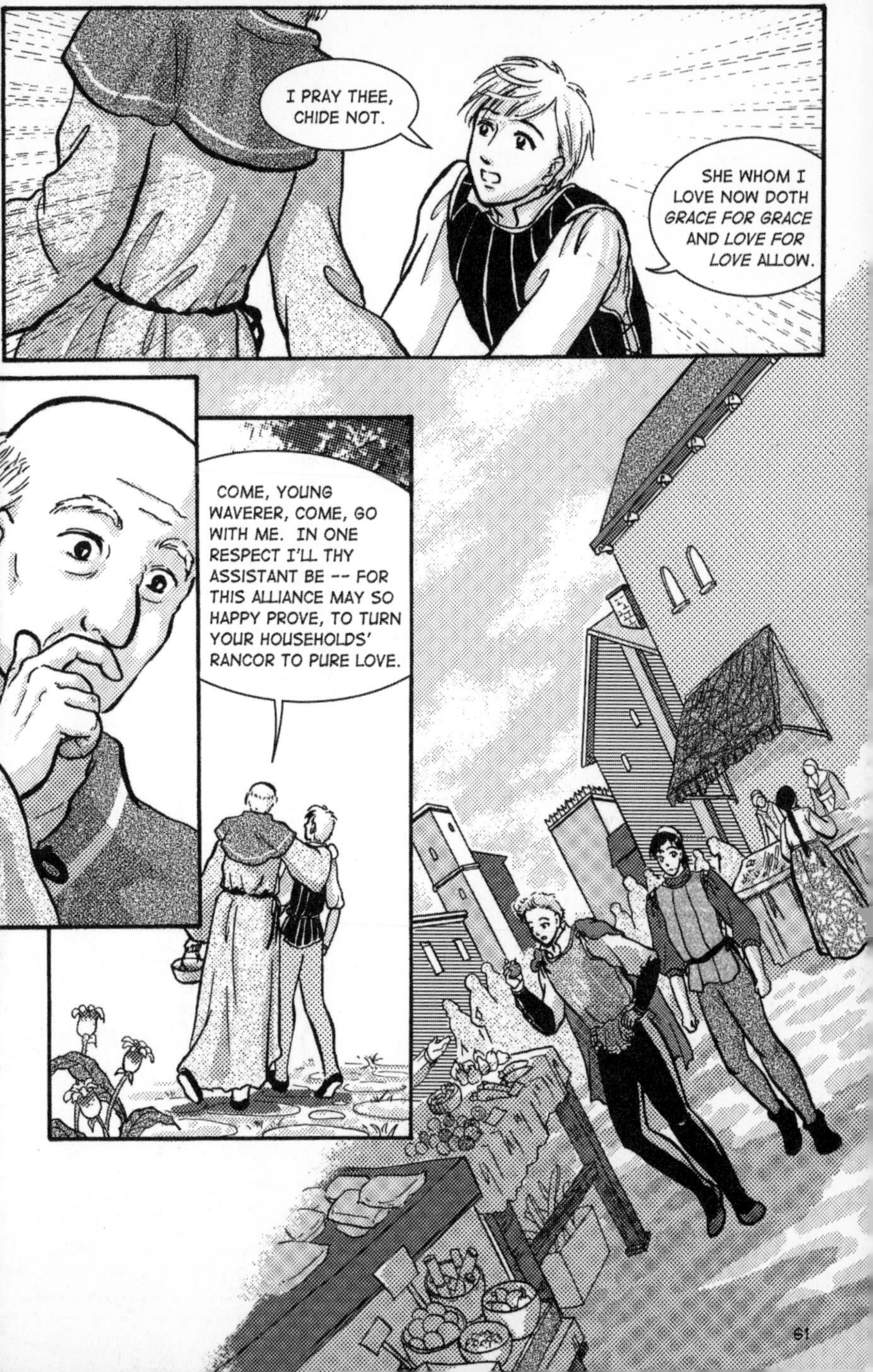
I PRAY THEE, CHIDE NOT.
SHE WHOM I LOVE NOW DOTH *GRACE FOR GRACE* AND *LOVE FOR LOVE* ALLOW.
COME, YOUNG WAVERER, COME, GO WITH ME. IN ONE RESPECT I'LL THY ASSISTANT BE -- FOR THIS ALLIANCE MAY SO HAPPY PROVE, TO TURN YOUR HOUSEHOLDS' RANCOR TO PURE LOVE.

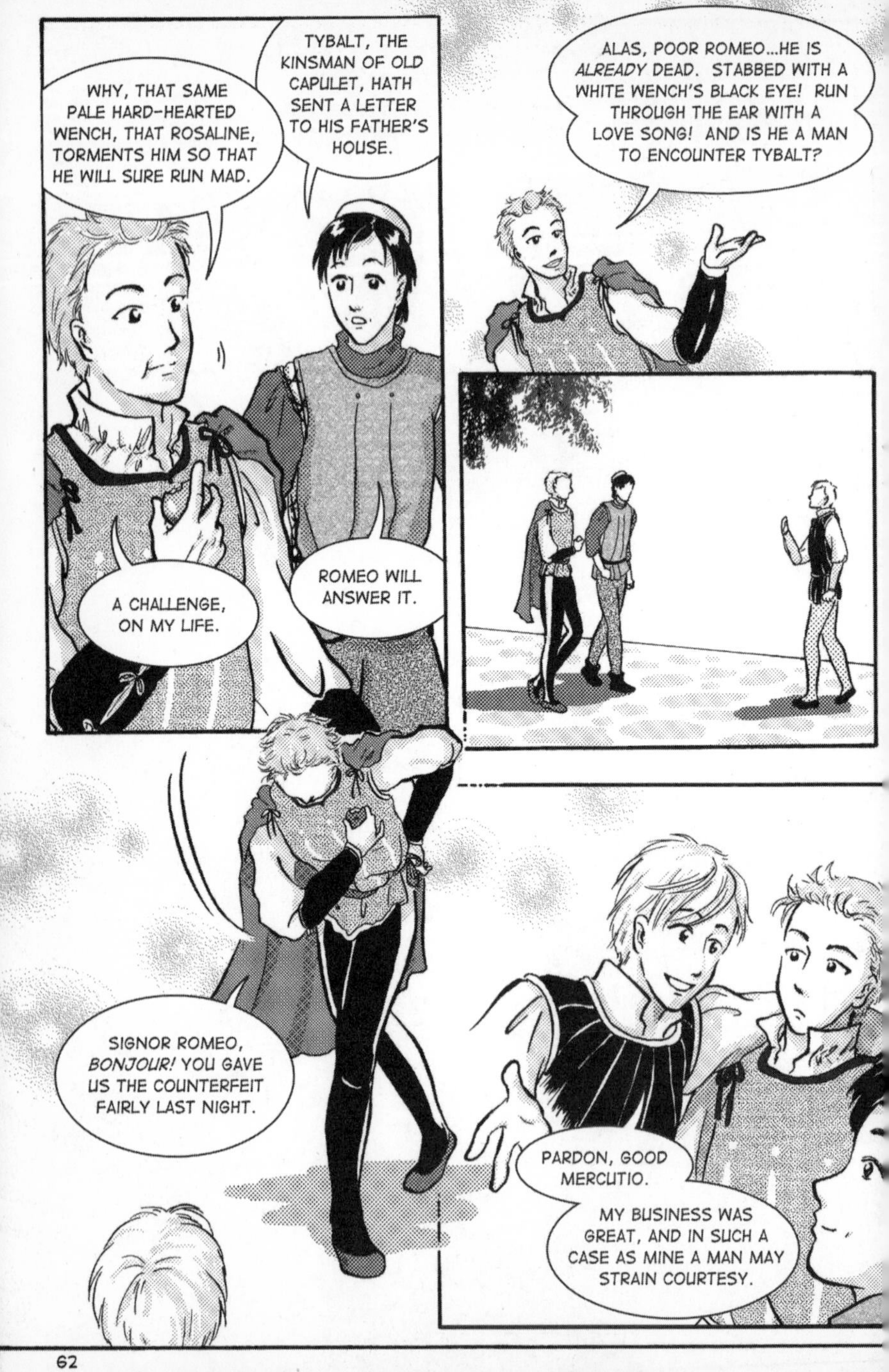
WHY, THAT SAME PALE HARD-HEARTED WENCH, THAT ROSALINE, TORMENTS HIM SO THAT HE WILL SURE RUN MAD.
TYBALT, THE KINSMAN OF OLD CAPULET, HATH SENT A LETTER TO HIS FATHER'S HOUSE.
A CHALLENGE, ON MY LIFE.
ROMEO WILL ANSWER IT.
ALAS, POOR ROMEO...HE IS *ALREADY* DEAD. STABBED WITH A WHITE WENCH'S BLACK EYE! RUN THROUGH THE EAR WITH A LOVE SONG! AND IS HE A MAN TO ENCOUNTER TYBALT?
SIGNOR ROMEO, *BONJOUR!* YOU GAVE US THE COUNTERFEIT FAIRLY LAST NIGHT.
PARDON, GOOD MERCUTIO.
MY BUSINESS WAS GREAT, AND IN SUCH A CASE AS MINE A MAN MAY STRAIN COURTESY.

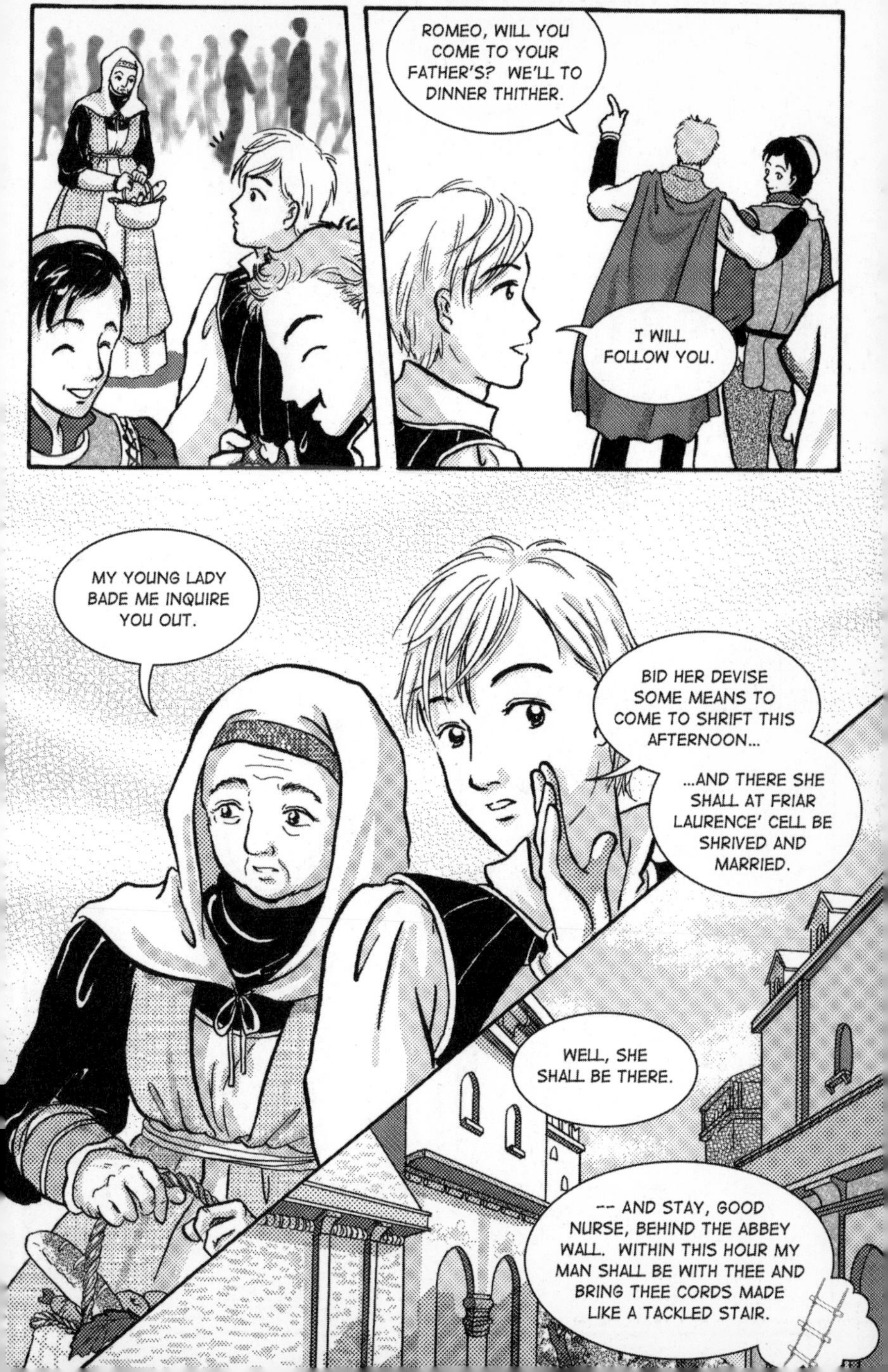
ROMEO, WILL YOU COME TO YOUR FATHER'S? WE'LL TO DINNER THITHER.
I WILL FOLLOW YOU.
MY YOUNG LADY BADE ME INQUIRE YOU OUT.
BID HER DEVISE SOME MEANS TO COME TO SHRIFT THIS AFTERNOON...
...AND THERE SHE SHALL AT FRIAR LAURENCE' CELL BE SHRIVED AND MARRIED.
WELL, SHE SHALL BE THERE.
-- AND STAY, GOOD NURSE, BEHIND THE ABBEY WALL. WITHIN THIS HOUR MY MAN SHALL BE WITH THEE AND BRING THEE CORDS MADE LIKE A TACKLED STAIR.

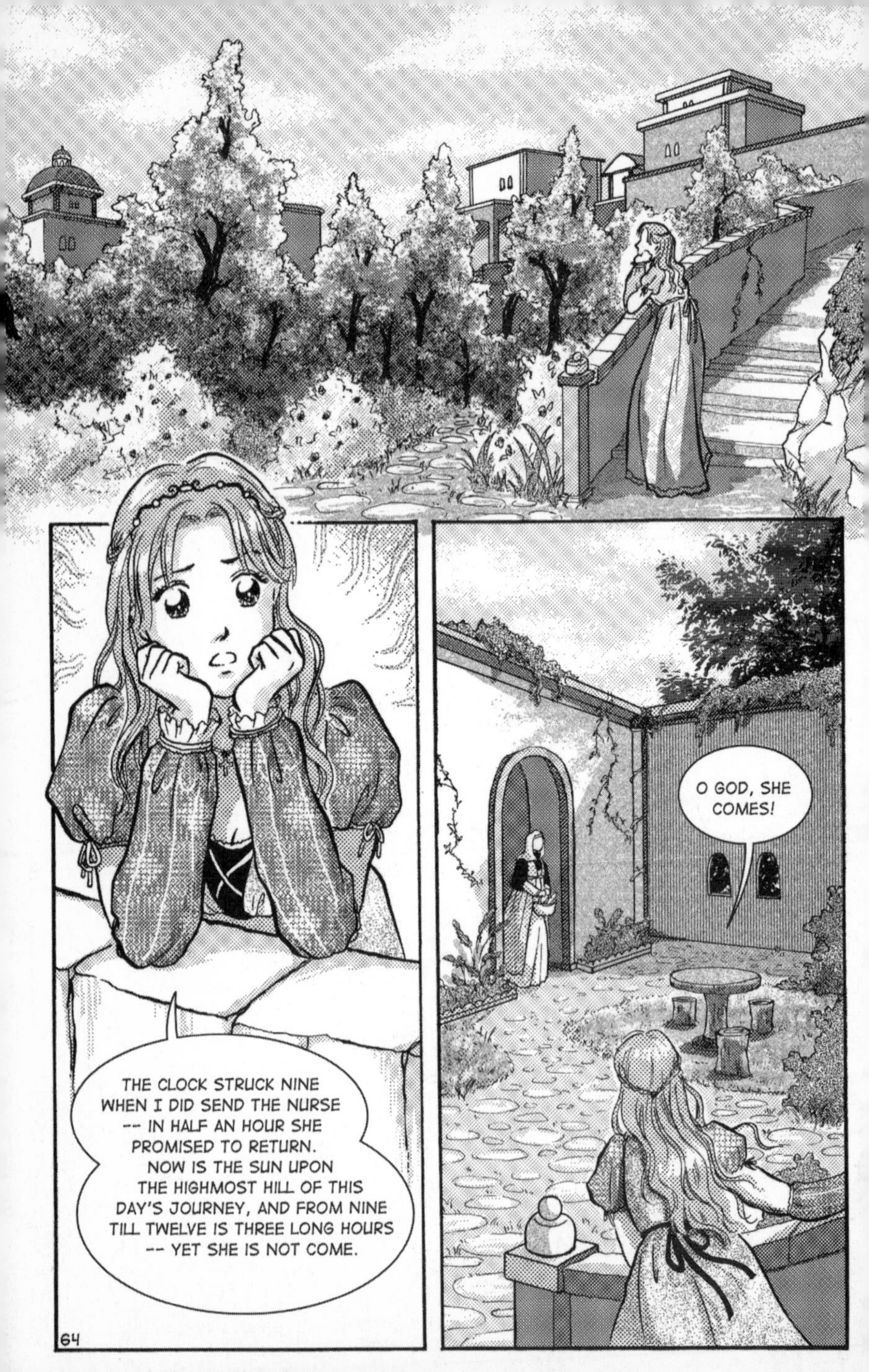
THE CLOCK STRUCK NINE WHEN I DID SEND THE NURSE -- IN HALF AN HOUR SHE PROMISED TO RETURN. NOW IS THE SUN UPON THE HIGHMOST HILL OF THIS DAY'S JOURNEY, AND FROM NINE TILL TWELVE IS THREE LONG HOURS -- YET SHE IS NOT COME.
O GOD, SHE COMES!

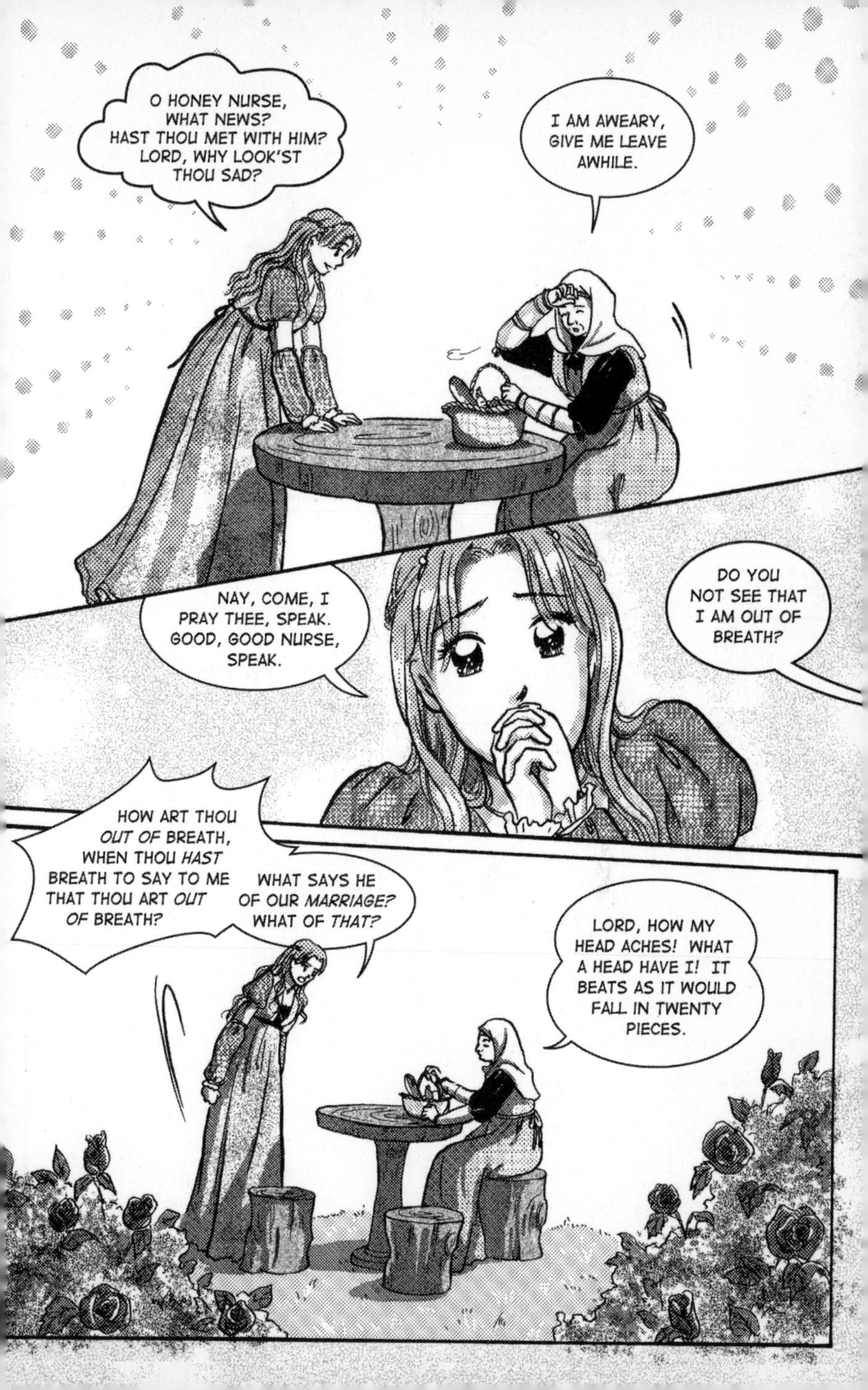
O HONEY NURSE, WHAT NEWS? HAST THOU MET WITH HIM? LORD, WHY LOOK'ST THOU SAD?
I AM AWEARY, GIVE ME LEAVE AWHILE.
NAY, COME, I PRAY THEE, SPEAK. GOOD, GOOD NURSE, SPEAK.
DO YOU NOT SEE THAT I AM OUT OF BREATH?
HOW ART THOU *OUT OF* BREATH, WHEN THOU *HAST* BREATH TO SAY TO ME THAT THOU ART *OUT OF* BREATH?
WHAT SAYS HE OF OUR *MARRIAGE?* WHAT OF *THAT?*
LORD, HOW MY HEAD ACHES! WHAT A HEAD HAVE I! IT BEATS AS IT WOULD FALL IN TWENTY PIECES.

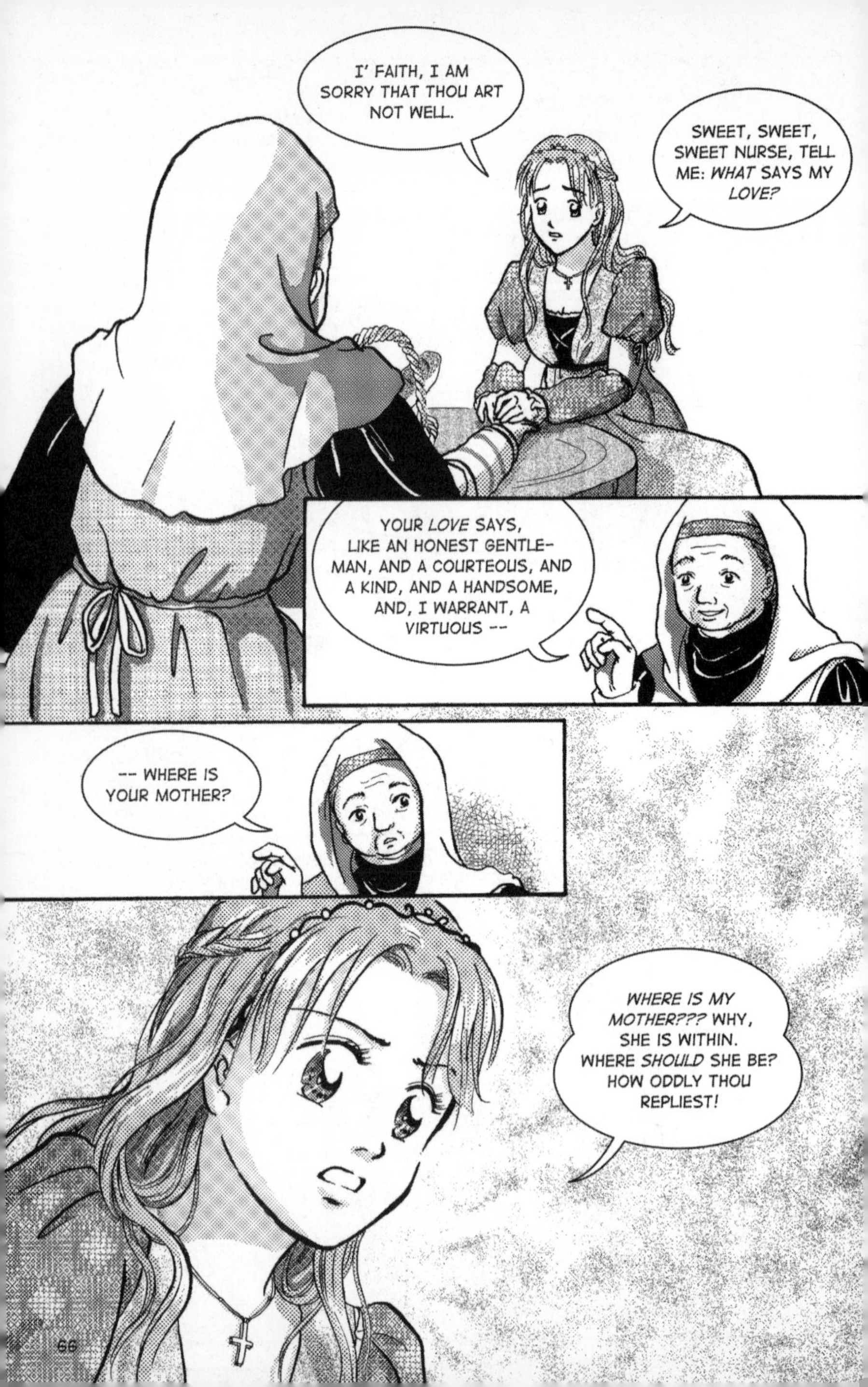
I' FAITH, I AM SORRY THAT THOU ART NOT WELL.
SWEET, SWEET, SWEET NURSE, TELL ME: *WHAT* SAYS MY *LOVE?*
YOUR *LOVE* SAYS, LIKE AN HONEST GENTLEMAN, AND A COURTEOUS, AND A KIND, AND A HANDSOME, AND, I WARRANT, A VIRTUOUS --
-- WHERE IS YOUR MOTHER?
WHERE IS MY MOTHER??? WHY, SHE IS WITHIN. WHERE *SHOULD* SHE BE? HOW ODDLY THOU REPLIEST!

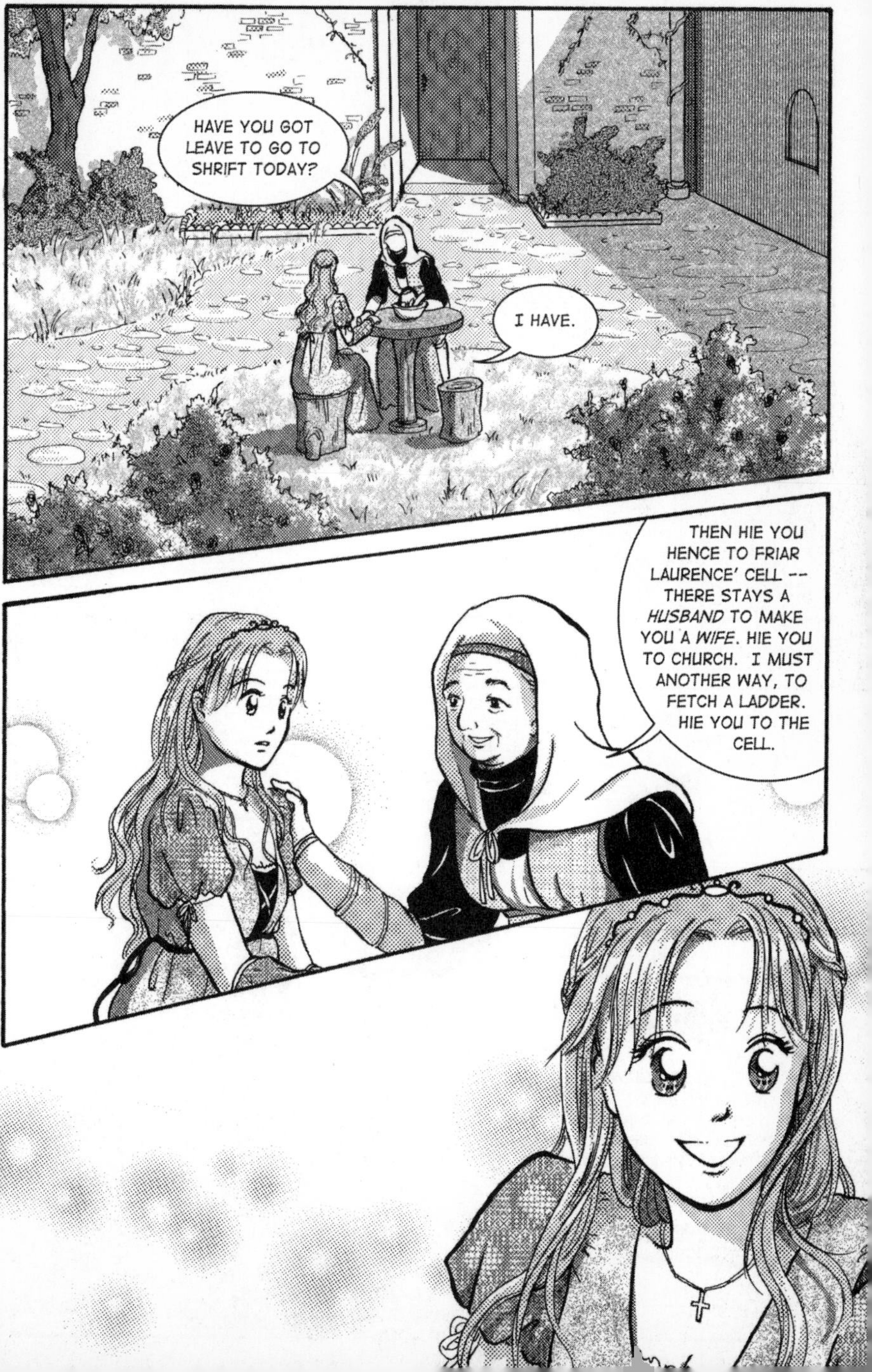
HAVE YOU GOT LEAVE TO GO TO SHRIFT TODAY?
I HAVE.
THEN HIE YOU HENCE TO FRIAR LAURENCE' CELL -- THERE STAYS A *HUSBAND* TO MAKE YOU A *WIFE*. HIE YOU TO CHURCH. I MUST ANOTHER WAY, TO FETCH A LADDER. HIE YOU TO THE CELL.

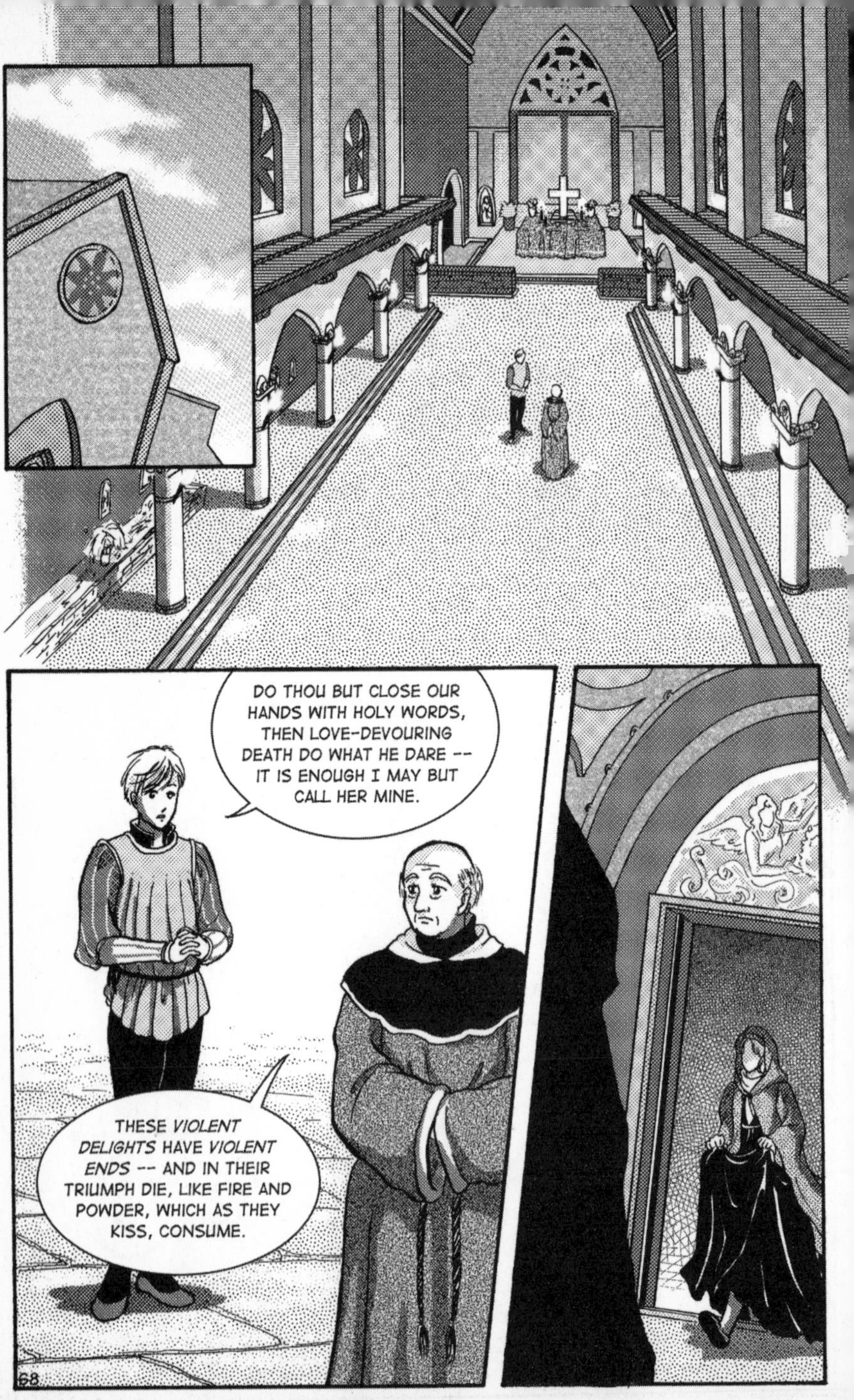
DO THOU BUT CLOSE OUR HANDS WITH HOLY WORDS, THEN LOVE-DEVOURING DEATH DO WHAT HE DARE -- IT IS ENOUGH I MAY BUT CALL HER MINE.
THESE *VIOLENT DELIGHTS* HAVE *VIOLENT ENDS* -- AND IN THEIR TRIUMPH DIE, LIKE FIRE AND POWDER, WHICH AS THEY KISS, CONSUME.

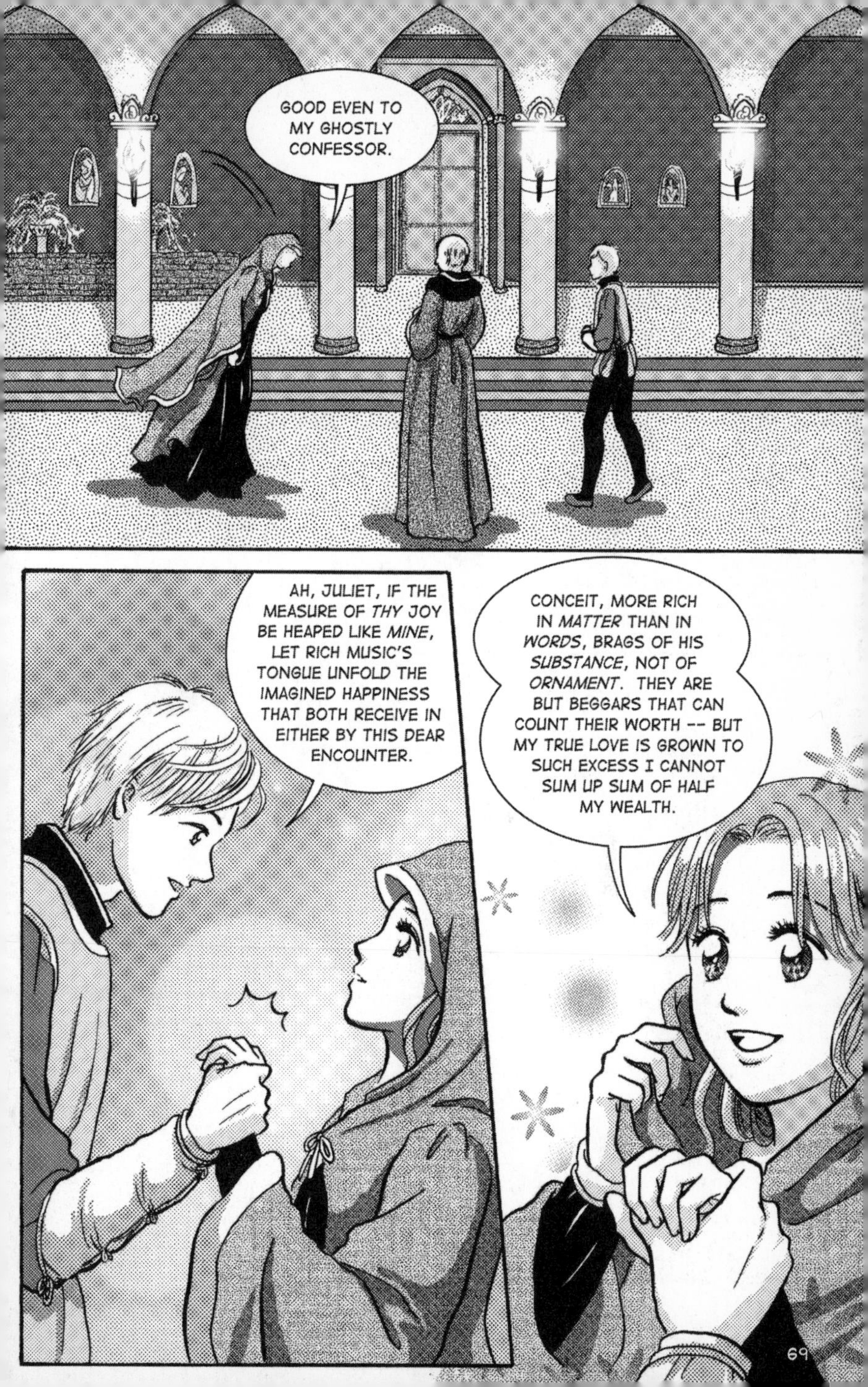
GOOD EVEN TO MY GHOSTLY CONFESSOR.
AH, JULIET, IF THE MEASURE OF *THY* JOY BE HEAPED LIKE *MINE*, LET RICH MUSIC'S TONGUE UNFOLD THE IMAGINED HAPPINESS THAT BOTH RECEIVE IN EITHER BY THIS DEAR ENCOUNTER.
CONCEIT, MORE RICH IN *MATTER* THAN IN *WORDS*, BRAGS OF HIS *SUBSTANCE*, NOT OF *ORNAMENT*. THEY ARE BUT BEGGARS THAT CAN COUNT THEIR WORTH -- BUT MY TRUE LOVE IS GROWN TO SUCH EXCESS I CANNOT SUM UP SUM OF HALF MY WEALTH.

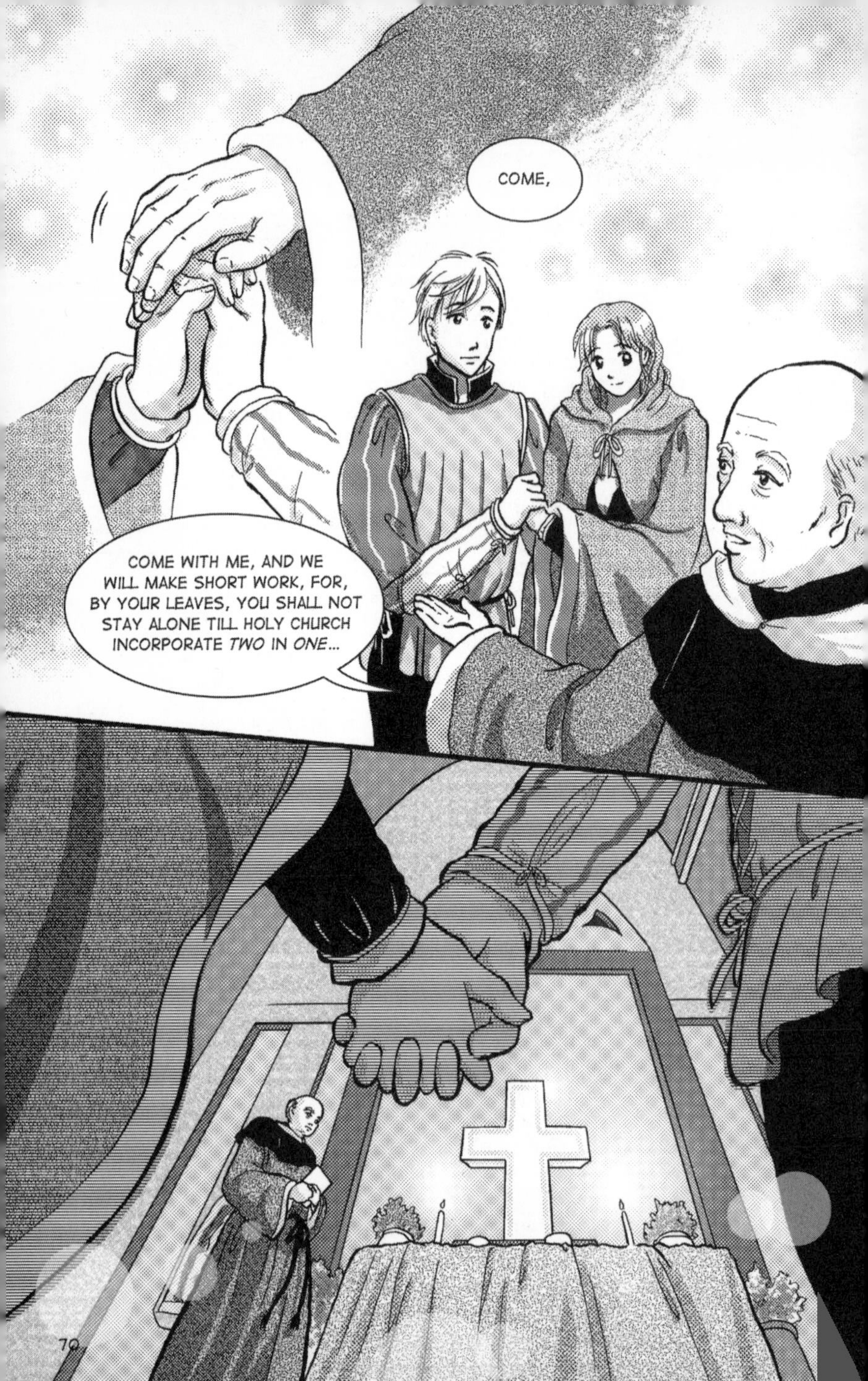
COME,
COME WITH ME, AND WE WILL MAKE SHORT WORK, FOR, BY YOUR LEAVES, YOU SHALL NOT STAY ALONE TILL HOLY CHURCH INCORPORATE *TWO* IN *ONE*...

ACT III

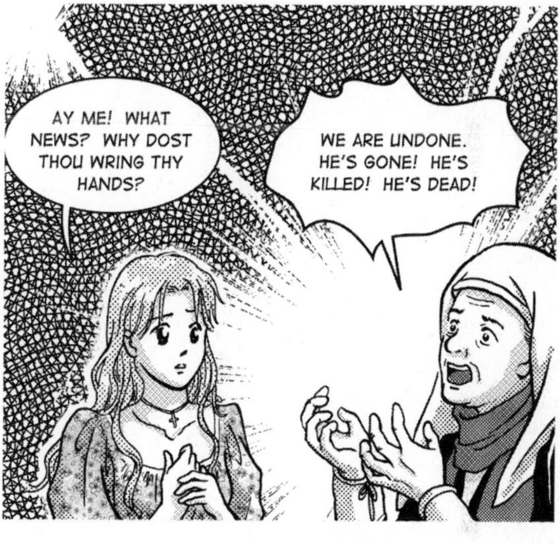
AY ME! WHAT NEWS? WHY DOST THOU WRING THY HANDS?
WE ARE UNDONE. HE'S GONE! HE'S KILLED! HE'S DEAD!

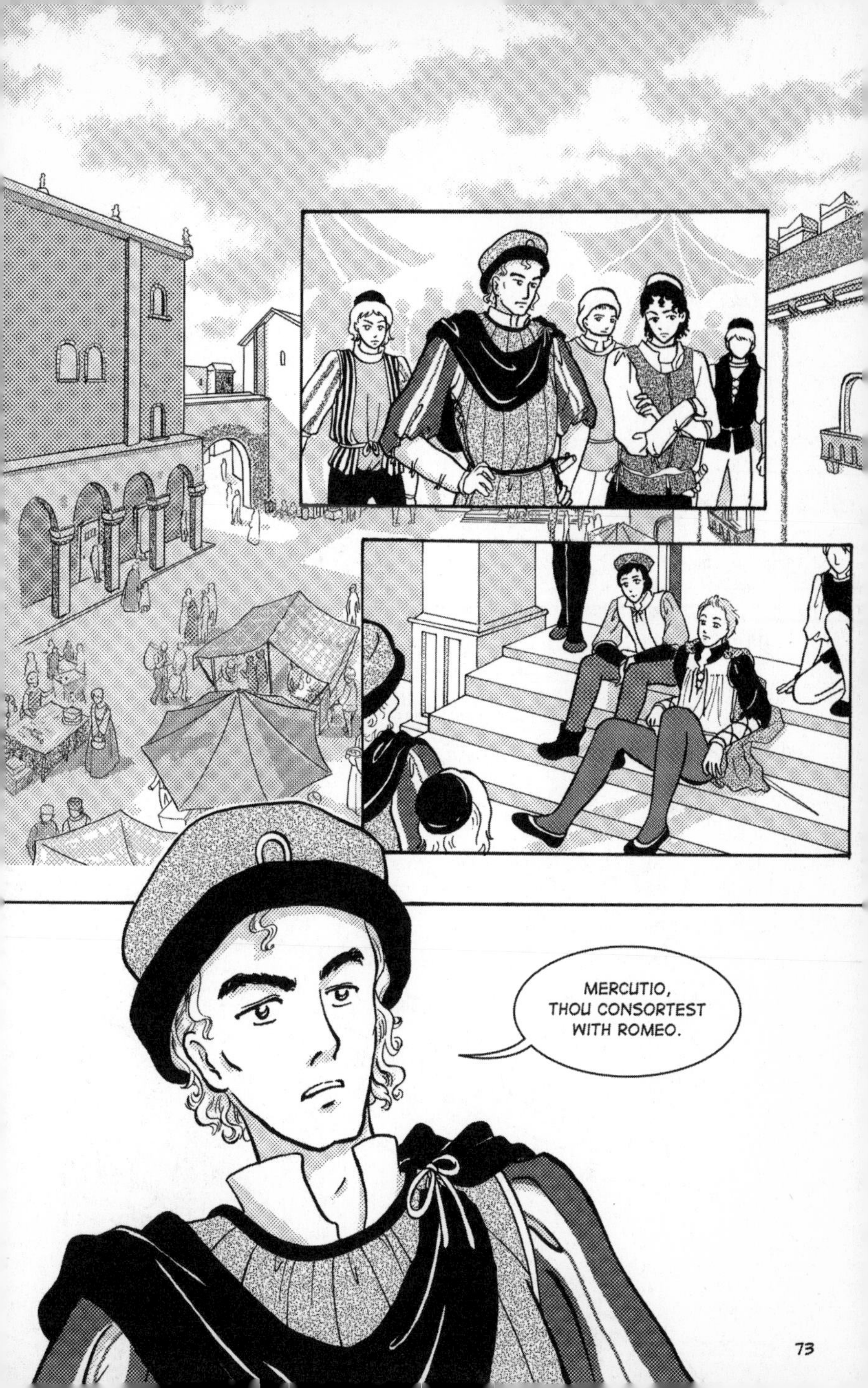
MERCUTIO, THOU CONSORTEST WITH ROMEO.

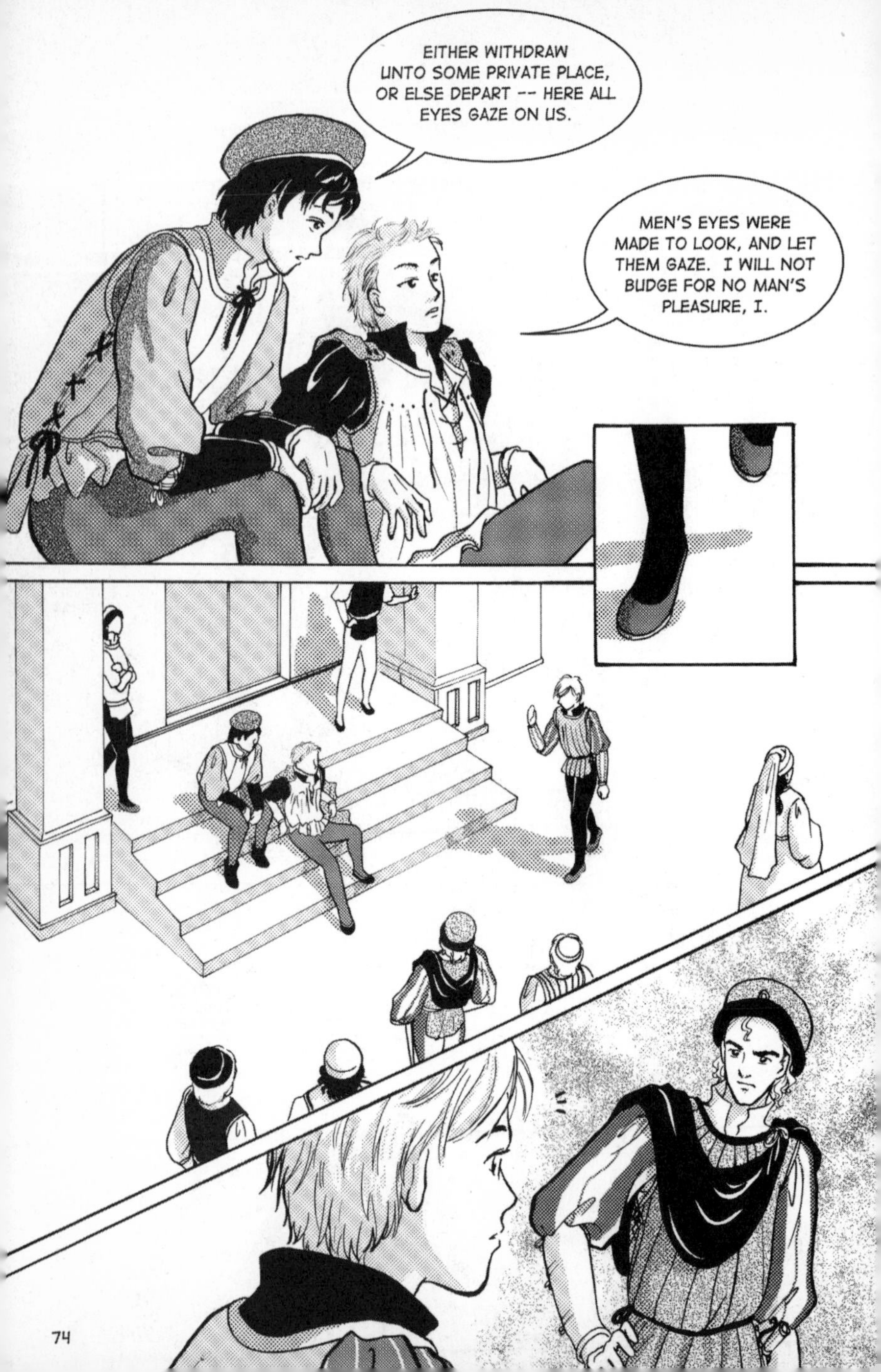
EITHER WITHDRAW UNTO SOME PRIVATE PLACE, OR ELSE DEPART -- HERE ALL EYES GAZE ON US.
MEN'S EYES WERE MADE TO LOOK, AND LET THEM GAZE. I WILL NOT BUDGE FOR NO MAN'S PLEASURE, I.

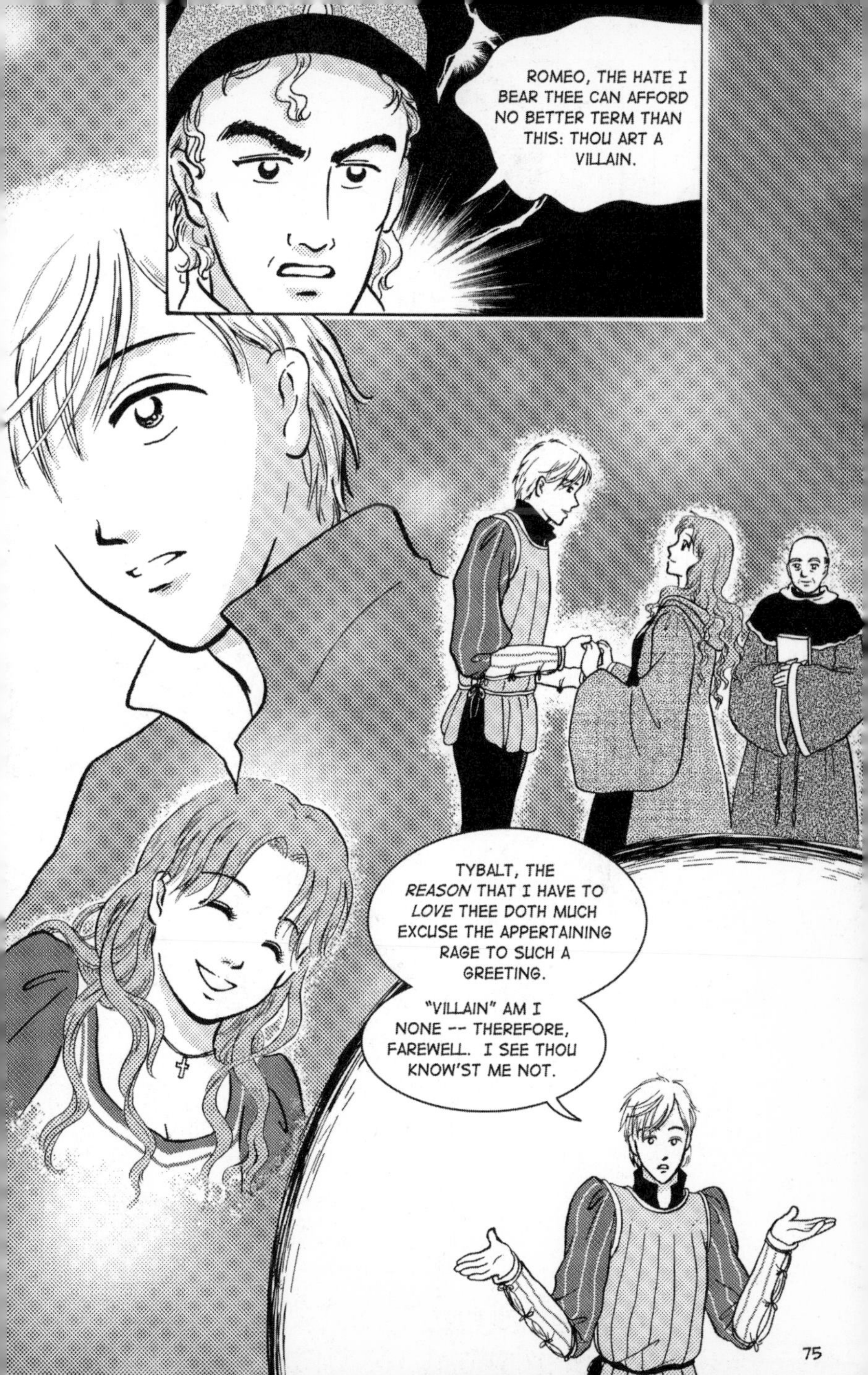
ROMEO, THE HATE I BEAR THEE CAN AFFORD NO BETTER TERM THAN THIS: THOU ART A VILLAIN.
TYBALT, THE *REASON* THAT I HAVE TO *LOVE* THEE DOTH MUCH EXCUSE THE APPERTAINING RAGE TO SUCH A GREETING.
"VILLAIN" AM I NONE -- THEREFORE, FAREWELL. I SEE THOU KNOW'ST ME NOT.

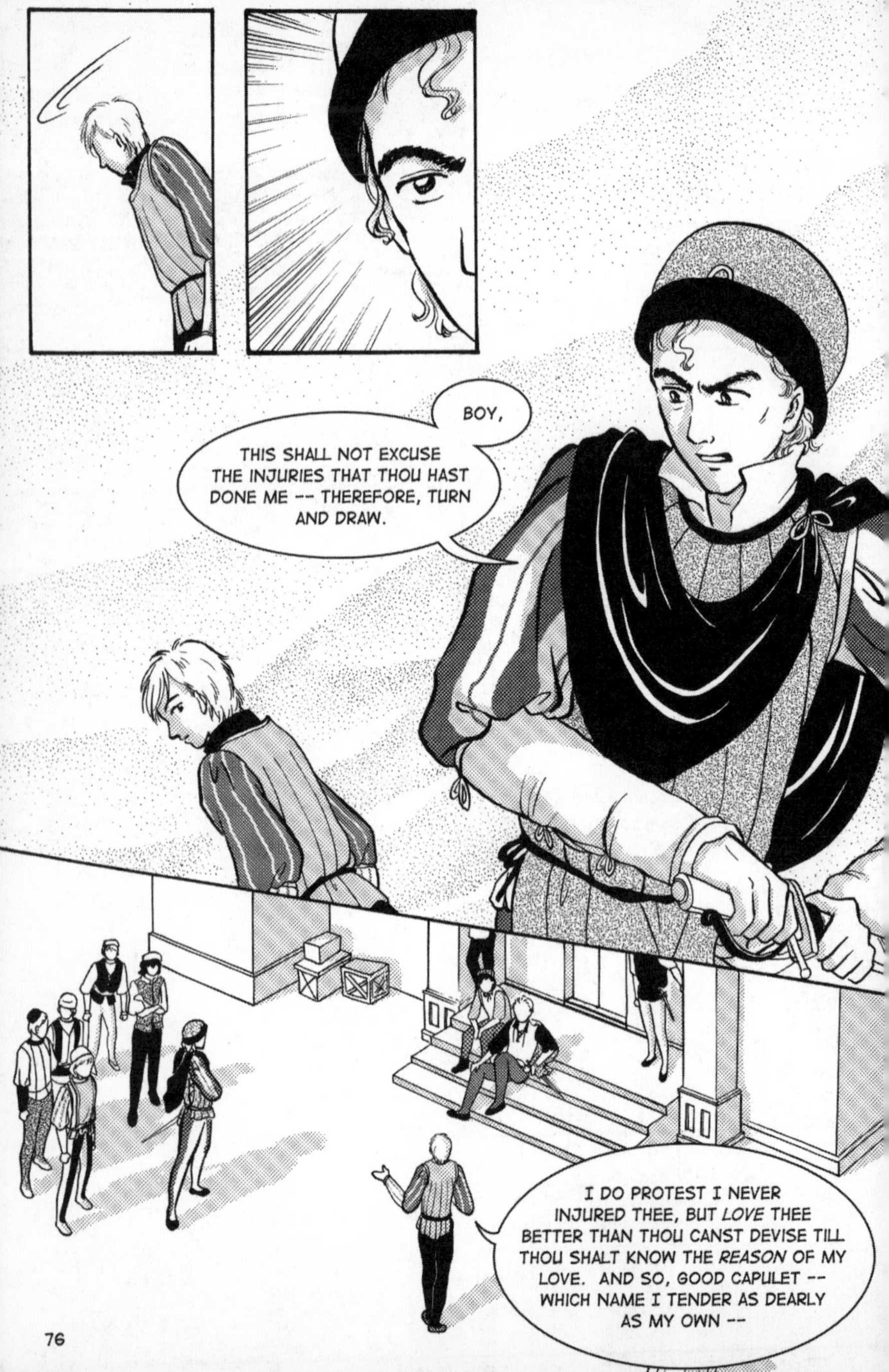
BOY,
THIS SHALL NOT EXCUSE THE INJURIES THAT THOU HAST DONE ME -- THEREFORE, TURN AND DRAW.
I DO PROTEST I NEVER INJURED THEE, BUT *LOVE* THEE BETTER THAN THOU CANST DEVISE TILL THOU SHALT KNOW THE *REASON* OF MY LOVE. AND SO, GOOD CAPULET -- WHICH NAME I TENDER AS DEARLY AS MY OWN --

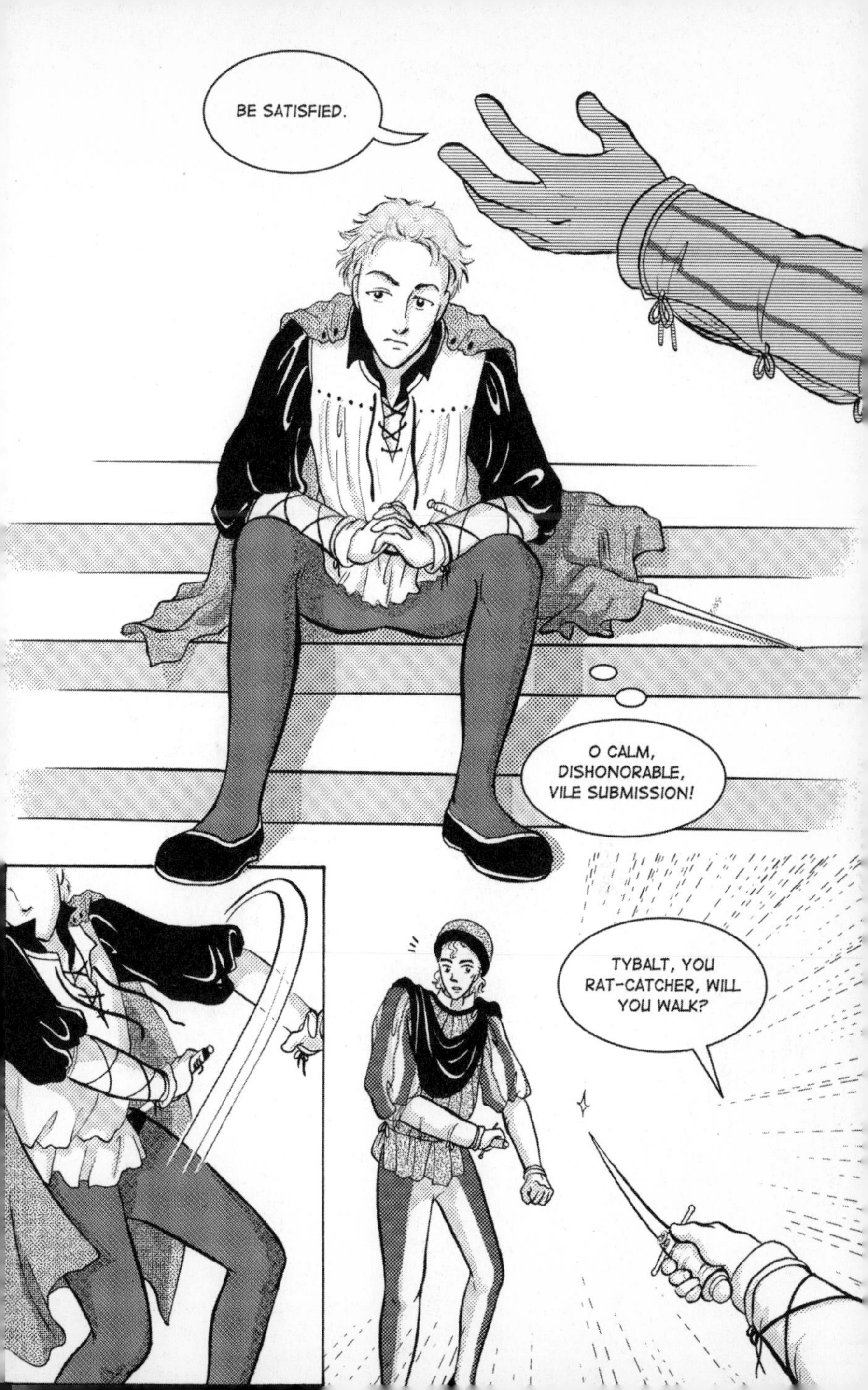
BE SATISFIED.
O CALM, DISHONORABLE, VILE SUBMISSION!
TYBALT, YOU RAT-CATCHER, WILL YOU WALK?

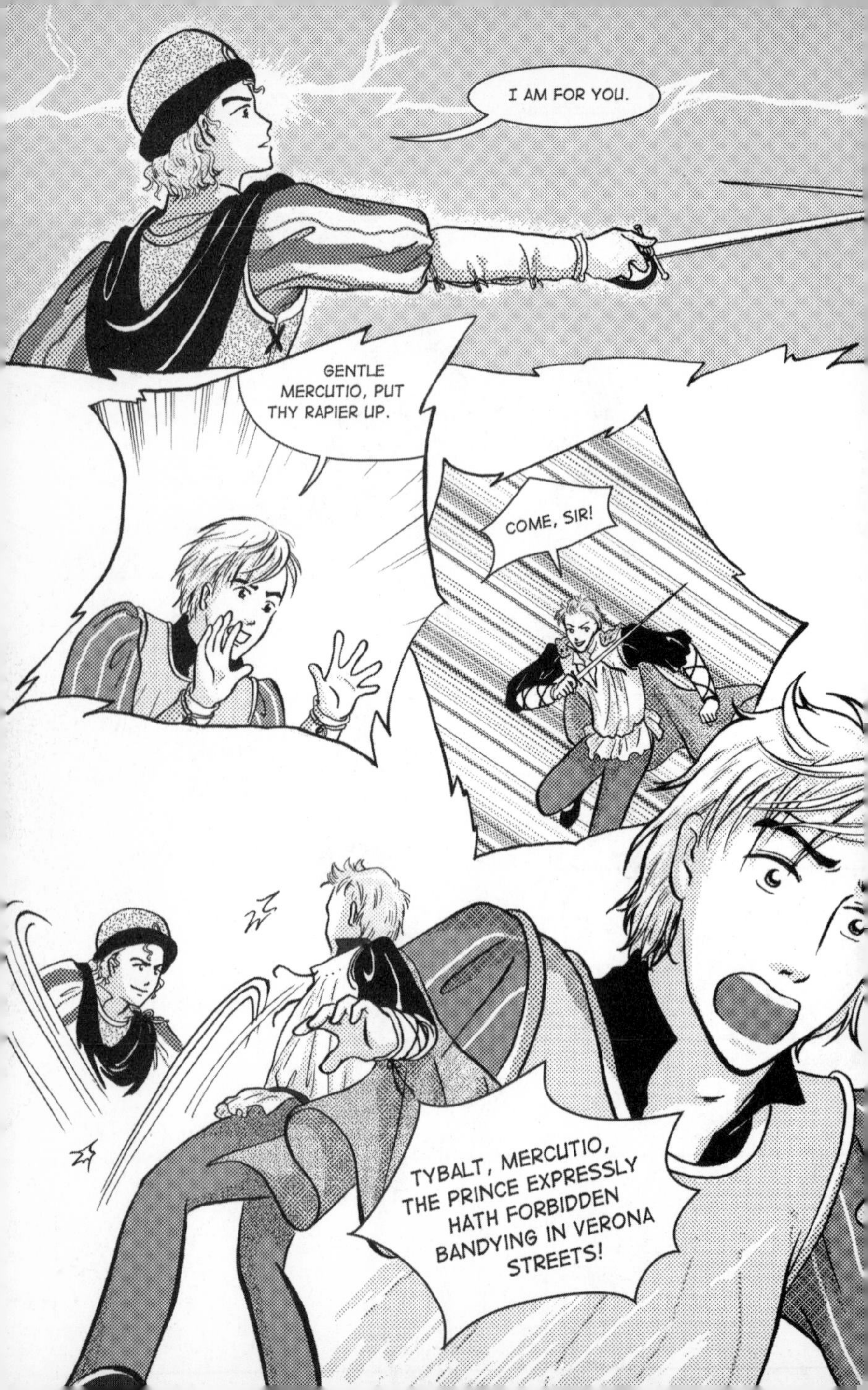
I AM FOR YOU.
GENTLE MERCUTIO, PUT THY RAPIER UP.
COME, SIR!
TYBALT, MERCUTIO, THE PRINCE EXPRESSLY HATH FORBIDDEN BANDYING IN VERONA STREETS!

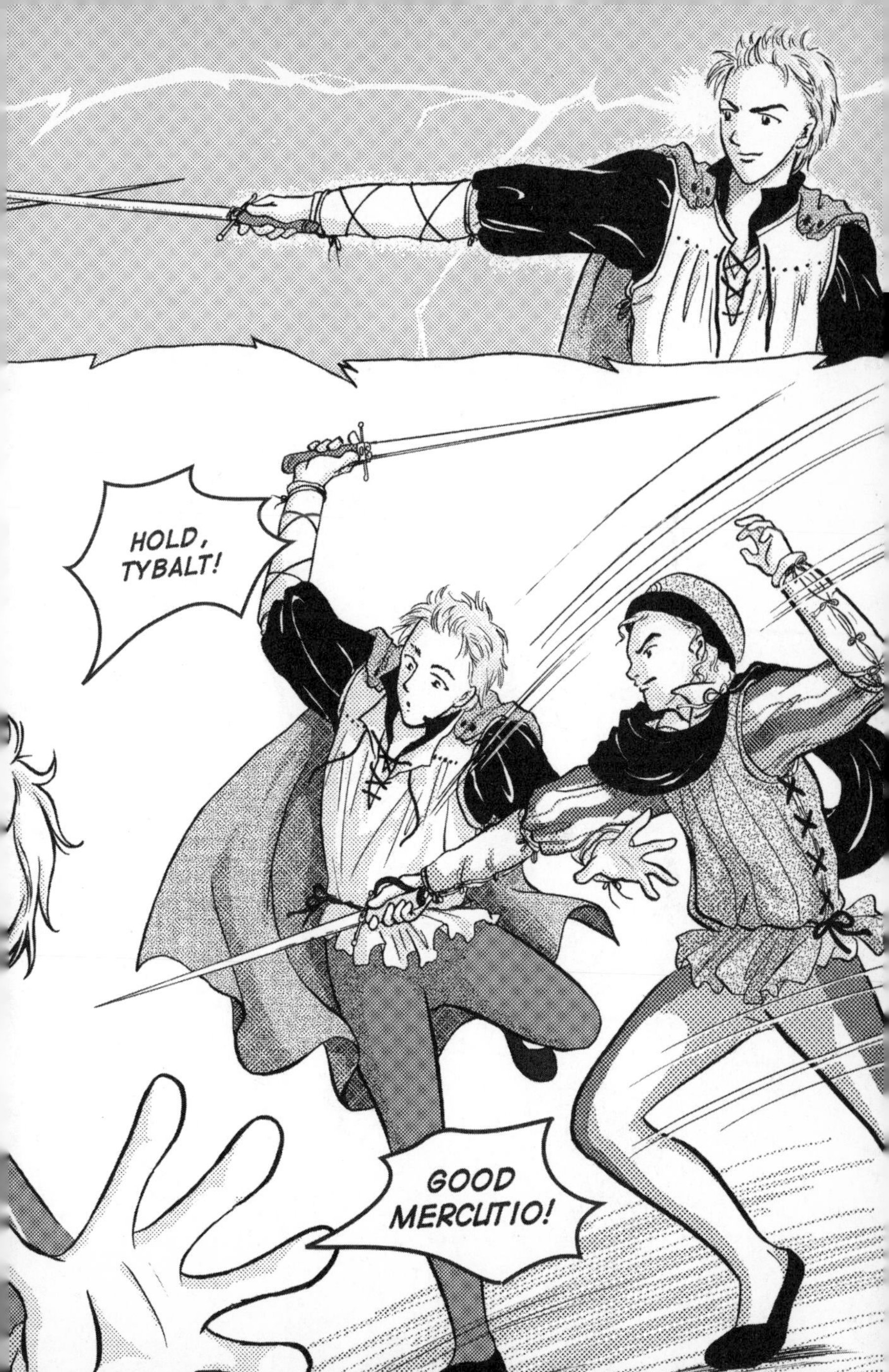
HOLD, TYBALT!
GOOD MERCUTIO!

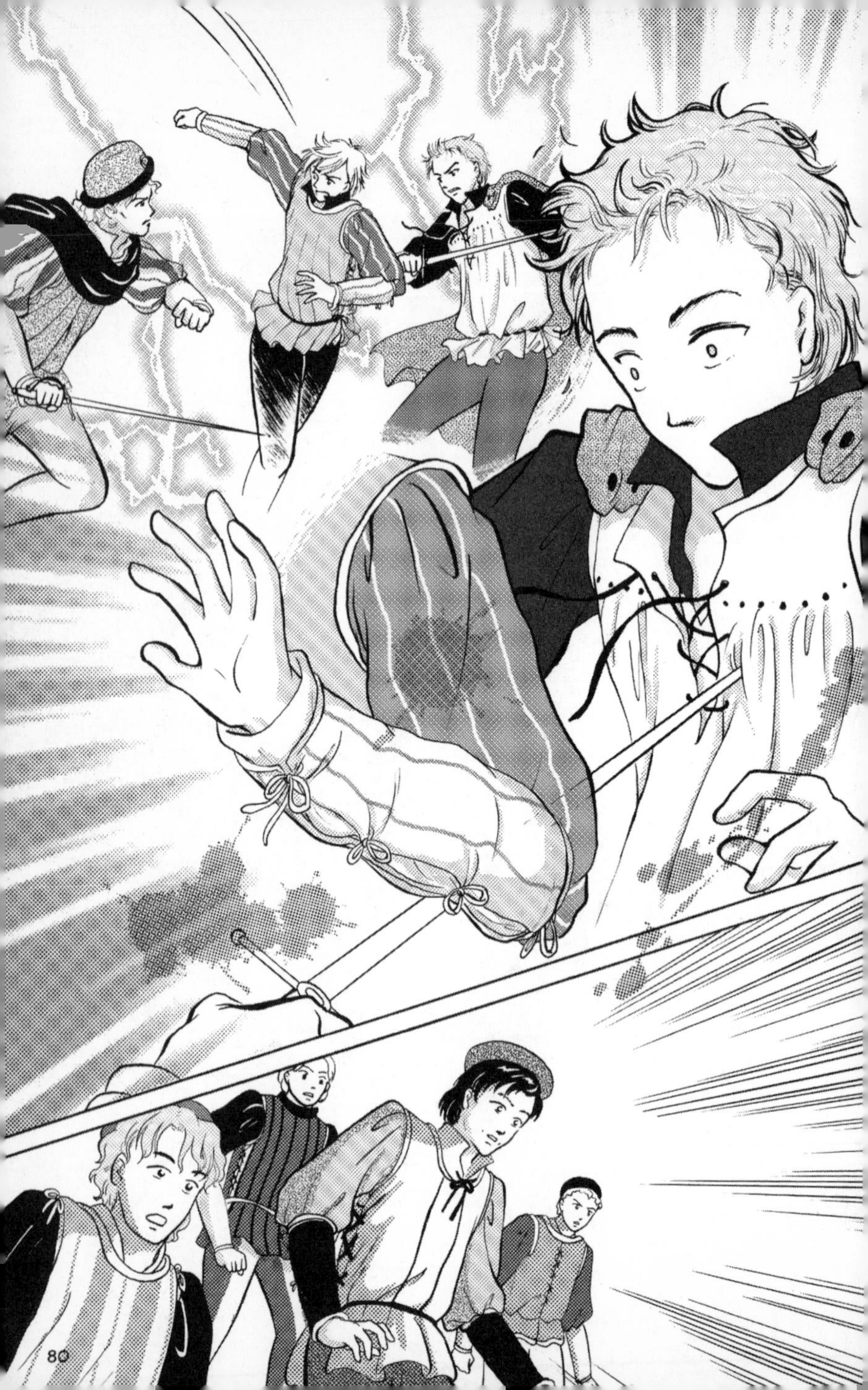

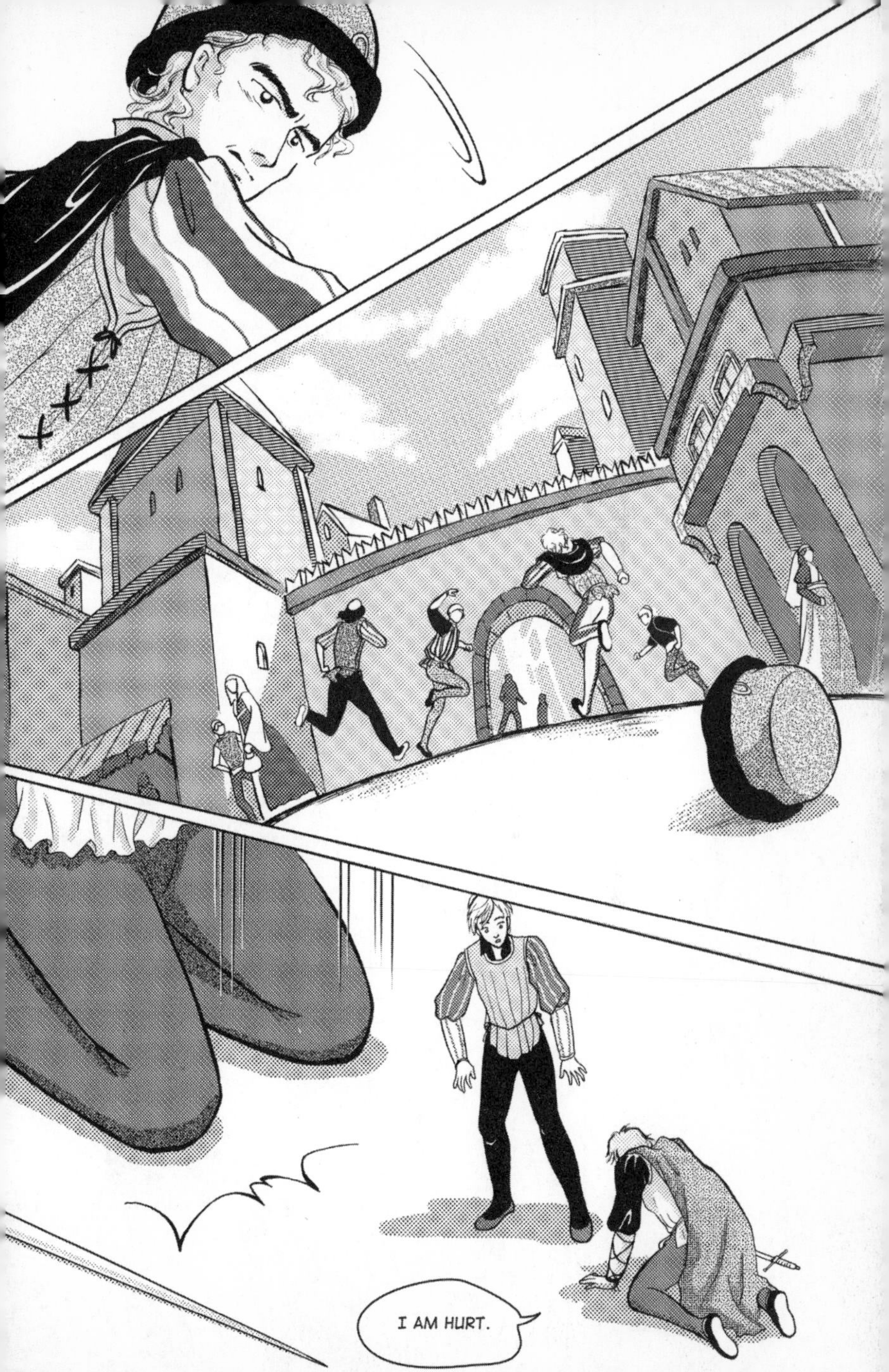
I AM HURT.

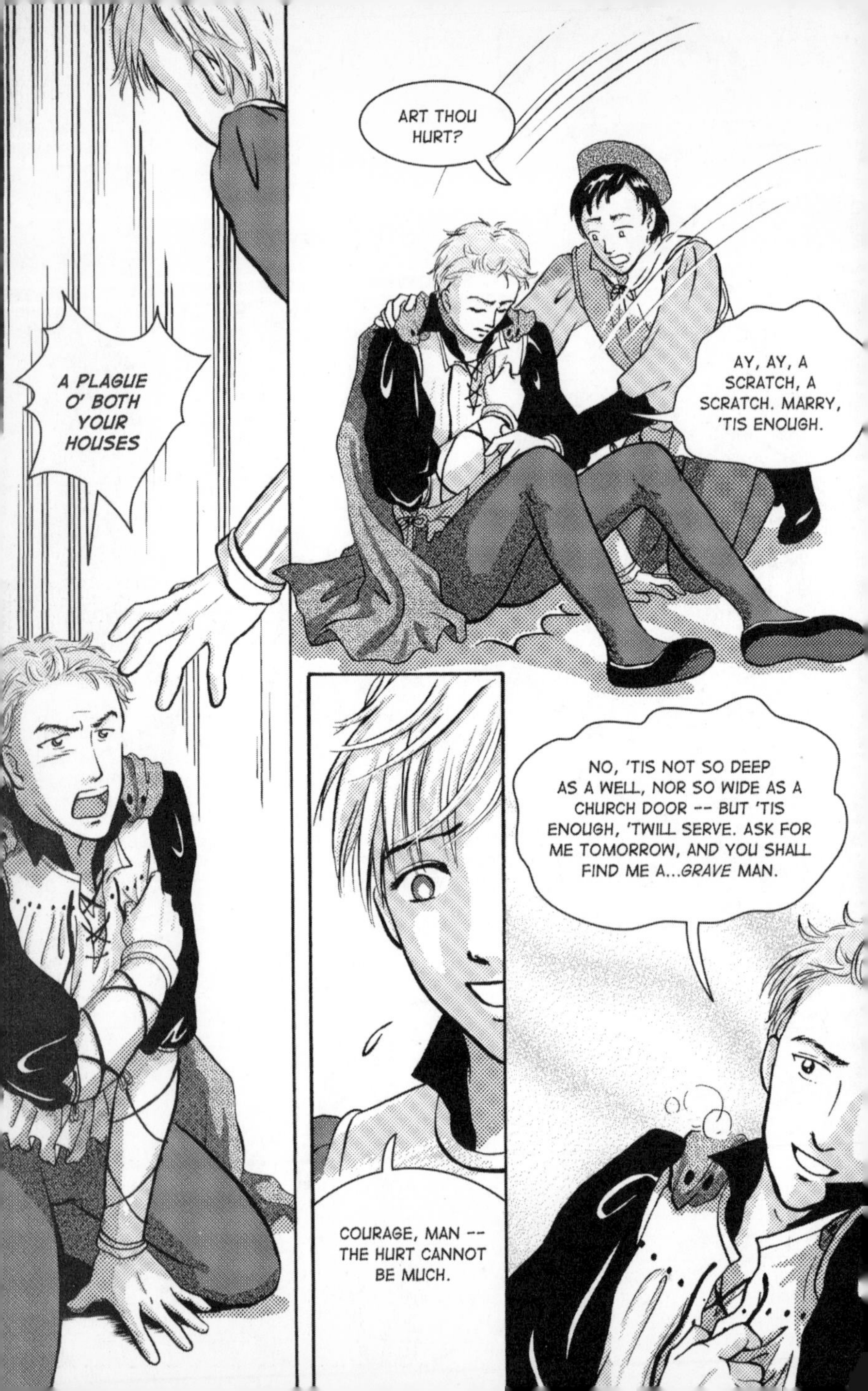
A PLAGUE O' BOTH YOUR HOUSES
ART THOU HURT?
AY, AY, A SCRATCH, A SCRATCH. MARRY, 'TIS ENOUGH.
COURAGE, MAN -- THE HURT CANNOT BE MUCH.
NO, 'TIS NOT SO DEEP AS A WELL, NOR SO WIDE AS A CHURCH DOOR -- BUT 'TIS ENOUGH, 'TWILL SERVE. ASK FOR ME TOMORROW, AND YOU SHALL FIND ME A...*GRAVE* MAN.

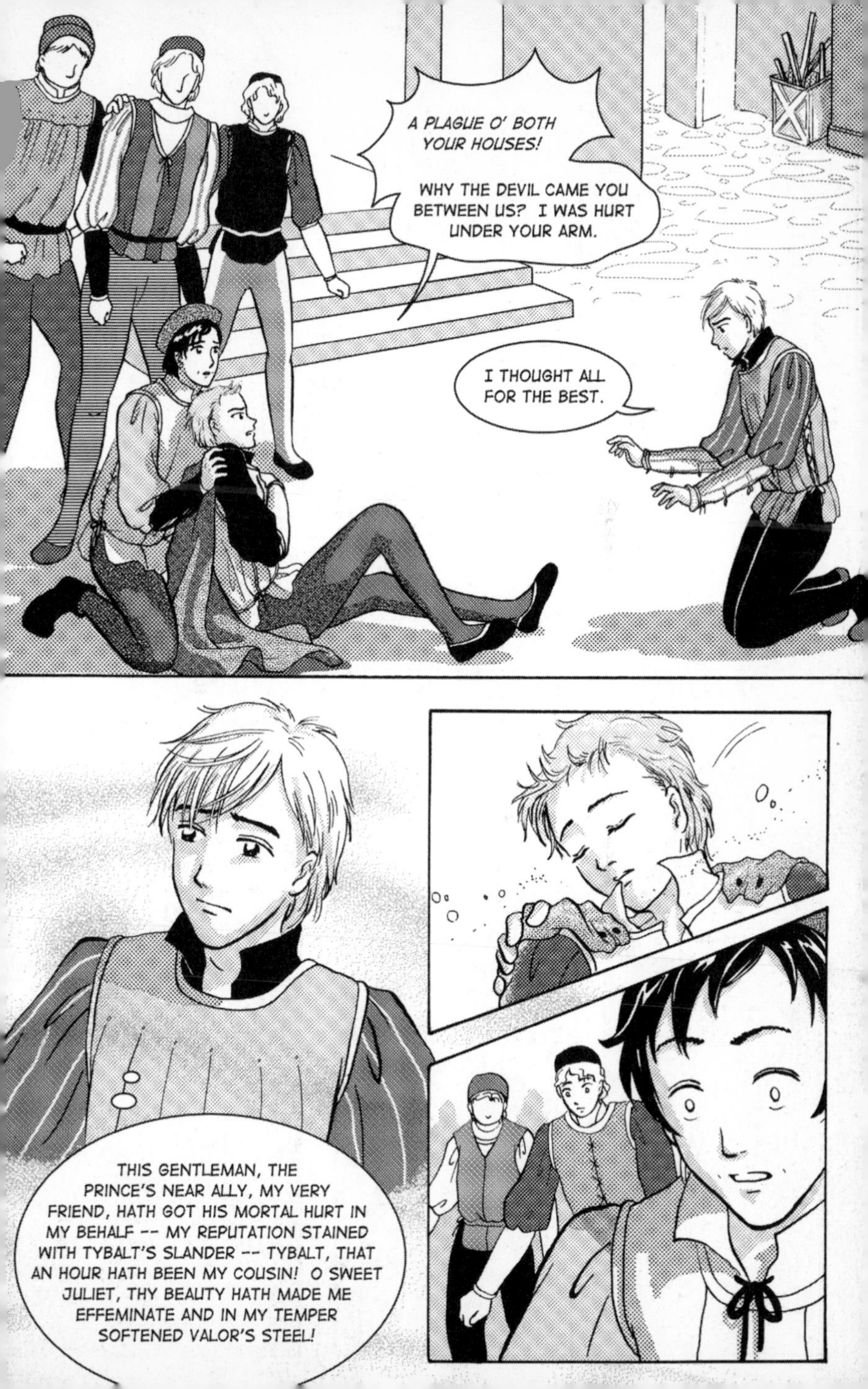
A PLAGUE O' BOTH YOUR HOUSES!
WHY THE DEVIL CAME YOU BETWEEN US? I WAS HURT UNDER YOUR ARM.
I THOUGHT ALL FOR THE BEST.
THIS GENTLEMAN, THE PRINCE'S NEAR ALLY, MY VERY FRIEND, HATH GOT HIS MORTAL HURT IN MY BEHALF -- MY REPUTATION STAINED WITH TYBALT'S SLANDER -- TYBALT, THAT AN HOUR HATH BEEN MY COUSIN! O SWEET JULIET, THY BEAUTY HATH MADE ME EFFEMINATE AND IN MY TEMPER SOFTENED VALOR'S STEEL!

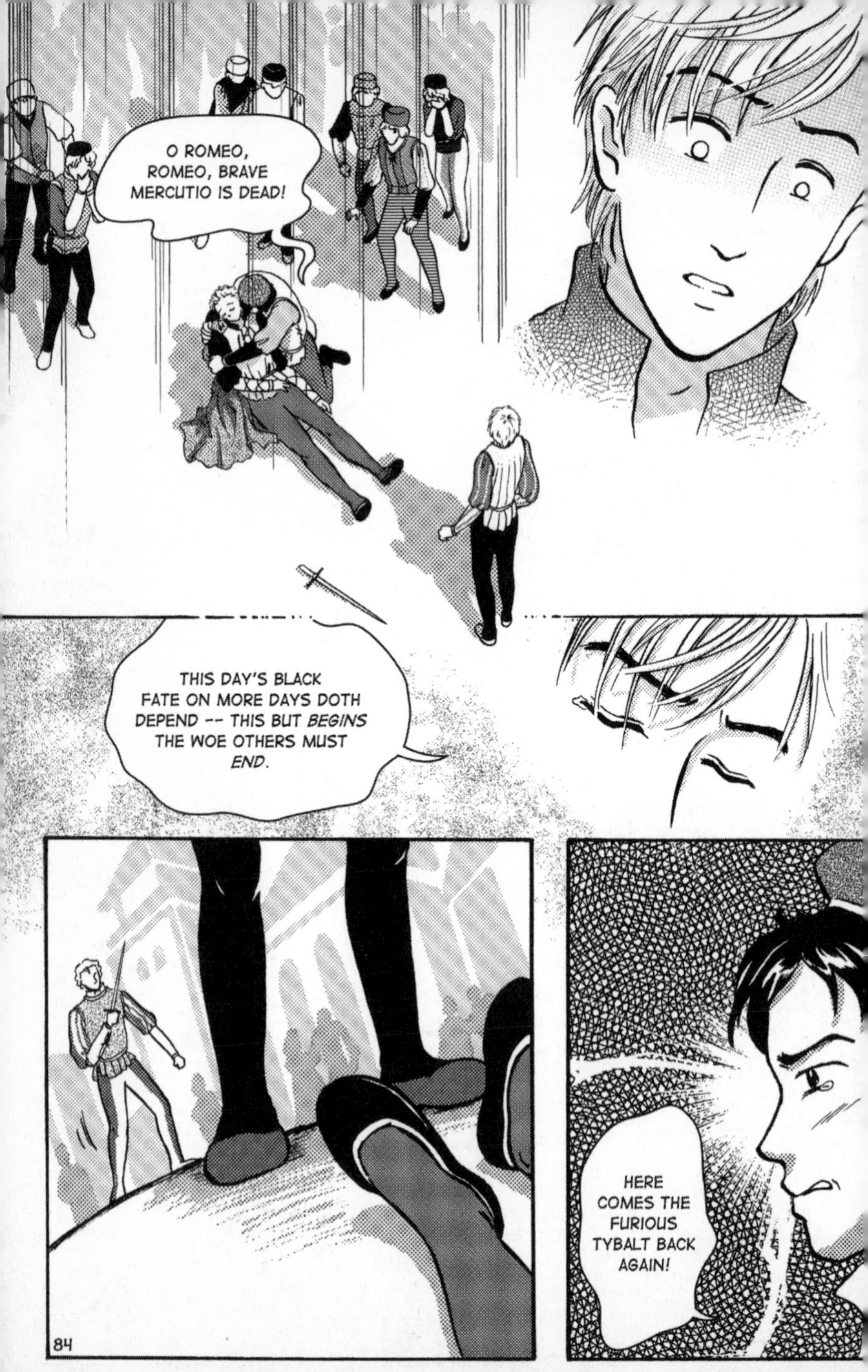
O ROMEO, ROMEO, BRAVE MERCUTIO IS DEAD!
THIS DAY'S BLACK FATE ON MORE DAYS DOTH DEPEND -- THIS BUT *BEGINS* THE WOE OTHERS MUST *END*.
HERE COMES THE FURIOUS TYBALT BACK AGAIN!

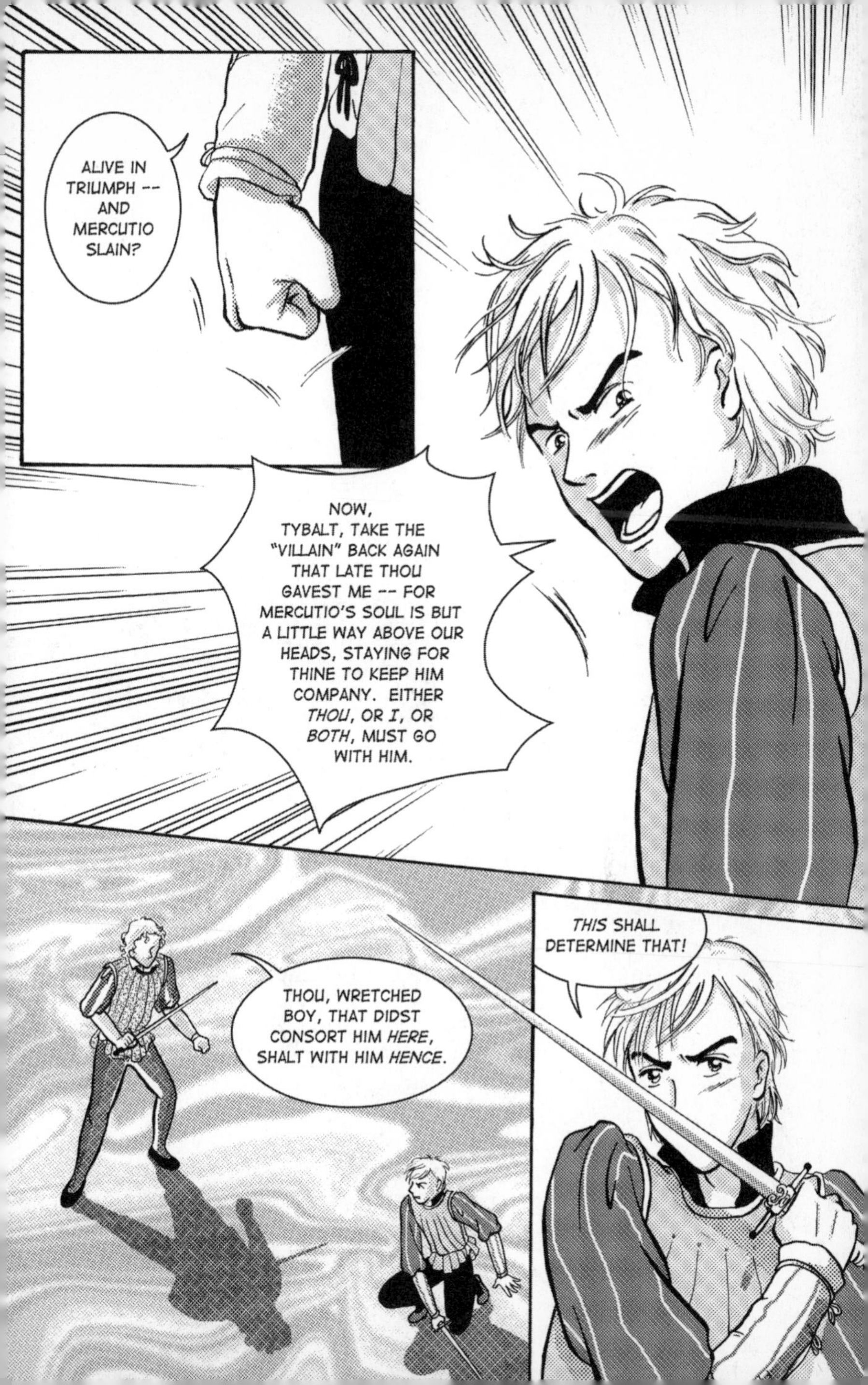
ALIVE IN TRIUMPH -- AND MERCUTIO SLAIN?
NOW, TYBALT, TAKE THE "VILLAIN" BACK AGAIN THAT LATE THOU GAVEST ME -- FOR MERCUTIO'S SOUL IS BUT A LITTLE WAY ABOVE OUR HEADS, STAYING FOR THINE TO KEEP HIM COMPANY. EITHER *THOU*, OR *I*, OR *BOTH*, MUST GO WITH HIM.
THOU, WRETCHED BOY, THAT DIDST CONSORT HIM *HERE*, SHALT WITH HIM *HENCE*.
THIS SHALL DETERMINE THAT!

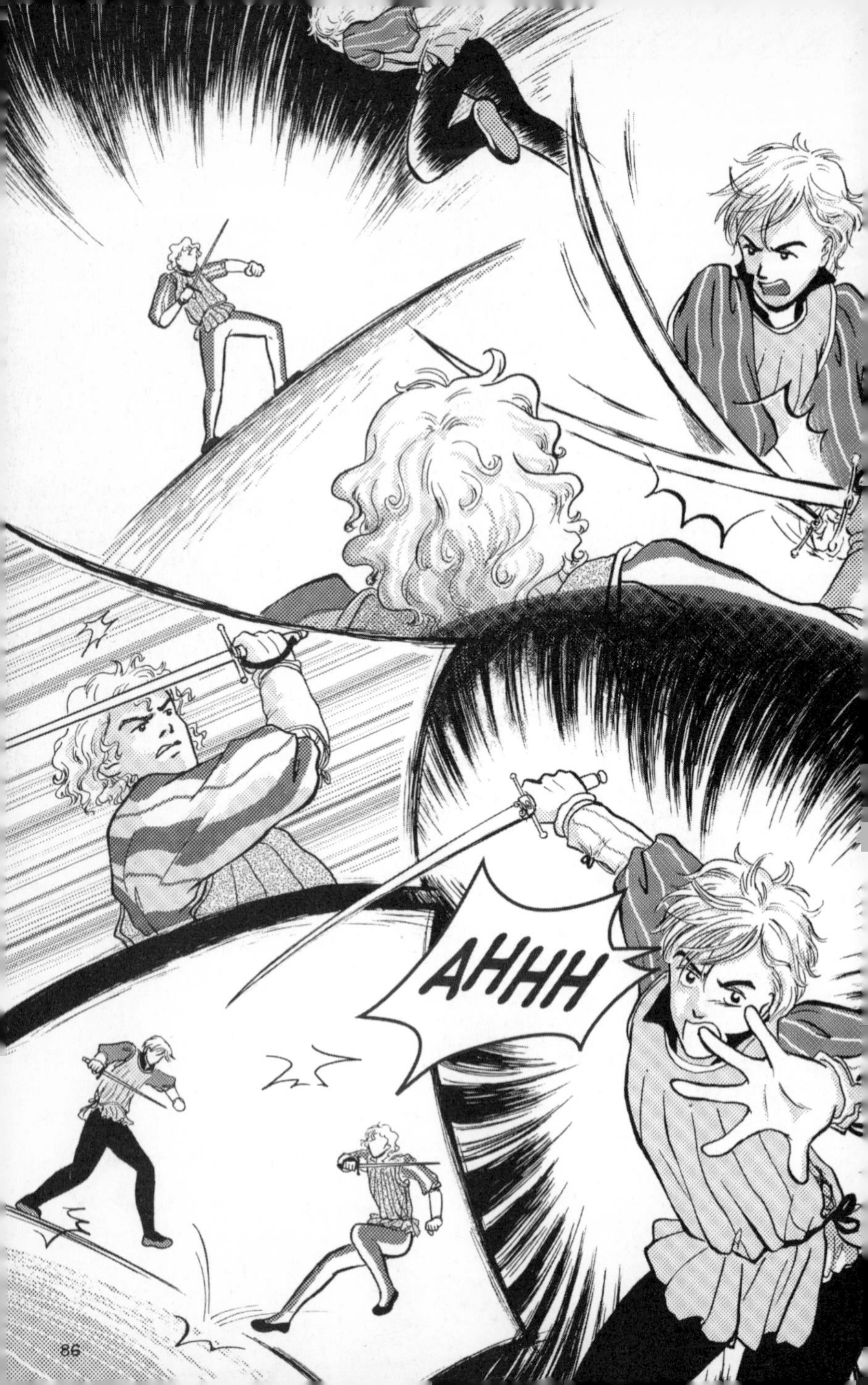
AHHH

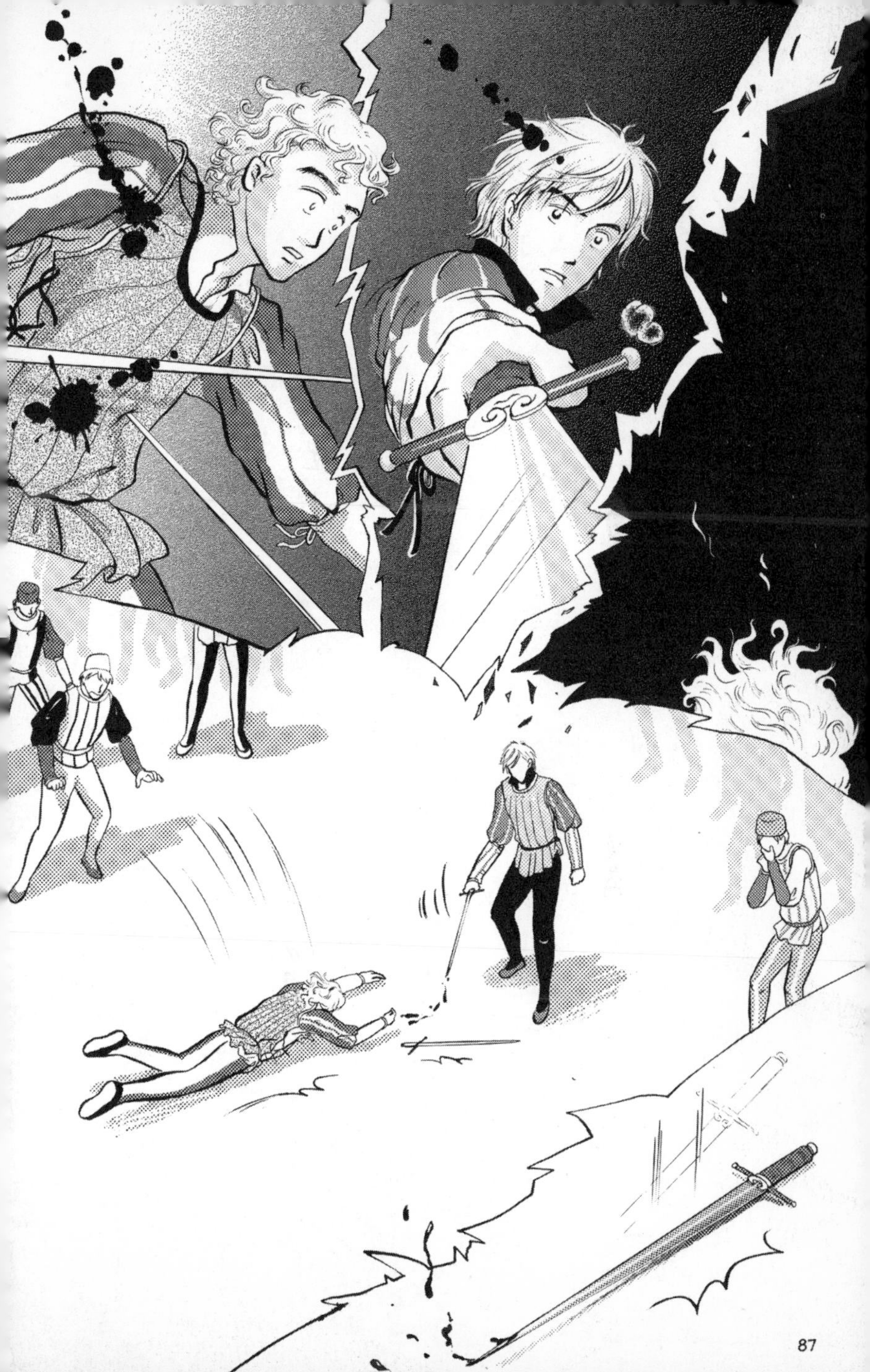

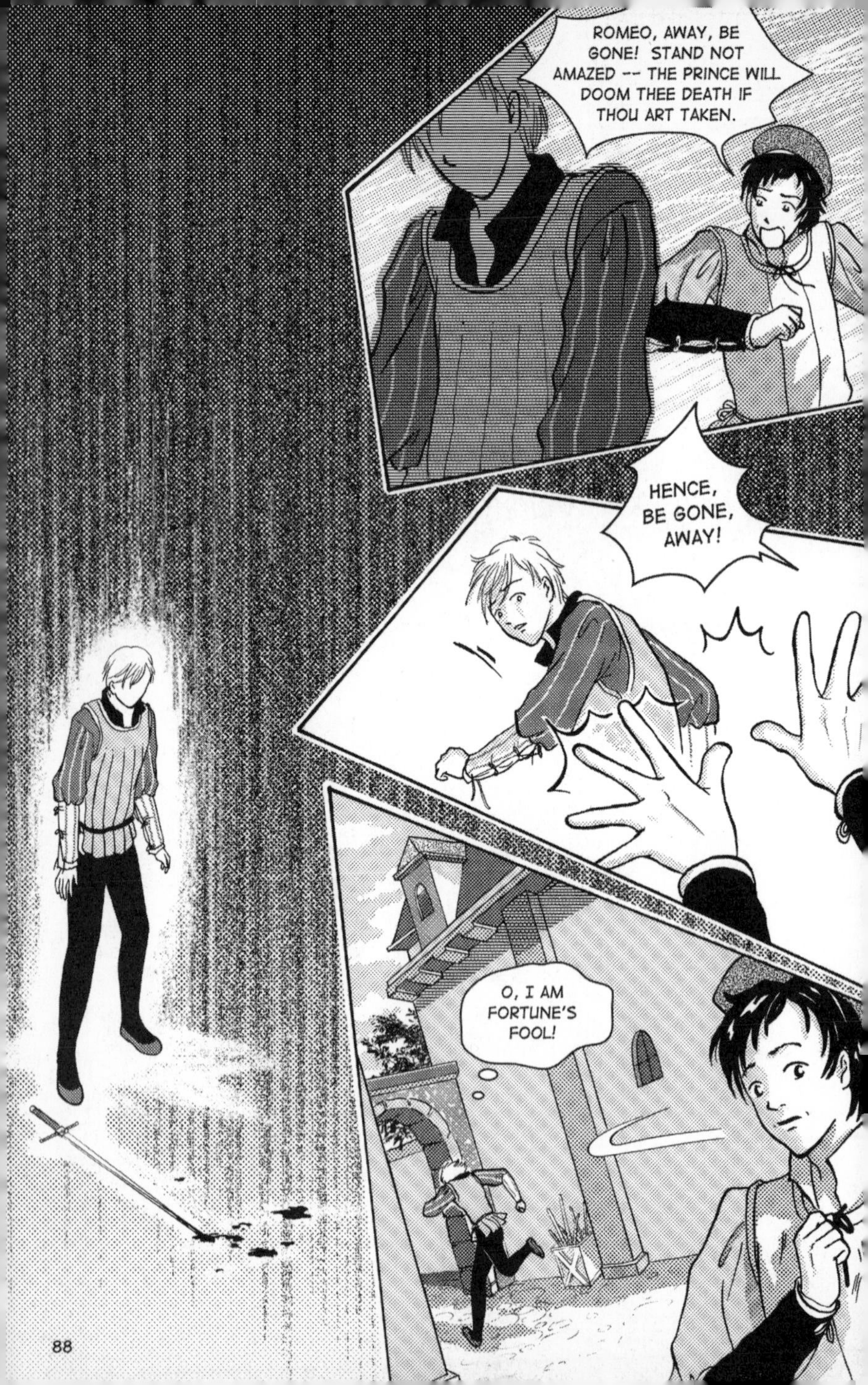
ROMEO, AWAY, BE GONE! STAND NOT AMAZED -- THE PRINCE WILL DOOM THEE DEATH IF THOU ART TAKEN.
HENCE, BE GONE, AWAY!
O, I AM FORTUNE'S FOOL!

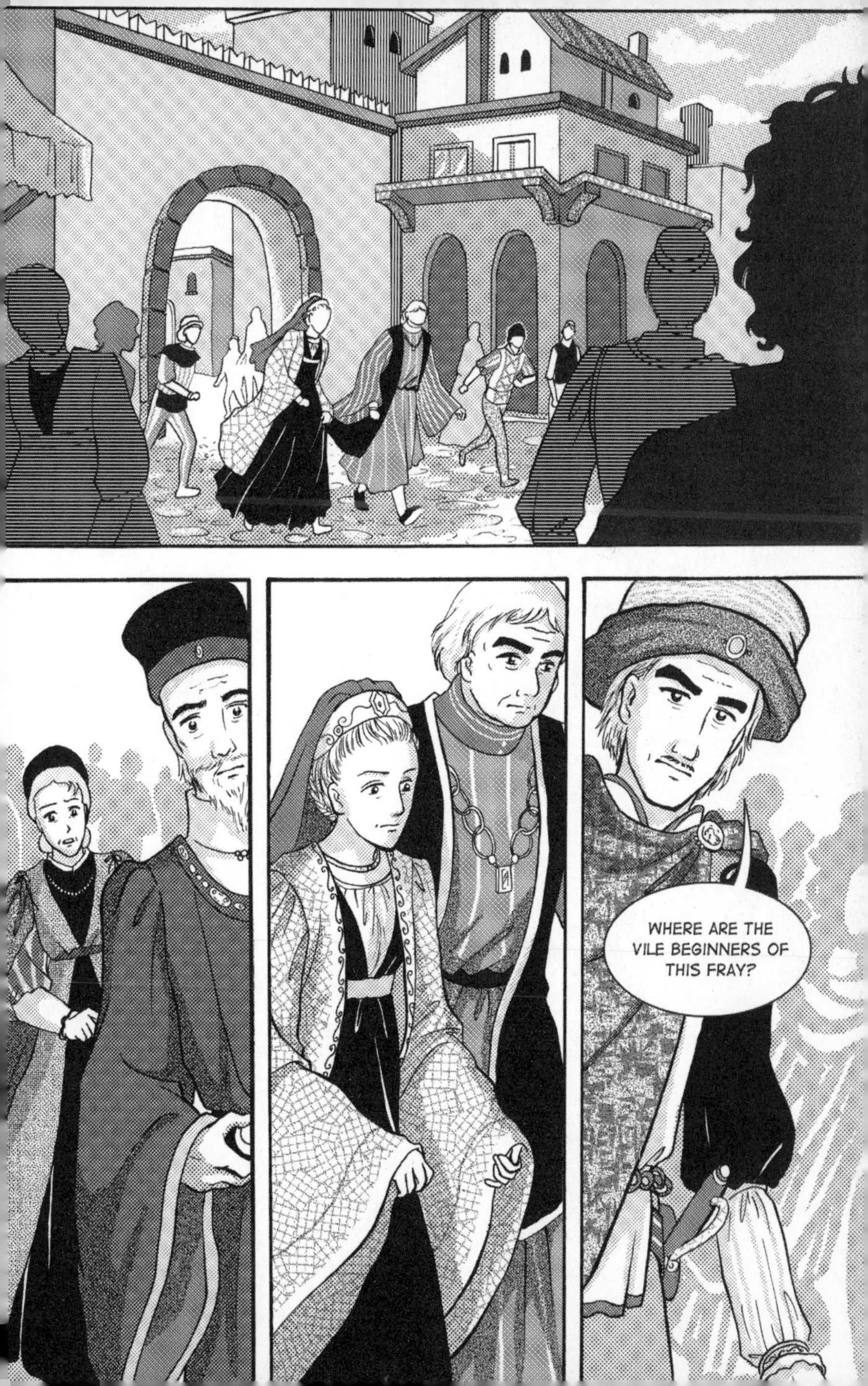
WHERE ARE THE VILE BEGINNERS OF THIS FRAY?

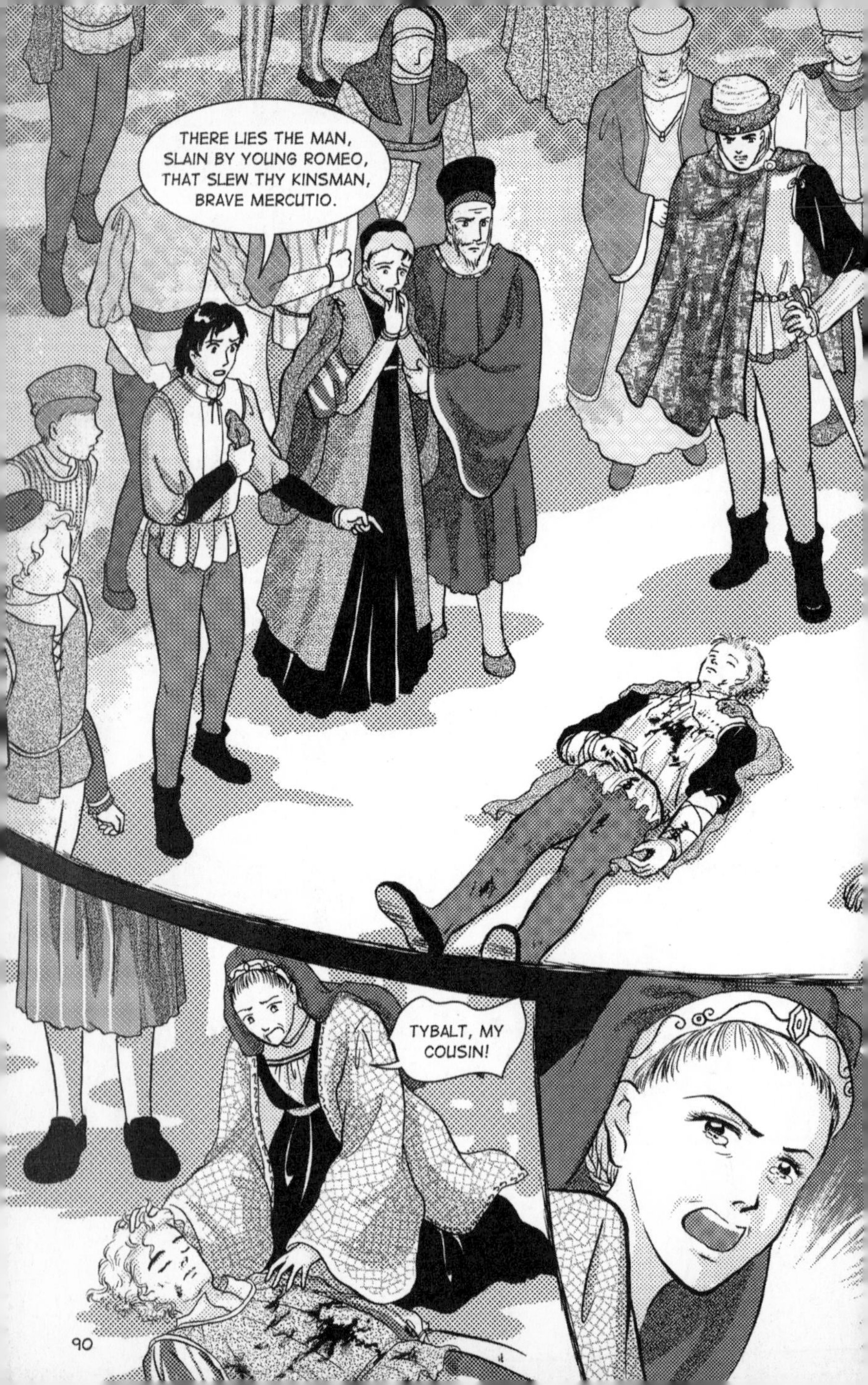
THERE LIES THE MAN, SLAIN BY YOUNG ROMEO, THAT SLEW THY KINSMAN, BRAVE MERCUTIO.
TYBALT, MY COUSIN!

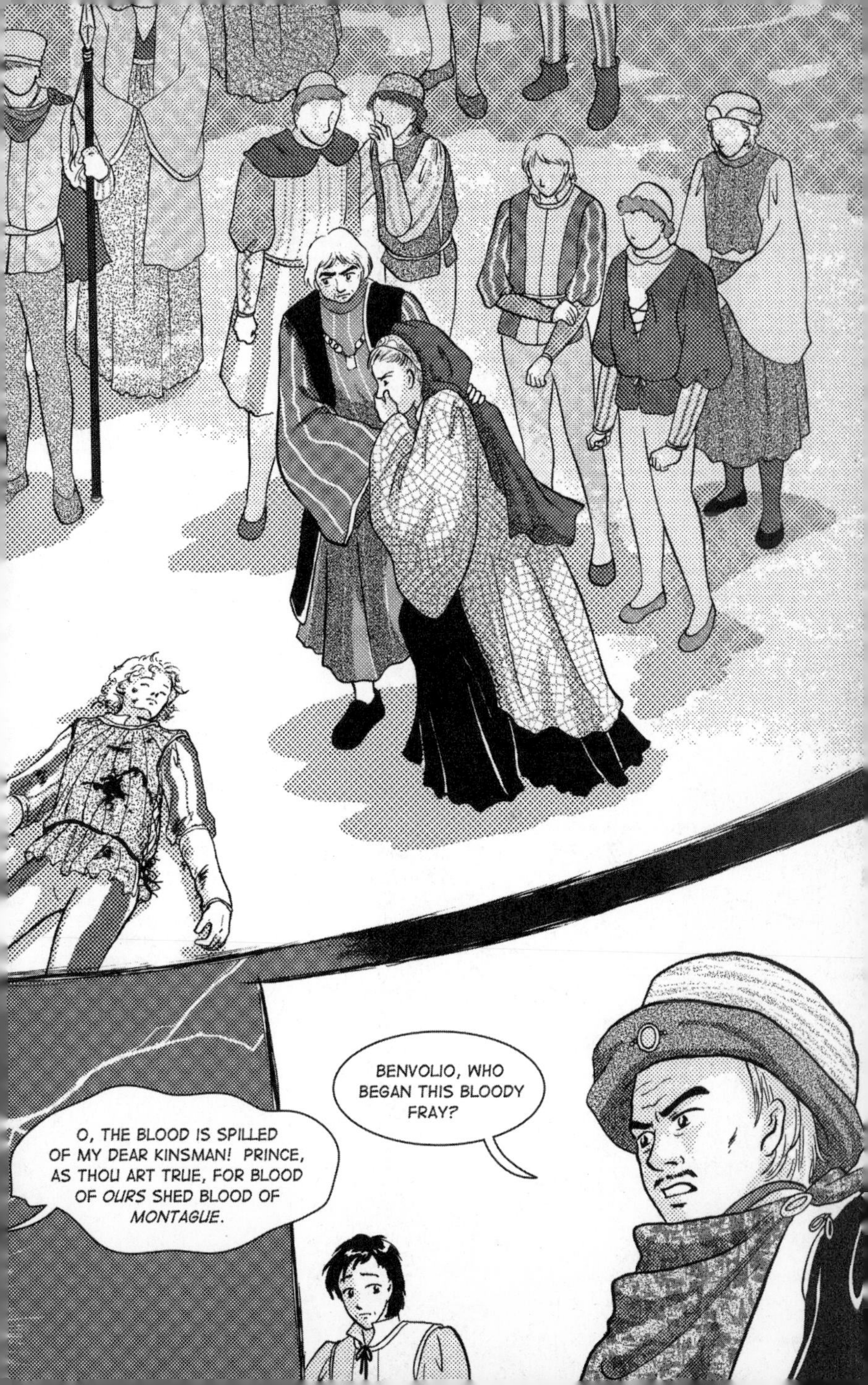
O, THE BLOOD IS SPILLED OF MY DEAR KINSMAN! PRINCE, AS THOU ART TRUE, FOR BLOOD OF *OURS* SHED BLOOD OF *MONTAGUE*.
BENVOLIO, WHO BEGAN THIS BLOODY FRAY?

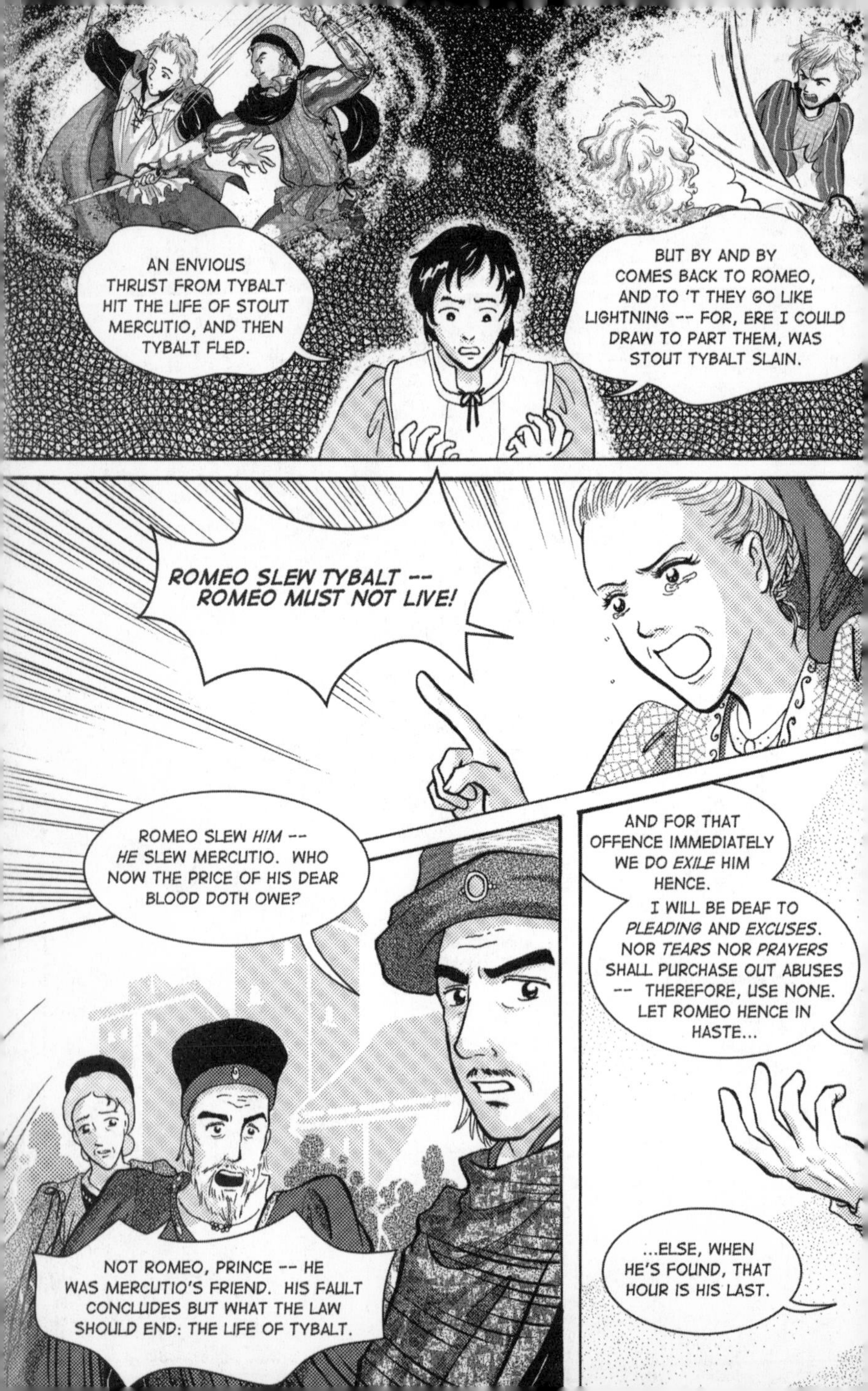
AN ENVIOUS THRUST FROM TYBALT HIT THE LIFE OF STOUT MERCUTIO, AND THEN TYBALT FLED.
BUT BY AND BY COMES BACK TO ROMEO, AND TO 'T THEY GO LIKE LIGHTNING -- FOR, ERE I COULD DRAW TO PART THEM, WAS STOUT TYBALT SLAIN.
ROMEO SLEW TYBALT -- ROMEO MUST NOT LIVE!
ROMEO SLEW *HIM* -- *HE* SLEW MERCUTIO. WHO NOW THE PRICE OF HIS DEAR BLOOD DOTH OWE?
NOT ROMEO, PRINCE -- HE WAS MERCUTIO'S FRIEND. HIS FAULT CONCLUDES BUT WHAT THE LAW SHOULD END: THE LIFE OF TYBALT.
AND FOR THAT OFFENCE IMMEDIATELY WE DO *EXILE* HIM HENCE.
I WILL BE DEAF TO *PLEADING* AND *EXCUSES*. NOR *TEARS* NOR *PRAYERS* SHALL PURCHASE OUT ABUSES -- THEREFORE, USE NONE. LET ROMEO HENCE IN HASTE...
...ELSE, WHEN HE'S FOUND, THAT HOUR IS HIS LAST.

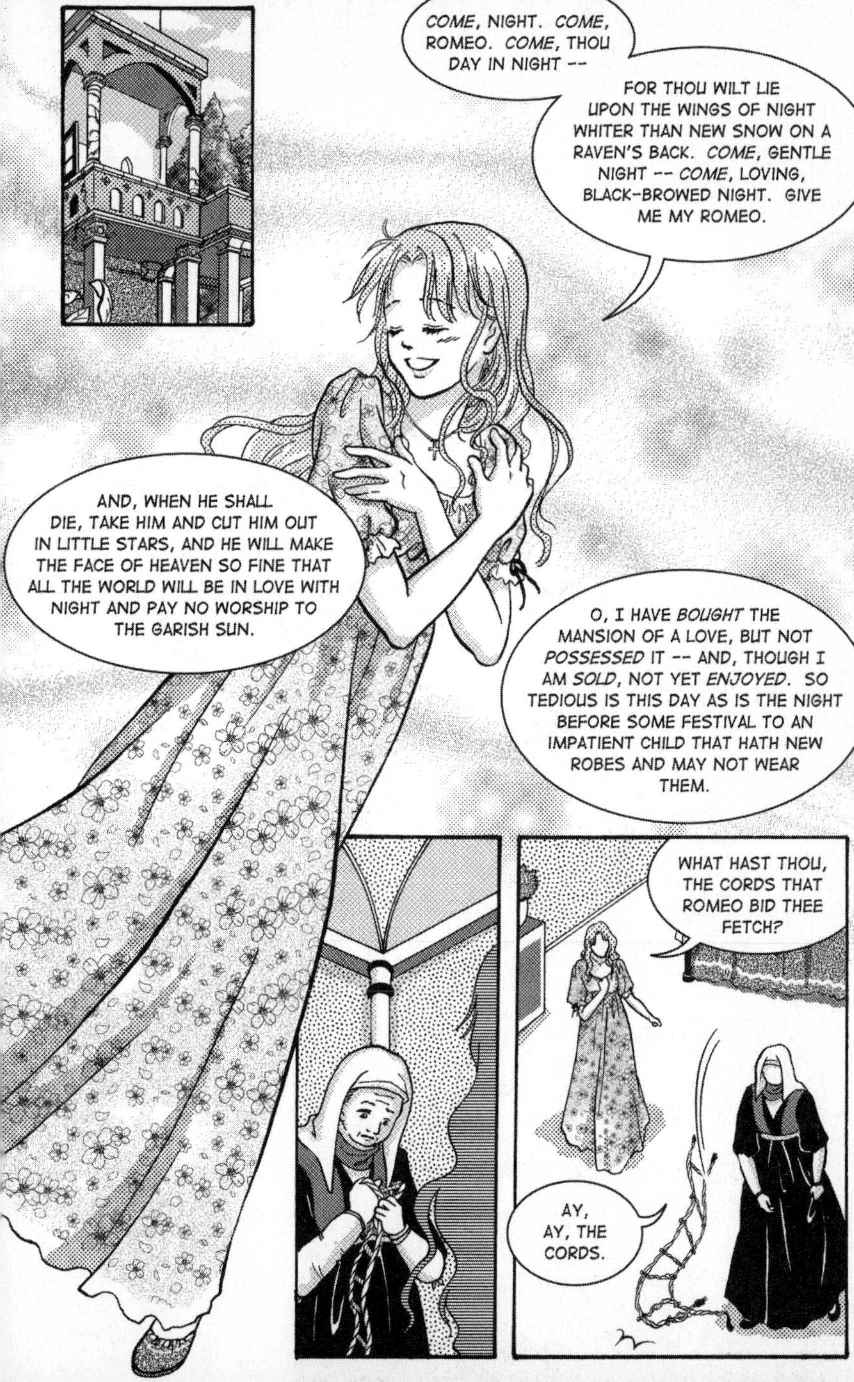
COME, NIGHT. *COME*, ROMEO. *COME*, THOU DAY IN NIGHT --
FOR THOU WILT LIE UPON THE WINGS OF NIGHT WHITER THAN NEW SNOW ON A RAVEN'S BACK. *COME*, GENTLE NIGHT -- *COME*, LOVING, BLACK-BROWED NIGHT. GIVE ME MY ROMEO.
AND, WHEN HE SHALL DIE, TAKE HIM AND CUT HIM OUT IN LITTLE STARS, AND HE WILL MAKE THE FACE OF HEAVEN SO FINE THAT ALL THE WORLD WILL BE IN LOVE WITH NIGHT AND PAY NO WORSHIP TO THE GARISH SUN.
O, I HAVE *BOUGHT* THE MANSION OF A LOVE, BUT NOT *POSSESSED* IT -- AND, THOUGH I AM *SOLD*, NOT YET *ENJOYED*. SO TEDIOUS IS THIS DAY AS IS THE NIGHT BEFORE SOME FESTIVAL TO AN IMPATIENT CHILD THAT HATH NEW ROBES AND MAY NOT WEAR THEM.
WHAT HAST THOU, THE CORDS THAT ROMEO BID THEE FETCH?
AY, AY, THE CORDS.

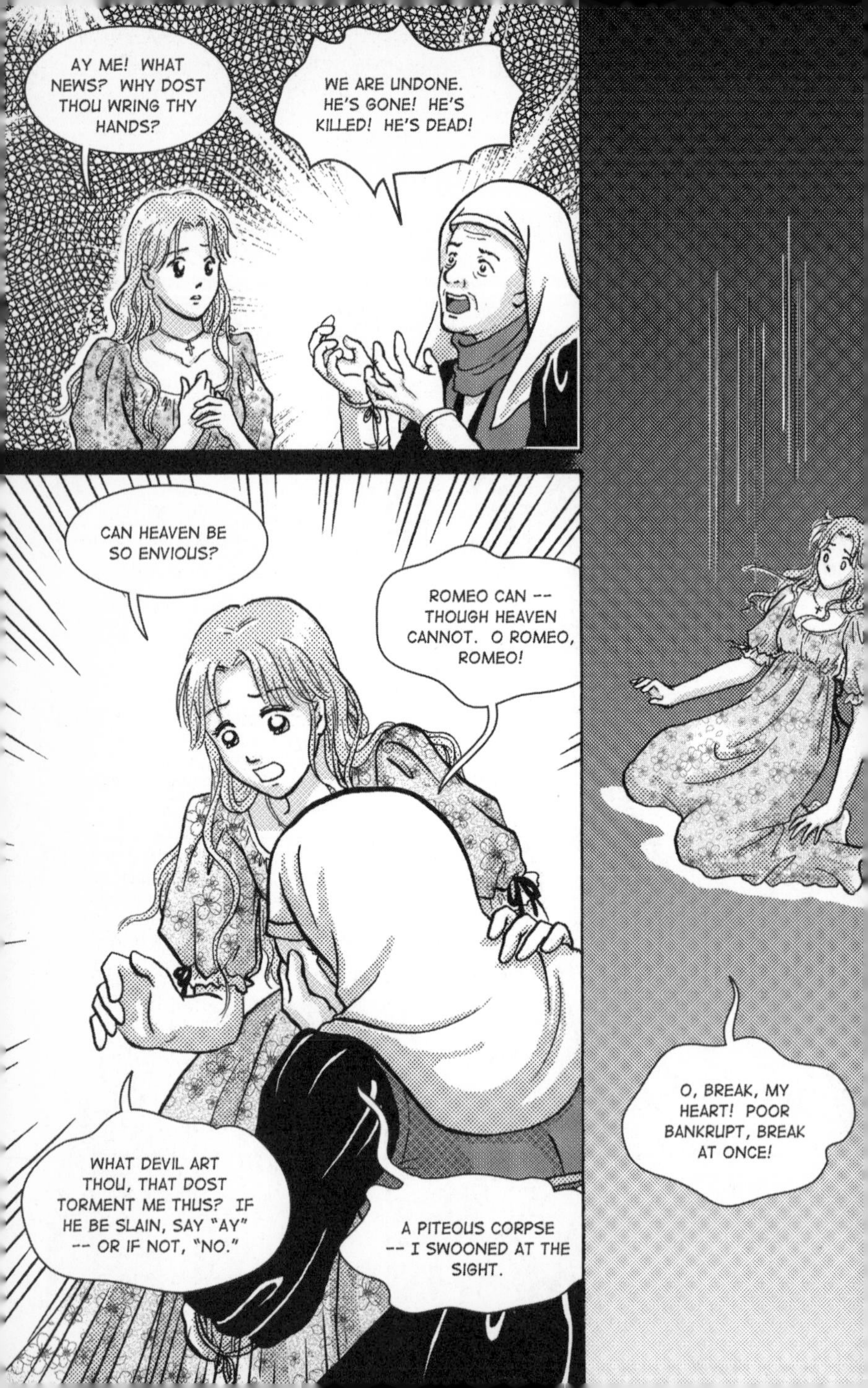
AY ME! WHAT NEWS? WHY DOST THOU WRING THY HANDS?
WE ARE UNDONE. HE'S GONE! HE'S KILLED! HE'S DEAD!
CAN HEAVEN BE SO ENVIOUS?
ROMEO CAN -- THOUGH HEAVEN CANNOT. O ROMEO, ROMEO!
WHAT DEVIL ART THOU, THAT DOST TORMENT ME THUS? IF HE BE SLAIN, SAY "AY" -- OR IF NOT, "NO."
A PITEOUS CORPSE -- I SWOONED AT THE SIGHT.
O, BREAK, MY HEART! POOR BANKRUPT, BREAK AT ONCE!

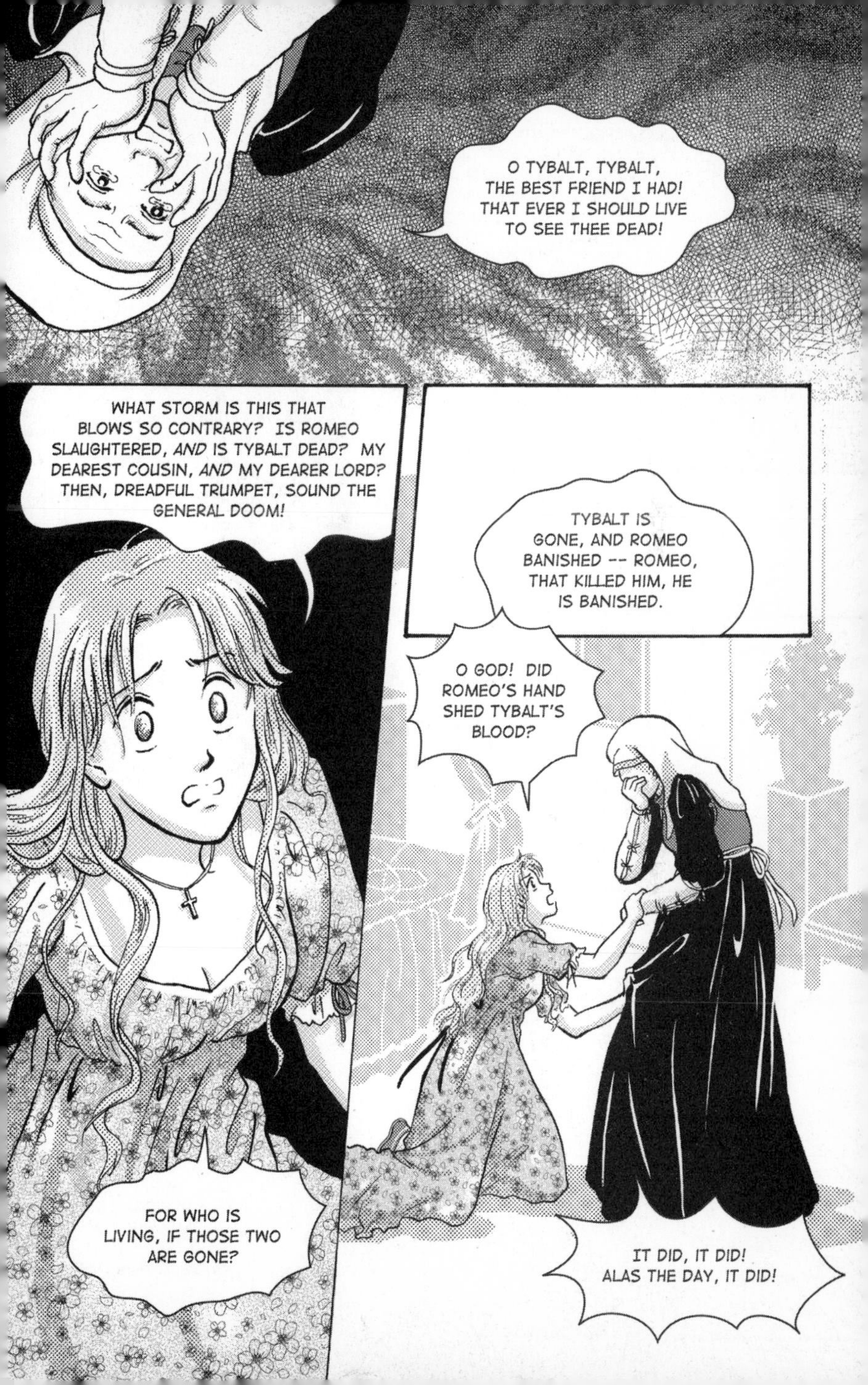
O TYBALT, TYBALT, THE BEST FRIEND I HAD! THAT EVER I SHOULD LIVE TO SEE THEE DEAD!
WHAT STORM IS THIS THAT BLOWS SO CONTRARY? IS ROMEO SLAUGHTERED, *AND* IS TYBALT DEAD? MY DEAREST COUSIN, *AND* MY DEARER LORD? THEN, DREADFUL TRUMPET, SOUND THE GENERAL DOOM!
FOR WHO IS LIVING, IF THOSE TWO ARE GONE?
TYBALT IS GONE, AND ROMEO BANISHED -- ROMEO, THAT KILLED HIM, HE IS BANISHED.
O GOD! DID ROMEO'S HAND SHED TYBALT'S BLOOD?
IT DID, IT DID! ALAS THE DAY, IT DID!

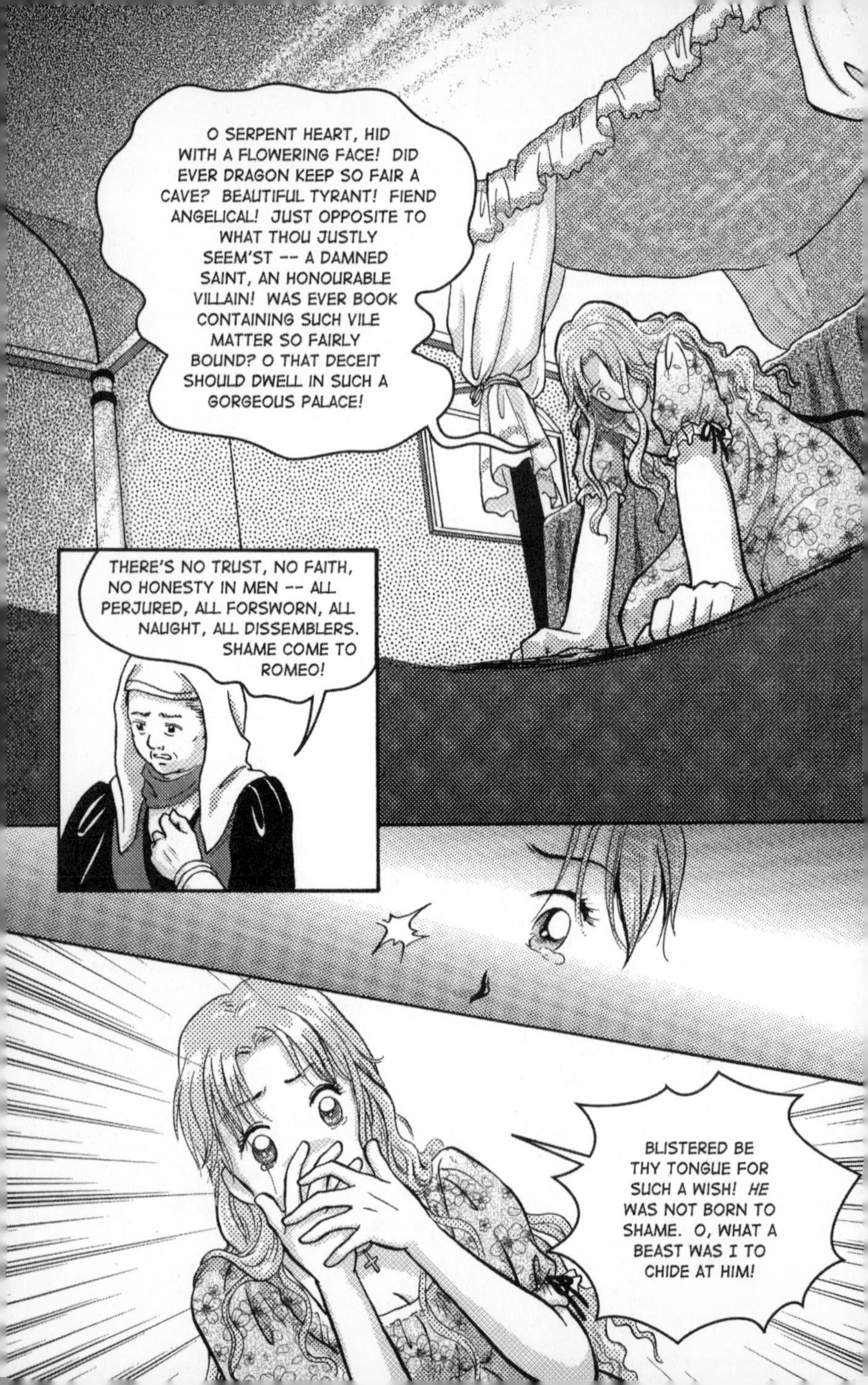
O SERPENT HEART, HID WITH A FLOWERING FACE! DID EVER DRAGON KEEP SO FAIR A CAVE? BEAUTIFUL TYRANT! FIEND ANGELICAL! JUST OPPOSITE TO WHAT THOU JUSTLY SEEM'ST -- A DAMNED SAINT, AN HONOURABLE VILLAIN! WAS EVER BOOK CONTAINING SUCH VILE MATTER SO FAIRLY BOUND? O THAT DECEIT SHOULD DWELL IN SUCH A GORGEOUS PALACE!
THERE'S NO TRUST, NO FAITH, NO HONESTY IN MEN -- ALL PERJURED, ALL FORSWORN, ALL NAUGHT, ALL DISSEMBLERS. SHAME COME TO ROMEO!
BLISTERED BE THY TONGUE FOR SUCH A WISH! *HE* WAS NOT BORN TO SHAME. O, WHAT A BEAST WAS I TO CHIDE AT HIM!

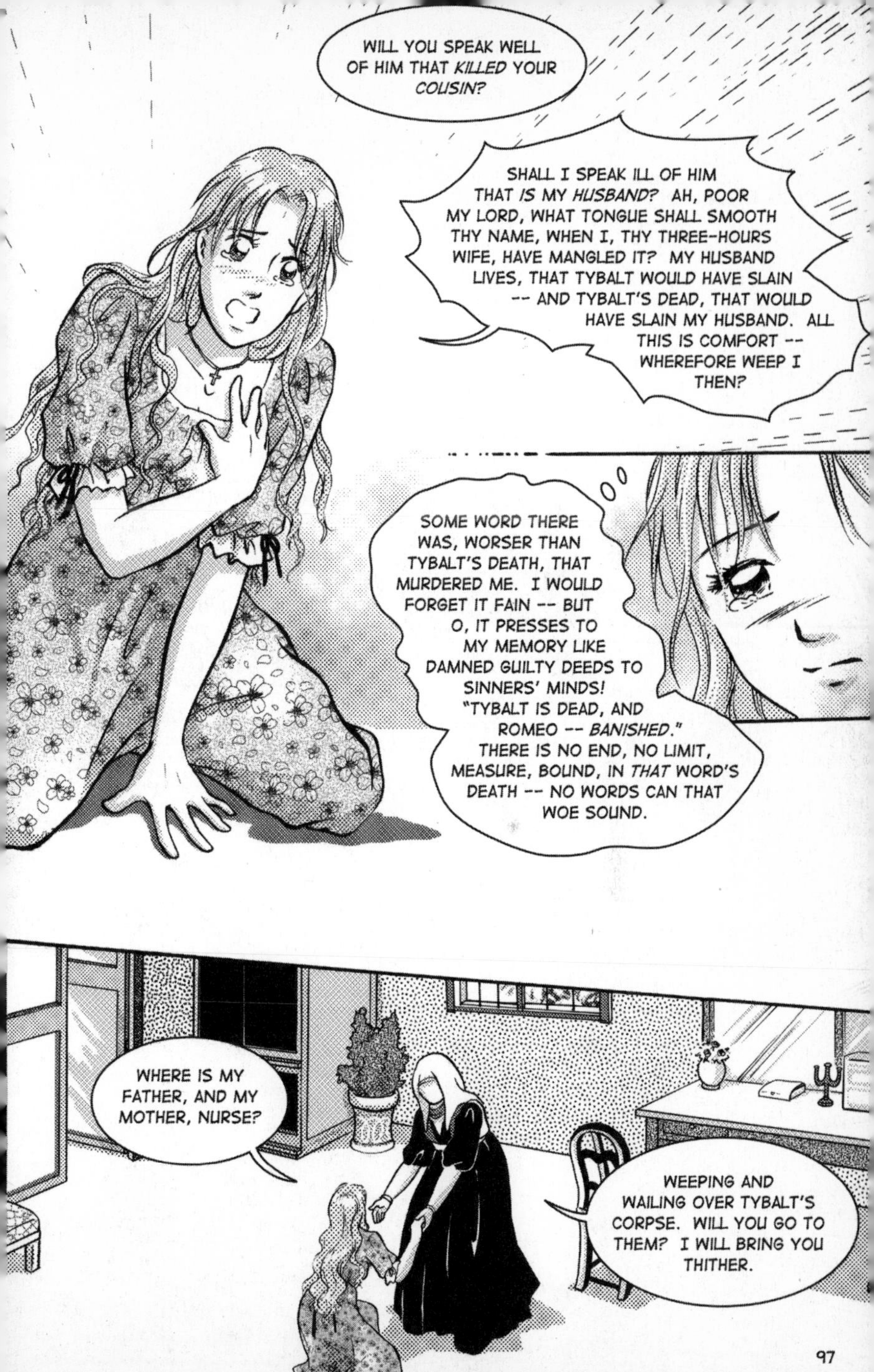
WILL YOU SPEAK WELL OF HIM THAT *KILLED* YOUR *COUSIN*?
SHALL I SPEAK ILL OF HIM THAT *IS* MY *HUSBAND*? AH, POOR MY LORD, WHAT TONGUE SHALL SMOOTH THY NAME, WHEN I, THY THREE-HOURS WIFE, HAVE MANGLED IT? MY HUSBAND LIVES, THAT TYBALT WOULD HAVE SLAIN -- AND TYBALT'S DEAD, THAT WOULD HAVE SLAIN MY HUSBAND. ALL THIS IS COMFORT -- WHEREFORE WEEP I THEN?
SOME WORD THERE WAS, WORSER THAN TYBALT'S DEATH, THAT MURDERED ME. I WOULD FORGET IT FAIN -- BUT O, IT PRESSES TO MY MEMORY LIKE DAMNED GUILTY DEEDS TO SINNERS' MINDS! "TYBALT IS DEAD, AND ROMEO -- *BANISHED*." THERE IS NO END, NO LIMIT, MEASURE, BOUND, IN *THAT* WORD'S DEATH -- NO WORDS CAN THAT WOE SOUND.
WHERE IS MY FATHER, AND MY MOTHER, NURSE?
WEEPING AND WAILING OVER TYBALT'S CORPSE. WILL YOU GO TO THEM? I WILL BRING YOU THITHER.

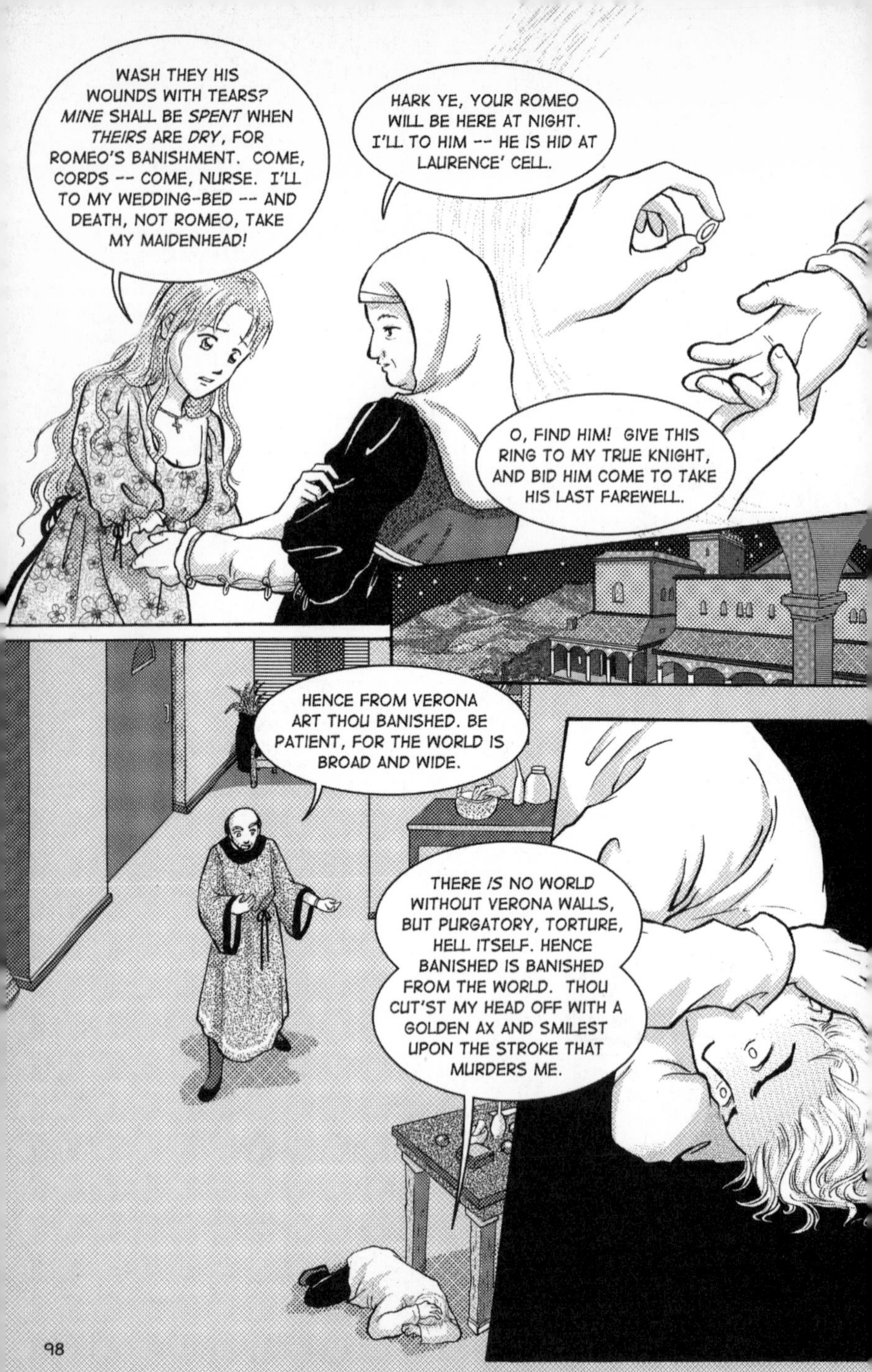
WASH THEY HIS WOUNDS WITH TEARS? *MINE* SHALL BE *SPENT* WHEN *THEIRS* ARE *DRY*, FOR ROMEO'S BANISHMENT. COME, CORDS -- COME, NURSE. I'LL TO MY WEDDING-BED -- AND DEATH, NOT ROMEO, TAKE MY MAIDENHEAD!
HARK YE, YOUR ROMEO WILL BE HERE AT NIGHT. I'LL TO HIM -- HE IS HID AT LAURENCE' CELL.
O, FIND HIM! GIVE THIS RING TO MY TRUE KNIGHT, AND BID HIM COME TO TAKE HIS LAST FAREWELL.
HENCE FROM VERONA ART THOU BANISHED. BE PATIENT, FOR THE WORLD IS BROAD AND WIDE.
THERE *IS* NO WORLD WITHOUT VERONA WALLS, BUT PURGATORY, TORTURE, HELL ITSELF. HENCE BANISHED IS BANISHED FROM THE WORLD. THOU CUT'ST MY HEAD OFF WITH A GOLDEN AX AND SMILEST UPON THE STROKE THAT MURDERS ME.

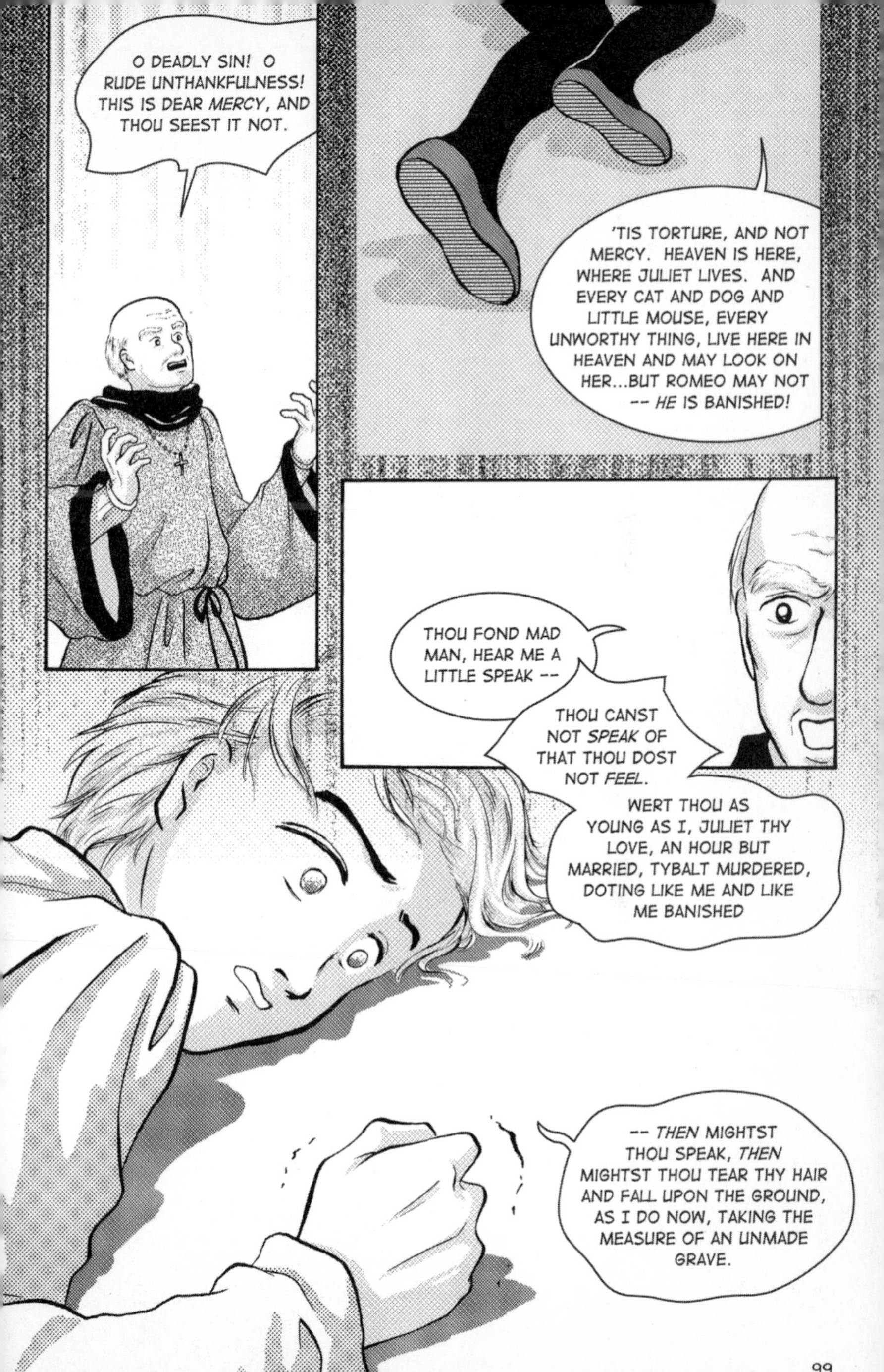
O DEADLY SIN! O RUDE UNTHANKFULNESS! THIS IS DEAR *MERCY*, AND THOU SEEST IT NOT.
'TIS TORTURE, AND NOT MERCY. HEAVEN IS HERE, WHERE JULIET LIVES. AND EVERY CAT AND DOG AND LITTLE MOUSE, EVERY UNWORTHY THING, LIVE HERE IN HEAVEN AND MAY LOOK ON HER...BUT ROMEO MAY NOT -- *HE* IS BANISHED!
THOU FOND MAD MAN, HEAR ME A LITTLE SPEAK --
THOU CANST NOT *SPEAK* OF THAT THOU DOST NOT *FEEL*.
WERT THOU AS YOUNG AS I, JULIET THY LOVE, AN HOUR BUT MARRIED, TYBALT MURDERED, DOTING LIKE ME AND LIKE ME BANISHED
-- *THEN* MIGHTST THOU SPEAK, *THEN* MIGHTST THOU TEAR THY HAIR AND FALL UPON THE GROUND, AS I DO NOW, TAKING THE MEASURE OF AN UNMADE GRAVE.

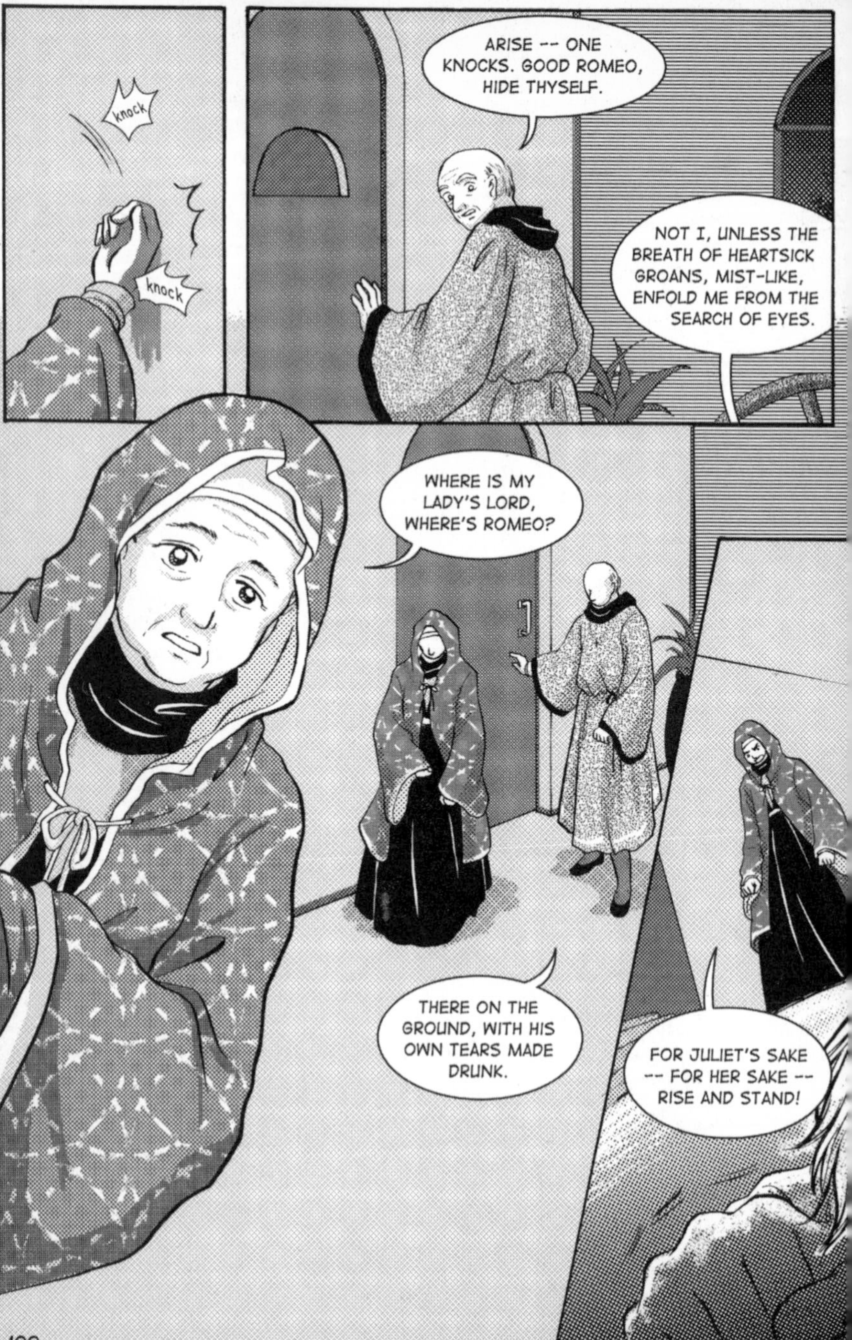
knock
knock
ARISE -- ONE KNOCKS. GOOD ROMEO, HIDE THYSELF.
NOT I, UNLESS THE BREATH OF HEARTSICK GROANS, MIST-LIKE, ENFOLD ME FROM THE SEARCH OF EYES.
WHERE IS MY LADY'S LORD, WHERE'S ROMEO?
THERE ON THE GROUND, WITH HIS OWN TEARS MADE DRUNK.
FOR JULIET'S SAKE -- FOR HER SAKE -- RISE AND STAND!

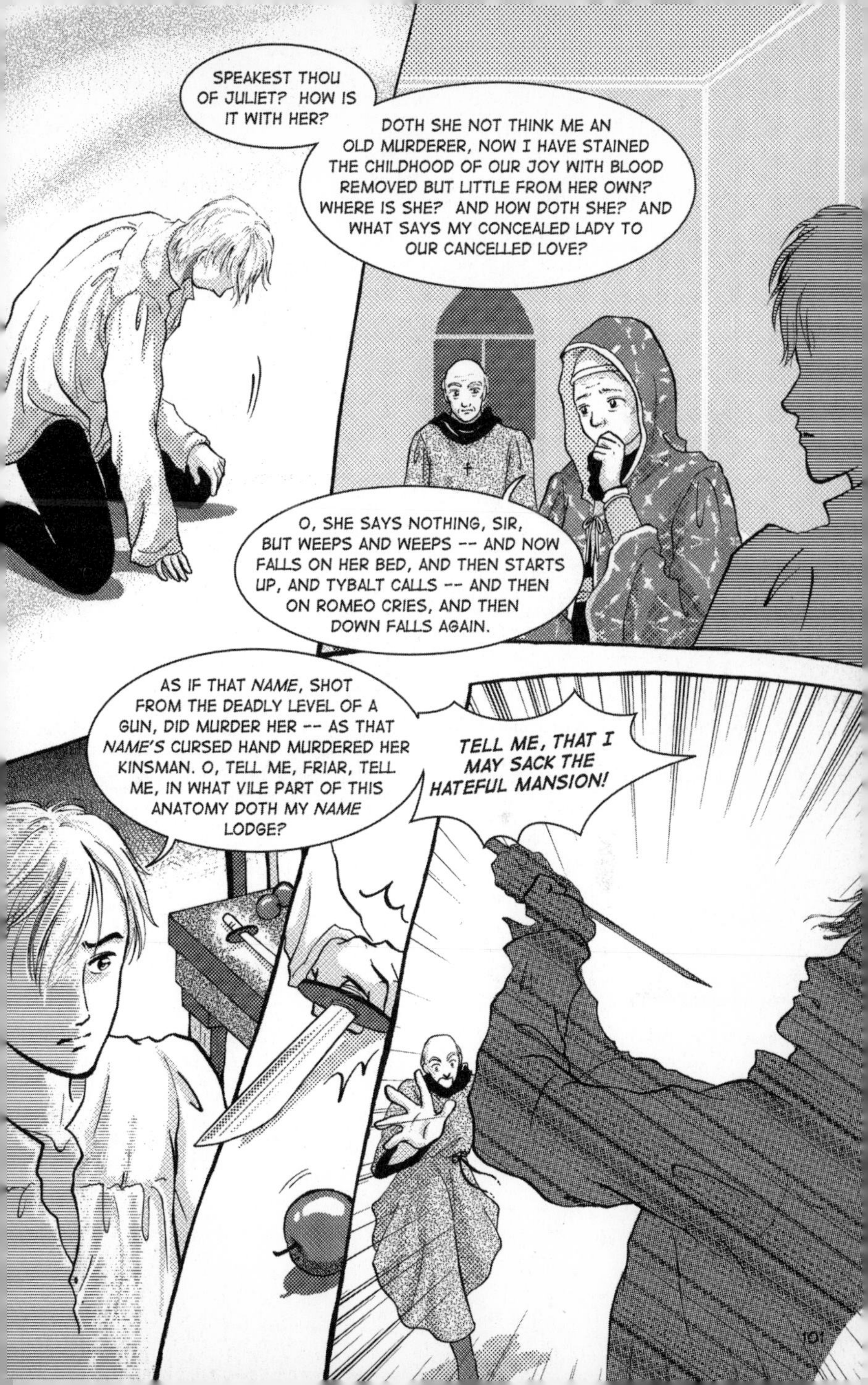
SPEAKEST THOU OF JULIET? HOW IS IT WITH HER?
DOTH SHE NOT THINK ME AN OLD MURDERER, NOW I HAVE STAINED THE CHILDHOOD OF OUR JOY WITH BLOOD REMOVED BUT LITTLE FROM HER OWN? WHERE IS SHE? AND HOW DOTH SHE? AND WHAT SAYS MY CONCEALED LADY TO OUR CANCELLED LOVE?
O, SHE SAYS NOTHING, SIR, BUT WEEPS AND WEEPS -- AND NOW FALLS ON HER BED, AND THEN STARTS UP, AND TYBALT CALLS -- AND THEN ON ROMEO CRIES, AND THEN DOWN FALLS AGAIN.
AS IF THAT *NAME*, SHOT FROM THE DEADLY LEVEL OF A GUN, DID MURDER HER -- AS THAT *NAME'S* CURSED HAND MURDERED HER KINSMAN. O, TELL ME, FRIAR, TELL ME, IN WHAT VILE PART OF THIS ANATOMY DOTH MY *NAME* LODGE?
TELL ME, THAT I MAY SACK THE HATEFUL MANSION!

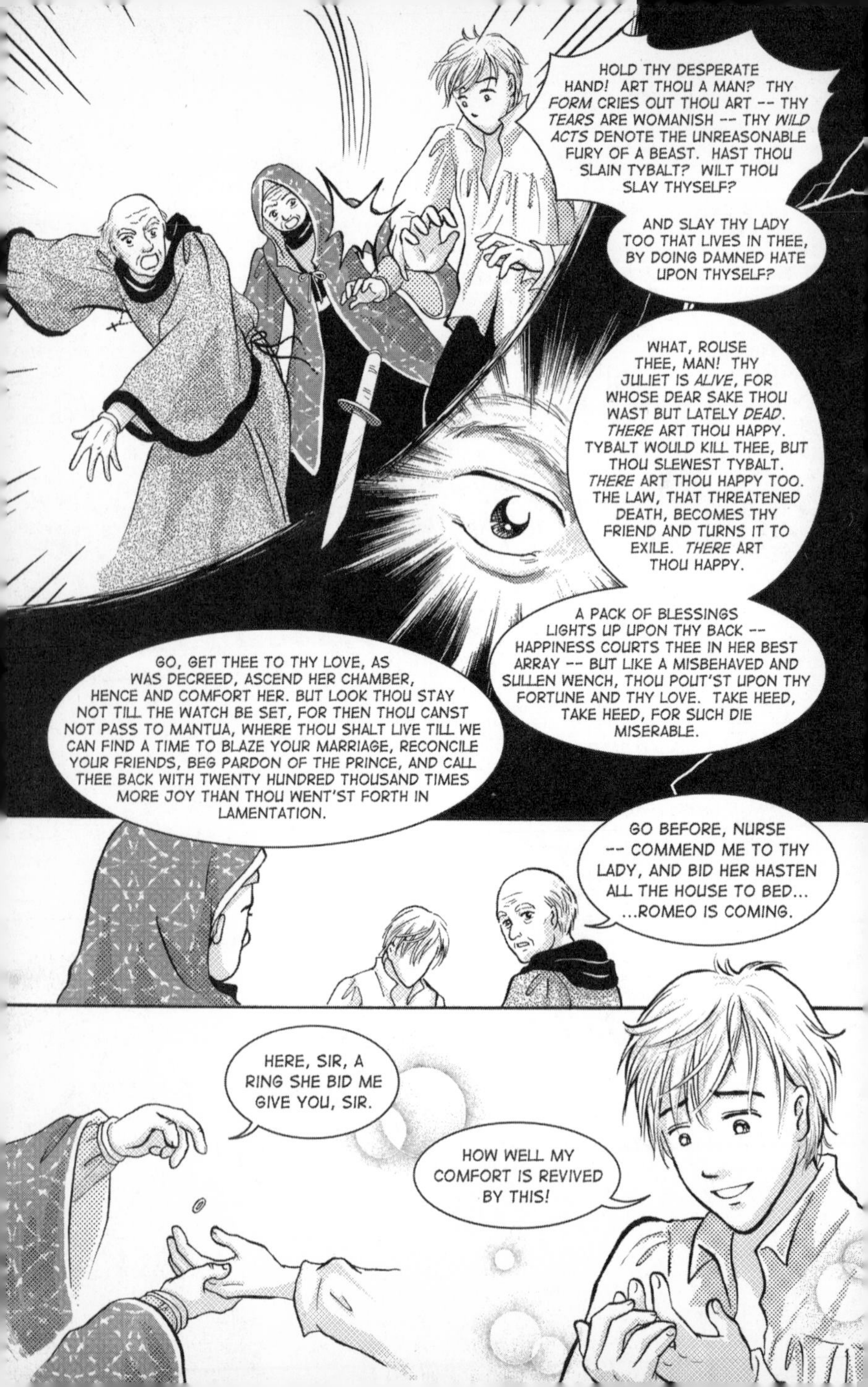
HOLD THY DESPERATE HAND! ART THOU A MAN? THY *FORM* CRIES OUT THOU ART -- THY *TEARS* ARE WOMANISH -- THY *WILD ACTS* DENOTE THE UNREASONABLE FURY OF A BEAST. HAST THOU SLAIN TYBALT? WILT THOU SLAY THYSELF?
AND SLAY THY LADY TOO THAT LIVES IN THEE, BY DOING DAMNED HATE UPON THYSELF?
WHAT, ROUSE THEE, MAN! THY JULIET IS *ALIVE*, FOR WHOSE DEAR SAKE THOU WAST BUT LATELY *DEAD*. *THERE* ART THOU HAPPY. TYBALT WOULD KILL THEE, BUT THOU SLEWEST TYBALT. *THERE* ART THOU HAPPY TOO. THE LAW, THAT THREATENED DEATH, BECOMES THY FRIEND AND TURNS IT TO EXILE. *THERE* ART THOU HAPPY.
A PACK OF BLESSINGS LIGHTS UP UPON THY BACK -- HAPPINESS COURTS THEE IN HER BEST ARRAY -- BUT LIKE A MISBEHAVED AND SULLEN WENCH, THOU POUT'ST UPON THY FORTUNE AND THY LOVE. TAKE HEED, TAKE HEED, FOR SUCH DIE MISERABLE.
GO, GET THEE TO THY LOVE, AS WAS DECREED, ASCEND HER CHAMBER, HENCE AND COMFORT HER. BUT LOOK THOU STAY NOT TILL THE WATCH BE SET, FOR THEN THOU CANST NOT PASS TO MANTUA, WHERE THOU SHALT LIVE TILL WE CAN FIND A TIME TO BLAZE YOUR MARRIAGE, RECONCILE YOUR FRIENDS, BEG PARDON OF THE PRINCE, AND CALL THEE BACK WITH TWENTY HUNDRED THOUSAND TIMES MORE JOY THAN THOU WENT'ST FORTH IN LAMENTATION.
GO BEFORE, NURSE -- COMMEND ME TO THY LADY, AND BID HER HASTEN ALL THE HOUSE TO BED... ...ROMEO IS COMING.
HERE, SIR, A RING SHE BID ME GIVE YOU, SIR.
HOW WELL MY COMFORT IS REVIVED BY THIS!

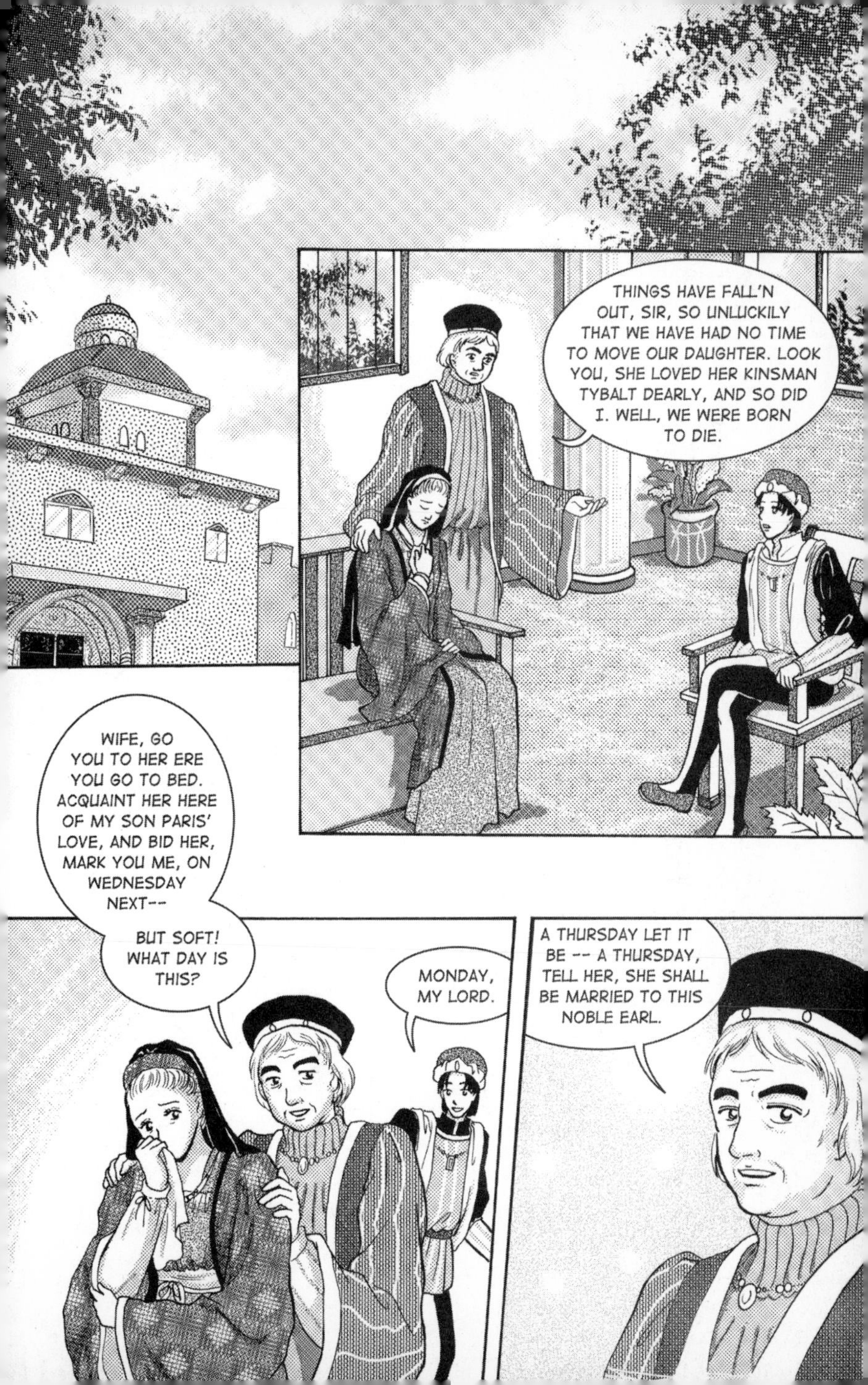
THINGS HAVE FALL'N OUT, SIR, SO UNLUCKILY THAT WE HAVE HAD NO TIME TO MOVE OUR DAUGHTER. LOOK YOU, SHE LOVED HER KINSMAN TYBALT DEARLY, AND SO DID I. WELL, WE WERE BORN TO DIE.
WIFE, GO YOU TO HER ERE YOU GO TO BED. ACQUAINT HER HERE OF MY SON PARIS' LOVE, AND BID HER, MARK YOU ME, ON WEDNESDAY NEXT--
BUT SOFT! WHAT DAY IS THIS?
MONDAY, MY LORD.
A THURSDAY LET IT BE -- A THURSDAY, TELL HER, SHE SHALL BE MARRIED TO THIS NOBLE EARL.

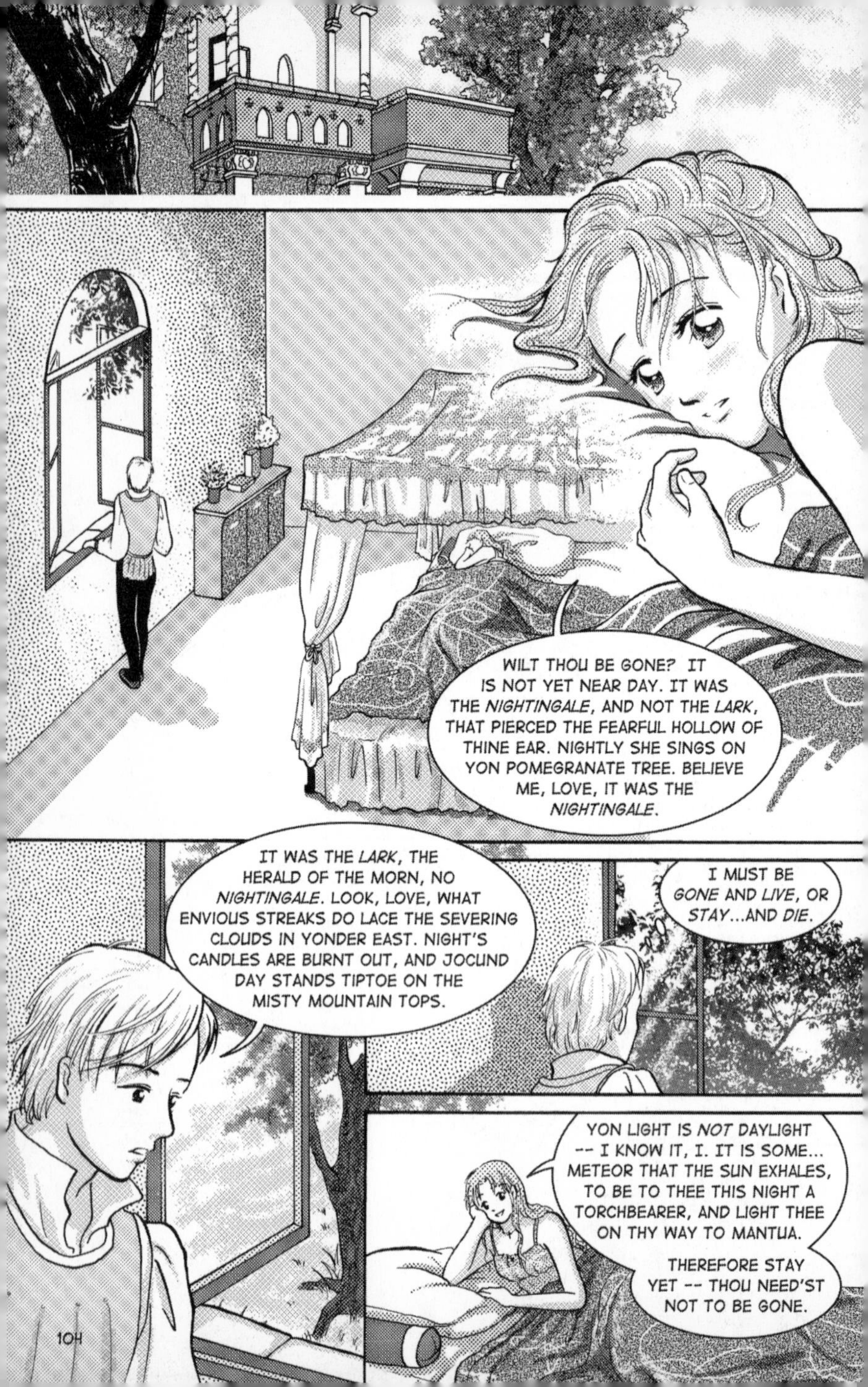
WILT THOU BE GONE? IT IS NOT YET NEAR DAY. IT WAS THE *NIGHTINGALE*, AND NOT THE *LARK*, THAT PIERCED THE FEARFUL HOLLOW OF THINE EAR. NIGHTLY SHE SINGS ON YON POMEGRANATE TREE. BELIEVE ME, LOVE, IT WAS THE *NIGHTINGALE*.
IT WAS THE *LARK*, THE HERALD OF THE MORN, NO *NIGHTINGALE*. LOOK, LOVE, WHAT ENVIOUS STREAKS DO LACE THE SEVERING CLOUDS IN YONDER EAST. NIGHT'S CANDLES ARE BURNT OUT, AND JOCUND DAY STANDS TIPTOE ON THE MISTY MOUNTAIN TOPS.
I MUST BE *GONE* AND *LIVE*, OR *STAY*...AND *DIE*.
YON LIGHT IS *NOT* DAYLIGHT -- I KNOW IT, I. IT IS SOME... METEOR THAT THE SUN EXHALES, TO BE TO THEE THIS NIGHT A TORCHBEARER, AND LIGHT THEE ON THY WAY TO MANTUA.
THEREFORE STAY YET -- THOU NEED'ST NOT TO BE GONE.

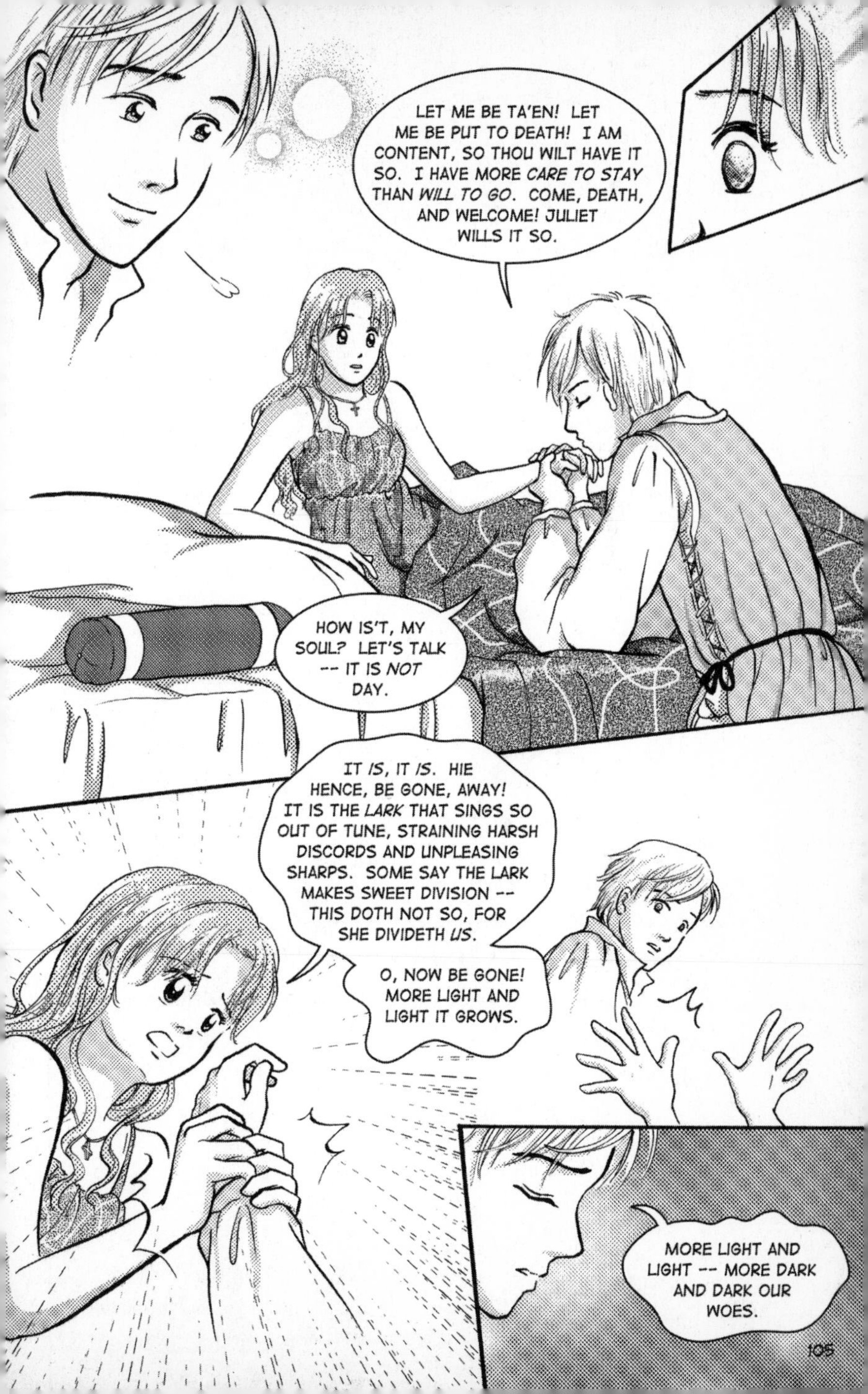

LET ME BE TA'EN! LET ME BE PUT TO DEATH! I AM CONTENT, SO THOU WILT HAVE IT SO. I HAVE MORE *CARE TO STAY* THAN *WILL TO GO*. COME, DEATH, AND WELCOME! JULIET WILLS IT SO.
HOW IS'T, MY SOUL? LET'S TALK -- IT IS *NOT* DAY.
IT *IS*, IT *IS*. HIE HENCE, BE GONE, AWAY! IT IS THE *LARK* THAT SINGS SO OUT OF TUNE, STRAINING HARSH DISCORDS AND UNPLEASING SHARPS. SOME SAY THE LARK MAKES SWEET DIVISION -- THIS DOTH NOT SO, FOR SHE DIVIDETH *US*.
O, NOW BE GONE! MORE LIGHT AND LIGHT IT GROWS.
MORE LIGHT AND LIGHT -- MORE DARK AND DARK OUR WOES.

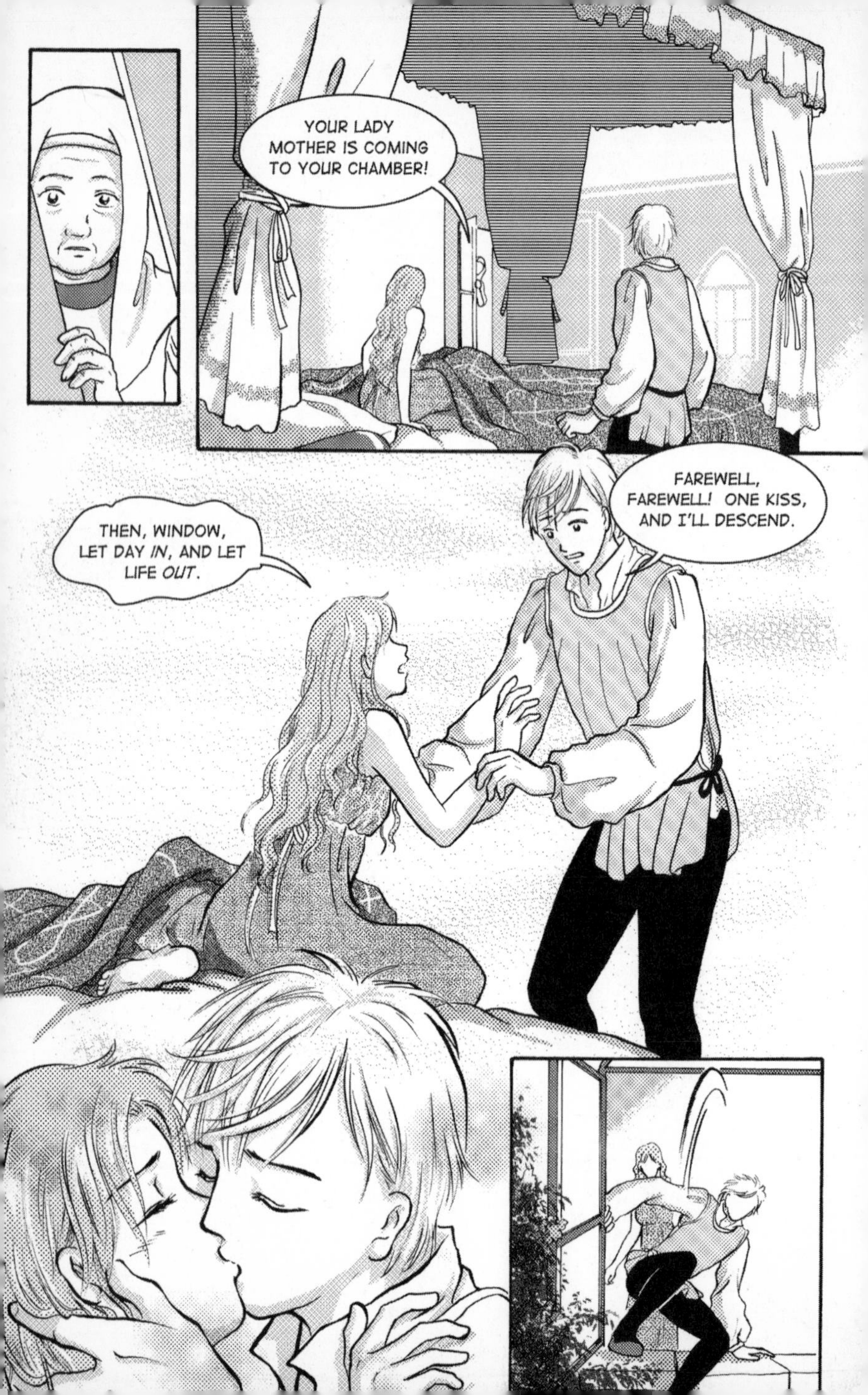
YOUR LADY MOTHER IS COMING TO YOUR CHAMBER!
FAREWELL, FAREWELL! ONE KISS, AND I'LL DESCEND.
THEN, WINDOW, LET DAY *IN*, AND LET LIFE *OUT*.

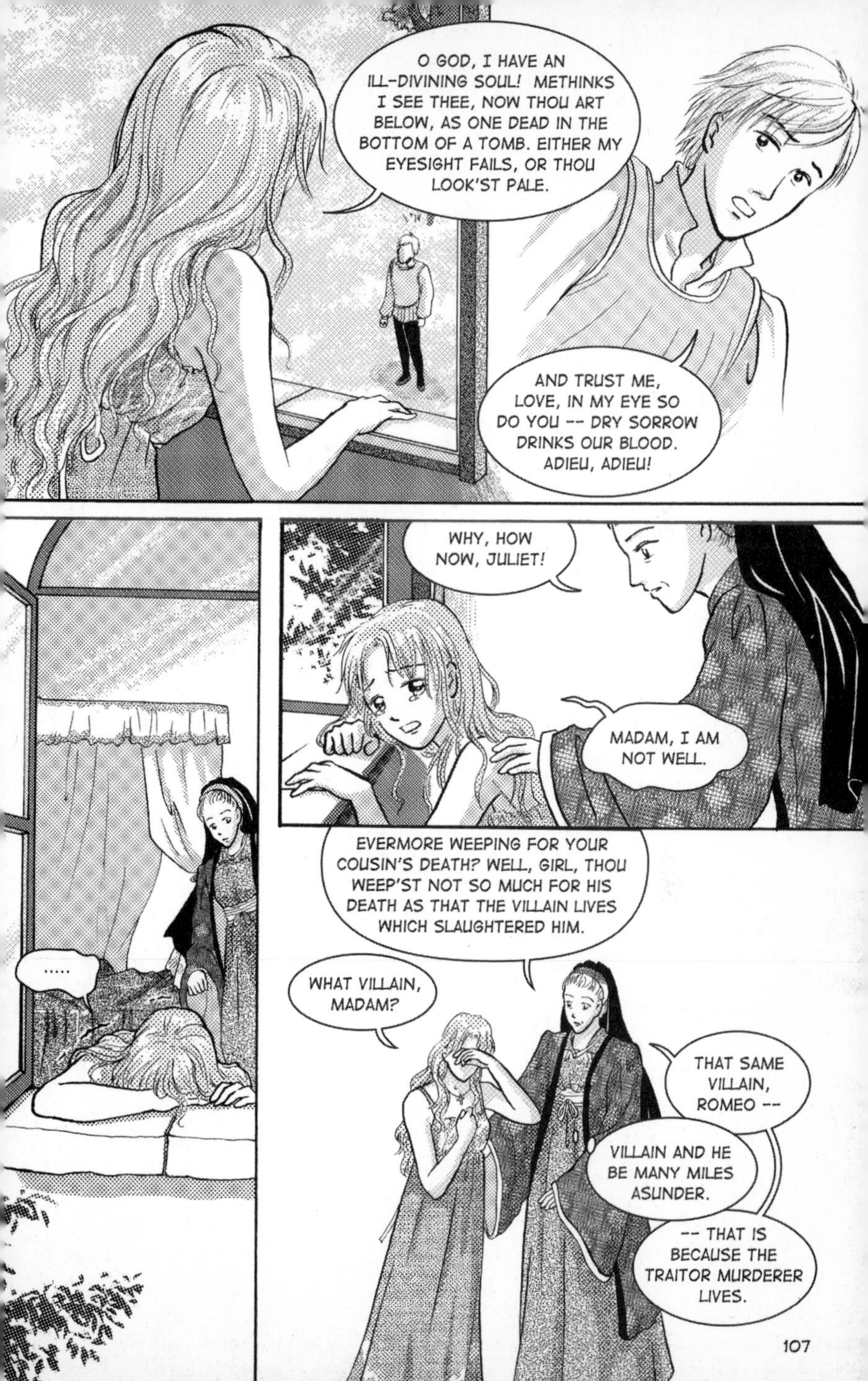
O GOD, I HAVE AN ILL-DIVINING SOUL! METHINKS I SEE THEE, NOW THOU ART BELOW, AS ONE DEAD IN THE BOTTOM OF A TOMB. EITHER MY EYESIGHT FAILS, OR THOU LOOK'ST PALE.
AND TRUST ME, LOVE, IN MY EYE SO DO YOU -- DRY SORROW DRINKS OUR BLOOD. ADIEU, ADIEU!
.....
WHY, HOW NOW, JULIET!
MADAM, I AM NOT WELL.
EVERMORE WEEPING FOR YOUR COUSIN'S DEATH? WELL, GIRL, THOU WEEP'ST NOT SO MUCH FOR HIS DEATH AS THAT THE VILLAIN LIVES WHICH SLAUGHTERED HIM.
WHAT VILLAIN, MADAM?
THAT SAME VILLAIN, ROMEO --
VILLAIN AND HE BE MANY MILES ASUNDER.
-- THAT IS BECAUSE THE TRAITOR MURDERER LIVES.

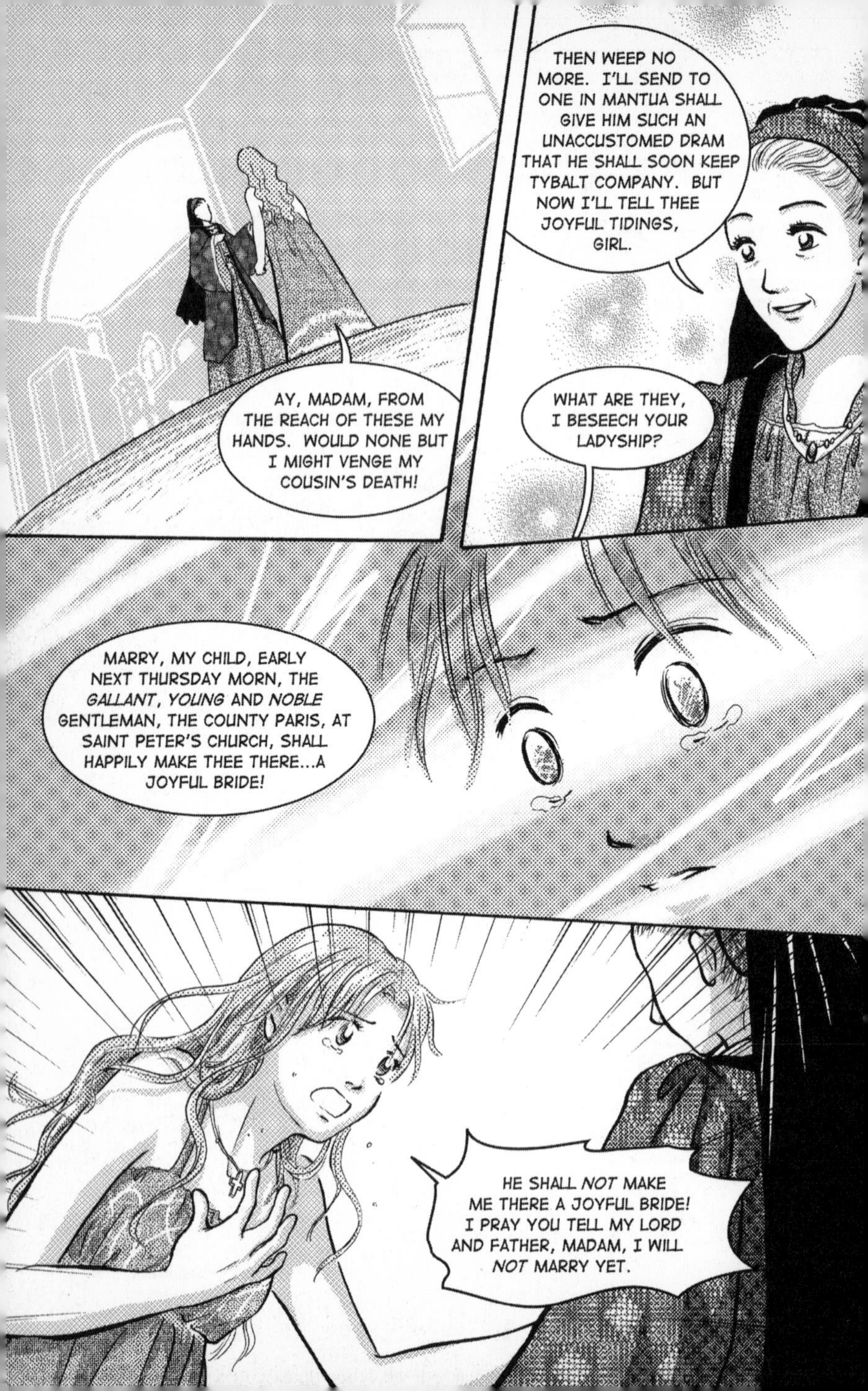
AY, MADAM, FROM THE REACH OF THESE MY HANDS. WOULD NONE BUT I MIGHT VENGE MY COUSIN'S DEATH!
THEN WEEP NO MORE. I'LL SEND TO ONE IN MANTUA SHALL GIVE HIM SUCH AN UNACCUSTOMED DRAM THAT HE SHALL SOON KEEP TYBALT COMPANY. BUT NOW I'LL TELL THEE JOYFUL TIDINGS, GIRL.
WHAT ARE THEY, I BESEECH YOUR LADYSHIP?
MARRY, MY CHILD, EARLY NEXT THURSDAY MORN, THE *GALLANT*, *YOUNG* AND *NOBLE* GENTLEMAN, THE COUNTY PARIS, AT SAINT PETER'S CHURCH, SHALL HAPPILY MAKE THEE THERE...A JOYFUL BRIDE!
HE SHALL *NOT* MAKE ME THERE A JOYFUL BRIDE! I PRAY YOU TELL MY LORD AND FATHER, MADAM, I WILL *NOT* MARRY YET.

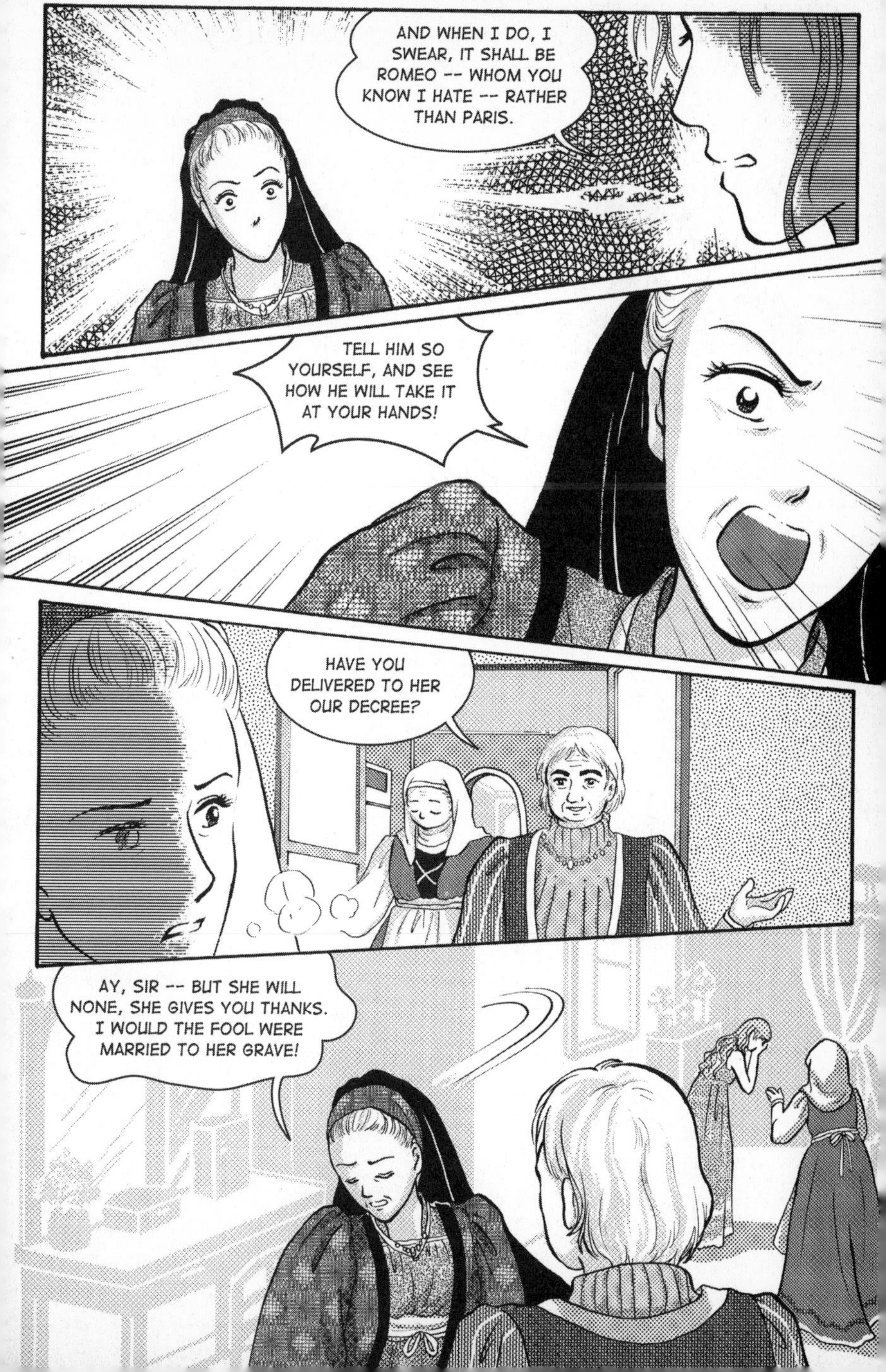
AND WHEN I DO, I SWEAR, IT SHALL BE ROMEO -- WHOM YOU KNOW I HATE -- RATHER THAN PARIS.
TELL HIM SO YOURSELF, AND SEE HOW HE WILL TAKE IT AT YOUR HANDS!
HAVE YOU DELIVERED TO HER OUR DECREE?
AY, SIR -- BUT SHE WILL NONE, SHE GIVES YOU THANKS. I WOULD THE FOOL WERE MARRIED TO HER GRAVE!

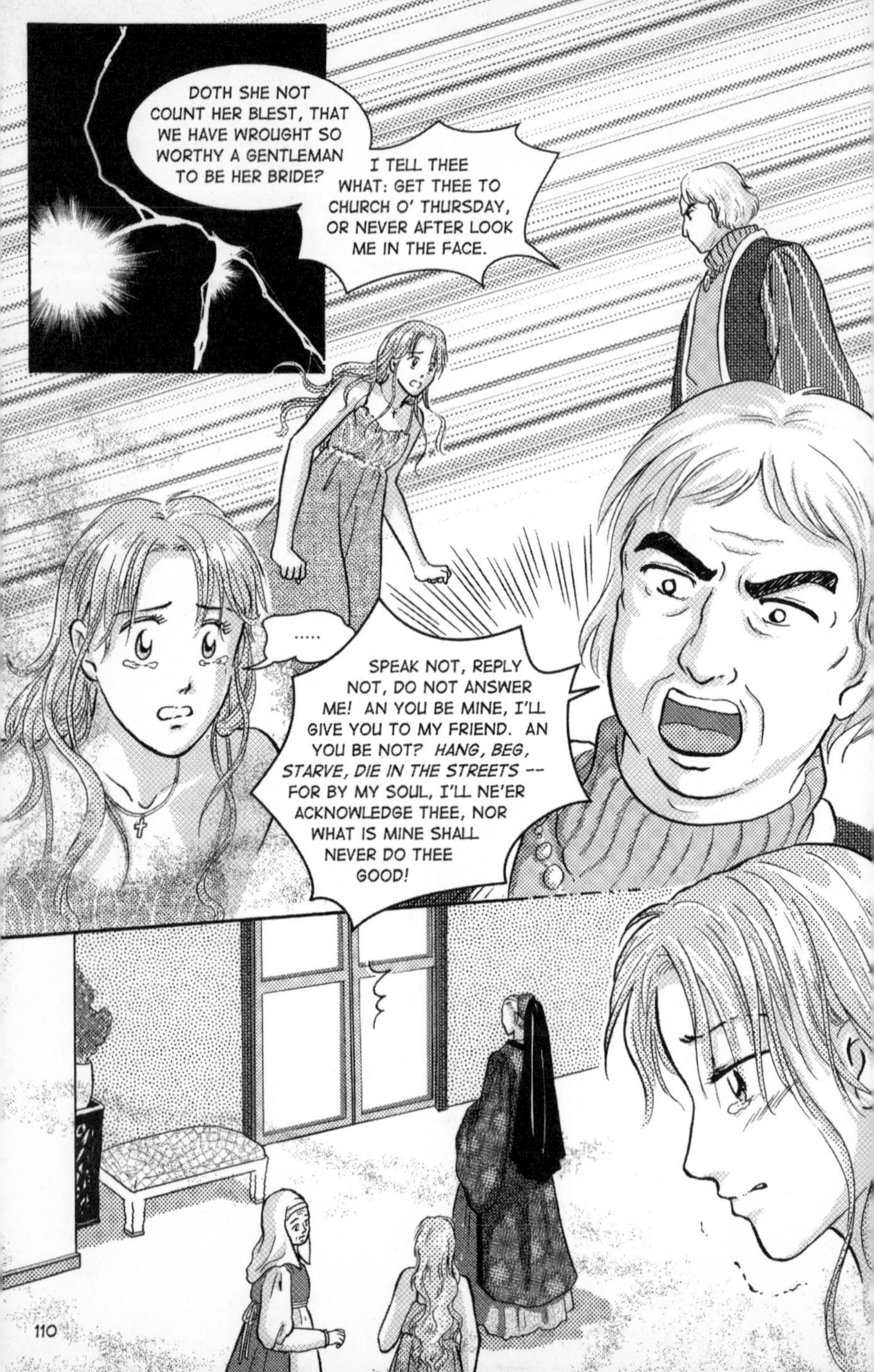
DOTH SHE NOT COUNT HER BLEST, THAT WE HAVE WROUGHT SO WORTHY A GENTLEMAN TO BE HER BRIDE?
I TELL THEE WHAT: GET THEE TO CHURCH O' THURSDAY, OR NEVER AFTER LOOK ME IN THE FACE.
.....
SPEAK NOT, REPLY NOT, DO NOT ANSWER ME! AN YOU BE MINE, I'LL GIVE YOU TO MY FRIEND. AN YOU BE NOT? *HANG, BEG, STARVE, DIE IN THE STREETS* -- FOR BY MY SOUL, I'LL NE'ER ACKNOWLEDGE THEE, NOR WHAT IS MINE SHALL NEVER DO THEE GOOD!

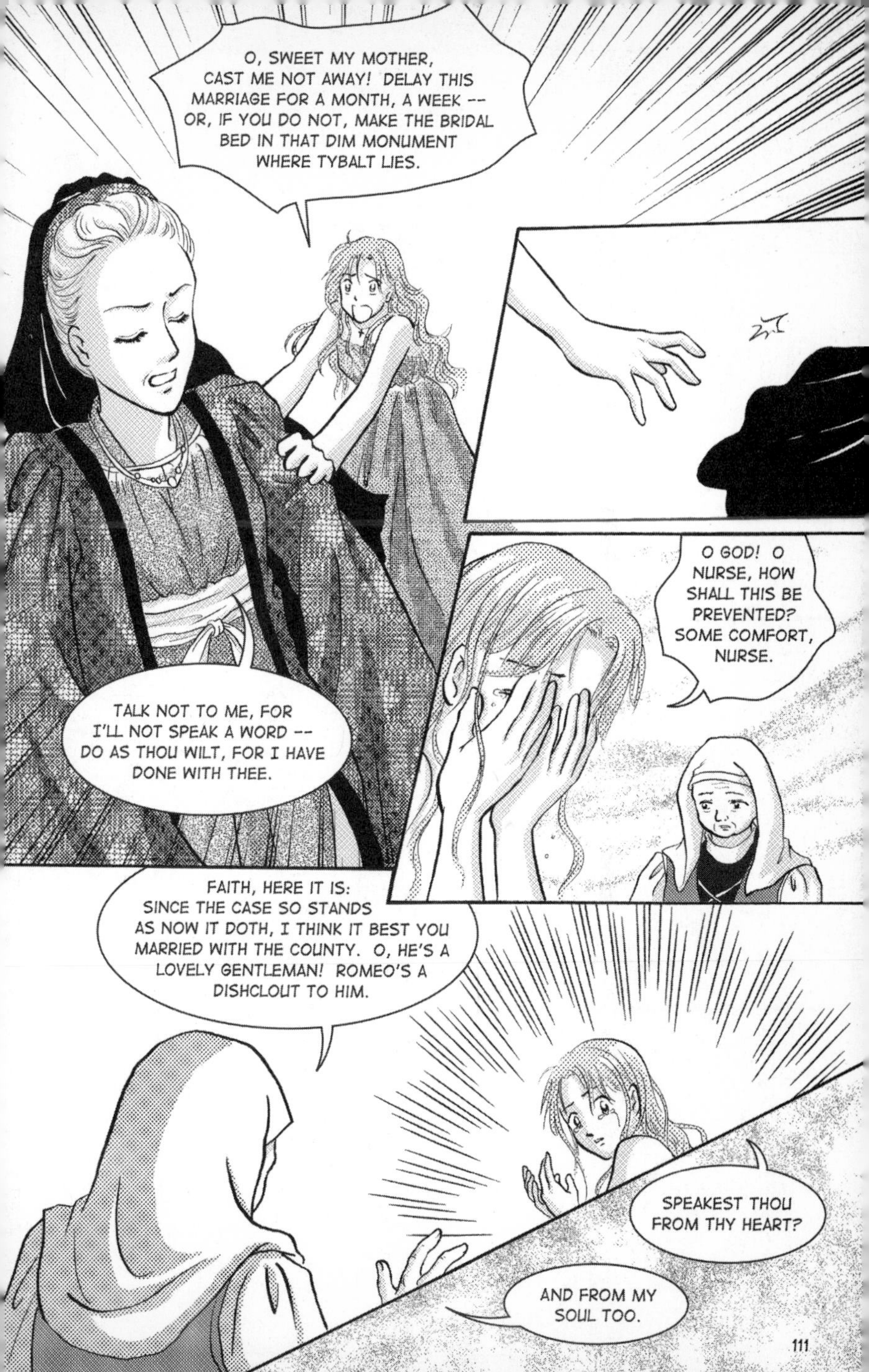
O, SWEET MY MOTHER, CAST ME NOT AWAY! DELAY THIS MARRIAGE FOR A MONTH, A WEEK -- OR, IF YOU DO NOT, MAKE THE BRIDAL BED IN THAT DIM MONUMENT WHERE TYBALT LIES.
TALK NOT TO ME, FOR I'LL NOT SPEAK A WORD -- DO AS THOU WILT, FOR I HAVE DONE WITH THEE.
O GOD! O NURSE, HOW SHALL THIS BE PREVENTED? SOME COMFORT, NURSE.
FAITH, HERE IT IS: SINCE THE CASE SO STANDS AS NOW IT DOTH, I THINK IT BEST YOU MARRIED WITH THE COUNTY. O, HE'S A LOVELY GENTLEMAN! ROMEO'S A DISHCLOUT TO HIM.
SPEAKEST THOU FROM THY HEART?
AND FROM MY SOUL TOO.

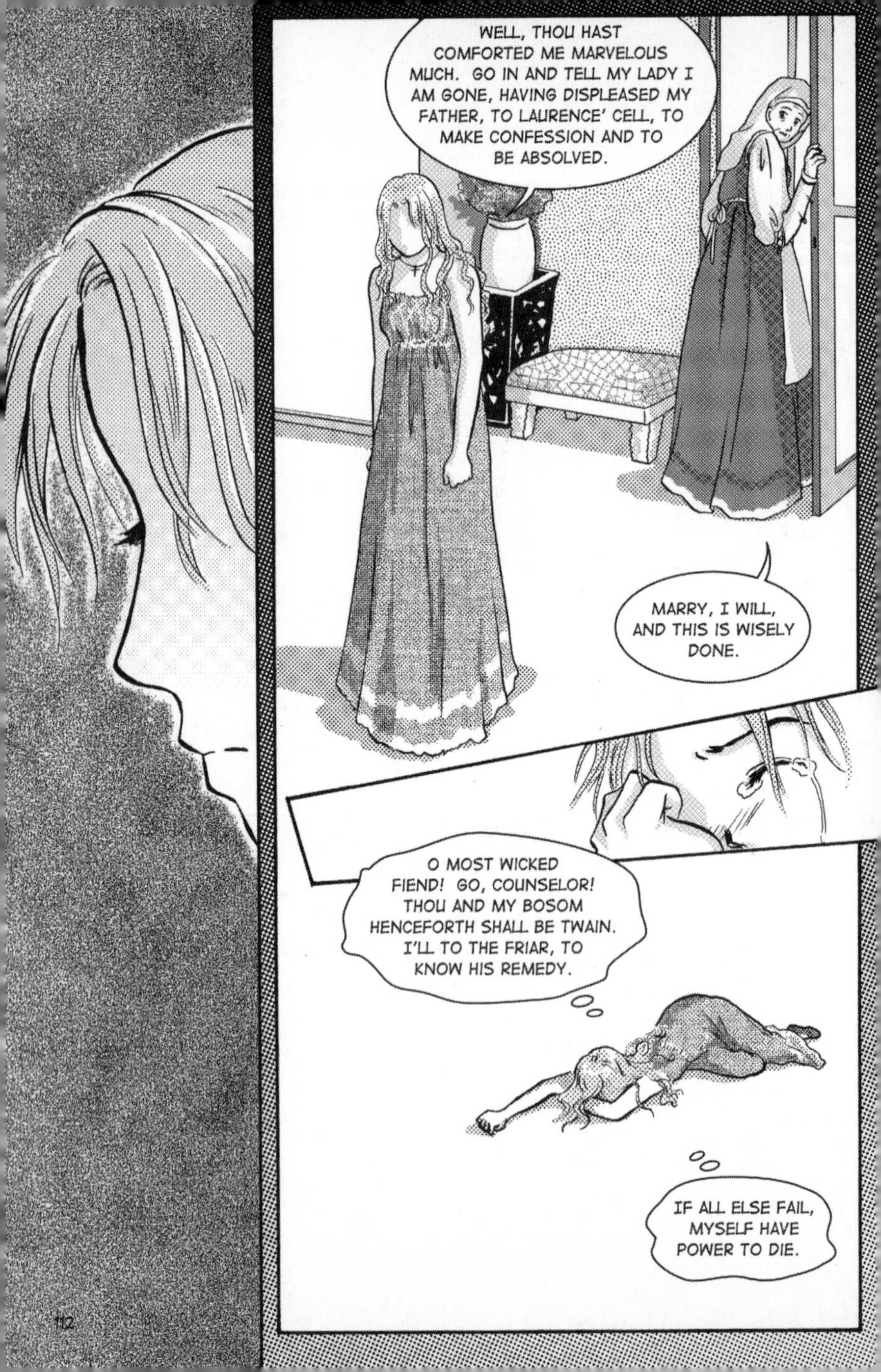
WELL, THOU HAST COMFORTED ME MARVELOUS MUCH. GO IN AND TELL MY LADY I AM GONE, HAVING DISPLEASED MY FATHER, TO LAURENCE' CELL, TO MAKE CONFESSION AND TO BE ABSOLVED.
MARRY, I WILL, AND THIS IS WISELY DONE.
O MOST WICKED FIEND! GO, COUNSELOR! THOU AND MY BOSOM HENCEFORTH SHALL BE TWAIN. I'LL TO THE FRIAR, TO KNOW HIS REMEDY.
IF ALL ELSE FAIL, MYSELF HAVE POWER TO DIE.

ACT IV

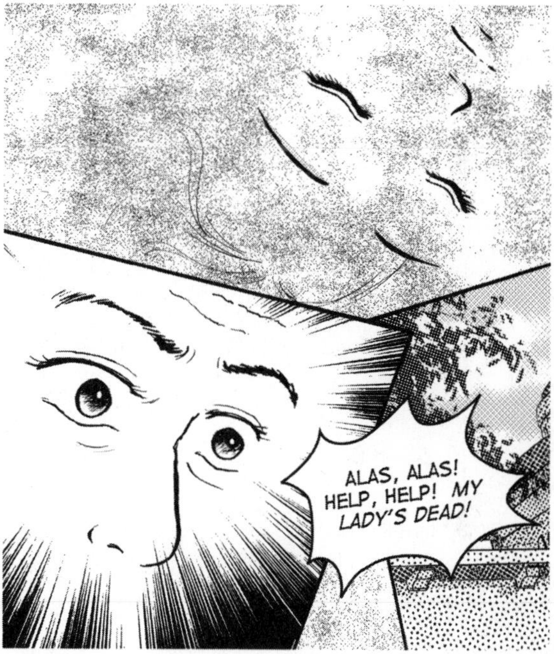
ALAS, ALAS! HELP, HELP! MY LADY'S DEAD!

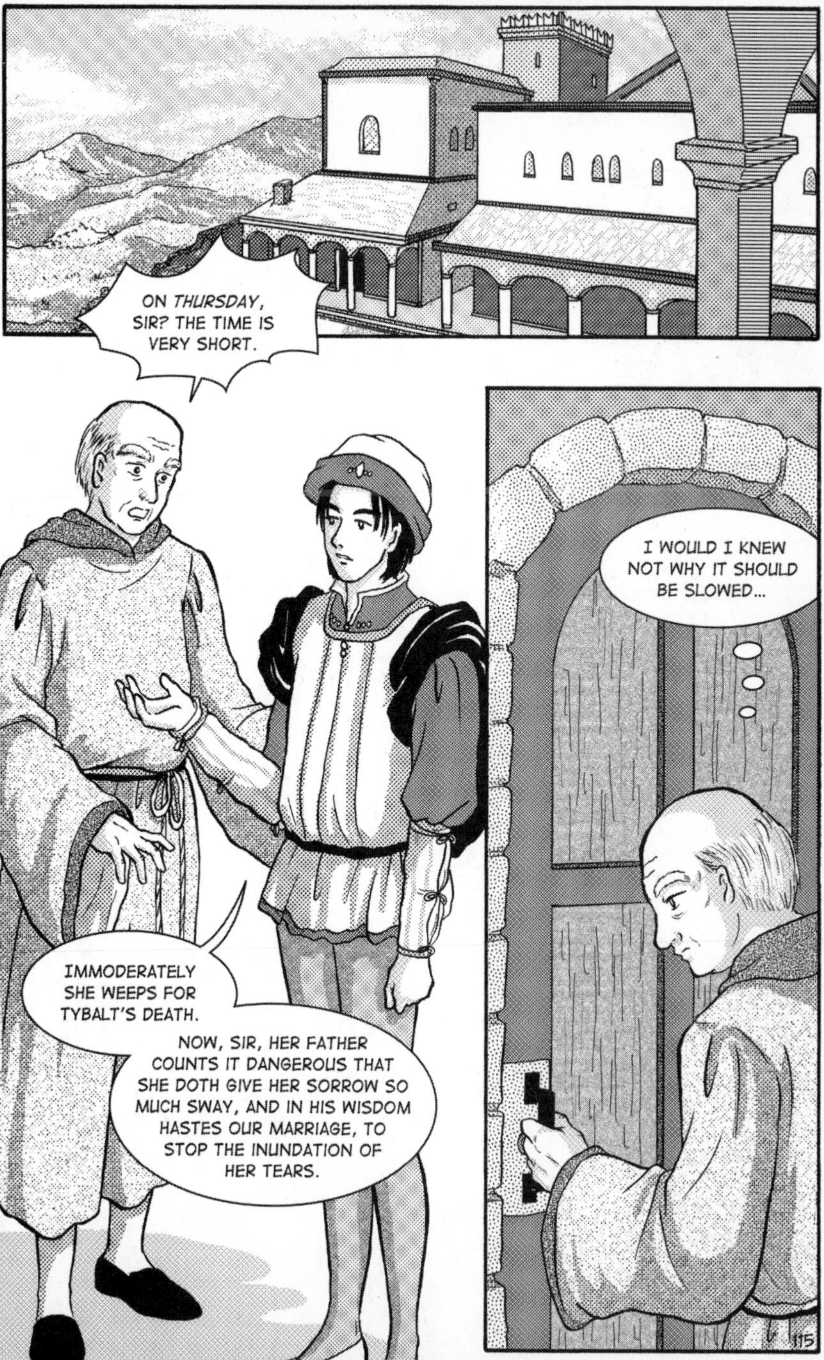
ON *THURSDAY*, SIR? THE TIME IS VERY SHORT.
IMMODERATELY SHE WEEPS FOR TYBALT'S DEATH.
NOW, SIR, HER FATHER COUNTS IT DANGEROUS THAT SHE DOTH GIVE HER SORROW SO MUCH SWAY, AND IN HIS WISDOM HASTES OUR MARRIAGE, TO STOP THE INUNDATION OF HER TEARS.
I WOULD I KNEW NOT WHY IT SHOULD BE SLOWED...

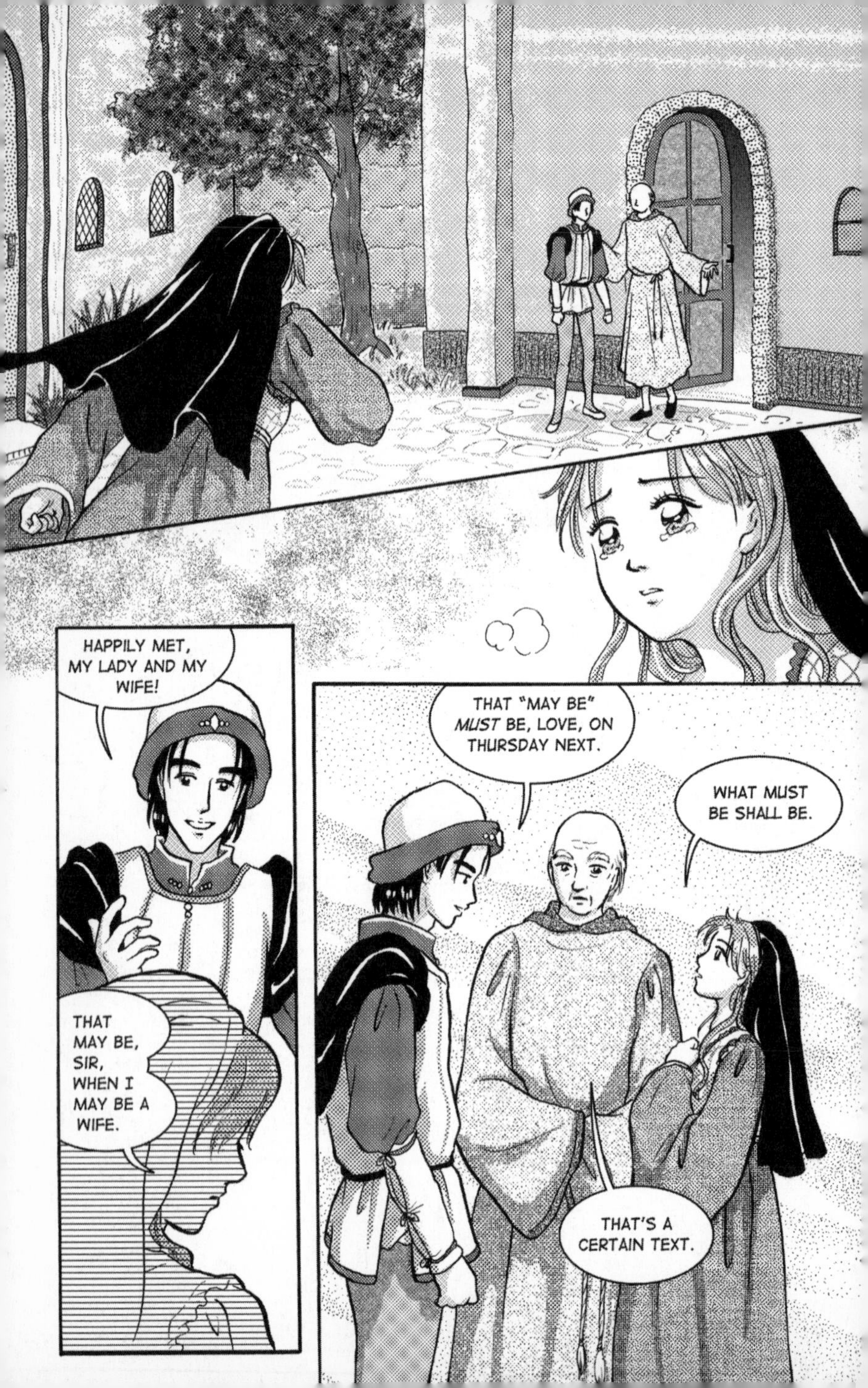
HAPPILY MET, MY LADY AND MY WIFE!
THAT MAY BE, SIR, WHEN I MAY BE A WIFE.
THAT "MAY BE" *MUST* BE, LOVE, ON THURSDAY NEXT.
WHAT MUST BE SHALL BE.
THAT'S A CERTAIN TEXT.

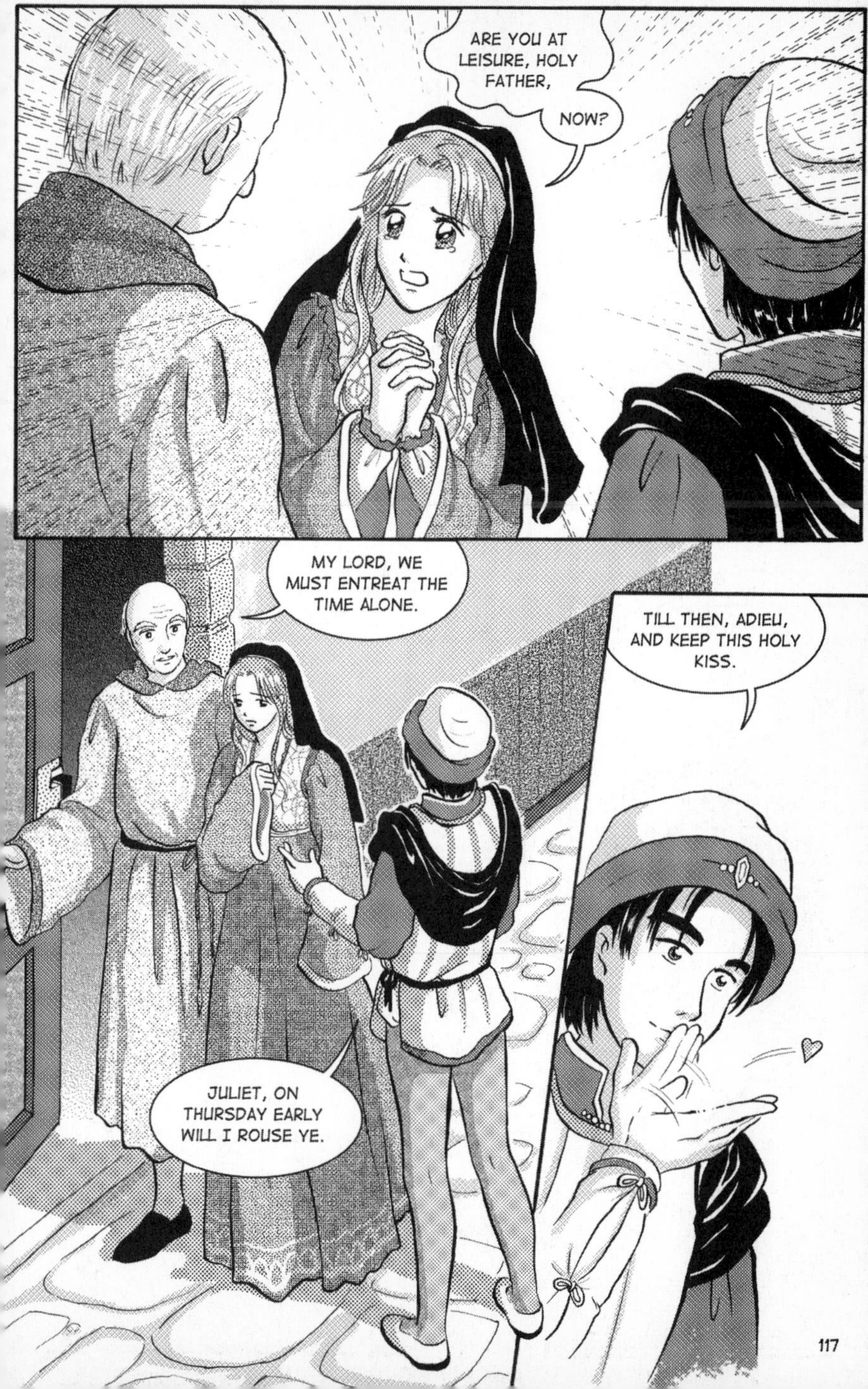
ARE YOU AT LEISURE, HOLY FATHER,
NOW?
MY LORD, WE MUST ENTREAT THE TIME ALONE.
JULIET, ON THURSDAY EARLY WILL I ROUSE YE.
TILL THEN, ADIEU, AND KEEP THIS HOLY KISS.

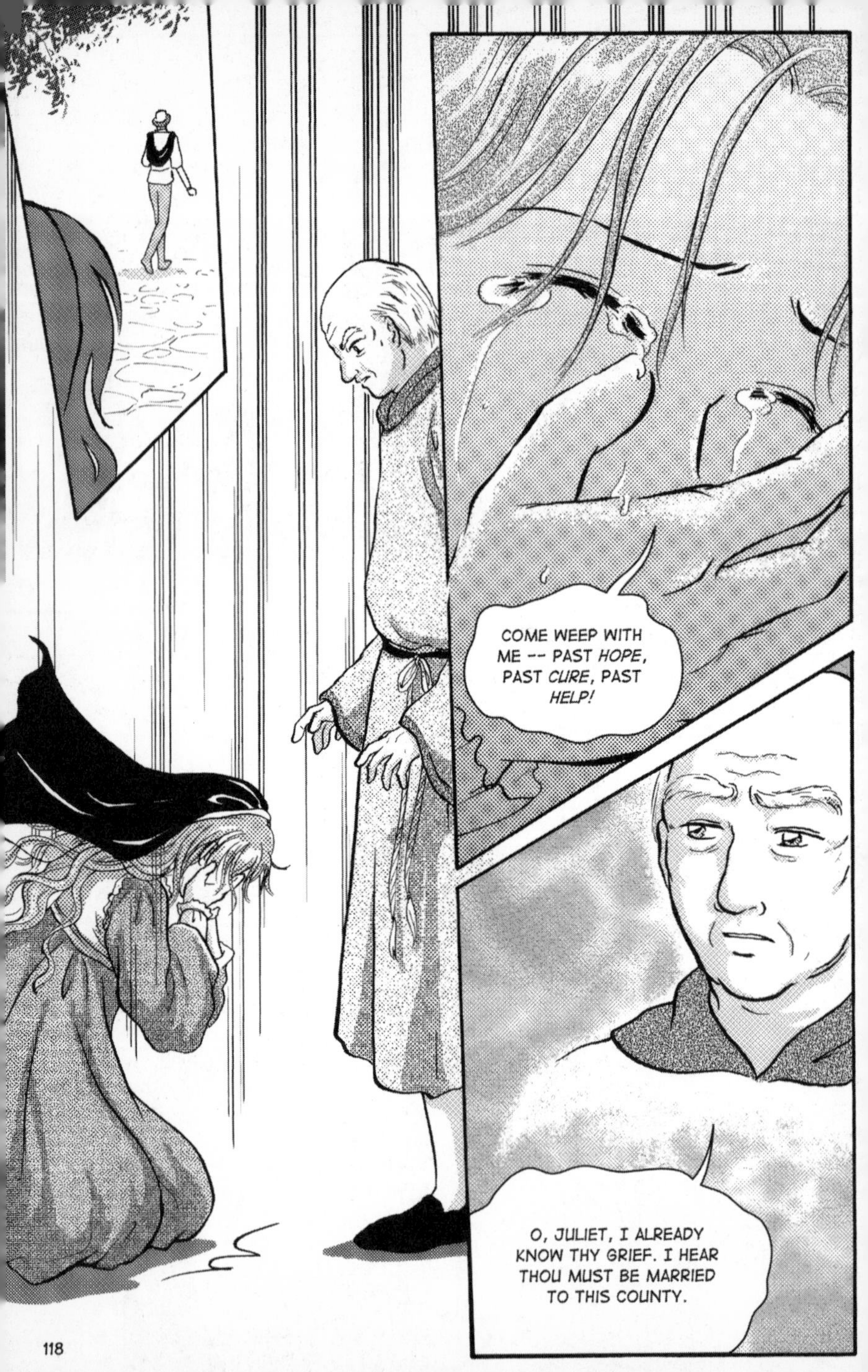
COME WEEP WITH ME -- PAST *HOPE*, PAST *CURE*, PAST *HELP!*
O, JULIET, I ALREADY KNOW THY GRIEF. I HEAR THOU MUST BE MARRIED TO THIS COUNTY.

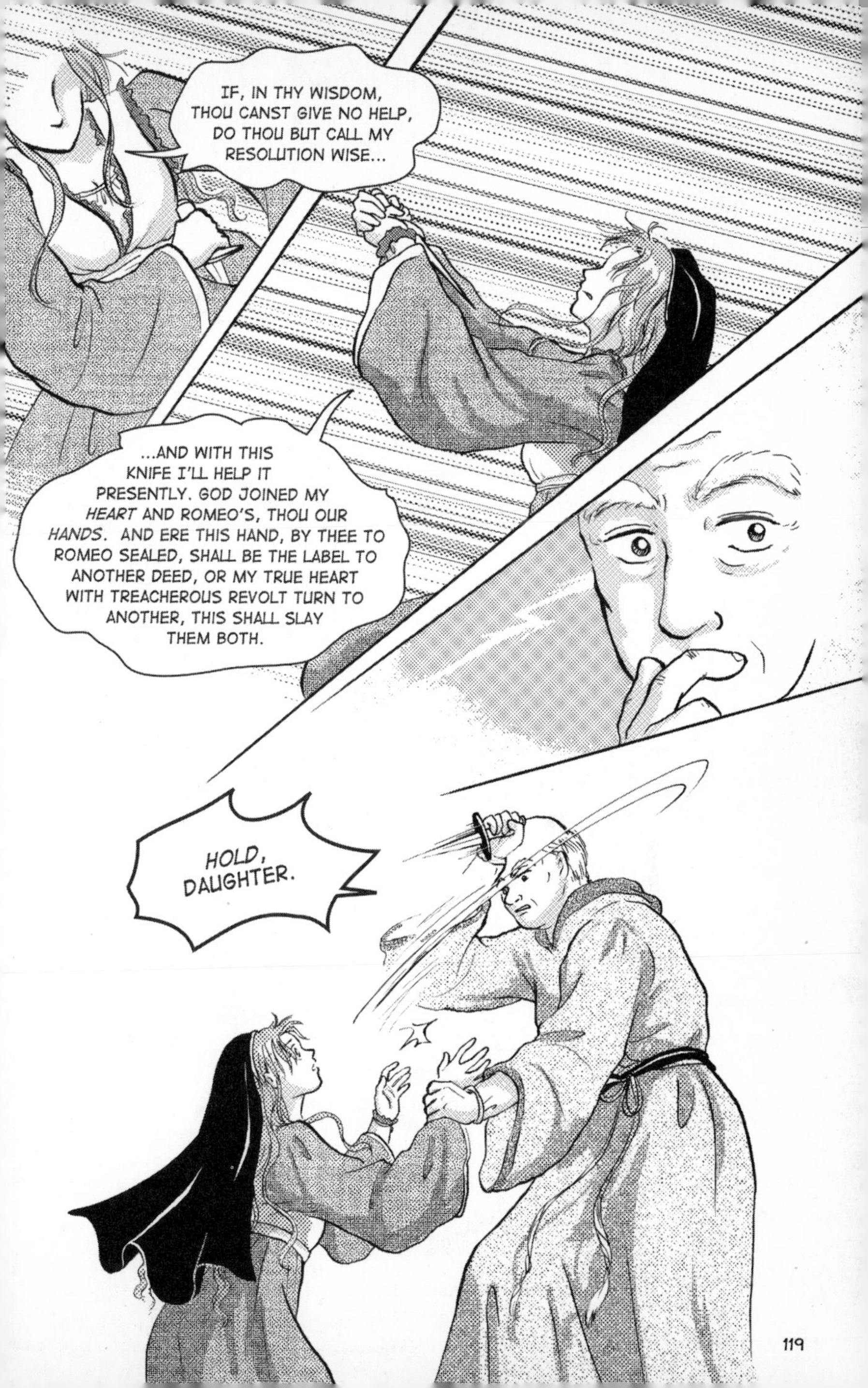
IF, IN THY WISDOM, THOU CANST GIVE NO HELP, DO THOU BUT CALL MY RESOLUTION WISE...
...AND WITH THIS KNIFE I'LL HELP IT PRESENTLY. GOD JOINED MY *HEART* AND ROMEO'S, THOU OUR *HANDS*. AND ERE THIS HAND, BY THEE TO ROMEO SEALED, SHALL BE THE LABEL TO ANOTHER DEED, OR MY TRUE HEART WITH TREACHEROUS REVOLT TURN TO ANOTHER, THIS SHALL SLAY THEM BOTH.
HOLD, DAUGHTER.

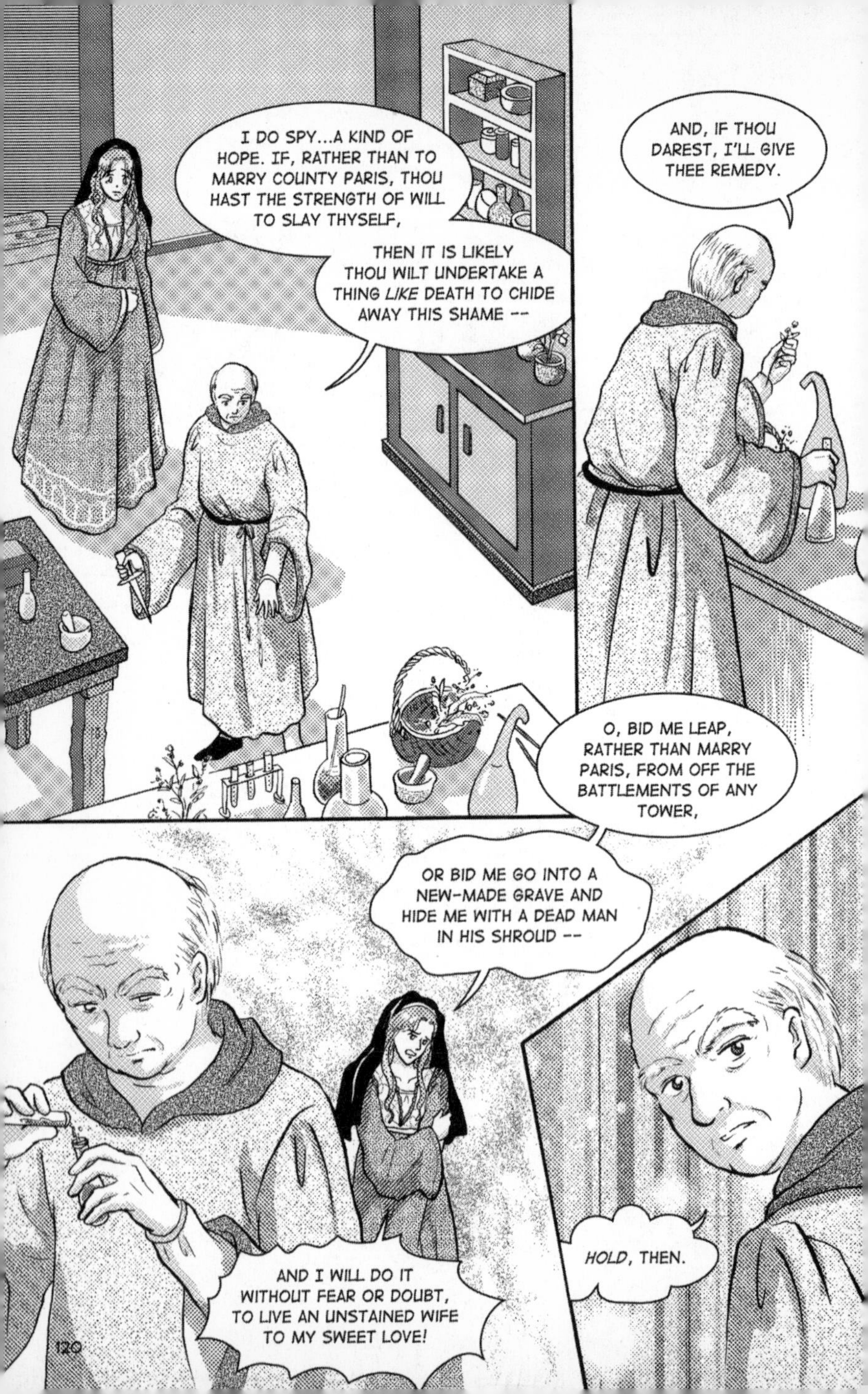
I DO SPY...A KIND OF HOPE. IF, RATHER THAN TO MARRY COUNTY PARIS, THOU HAST THE STRENGTH OF WILL TO SLAY THYSELF,
THEN IT IS LIKELY THOU WILT UNDERTAKE A THING *LIKE* DEATH TO CHIDE AWAY THIS SHAME --
AND, IF THOU DAREST, I'LL GIVE THEE REMEDY.
O, BID ME LEAP, RATHER THAN MARRY PARIS, FROM OFF THE BATTLEMENTS OF ANY TOWER,
OR BID ME GO INTO A NEW-MADE GRAVE AND HIDE ME WITH A DEAD MAN IN HIS SHROUD --
AND I WILL DO IT WITHOUT FEAR OR DOUBT, TO LIVE AN UNSTAINED WIFE TO MY SWEET LOVE!
HOLD, THEN.

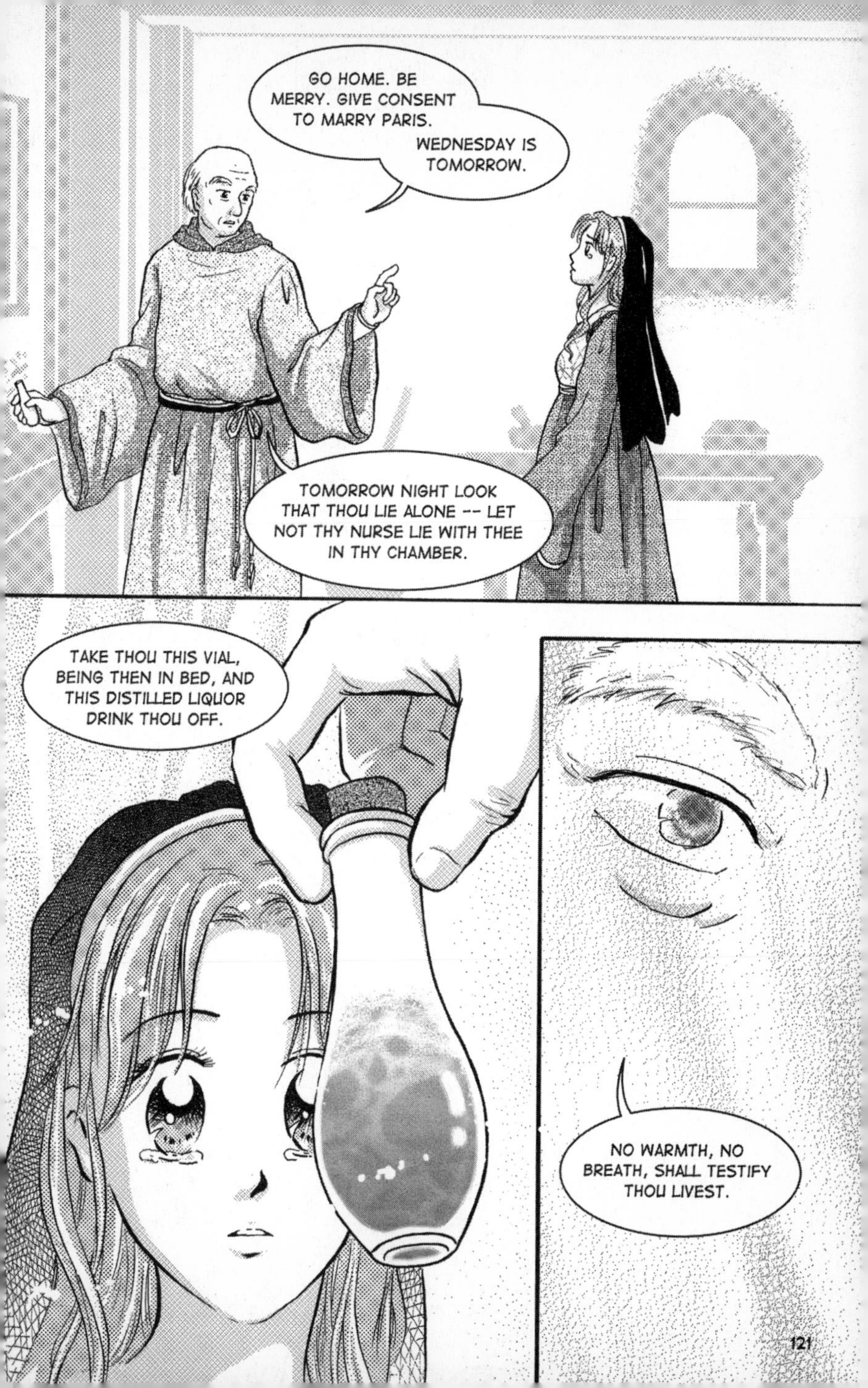
GO HOME. BE MERRY. GIVE CONSENT TO MARRY PARIS.
WEDNESDAY IS TOMORROW.
TOMORROW NIGHT LOOK THAT THOU LIE ALONE -- LET NOT THY NURSE LIE WITH THEE IN THY CHAMBER.
TAKE THOU THIS VIAL, BEING THEN IN BED, AND THIS DISTILLED LIQUOR DRINK THOU OFF.
NO WARMTH, NO BREATH, SHALL TESTIFY THOU LIVEST.

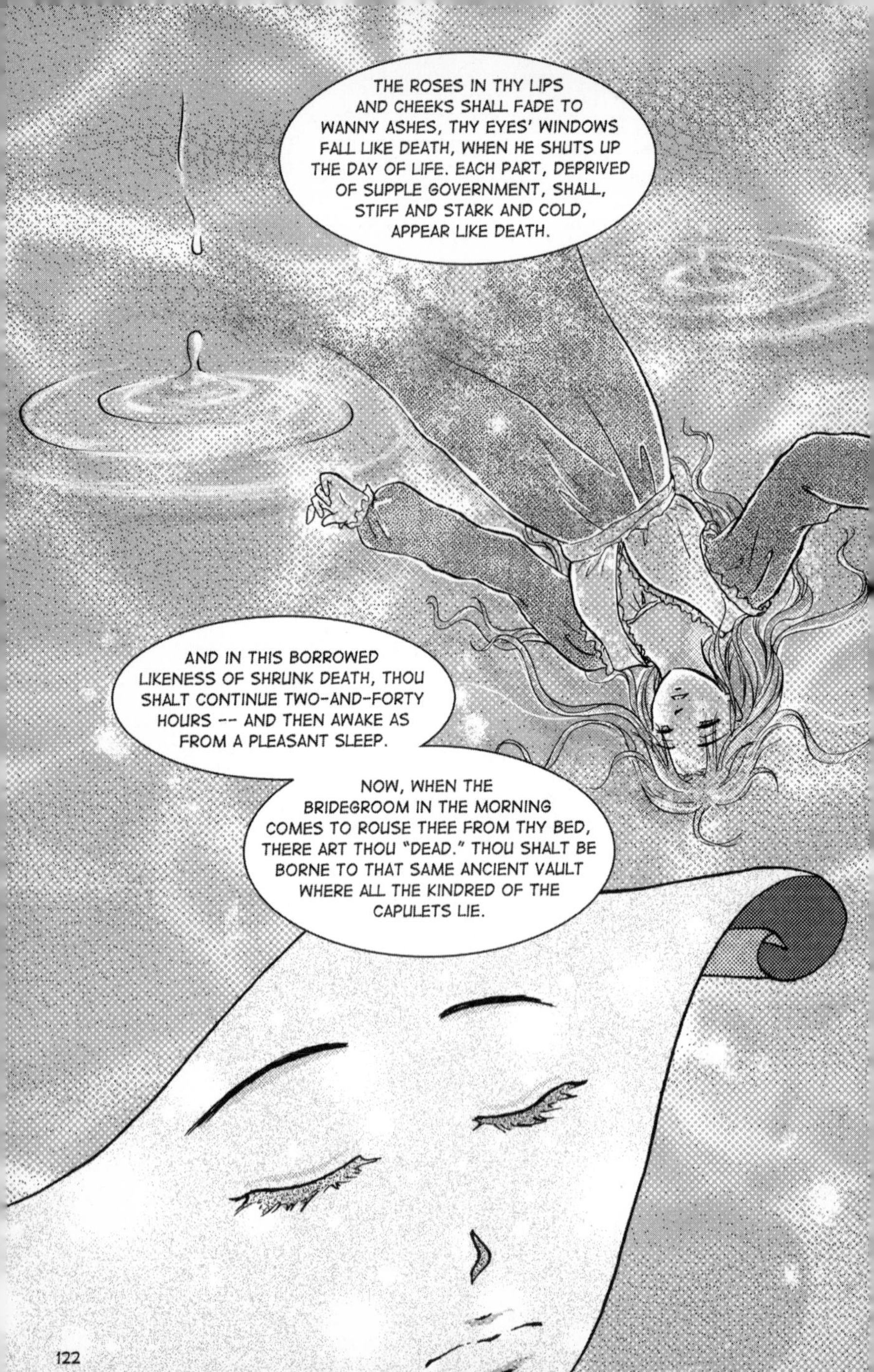
THE ROSES IN THY LIPS AND CHEEKS SHALL FADE TO WANNY ASHES, THY EYES' WINDOWS FALL LIKE DEATH, WHEN HE SHUTS UP THE DAY OF LIFE. EACH PART, DEPRIVED OF SUPPLE GOVERNMENT, SHALL, STIFF AND STARK AND COLD, APPEAR LIKE DEATH.
AND IN THIS BORROWED LIKENESS OF SHRUNK DEATH, THOU SHALT CONTINUE TWO-AND-FORTY HOURS -- AND THEN AWAKE AS FROM A PLEASANT SLEEP.
NOW, WHEN THE BRIDEGROOM IN THE MORNING COMES TO ROUSE THEE FROM THY BED, THERE ART THOU "DEAD." THOU SHALT BE BORNE TO THAT SAME ANCIENT VAULT WHERE ALL THE KINDRED OF THE CAPULETS LIE.

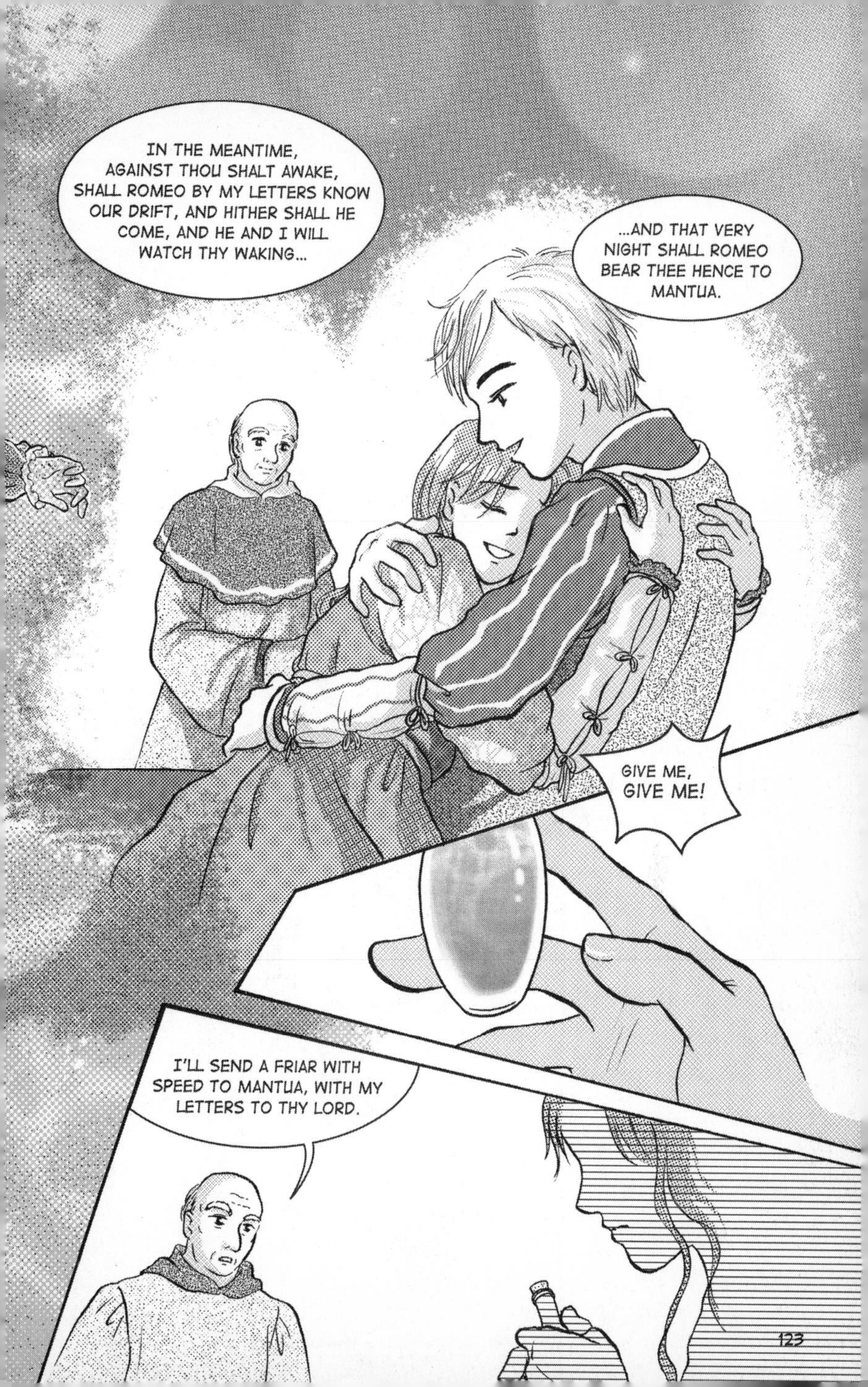
IN THE MEANTIME, AGAINST THOU SHALT AWAKE, SHALL ROMEO BY MY LETTERS KNOW OUR DRIFT, AND HITHER SHALL HE COME, AND HE AND I WILL WATCH THY WAKING...
...AND THAT VERY NIGHT SHALL ROMEO BEAR THEE HENCE TO MANTUA.
GIVE ME, GIVE ME!
I'LL SEND A FRIAR WITH SPEED TO MANTUA, WITH MY LETTERS TO THY LORD.

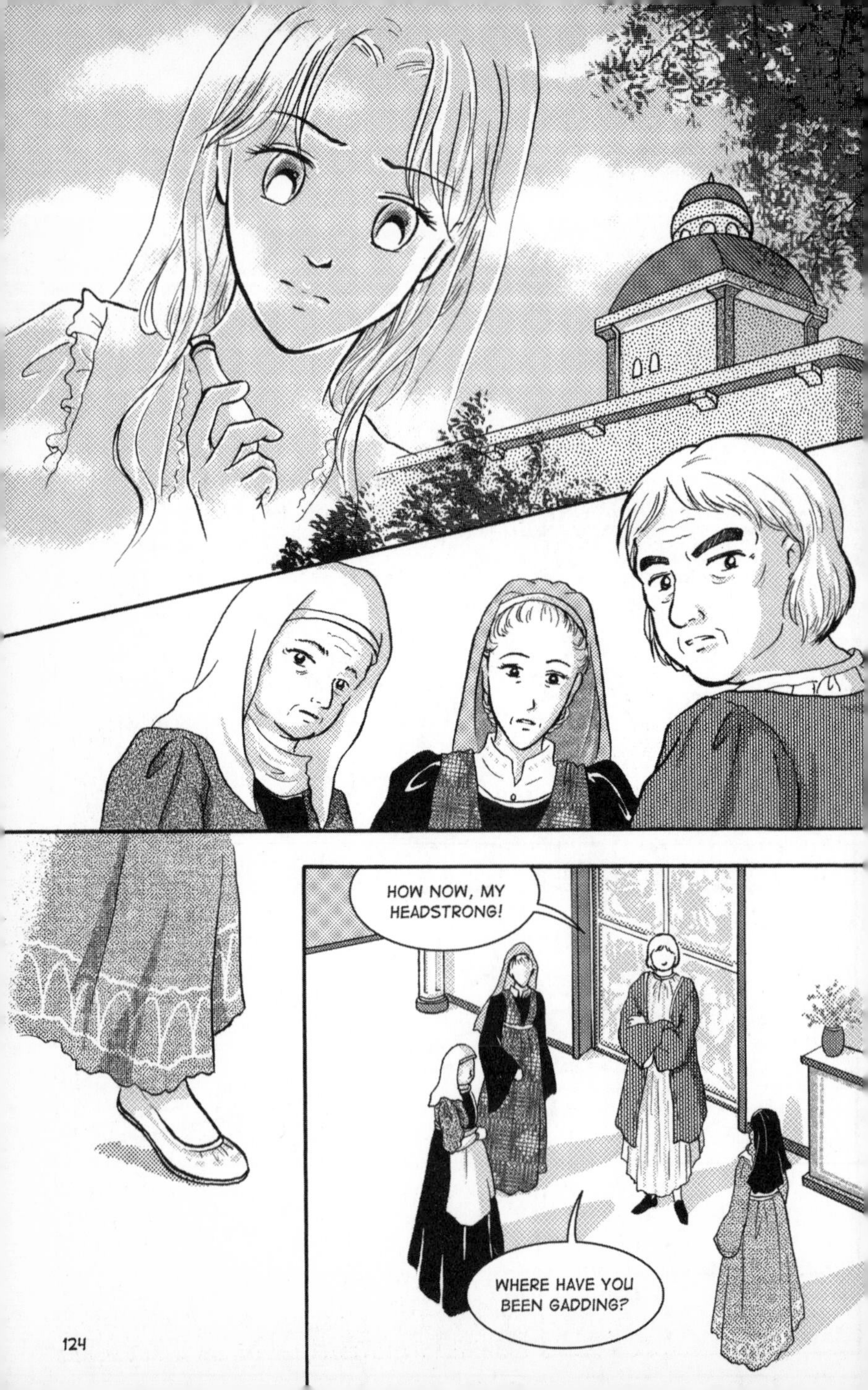
HOW NOW, MY HEADSTRONG!
WHERE HAVE YOU BEEN GADDING?

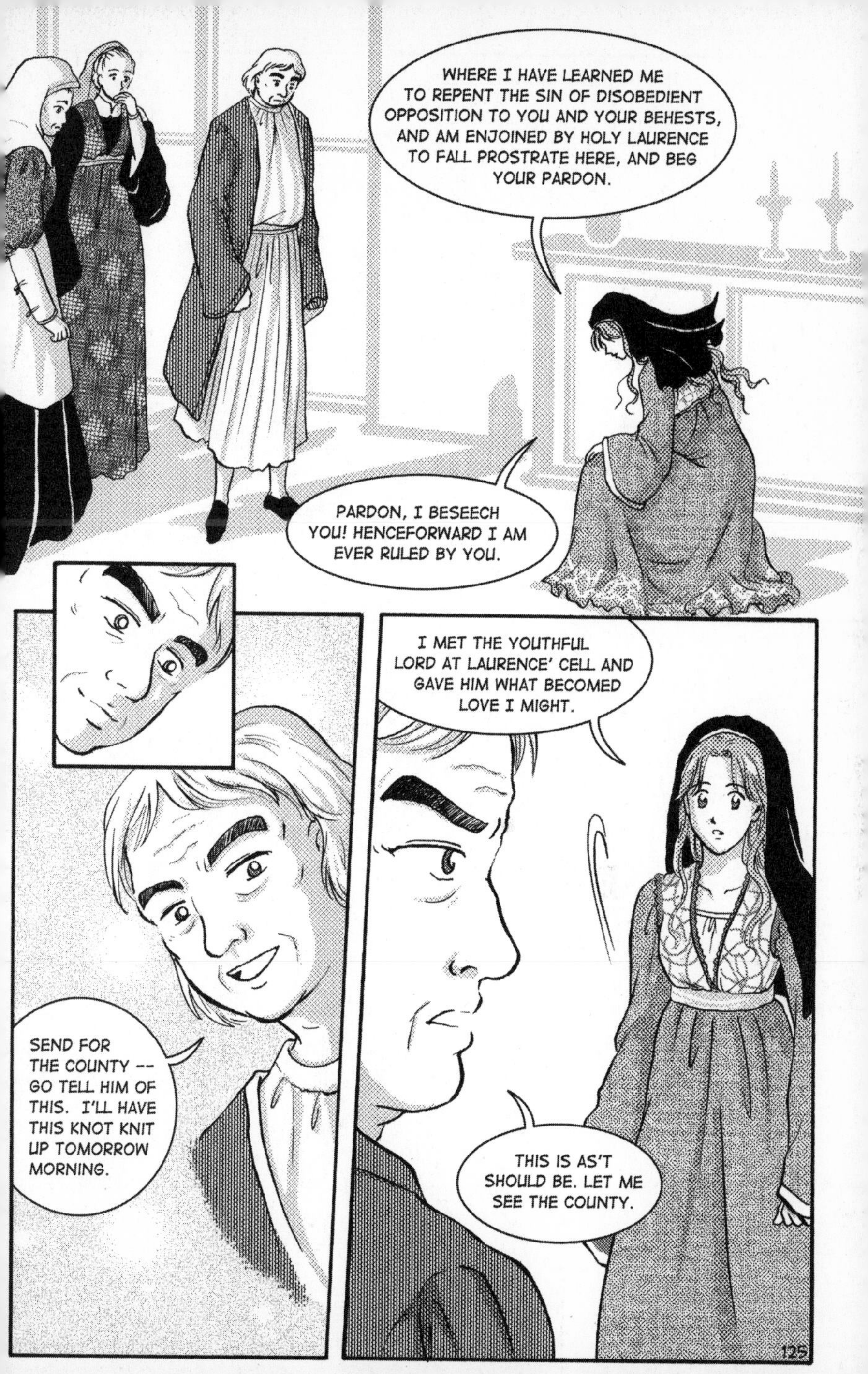
WHERE I HAVE LEARNED ME TO REPENT THE SIN OF DISOBEDIENT OPPOSITION TO YOU AND YOUR BEHESTS, AND AM ENJOINED BY HOLY LAURENCE TO FALL PROSTRATE HERE, AND BEG YOUR PARDON.
PARDON, I BESEECH YOU! HENCEFORWARD I AM EVER RULED BY YOU.
SEND FOR THE COUNTY -- GO TELL HIM OF THIS. I'LL HAVE THIS KNOT KNIT UP TOMORROW MORNING.
I MET THE YOUTHFUL LORD AT LAURENCE' CELL AND GAVE HIM WHAT BECOMED LOVE I MIGHT.
THIS IS AS'T SHOULD BE. LET ME SEE THE COUNTY.

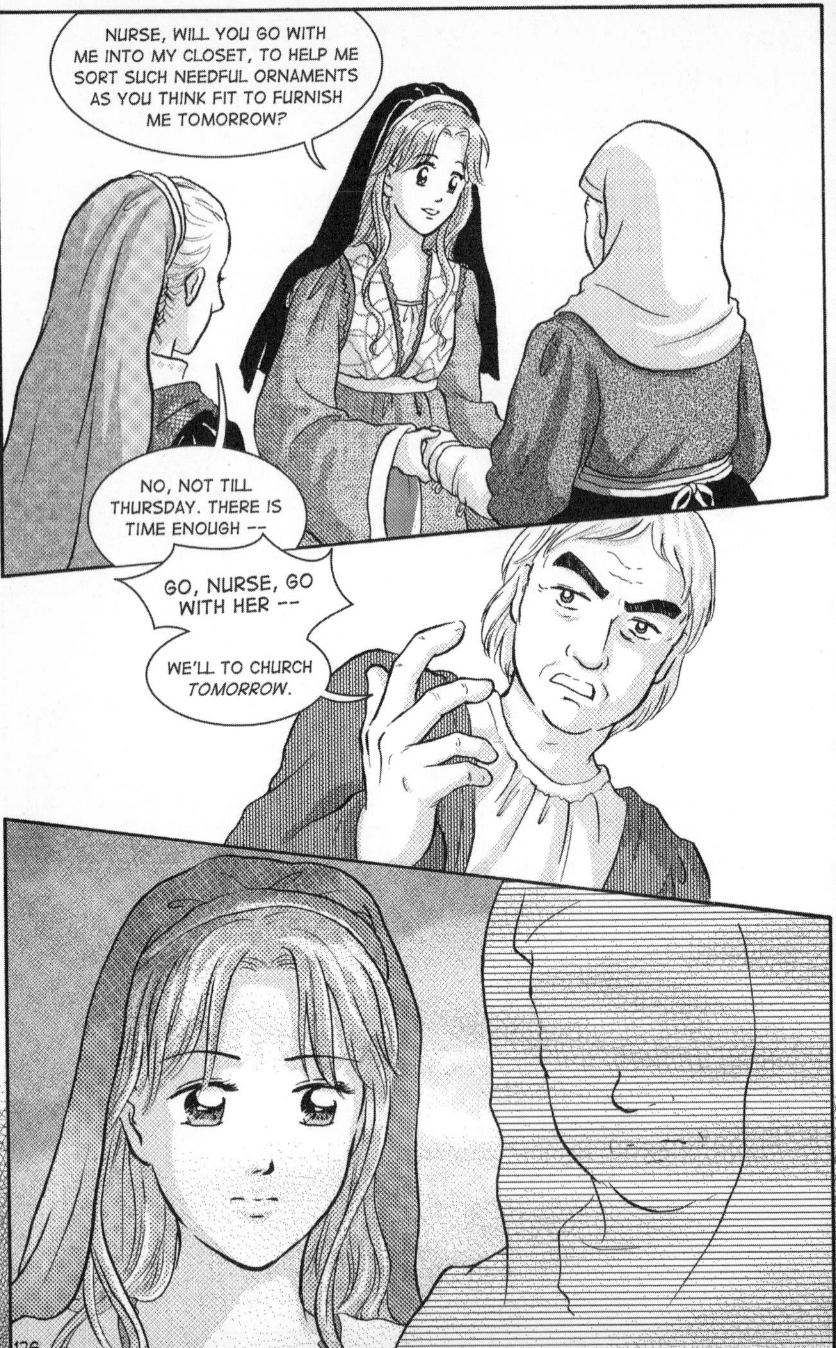
NURSE, WILL YOU GO WITH ME INTO MY CLOSET, TO HELP ME SORT SUCH NEEDFUL ORNAMENTS AS YOU THINK FIT TO FURNISH ME TOMORROW?
NO, NOT TILL THURSDAY. THERE IS TIME ENOUGH --
GO, NURSE, GO WITH HER --
WE'LL TO CHURCH *TOMORROW*.

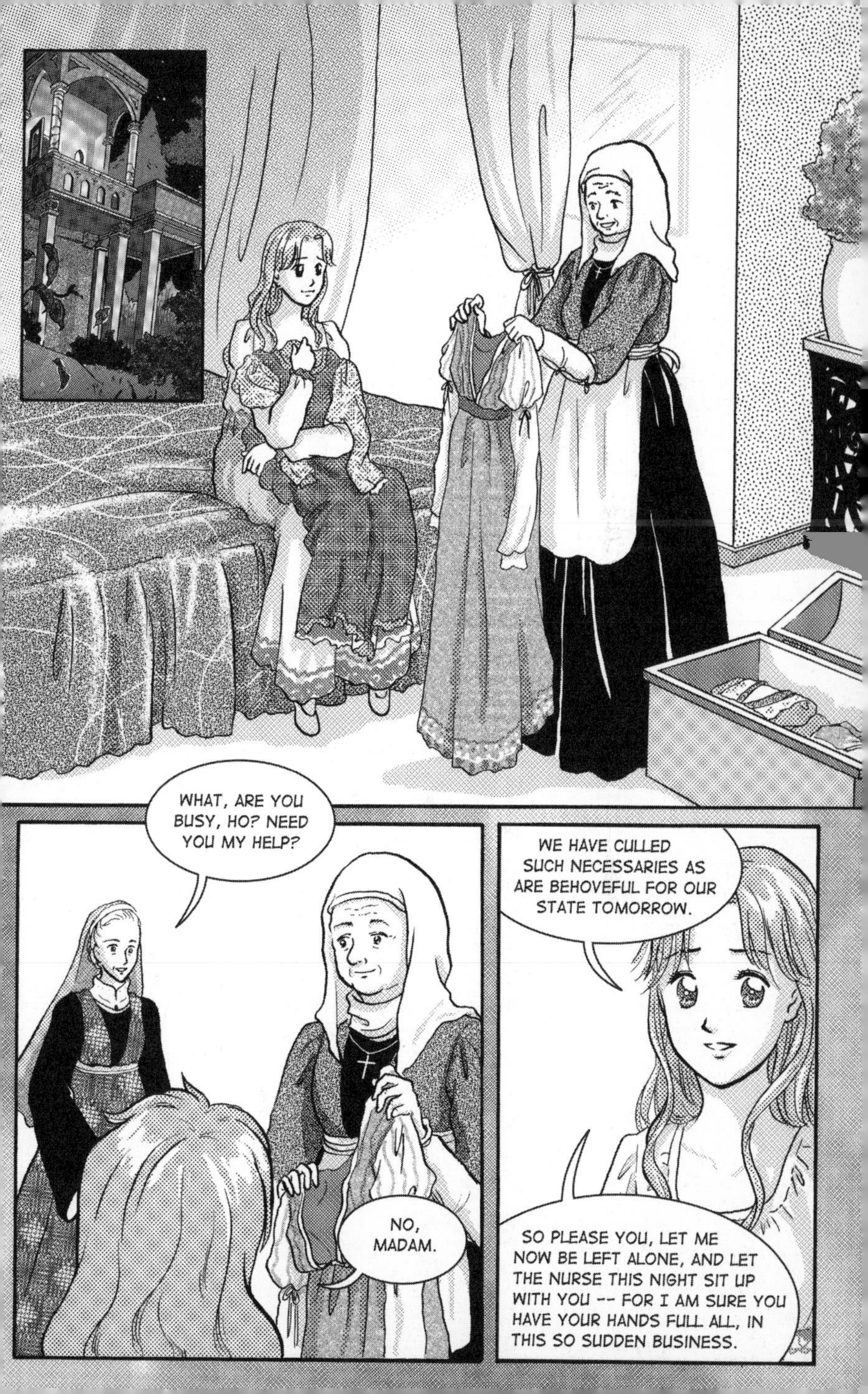
WHAT, ARE YOU BUSY, HO? NEED YOU MY HELP?
NO, MADAM.
WE HAVE CULLED SUCH NECESSARIES AS ARE BEHOVEFUL FOR OUR STATE TOMORROW.
SO PLEASE YOU, LET ME NOW BE LEFT ALONE, AND LET THE NURSE THIS NIGHT SIT UP WITH YOU -- FOR I AM SURE YOU HAVE YOUR HANDS FULL ALL, IN THIS SO SUDDEN BUSINESS.

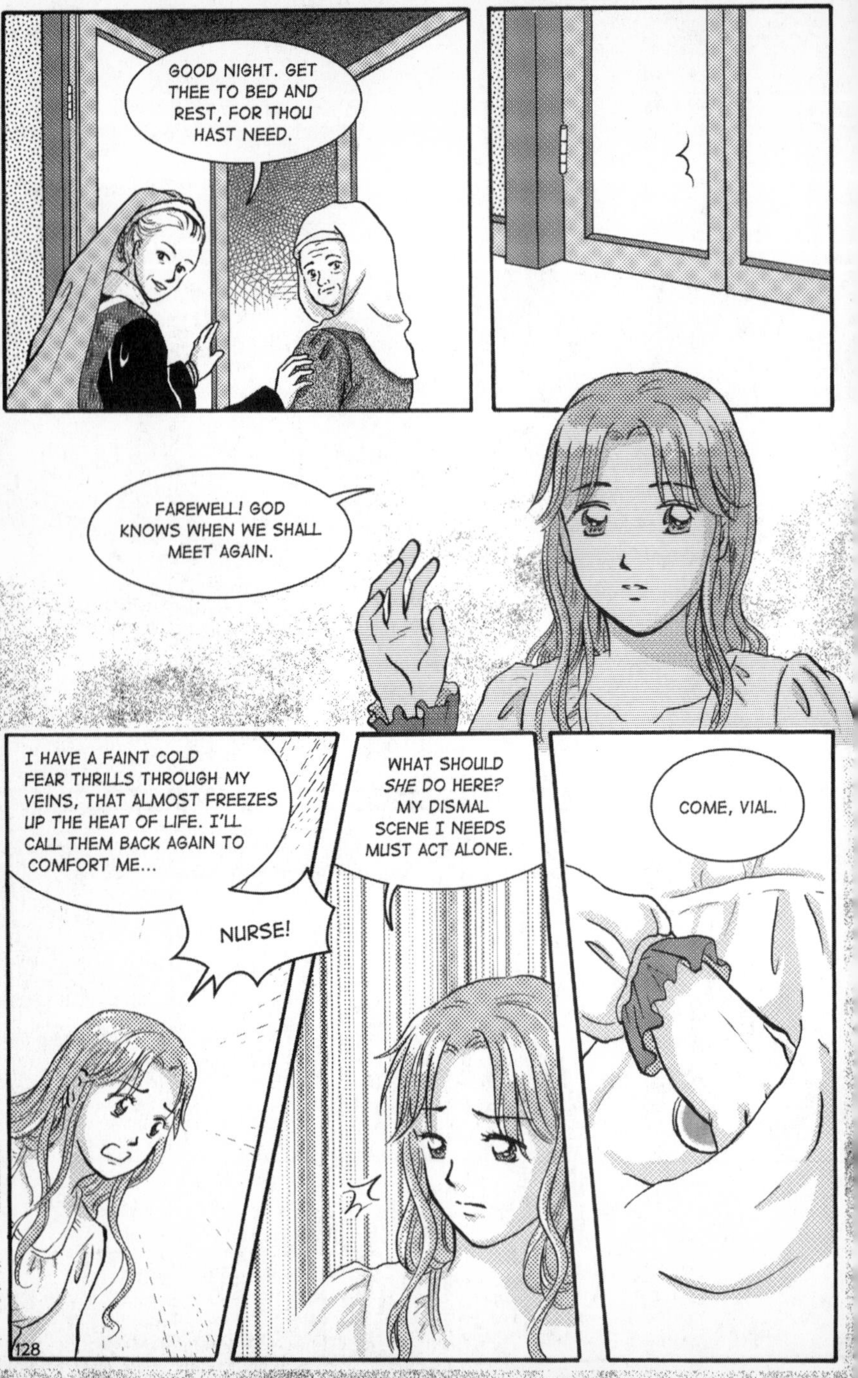
GOOD NIGHT. GET THEE TO BED AND REST, FOR THOU HAST NEED.
FAREWELL! GOD KNOWS WHEN WE SHALL MEET AGAIN.
I HAVE A FAINT COLD FEAR THRILLS THROUGH MY VEINS, THAT ALMOST FREEZES UP THE HEAT OF LIFE. I'LL CALL THEM BACK AGAIN TO COMFORT ME...
NURSE!
WHAT SHOULD *SHE* DO HERE? MY DISMAL SCENE I NEEDS MUST ACT ALONE.
COME, VIAL.

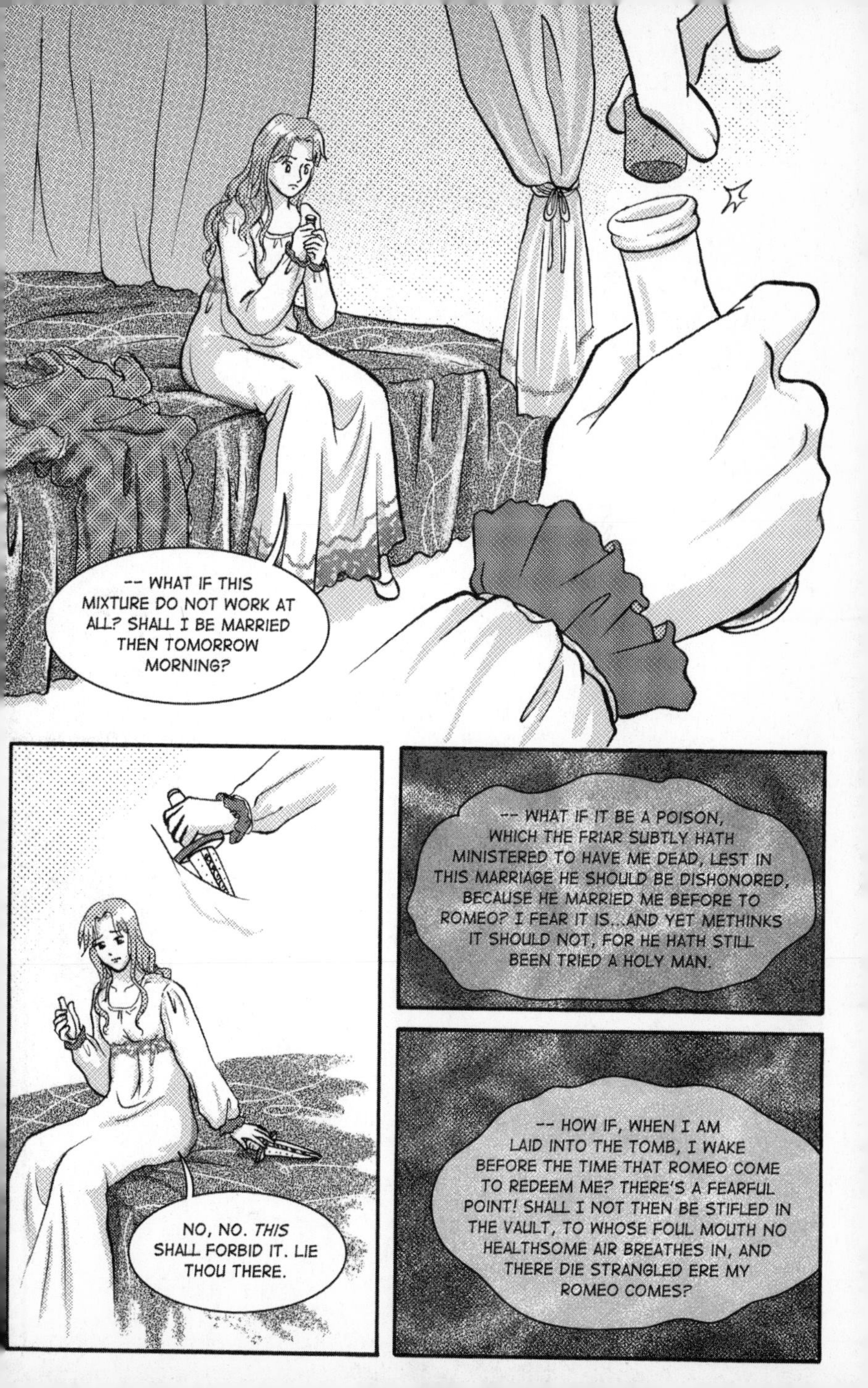
-- WHAT IF THIS MIXTURE DO NOT WORK AT ALL? SHALL I BE MARRIED THEN TOMORROW MORNING?
NO, NO. *THIS* SHALL FORBID IT. LIE THOU THERE.
-- WHAT IF IT BE A POISON, WHICH THE FRIAR SUBTLY HATH MINISTERED TO HAVE ME DEAD, LEST IN THIS MARRIAGE HE SHOULD BE DISHONORED, BECAUSE HE MARRIED ME BEFORE TO ROMEO? I FEAR IT IS...AND YET METHINKS IT SHOULD NOT, FOR HE HATH STILL BEEN TRIED A HOLY MAN.
-- HOW IF, WHEN I AM LAID INTO THE TOMB, I WAKE BEFORE THE TIME THAT ROMEO COME TO REDEEM ME? THERE'S A FEARFUL POINT! SHALL I NOT THEN BE STIFLED IN THE VAULT, TO WHOSE FOUL MOUTH NO HEALTHSOME AIR BREATHES IN, AND THERE DIE STRANGLED ERE MY ROMEO COMES?

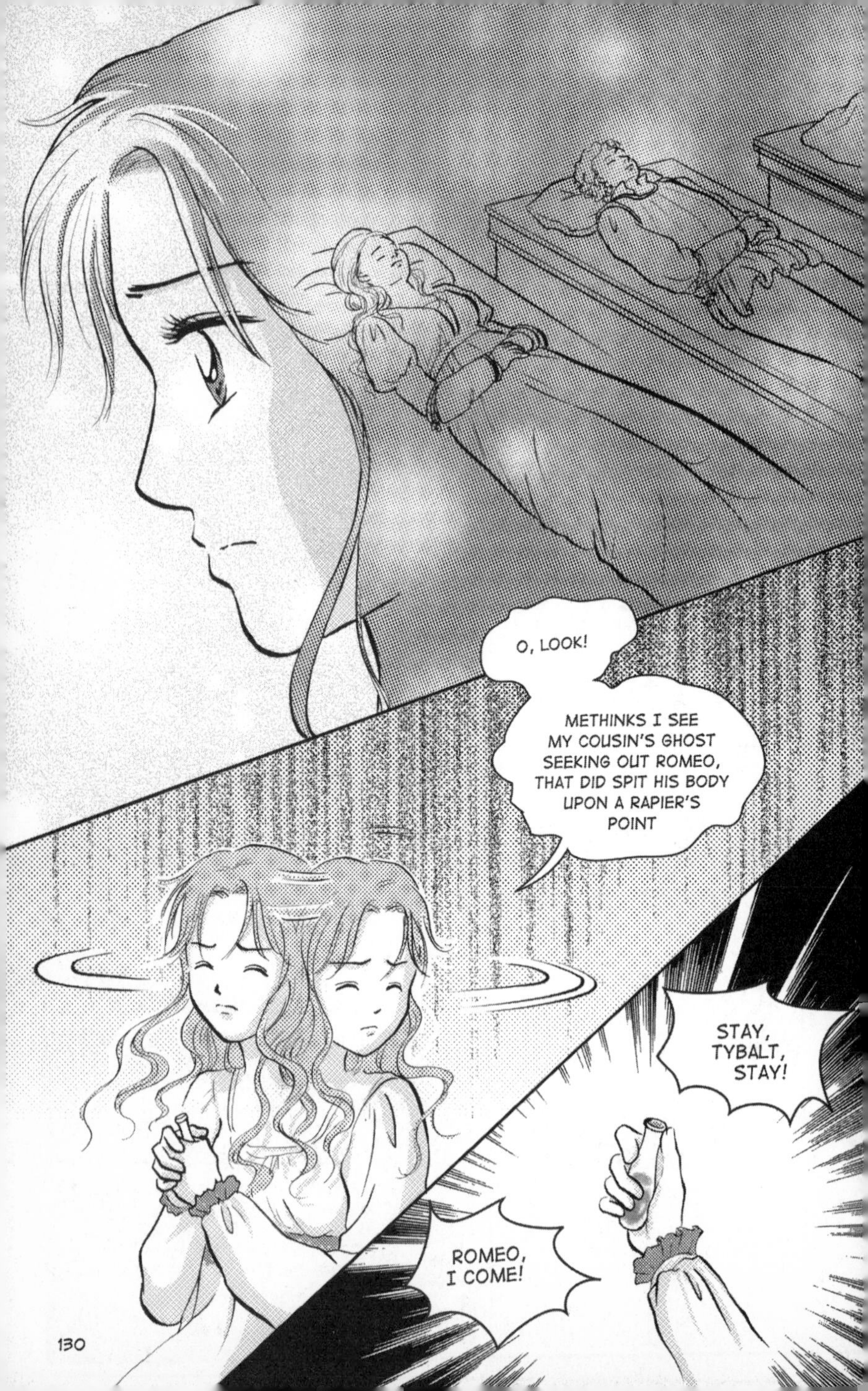
O, LOOK!
METHINKS I SEE MY COUSIN'S GHOST SEEKING OUT ROMEO, THAT DID SPIT HIS BODY UPON A RAPIER'S POINT
STAY, TYBALT, STAY!
ROMEO, I COME!

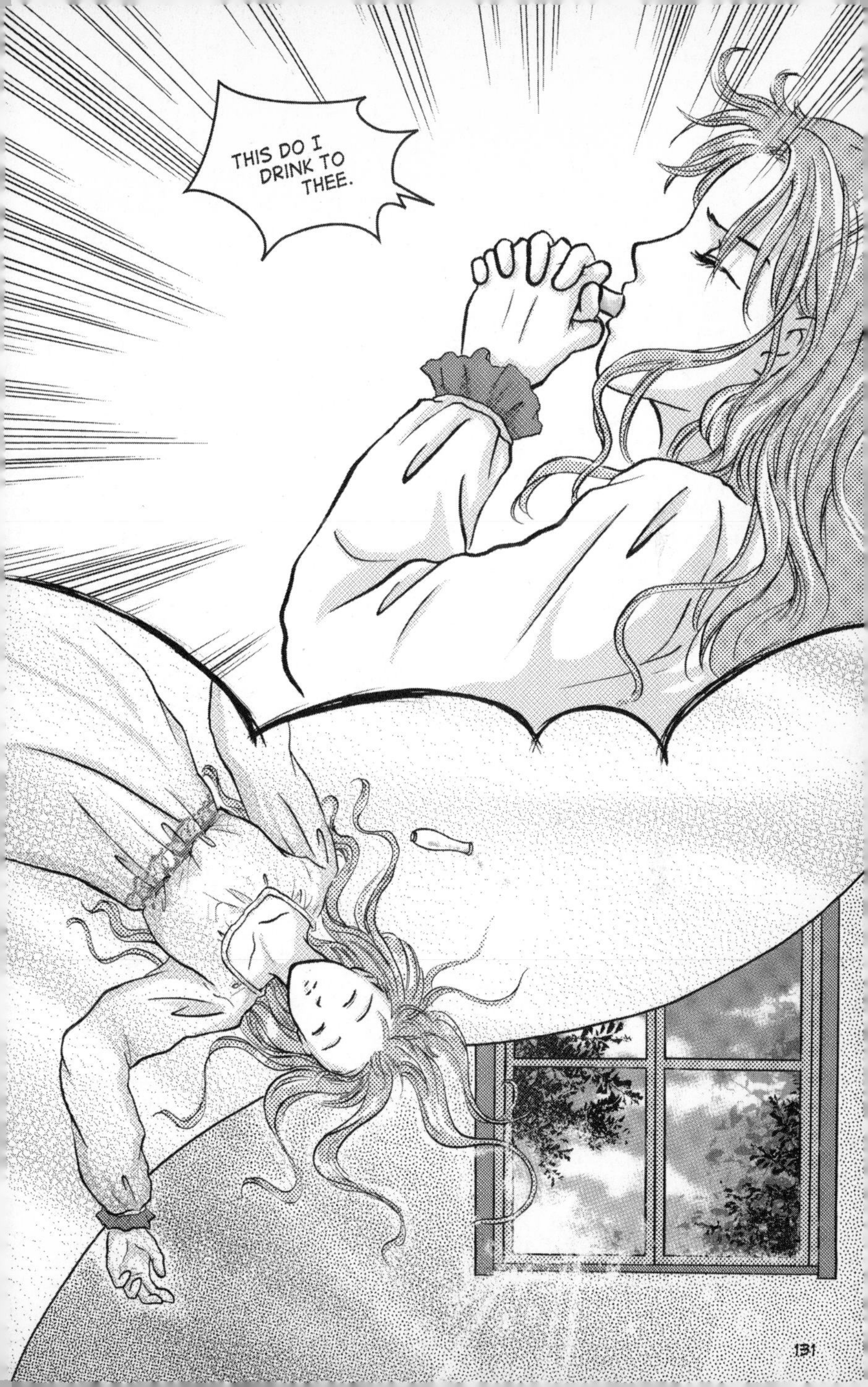
THIS DO I DRINK TO THEE.

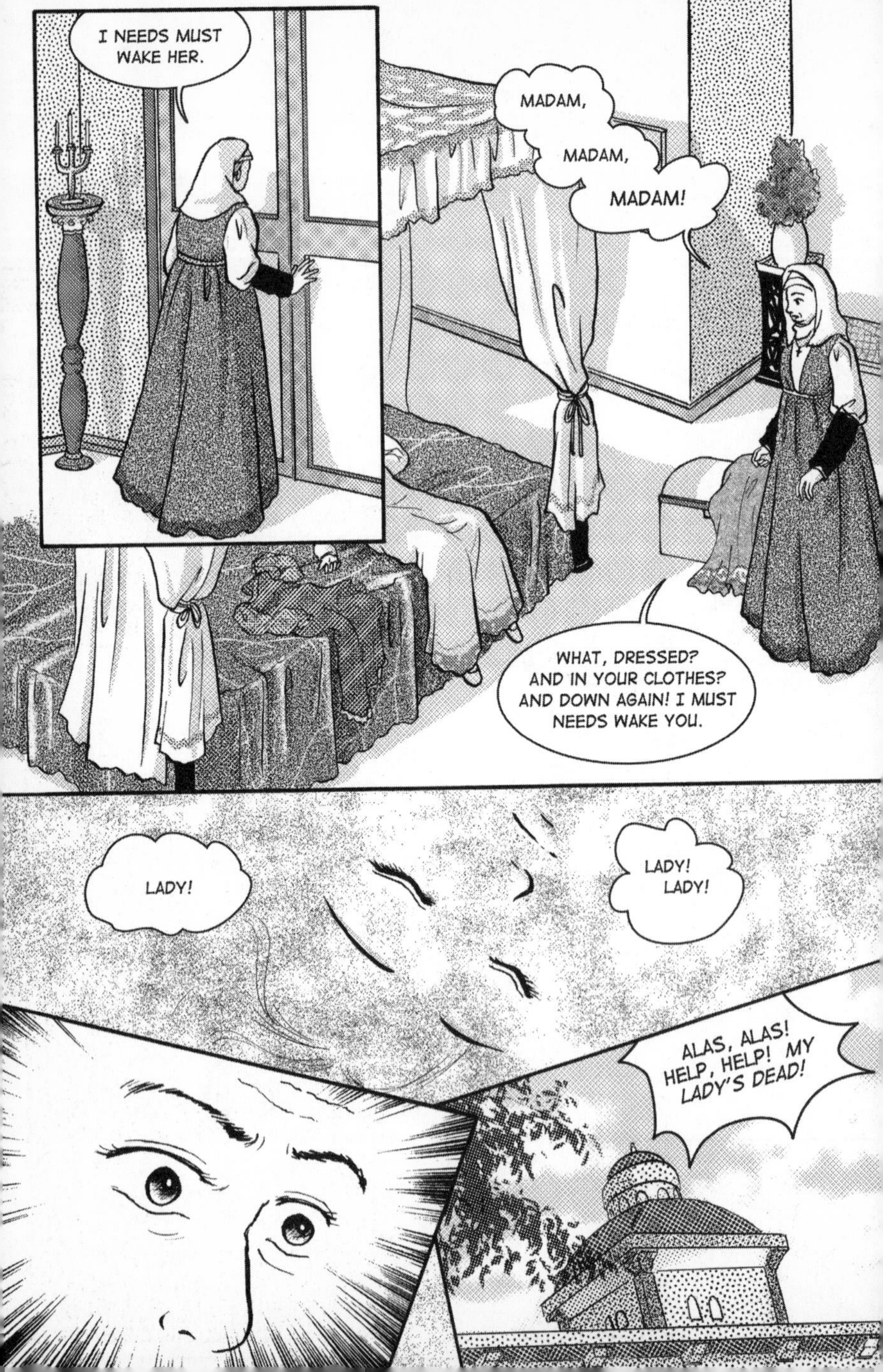
I NEEDS MUST WAKE HER.
MADAM,
MADAM,
MADAM!
WHAT, DRESSED? AND IN YOUR CLOTHES? AND DOWN AGAIN! I MUST NEEDS WAKE YOU.
LADY!
LADY! LADY!
ALAS, ALAS! HELP, HELP! MY LADY'S DEAD!

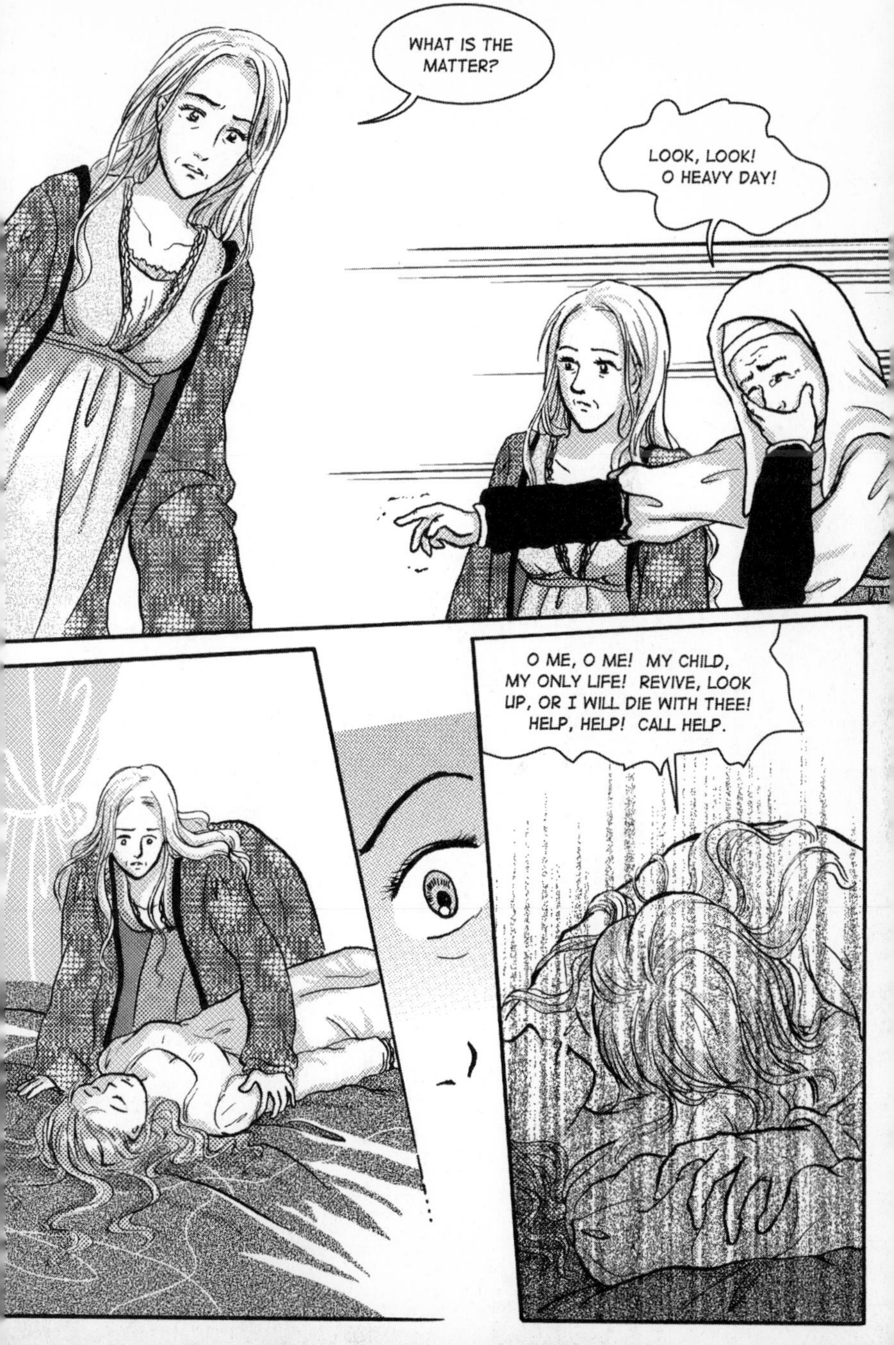
WHAT IS THE MATTER?
LOOK, LOOK! O HEAVY DAY!
O ME, O ME! MY CHILD, MY ONLY LIFE! REVIVE, LOOK UP, OR I WILL DIE WITH THEE! HELP, HELP! CALL HELP.

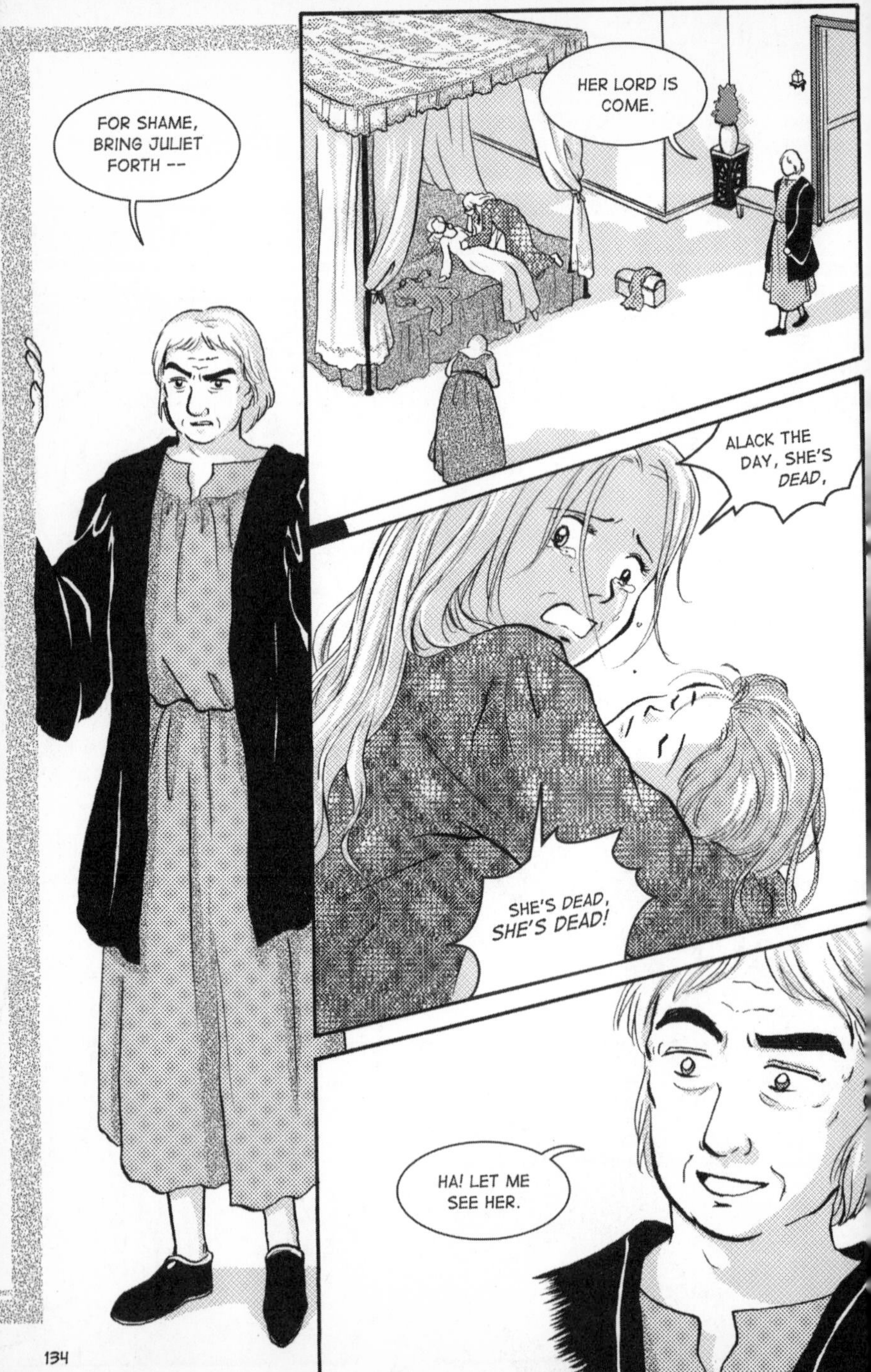
FOR SHAME, BRING JULIET FORTH --
HER LORD IS COME.
ALACK THE DAY, SHE'S *DEAD*,
SHE'S *DEAD*, SHE'S DEAD!
HA! LET ME SEE HER.

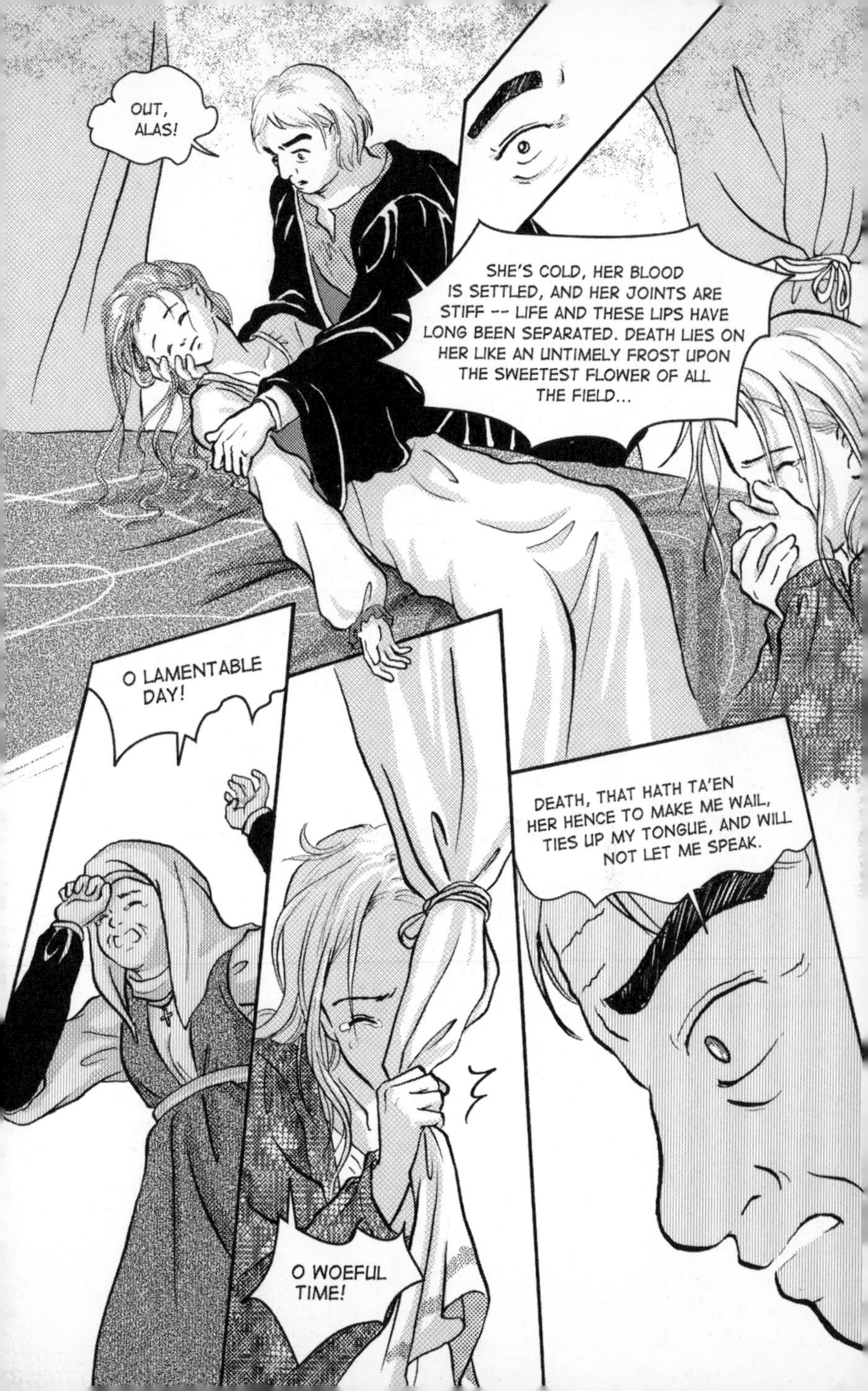
OUT, ALAS!
SHE'S COLD, HER BLOOD IS SETTLED, AND HER JOINTS ARE STIFF -- LIFE AND THESE LIPS HAVE LONG BEEN SEPARATED. DEATH LIES ON HER LIKE AN UNTIMELY FROST UPON THE SWEETEST FLOWER OF ALL THE FIELD...
O LAMENTABLE DAY!
O WOEFUL TIME!
DEATH, THAT HATH TA'EN HER HENCE TO MAKE ME WAIL, TIES UP MY TONGUE, AND WILL NOT LET ME SPEAK.

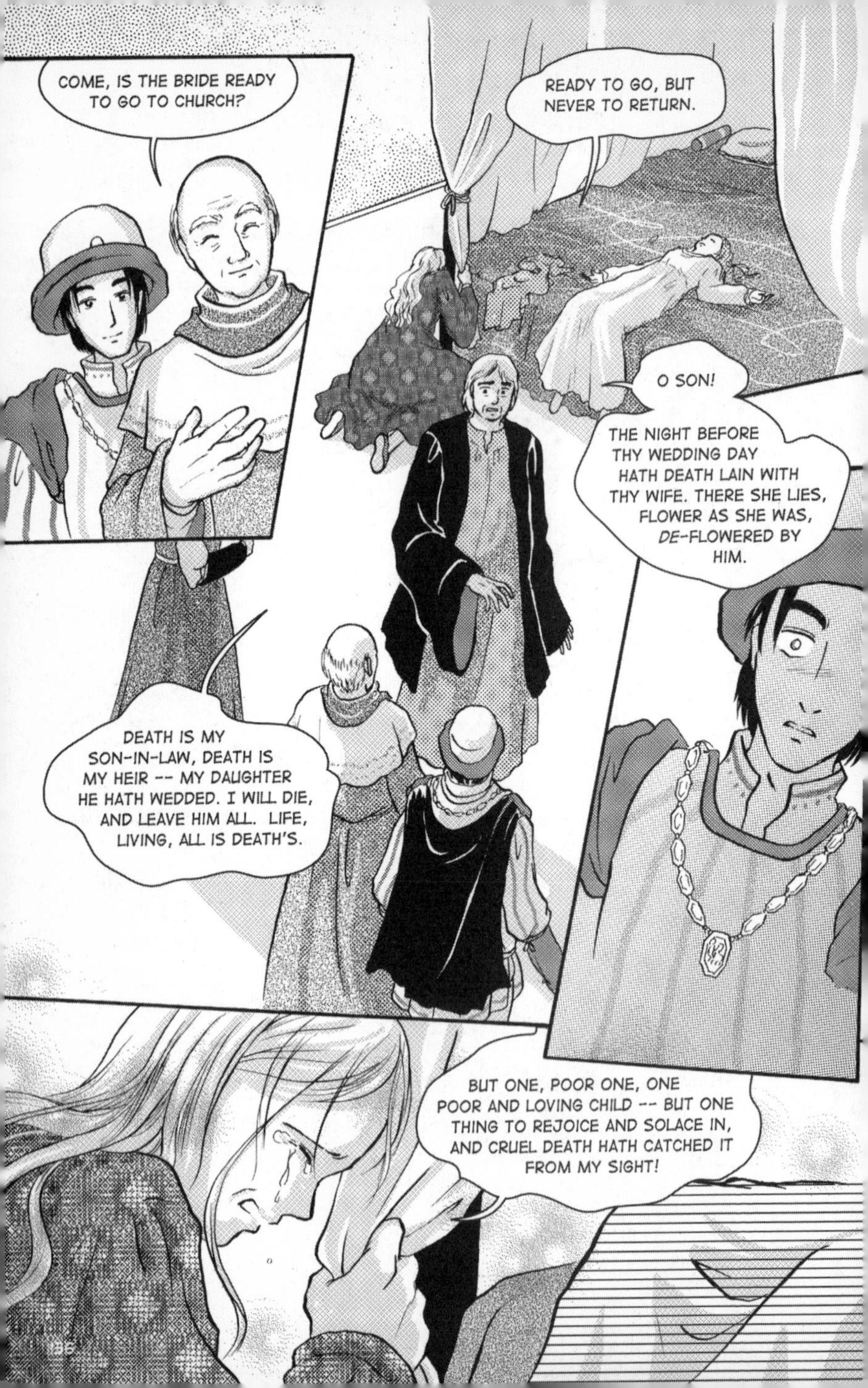
COME, IS THE BRIDE READY TO GO TO CHURCH?
READY TO GO, BUT NEVER TO RETURN.
O SON!
THE NIGHT BEFORE THY WEDDING DAY HATH DEATH LAIN WITH THY WIFE. THERE SHE LIES, FLOWER AS SHE WAS, *DE*-FLOWERED BY HIM.
DEATH IS MY SON-IN-LAW, DEATH IS MY HEIR -- MY DAUGHTER HE HATH WEDDED. I WILL DIE, AND LEAVE HIM ALL. LIFE, LIVING, ALL IS DEATH'S.
BUT ONE, POOR ONE, ONE POOR AND LOVING CHILD -- BUT ONE THING TO REJOICE AND SOLACE IN, AND CRUEL DEATH HATH CATCHED IT FROM MY SIGHT!

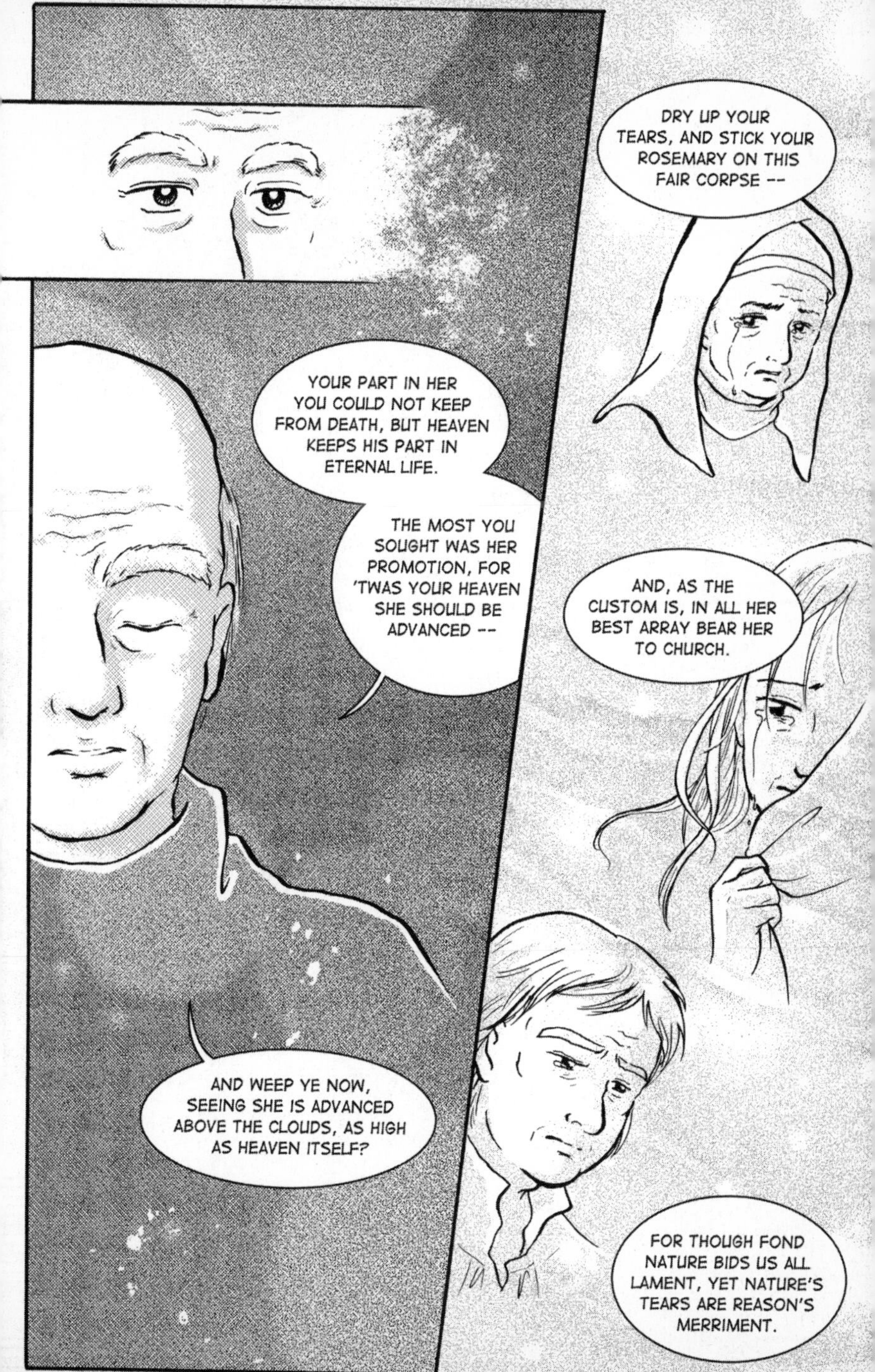
YOUR PART IN HER YOU COULD NOT KEEP FROM DEATH, BUT HEAVEN KEEPS HIS PART IN ETERNAL LIFE.
THE MOST YOU SOUGHT WAS HER PROMOTION, FOR 'TWAS YOUR HEAVEN SHE SHOULD BE ADVANCED --
AND WEEP YE NOW, SEEING SHE IS ADVANCED ABOVE THE CLOUDS, AS HIGH AS HEAVEN ITSELF?
DRY UP YOUR TEARS, AND STICK YOUR ROSEMARY ON THIS FAIR CORPSE --
AND, AS THE CUSTOM IS, IN ALL HER BEST ARRAY BEAR HER TO CHURCH.
FOR THOUGH FOND NATURE BIDS US ALL LAMENT, YET NATURE'S TEARS ARE REASON'S MERRIMENT.

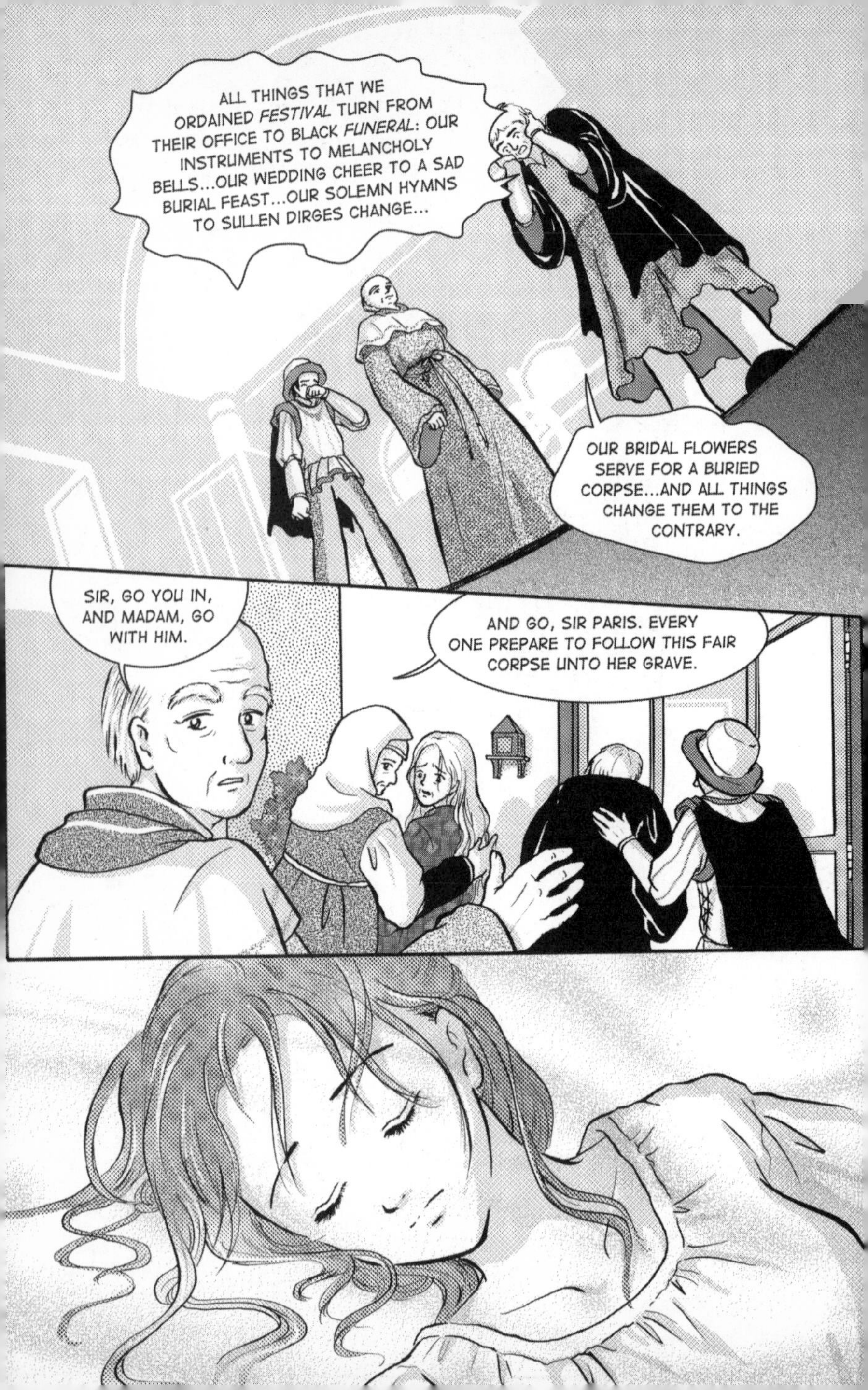
ALL THINGS THAT WE ORDAINED *FESTIVAL* TURN FROM THEIR OFFICE TO BLACK *FUNERAL*: OUR INSTRUMENTS TO MELANCHOLY BELLS...OUR WEDDING CHEER TO A SAD BURIAL FEAST...OUR SOLEMN HYMNS TO SULLEN DIRGES CHANGE...
OUR BRIDAL FLOWERS SERVE FOR A BURIED CORPSE...AND ALL THINGS CHANGE THEM TO THE CONTRARY.
SIR, GO YOU IN, AND MADAM, GO WITH HIM.
AND GO, SIR PARIS. EVERY ONE PREPARE TO FOLLOW THIS FAIR CORPSE UNTO HER GRAVE.

Act V

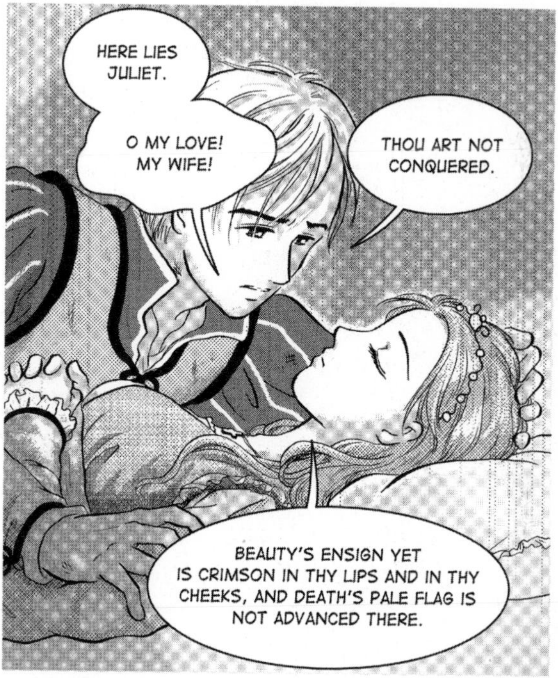
HERE LIES JULIET.
O MY LOVE! MY WIFE!
THOU ART NOT CONQUERED.
BEAUTY'S ENSIGN YET IS CRIMSON IN THY LIPS AND IN THY CHEEKS, AND DEATH'S PALE FLAG IS NOT ADVANCED THERE.

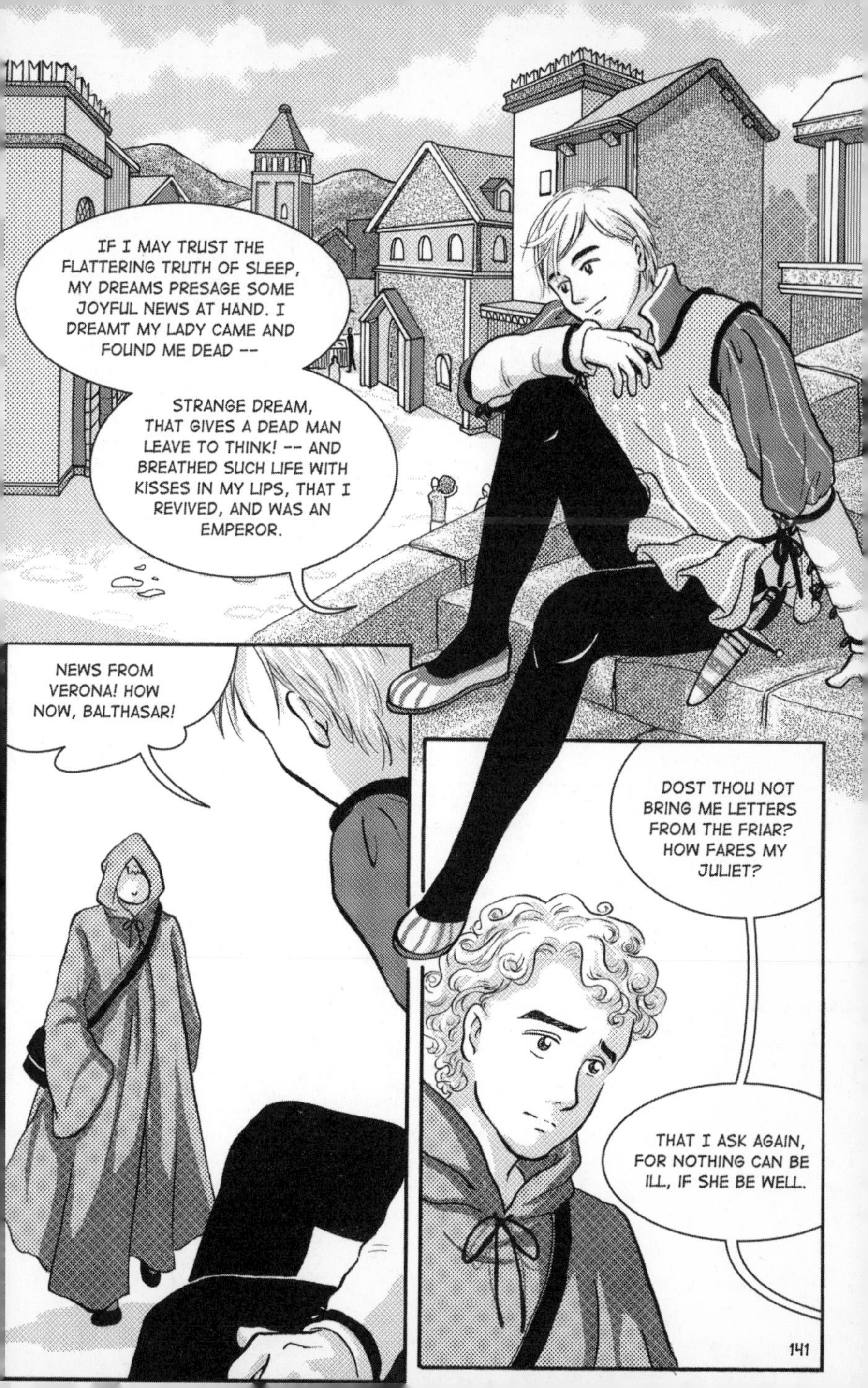

IF I MAY TRUST THE FLATTERING TRUTH OF SLEEP, MY DREAMS PRESAGE SOME JOYFUL NEWS AT HAND. I DREAMT MY LADY CAME AND FOUND ME DEAD --
STRANGE DREAM, THAT GIVES A DEAD MAN LEAVE TO THINK! -- AND BREATHED SUCH LIFE WITH KISSES IN MY LIPS, THAT I REVIVED, AND WAS AN EMPEROR.
NEWS FROM VERONA! HOW NOW, BALTHASAR!
DOST THOU NOT BRING ME LETTERS FROM THE FRIAR? HOW FARES MY JULIET?
THAT I ASK AGAIN, FOR NOTHING CAN BE ILL, IF SHE BE WELL.

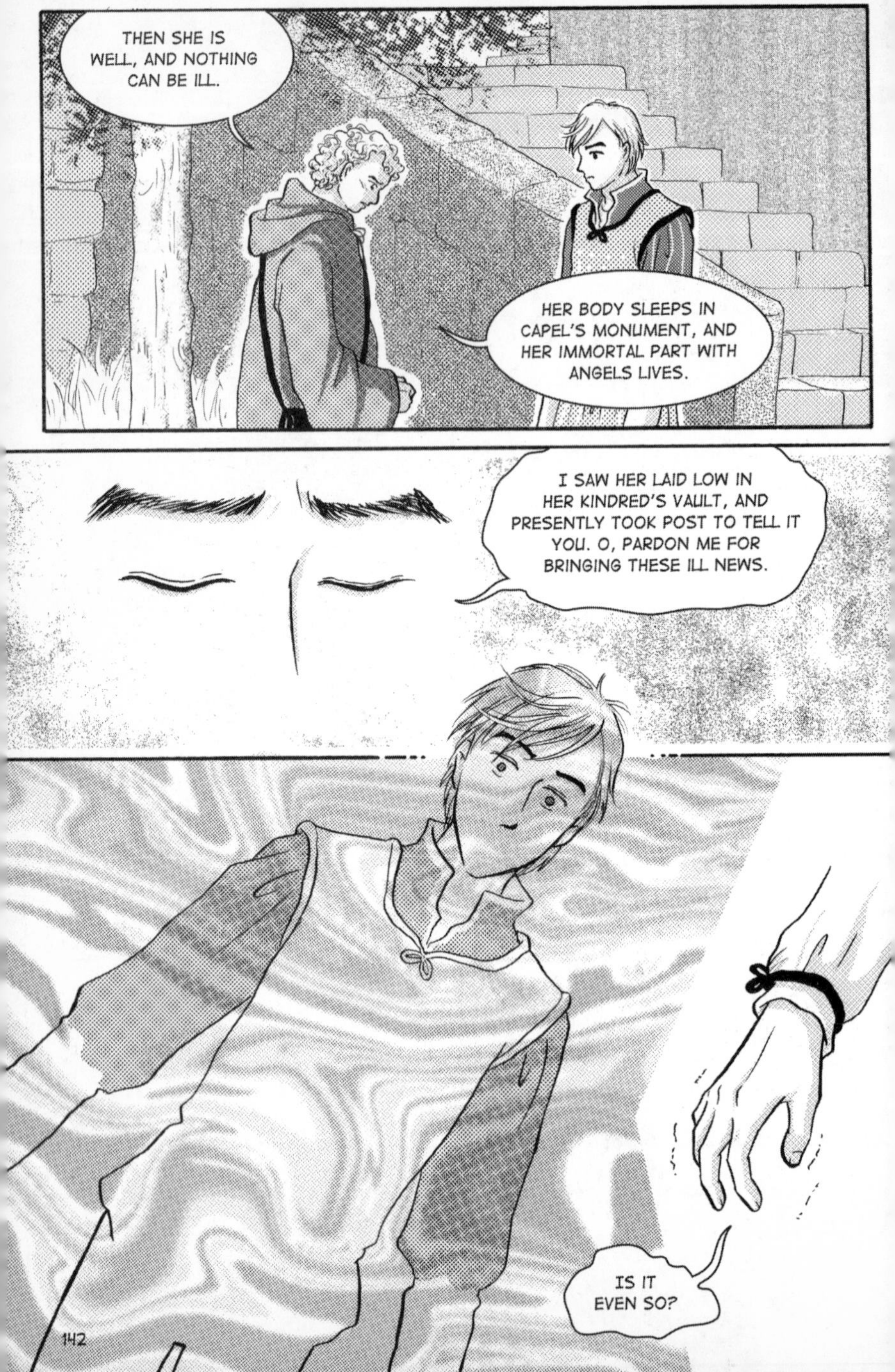
THEN SHE IS WELL, AND NOTHING CAN BE ILL.
HER BODY SLEEPS IN CAPEL'S MONUMENT, AND HER IMMORTAL PART WITH ANGELS LIVES.
I SAW HER LAID LOW IN HER KINDRED'S VAULT, AND PRESENTLY TOOK POST TO TELL IT YOU. O, PARDON ME FOR BRINGING THESE ILL NEWS.
IS IT EVEN SO?

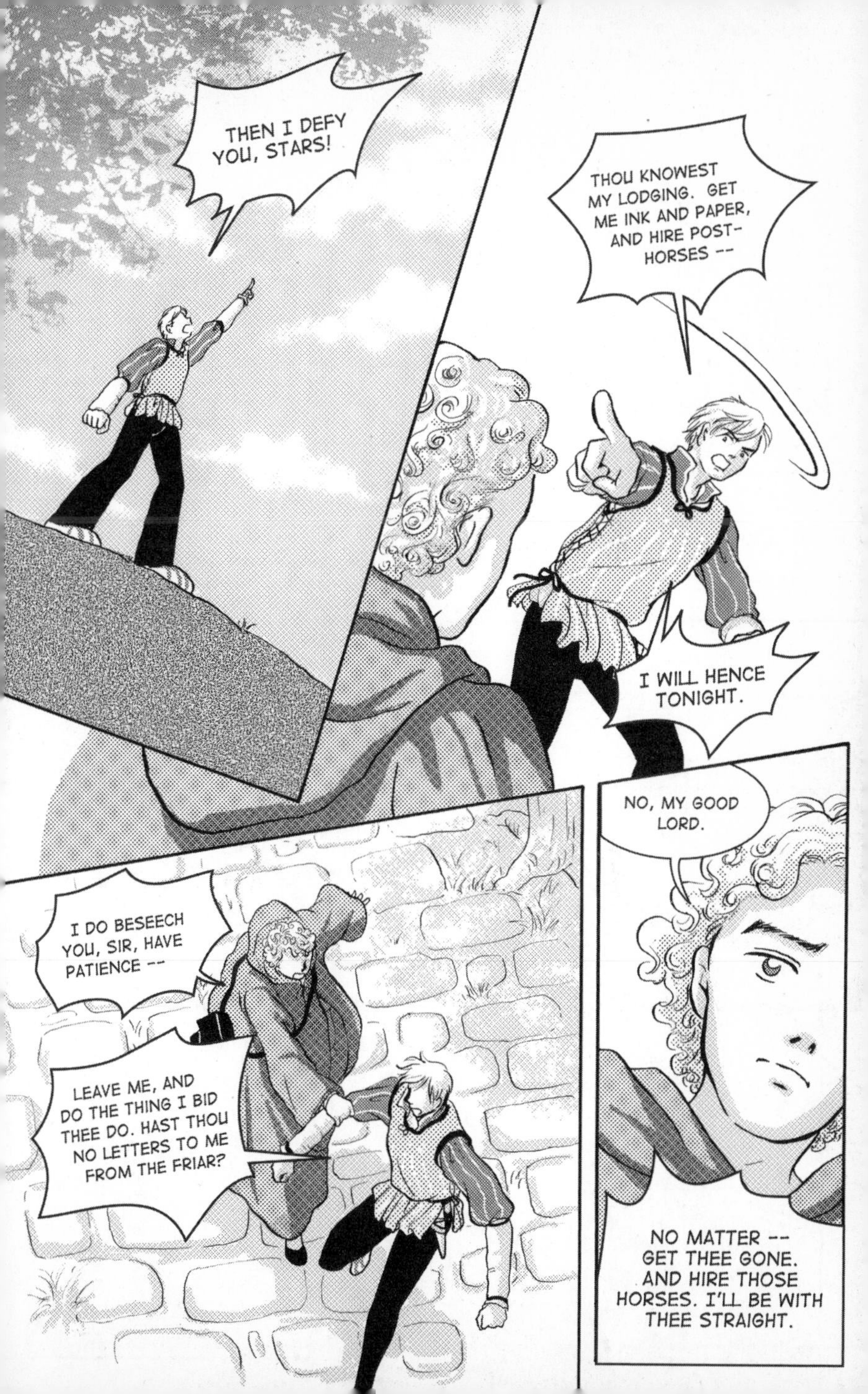
THEN I DEFY YOU, STARS!
THOU KNOWEST MY LODGING. GET ME INK AND PAPER, AND HIRE POST-HORSES --
I WILL HENCE TONIGHT.
I DO BESEECH YOU, SIR, HAVE PATIENCE --
LEAVE ME, AND DO THE THING I BID THEE DO. HAST THOU NO LETTERS TO ME FROM THE FRIAR?
NO, MY GOOD LORD.
NO MATTER -- GET THEE GONE. AND HIRE THOSE HORSES. I'LL BE WITH THEE STRAIGHT.

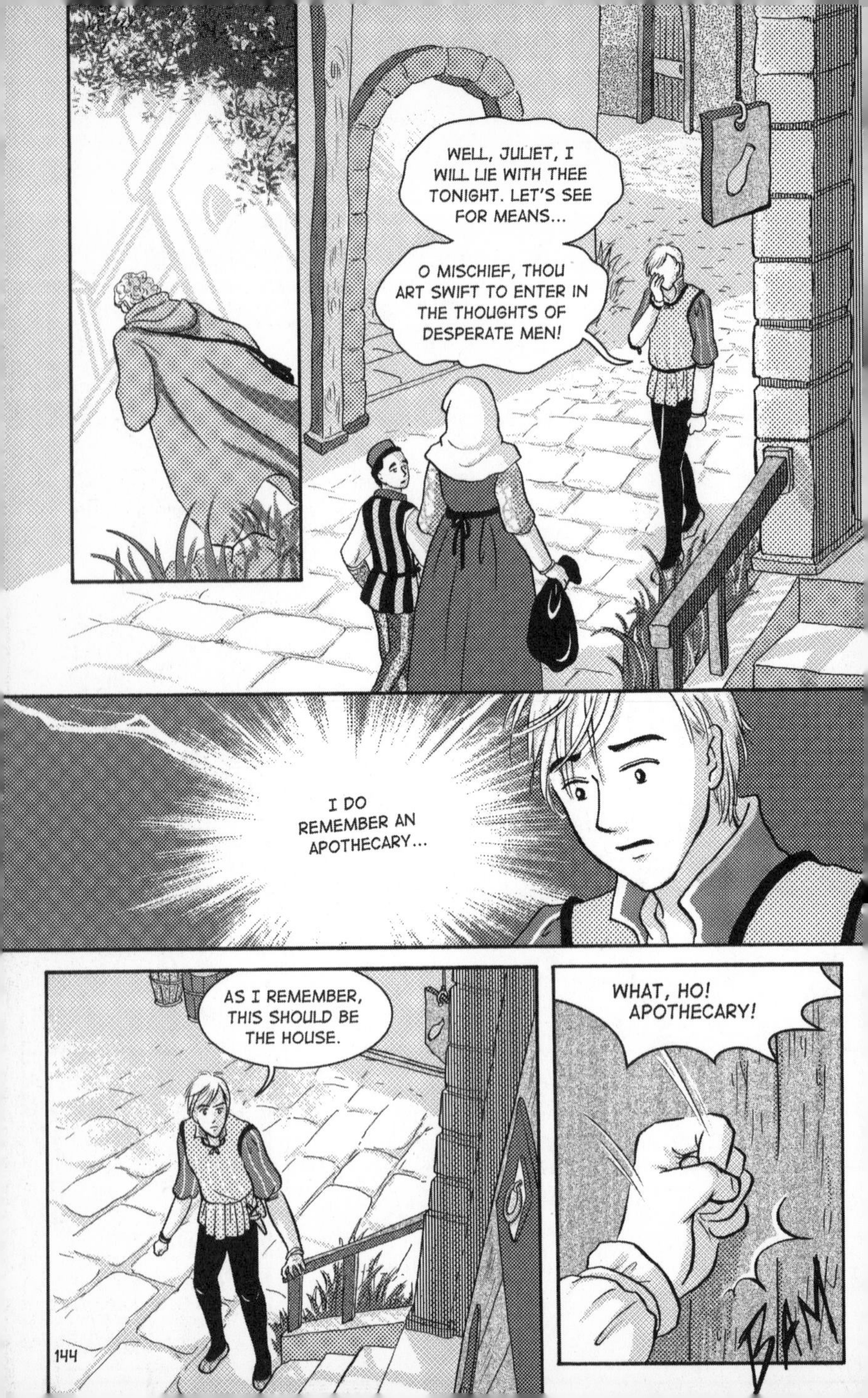
WELL, JULIET, I WILL LIE WITH THEE TONIGHT. LET'S SEE FOR MEANS...
O MISCHIEF, THOU ART SWIFT TO ENTER IN THE THOUGHTS OF DESPERATE MEN!
I DO REMEMBER AN APOTHECARY...
AS I REMEMBER, THIS SHOULD BE THE HOUSE.
WHAT, HO! APOTHECARY!
BAM

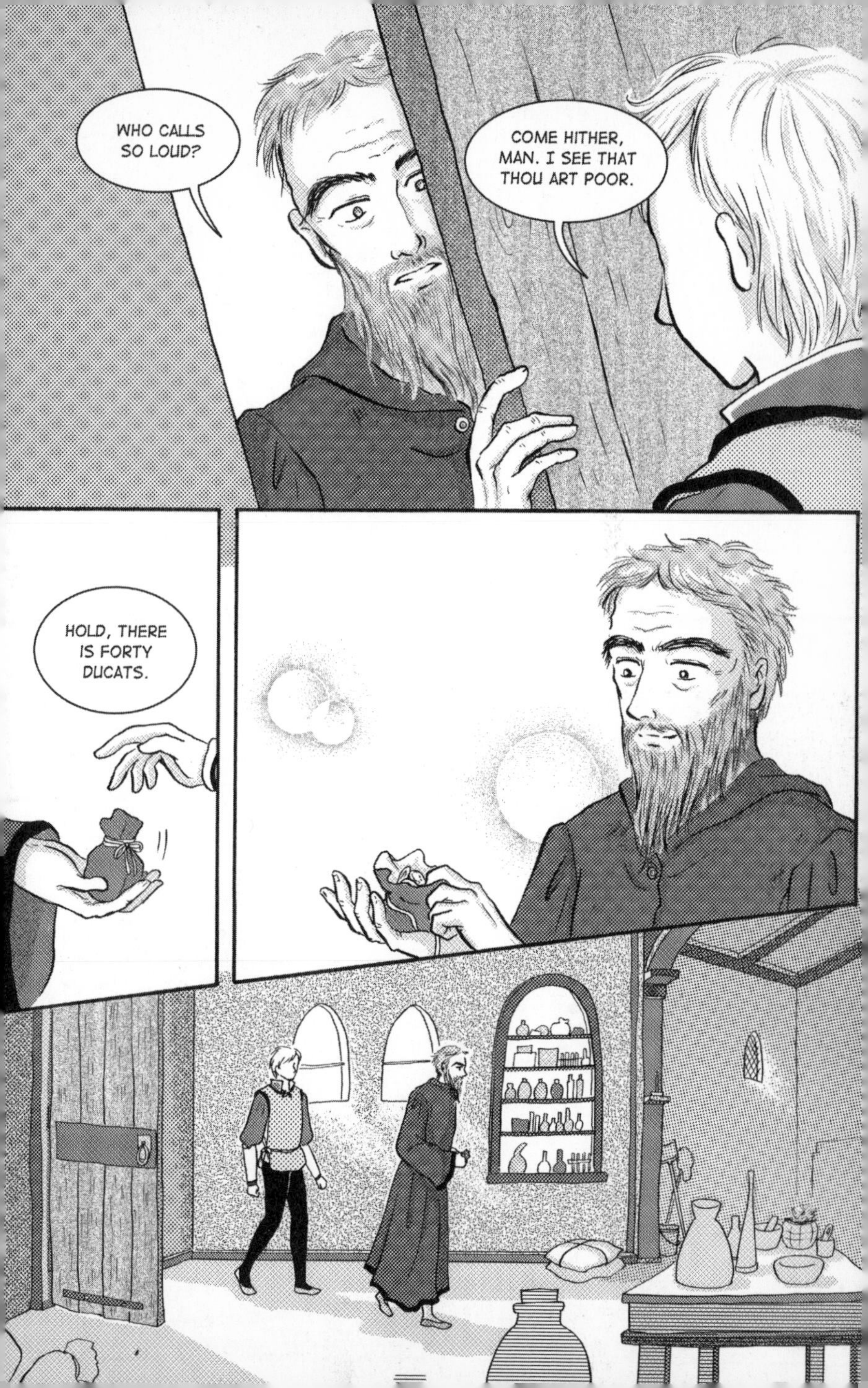
WHO CALLS SO LOUD?
COME HITHER, MAN. I SEE THAT THOU ART POOR.
HOLD, THERE IS FORTY DUCATS.

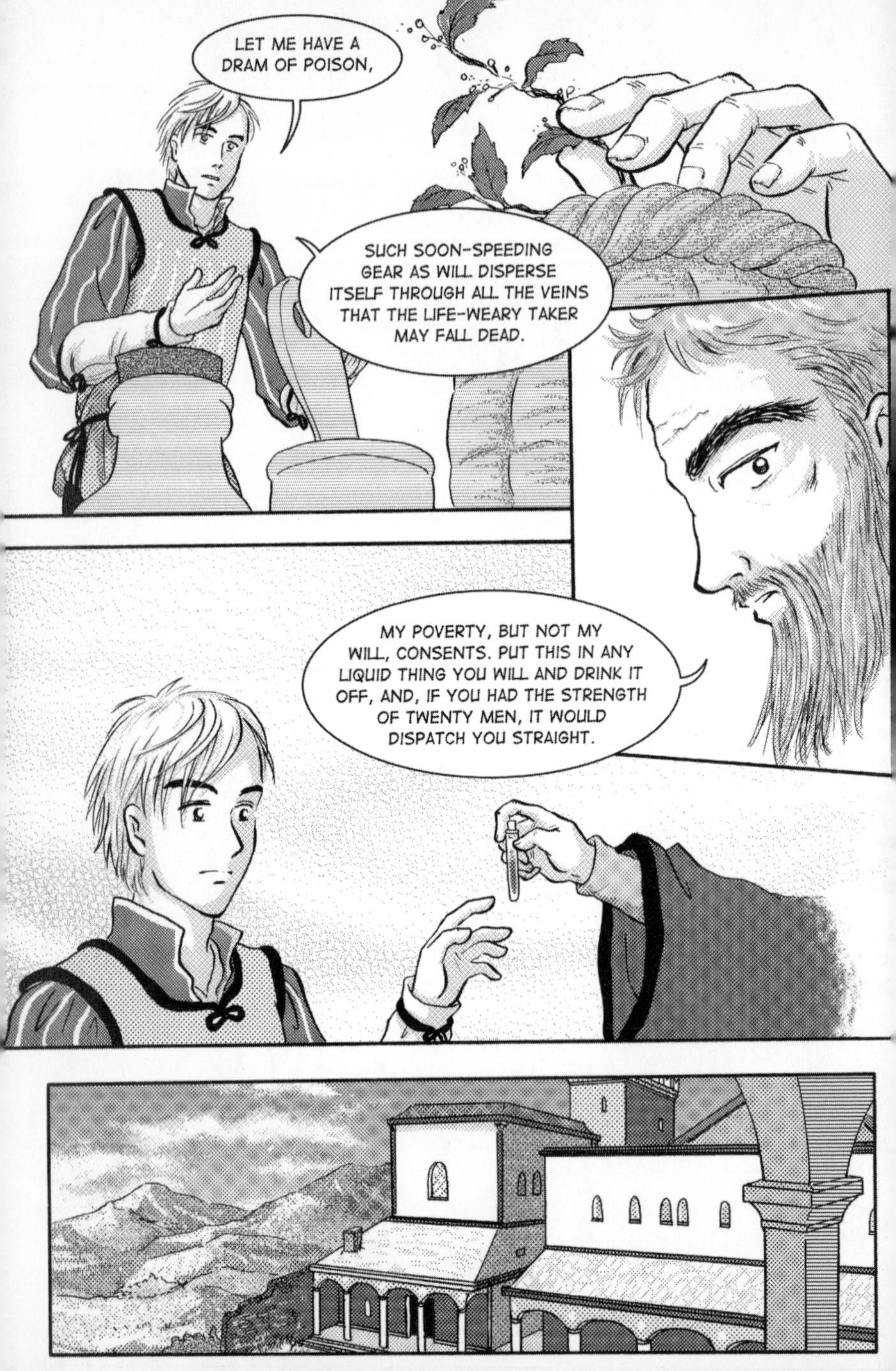
LET ME HAVE A DRAM OF POISON,
SUCH SOON-SPEEDING GEAR AS WILL DISPERSE ITSELF THROUGH ALL THE VEINS THAT THE LIFE-WEARY TAKER MAY FALL DEAD.
MY POVERTY, BUT NOT MY WILL, CONSENTS. PUT THIS IN ANY LIQUID THING YOU WILL AND DRINK IT OFF, AND, IF YOU HAD THE STRENGTH OF TWENTY MEN, IT WOULD DISPATCH YOU STRAIGHT.

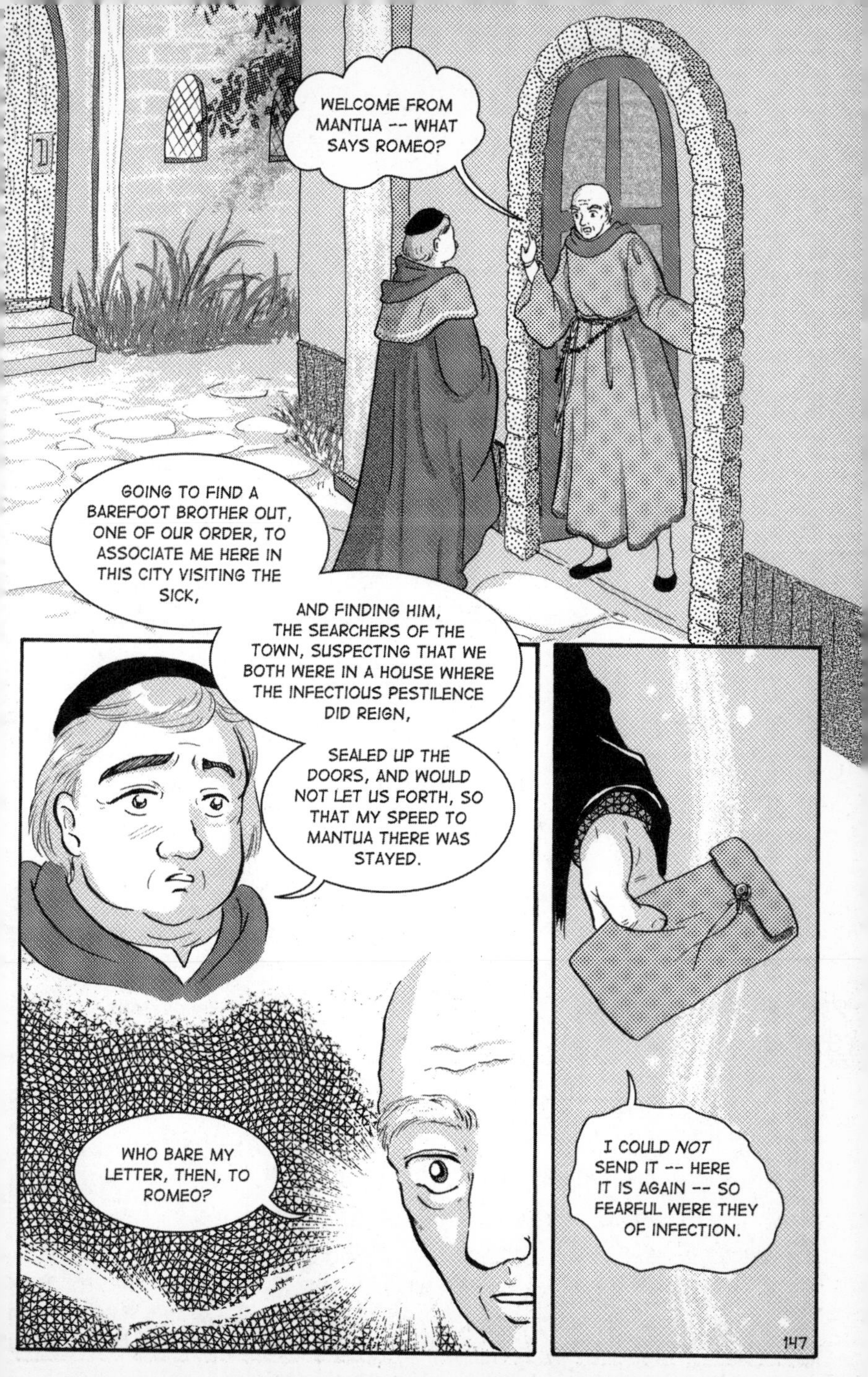
WELCOME FROM MANTUA -- WHAT SAYS ROMEO?
GOING TO FIND A BAREFOOT BROTHER OUT, ONE OF OUR ORDER, TO ASSOCIATE ME HERE IN THIS CITY VISITING THE SICK,
AND FINDING HIM, THE SEARCHERS OF THE TOWN, SUSPECTING THAT WE BOTH WERE IN A HOUSE WHERE THE INFECTIOUS PESTILENCE DID REIGN,
SEALED UP THE DOORS, AND WOULD NOT LET US FORTH, SO THAT MY SPEED TO MANTUA THERE WAS STAYED.
WHO BARE MY LETTER, THEN, TO ROMEO?
I COULD *NOT* SEND IT -- HERE IT IS AGAIN -- SO FEARFUL WERE THEY OF INFECTION.

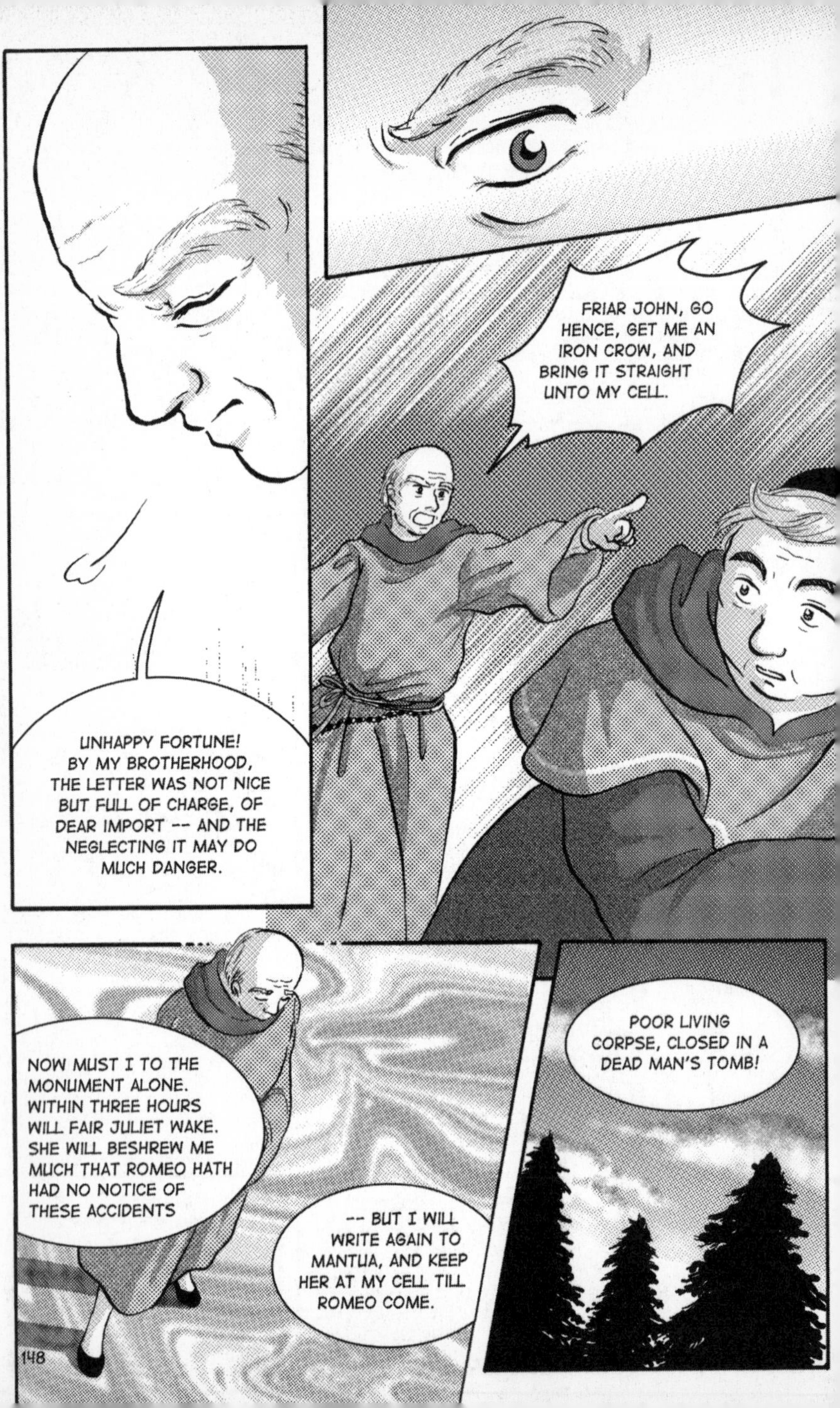
UNHAPPY FORTUNE! BY MY BROTHERHOOD, THE LETTER WAS NOT NICE BUT FULL OF CHARGE, OF DEAR IMPORT -- AND THE NEGLECTING IT MAY DO MUCH DANGER.
FRIAR JOHN, GO HENCE, GET ME AN IRON CROW, AND BRING IT STRAIGHT UNTO MY CELL.
NOW MUST I TO THE MONUMENT ALONE. WITHIN THREE HOURS WILL FAIR JULIET WAKE. SHE WILL BESHREW ME MUCH THAT ROMEO HATH HAD NO NOTICE OF THESE ACCIDENTS
-- BUT I WILL WRITE AGAIN TO MANTUA, AND KEEP HER AT MY CELL TILL ROMEO COME.
POOR LIVING CORPSE, CLOSED IN A DEAD MAN'S TOMB!

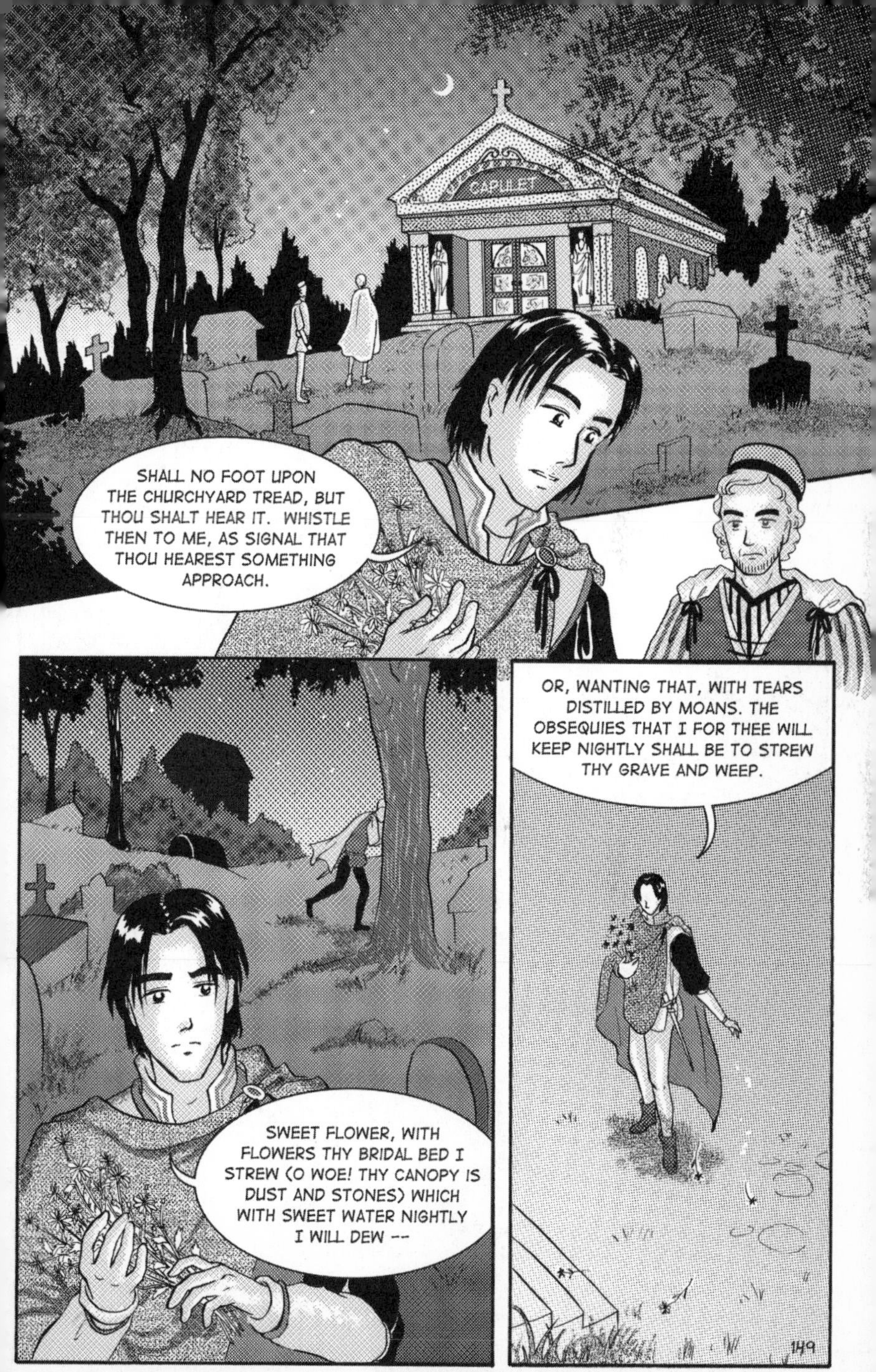
CAPULET
SHALL NO FOOT UPON THE CHURCHYARD TREAD, BUT THOU SHALT HEAR IT. WHISTLE THEN TO ME, AS SIGNAL THAT THOU HEAREST SOMETHING APPROACH.
SWEET FLOWER, WITH FLOWERS THY BRIDAL BED I STREW (O WOE! THY CANOPY IS DUST AND STONES) WHICH WITH SWEET WATER NIGHTLY I WILL DEW --
OR, WANTING THAT, WITH TEARS DISTILLED BY MOANS. THE OBSEQUIES THAT I FOR THEE WILL KEEP NIGHTLY SHALL BE TO STREW THY GRAVE AND WEEP.

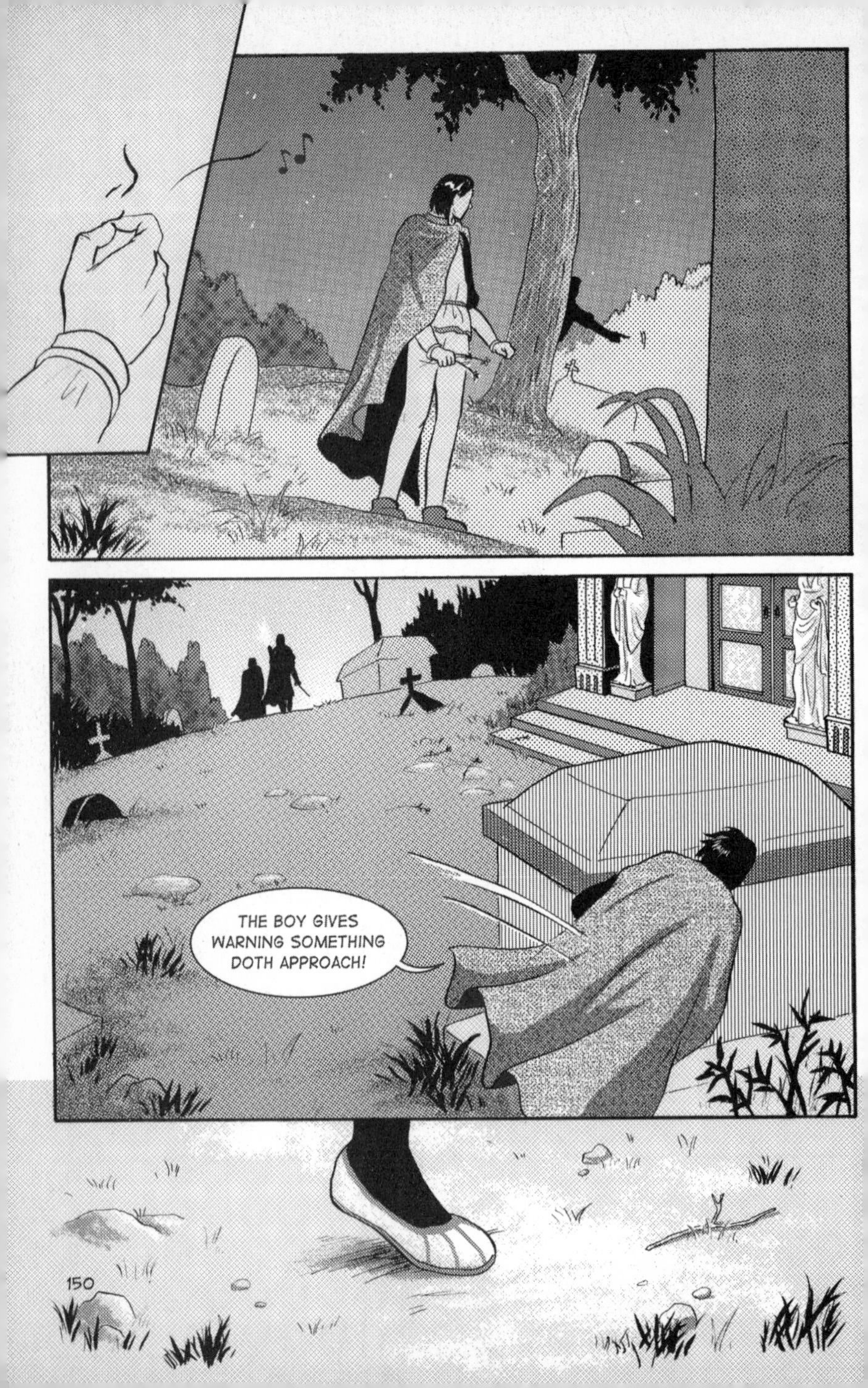
THE BOY GIVES WARNING SOMETHING DOTH APPROACH!

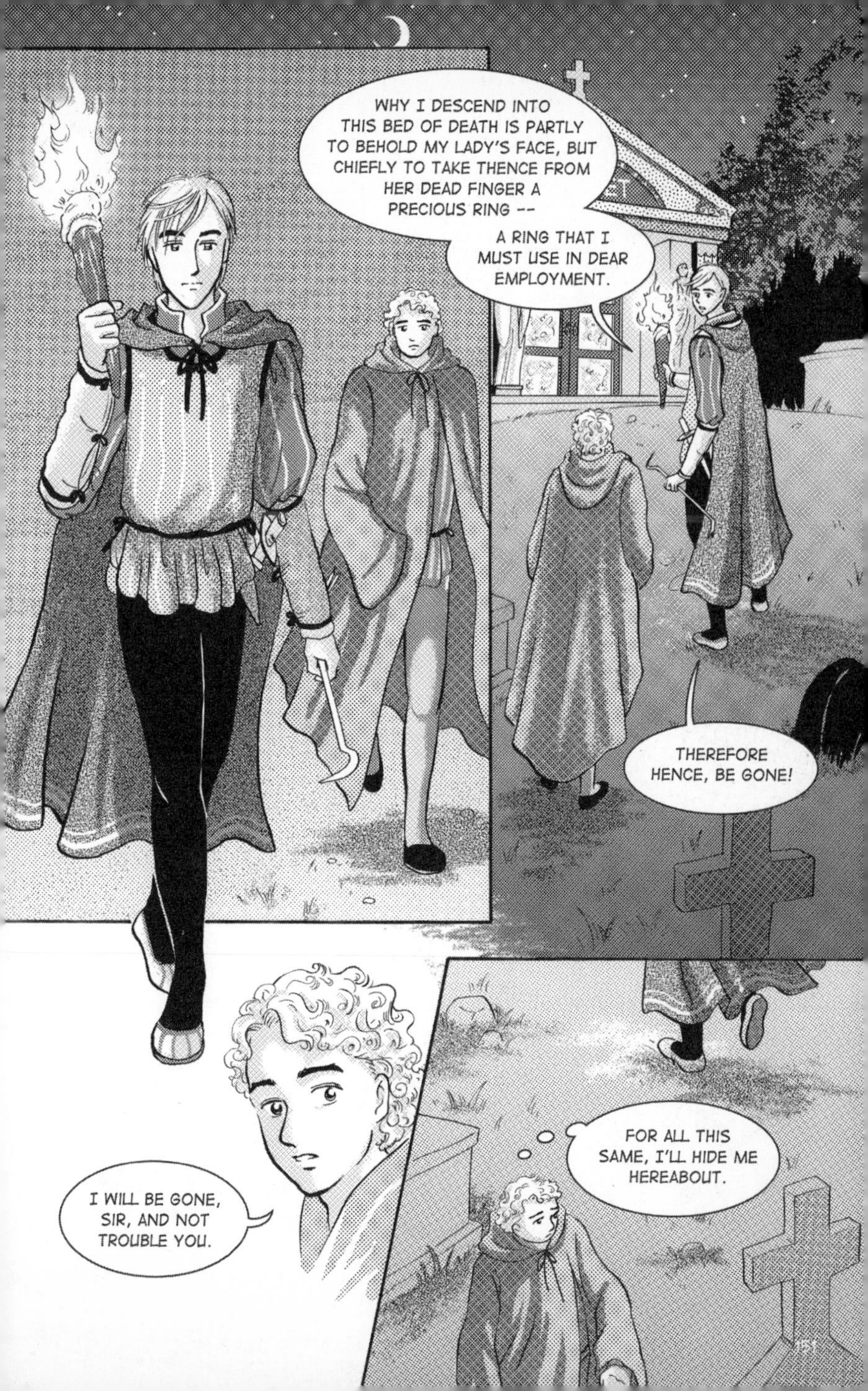
WHY I DESCEND INTO THIS BED OF DEATH IS PARTLY TO BEHOLD MY LADY'S FACE, BUT CHIEFLY TO TAKE THENCE FROM HER DEAD FINGER A PRECIOUS RING --
A RING THAT I MUST USE IN DEAR EMPLOYMENT.
THEREFORE HENCE, BE GONE!
I WILL BE GONE, SIR, AND NOT TROUBLE YOU.
FOR ALL THIS SAME, I'LL HIDE ME HEREABOUT.

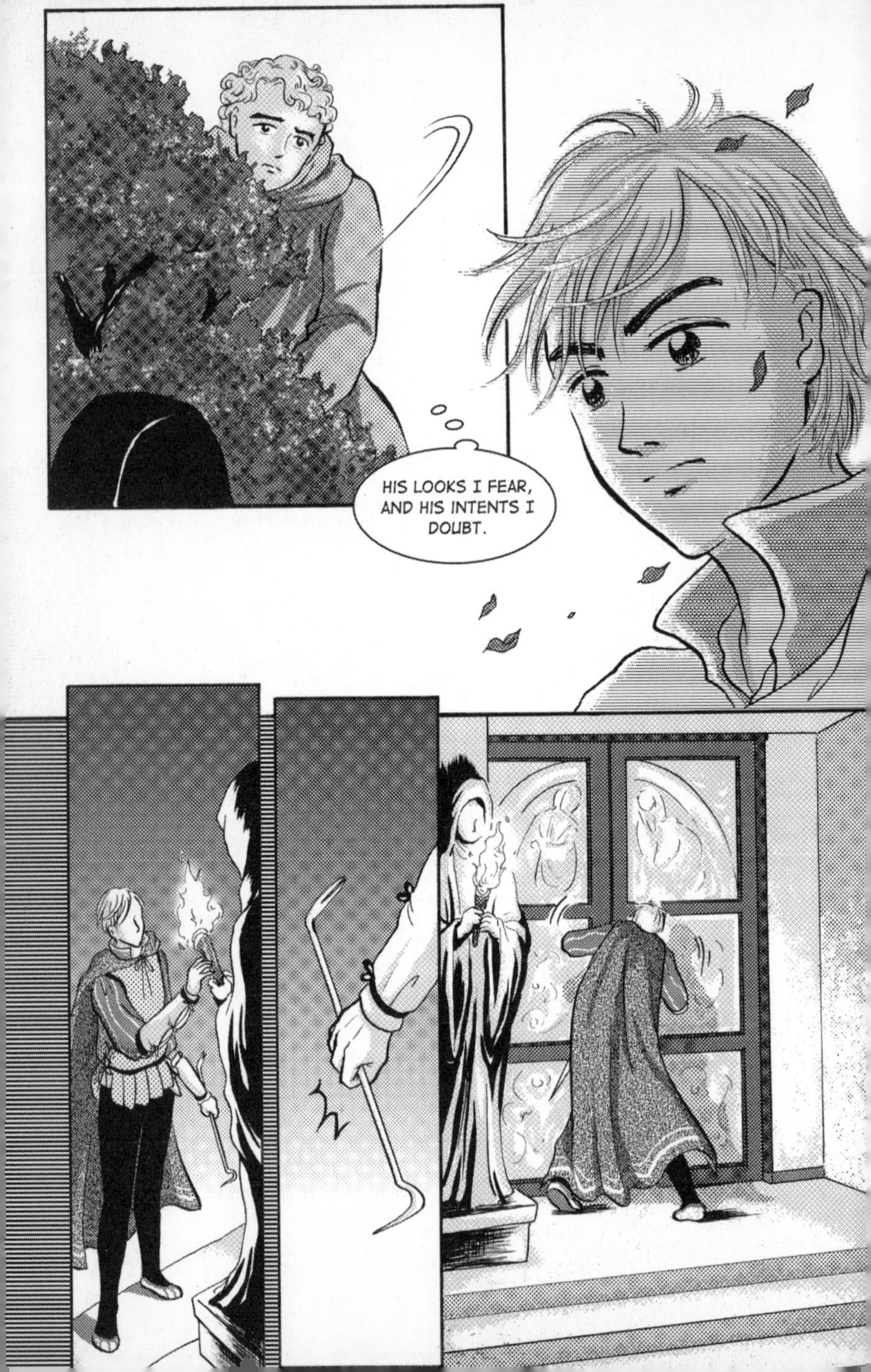
HIS LOOKS I FEAR, AND HIS INTENTS I DOUBT.

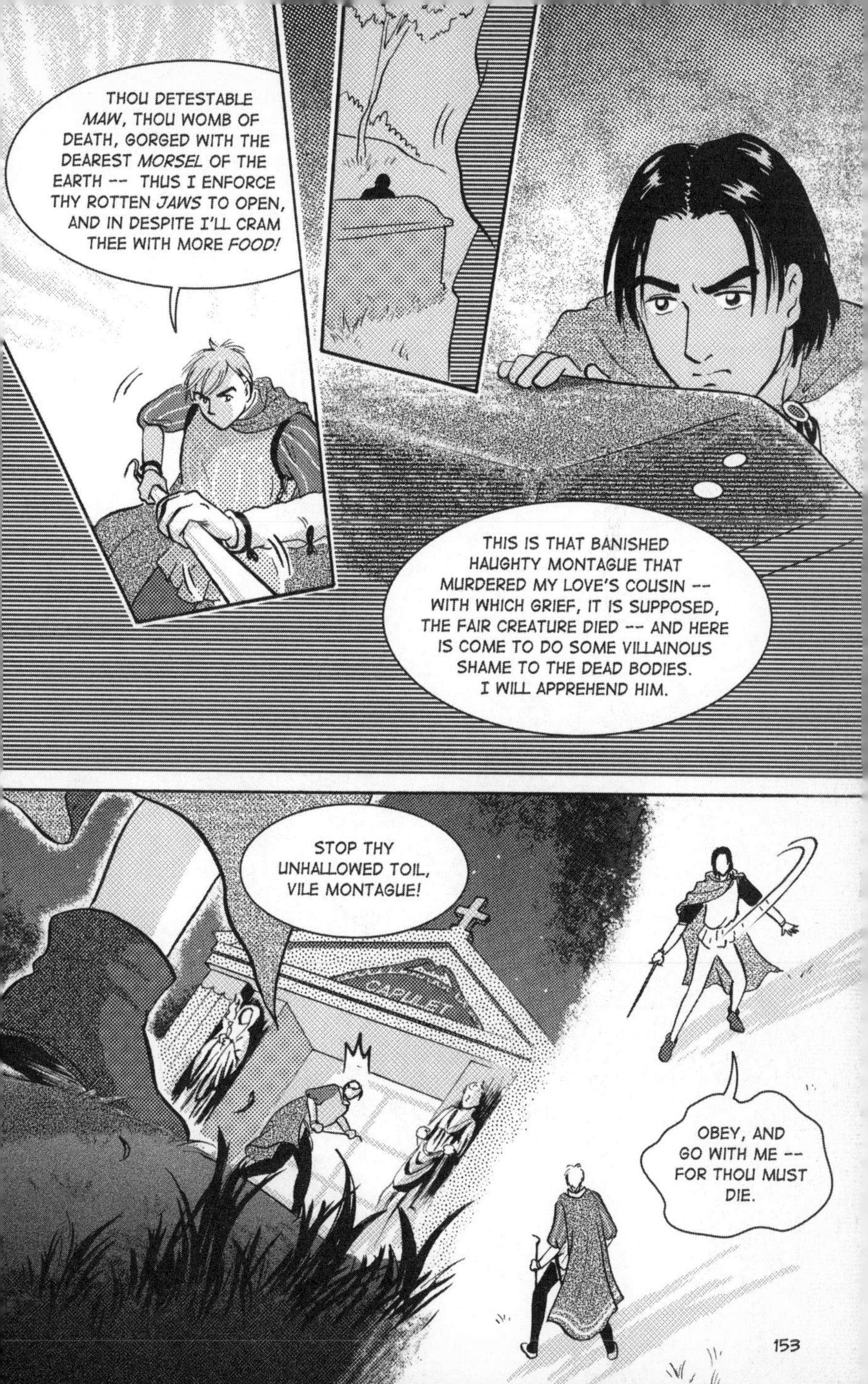
THOU DETESTABLE *MAW*, THOU WOMB OF DEATH, GORGED WITH THE DEAREST *MORSEL* OF THE EARTH -- THUS I ENFORCE THY ROTTEN *JAWS* TO OPEN, AND IN DESPITE I'LL CRAM THEE WITH MORE *FOOD!*
THIS IS THAT BANISHED HAUGHTY MONTAGUE THAT MURDERED MY LOVE'S COUSIN -- WITH WHICH GRIEF, IT IS SUPPOSED, THE FAIR CREATURE DIED -- AND HERE IS COME TO DO SOME VILLAINOUS SHAME TO THE DEAD BODIES. I WILL APPREHEND HIM.
STOP THY UNHALLOWED TOIL, VILE MONTAGUE!
CAPULET
OBEY, AND GO WITH ME -- FOR THOU MUST DIE.

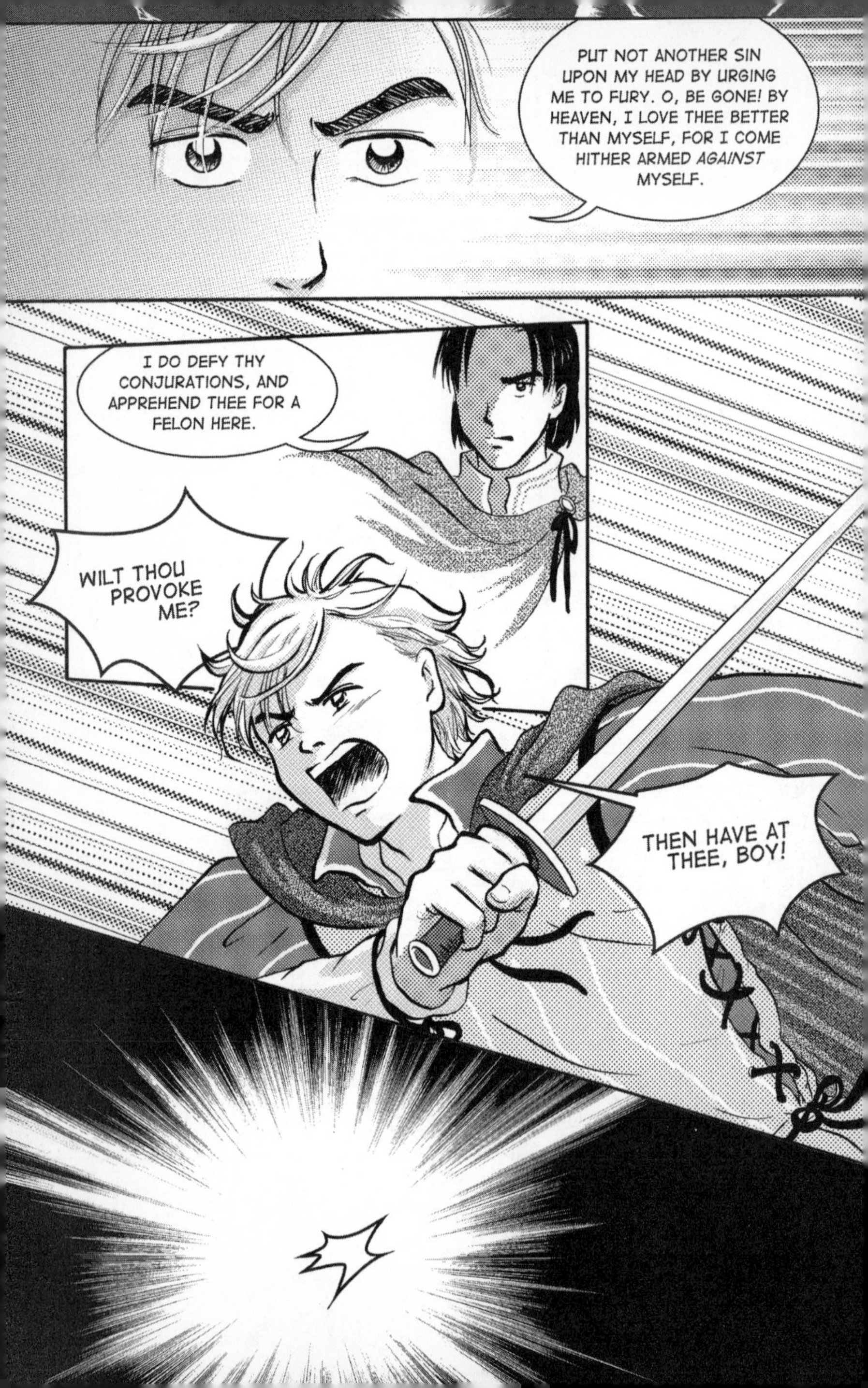
PUT NOT ANOTHER SIN UPON MY HEAD BY URGING ME TO FURY. O, BE GONE! BY HEAVEN, I LOVE THEE BETTER THAN MYSELF, FOR I COME HITHER ARMED *AGAINST* MYSELF.
I DO DEFY THY CONJURATIONS, AND APPREHEND THEE FOR A FELON HERE.
WILT THOU PROVOKE ME?
THEN HAVE AT THEE, BOY!

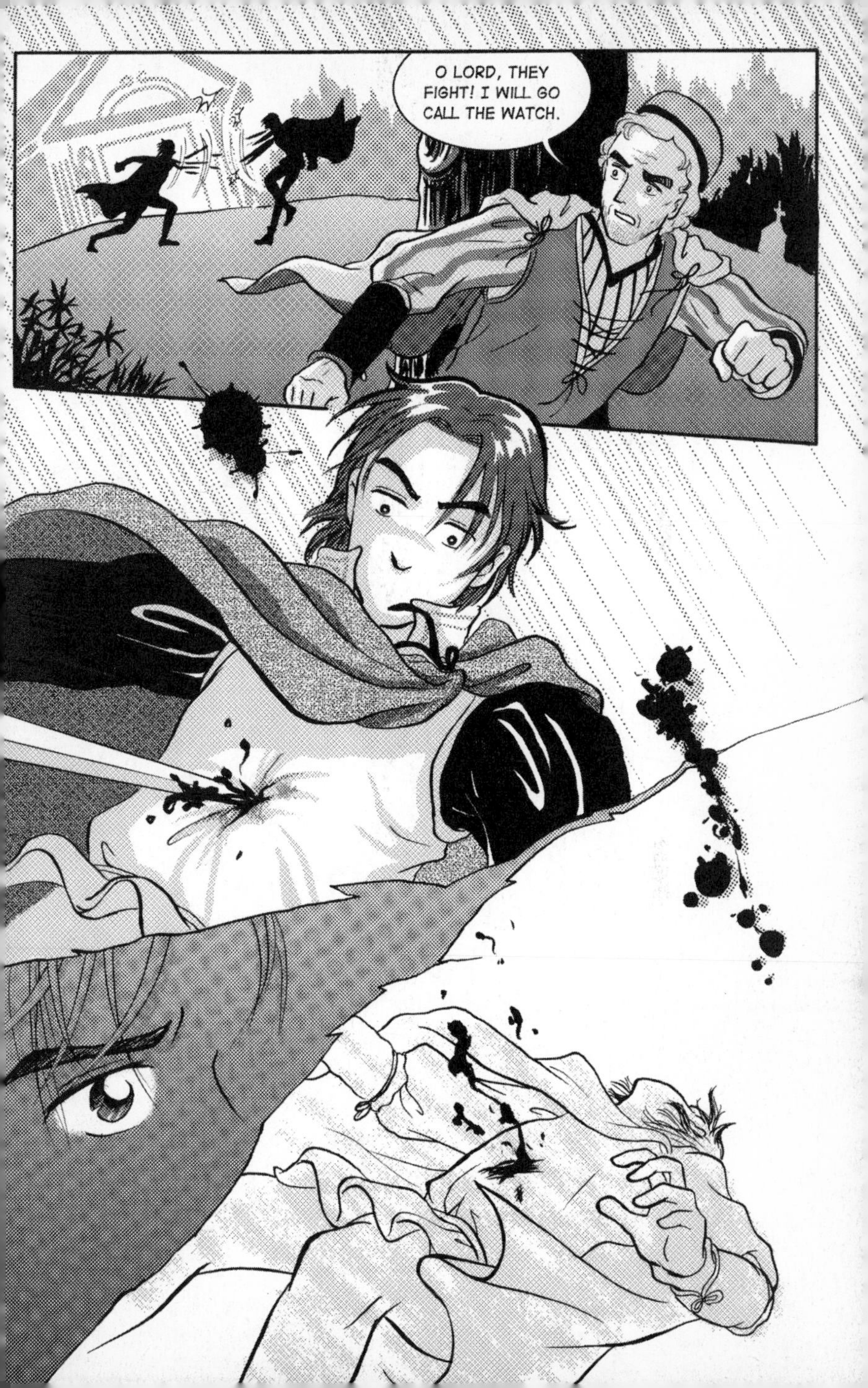
O LORD, THEY FIGHT! I WILL GO CALL THE WATCH.

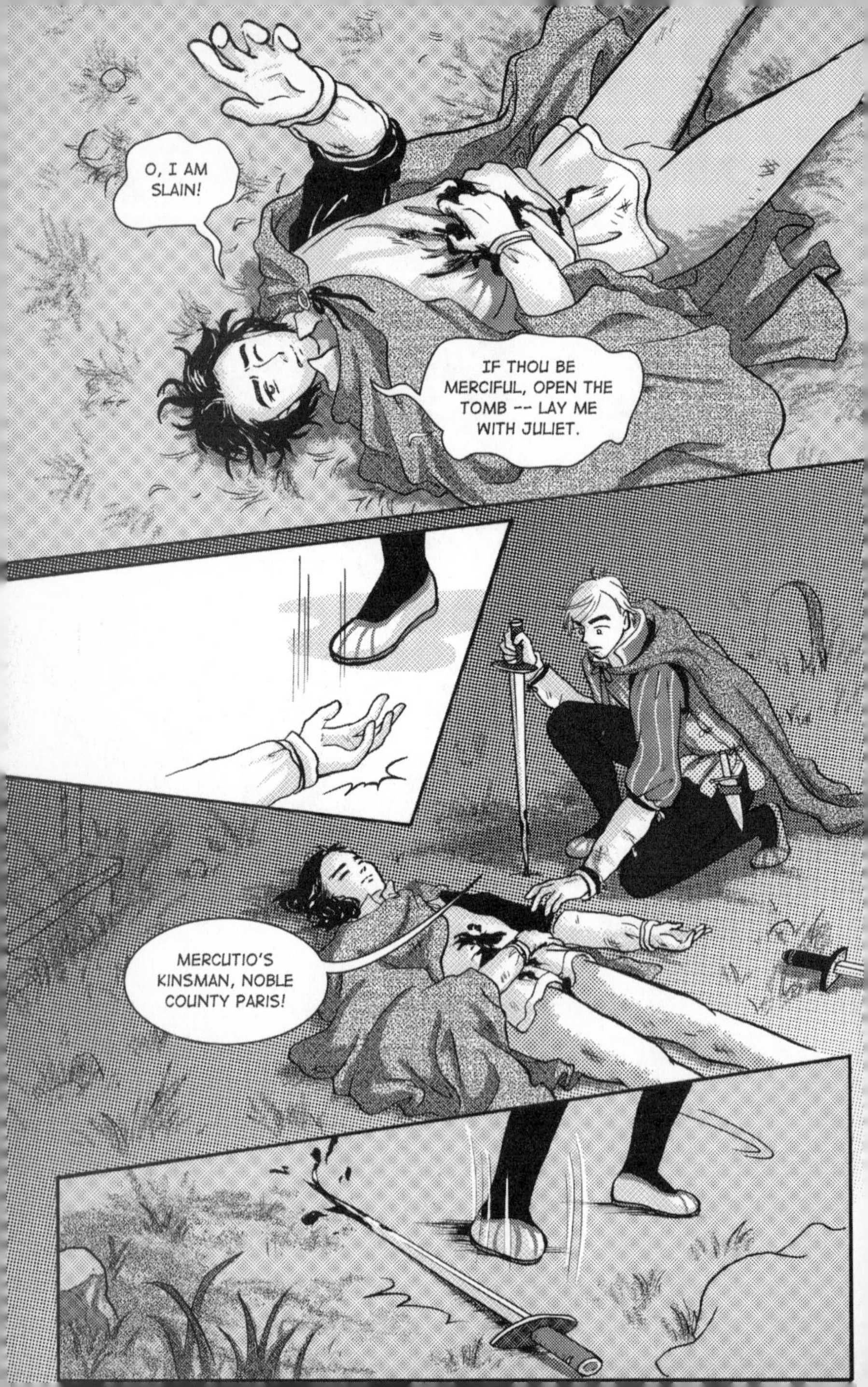
O, I AM SLAIN!
IF THOU BE MERCIFUL, OPEN THE TOMB -- LAY ME WITH JULIET.
MERCUTIO'S KINSMAN, NOBLE COUNTY PARIS!

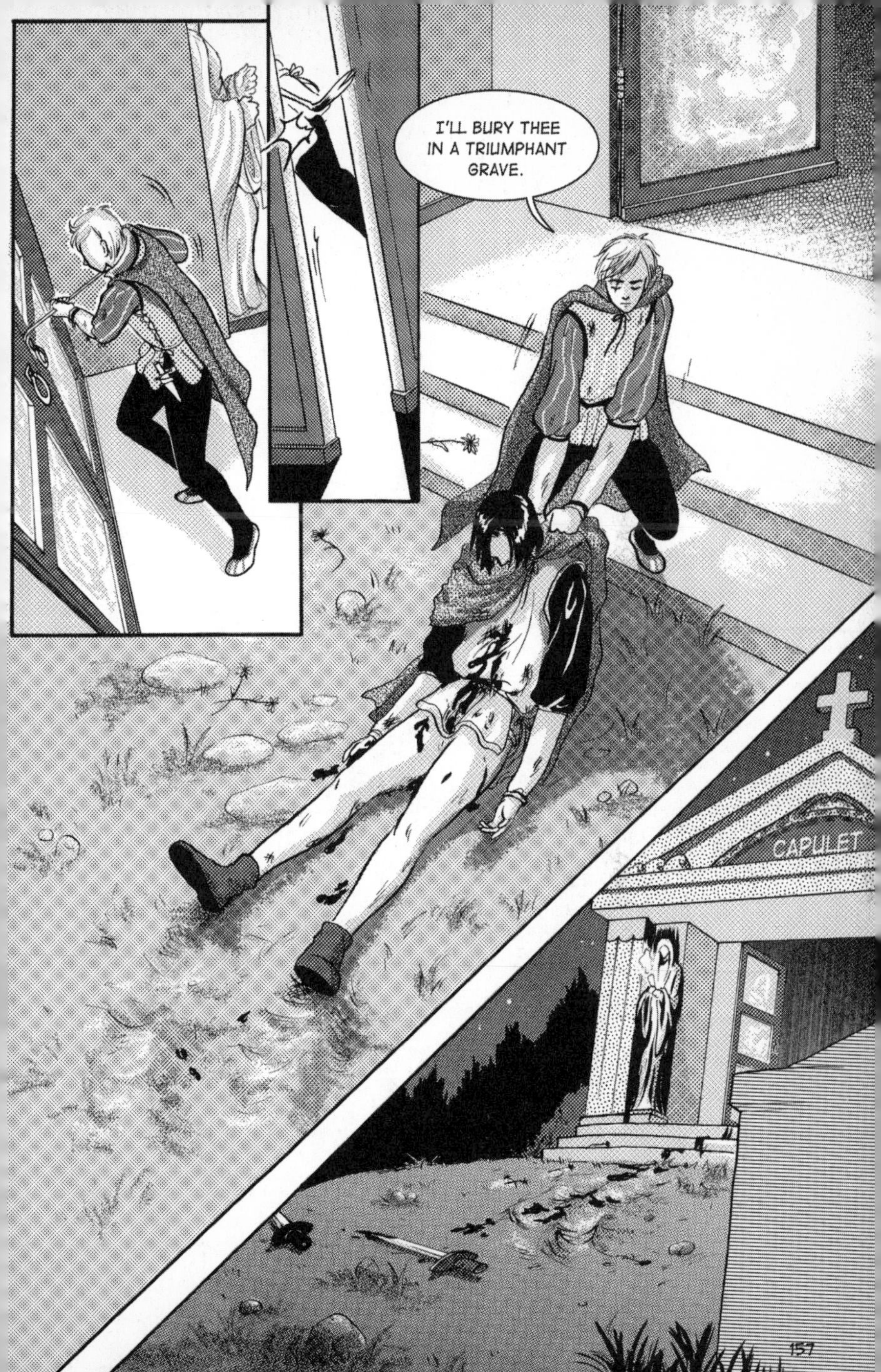
I'LL BURY THEE IN A TRIUMPHANT GRAVE.
CAPULET

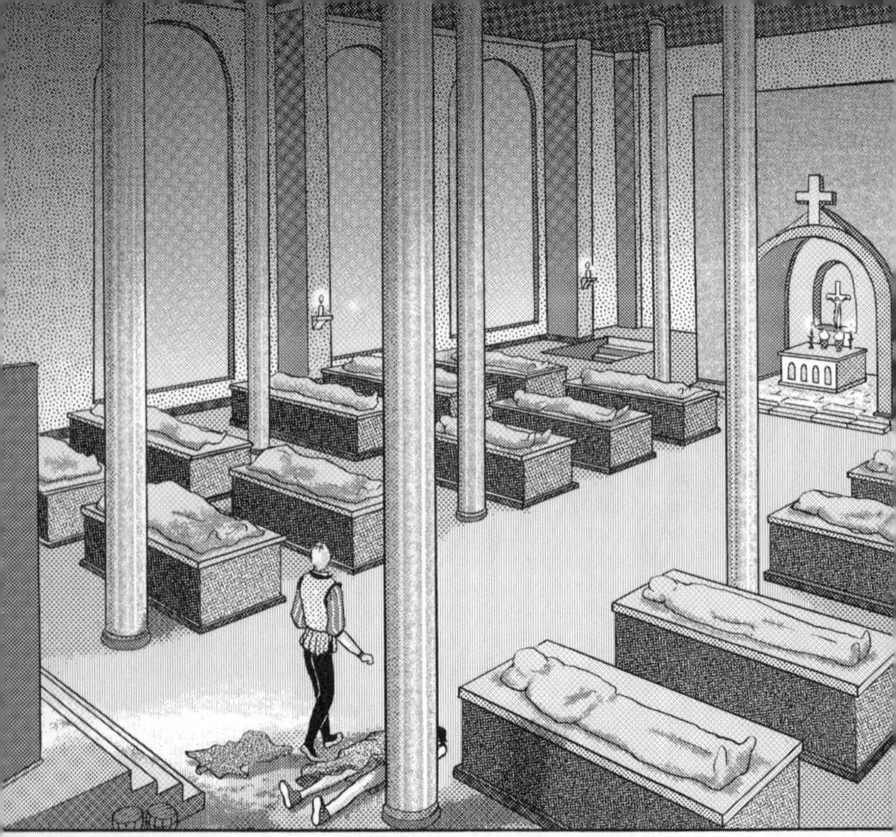

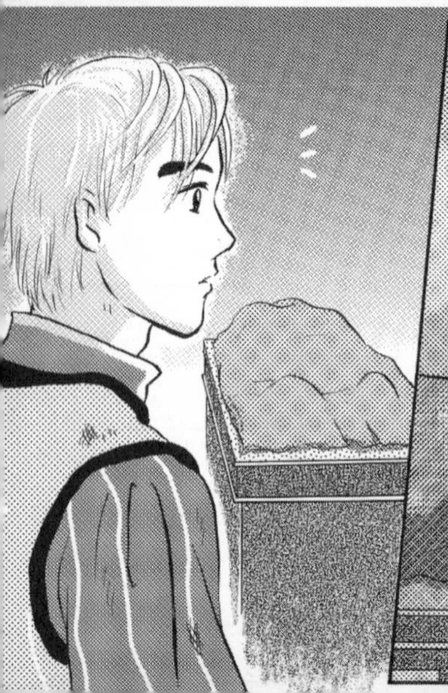

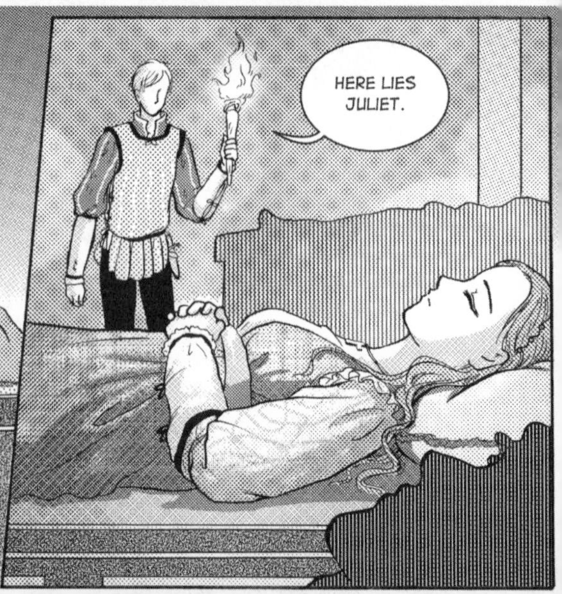
HERE LIES JULIET.

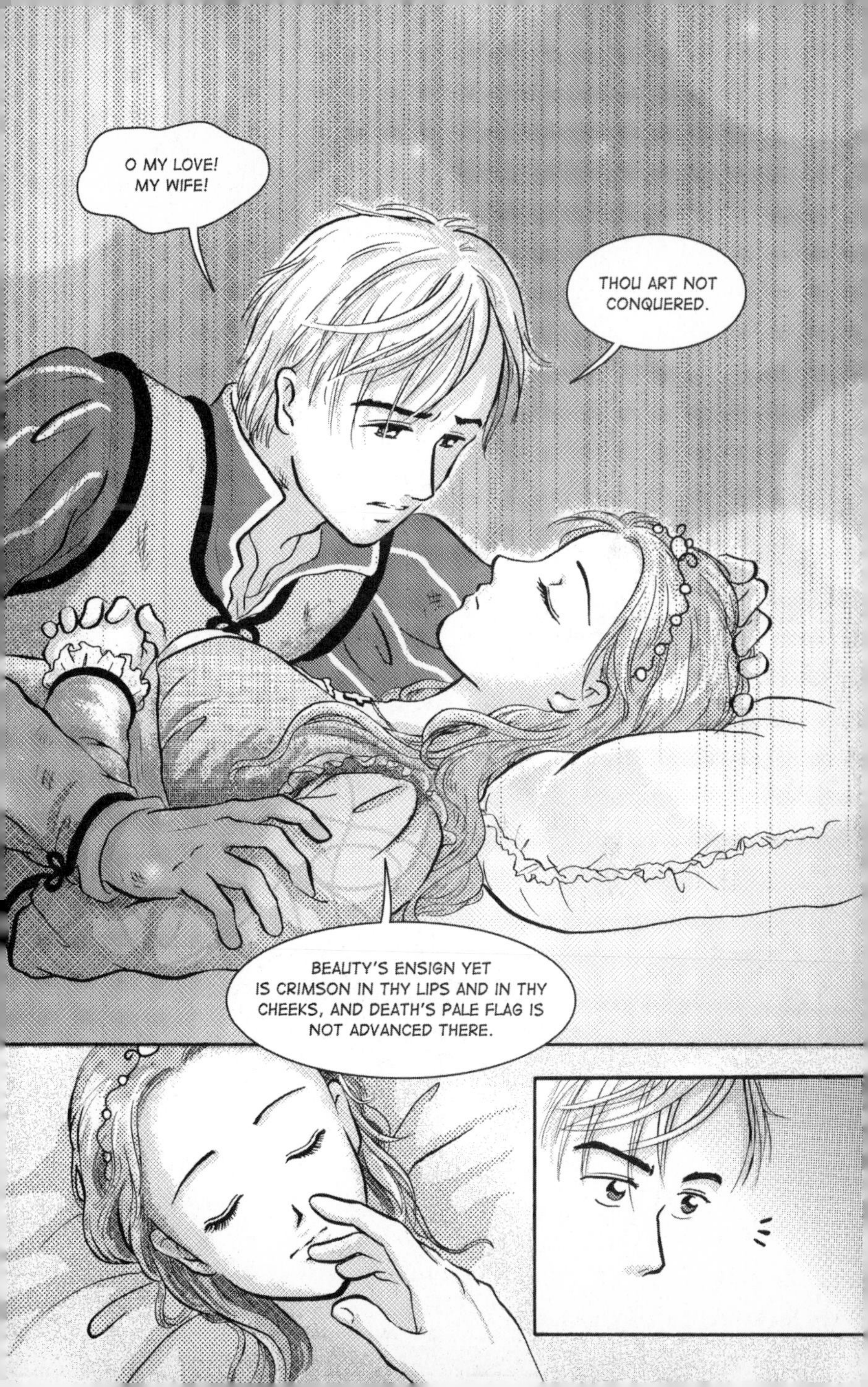
O MY LOVE! MY WIFE!
THOU ART NOT CONQUERED.
BEAUTY'S ENSIGN YET IS CRIMSON IN THY LIPS AND IN THY CHEEKS, AND DEATH'S PALE FLAG IS NOT ADVANCED THERE.

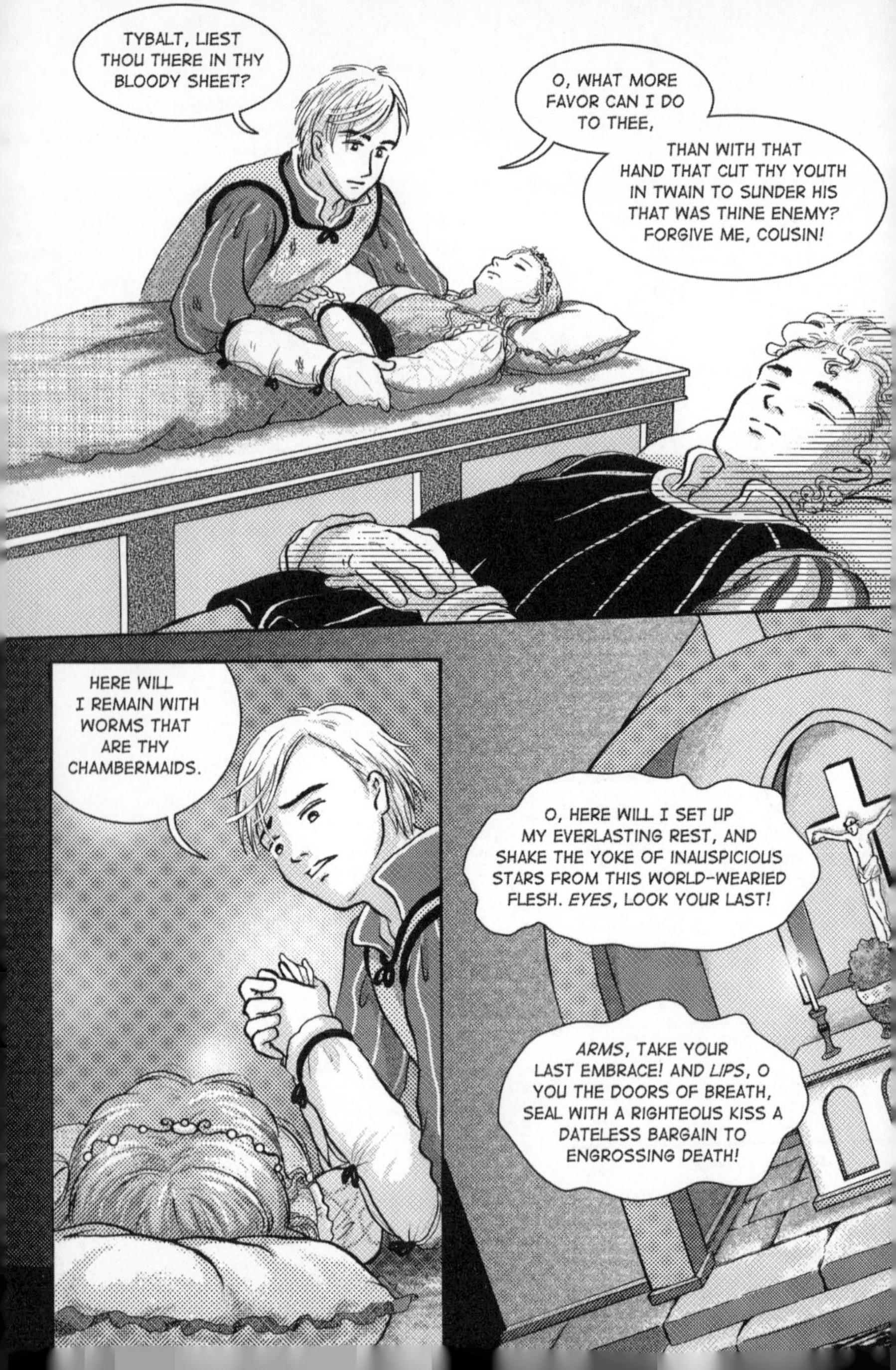
TYBALT, LIEST THOU THERE IN THY BLOODY SHEET?
O, WHAT MORE FAVOR CAN I DO TO THEE,
THAN WITH THAT HAND THAT CUT THY YOUTH IN TWAIN TO SUNDER HIS THAT WAS THINE ENEMY? FORGIVE ME, COUSIN!
HERE WILL I REMAIN WITH WORMS THAT ARE THY CHAMBERMAIDS.
O, HERE WILL I SET UP MY EVERLASTING REST, AND SHAKE THE YOKE OF INAUSPICIOUS STARS FROM THIS WORLD-WEARIED FLESH. *EYES*, LOOK YOUR LAST!
ARMS, TAKE YOUR LAST EMBRACE! AND *LIPS*, O YOU THE DOORS OF BREATH, SEAL WITH A RIGHTEOUS KISS A DATELESS BARGAIN TO ENGROSSING DEATH!

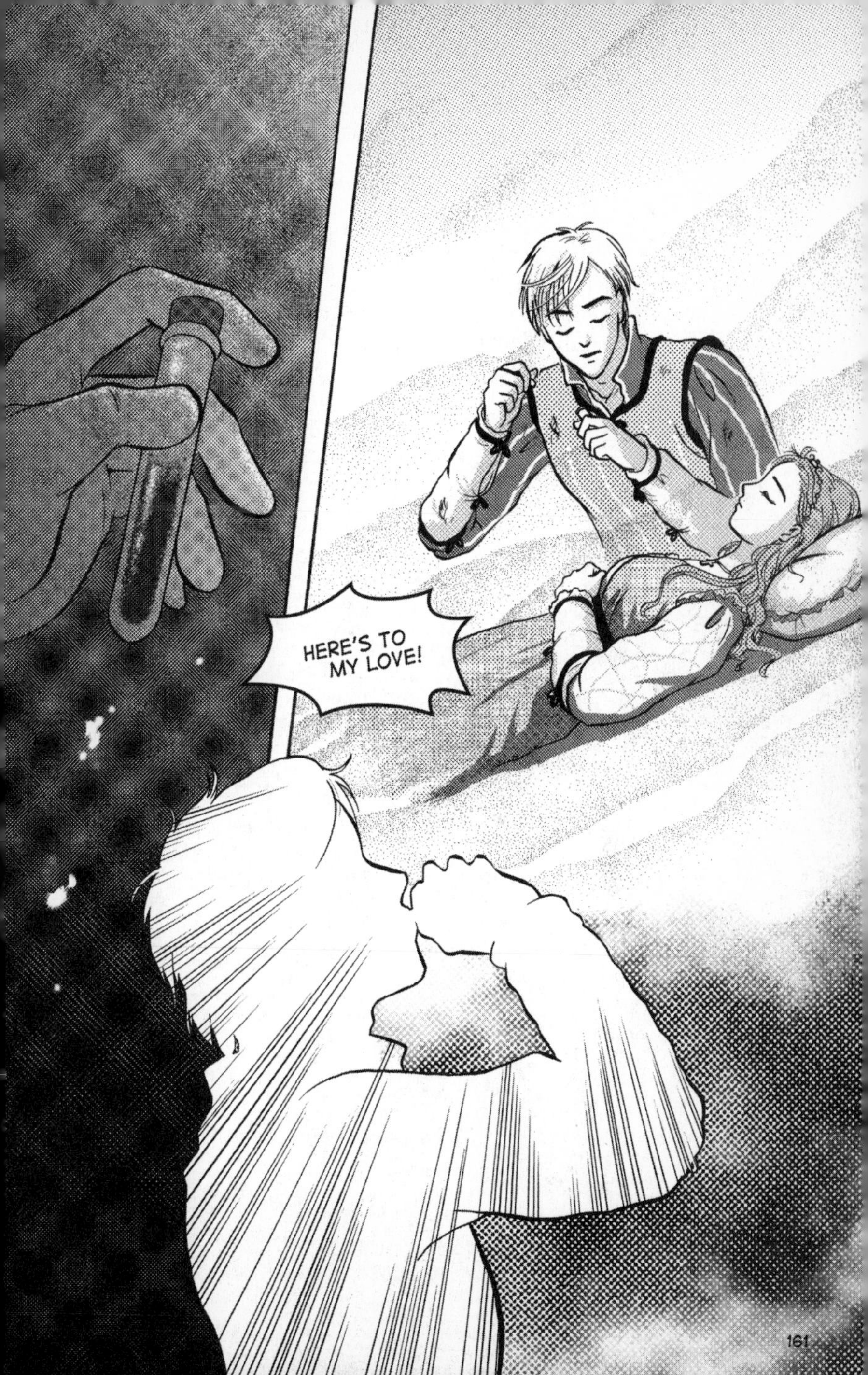
HERE'S TO MY LOVE!

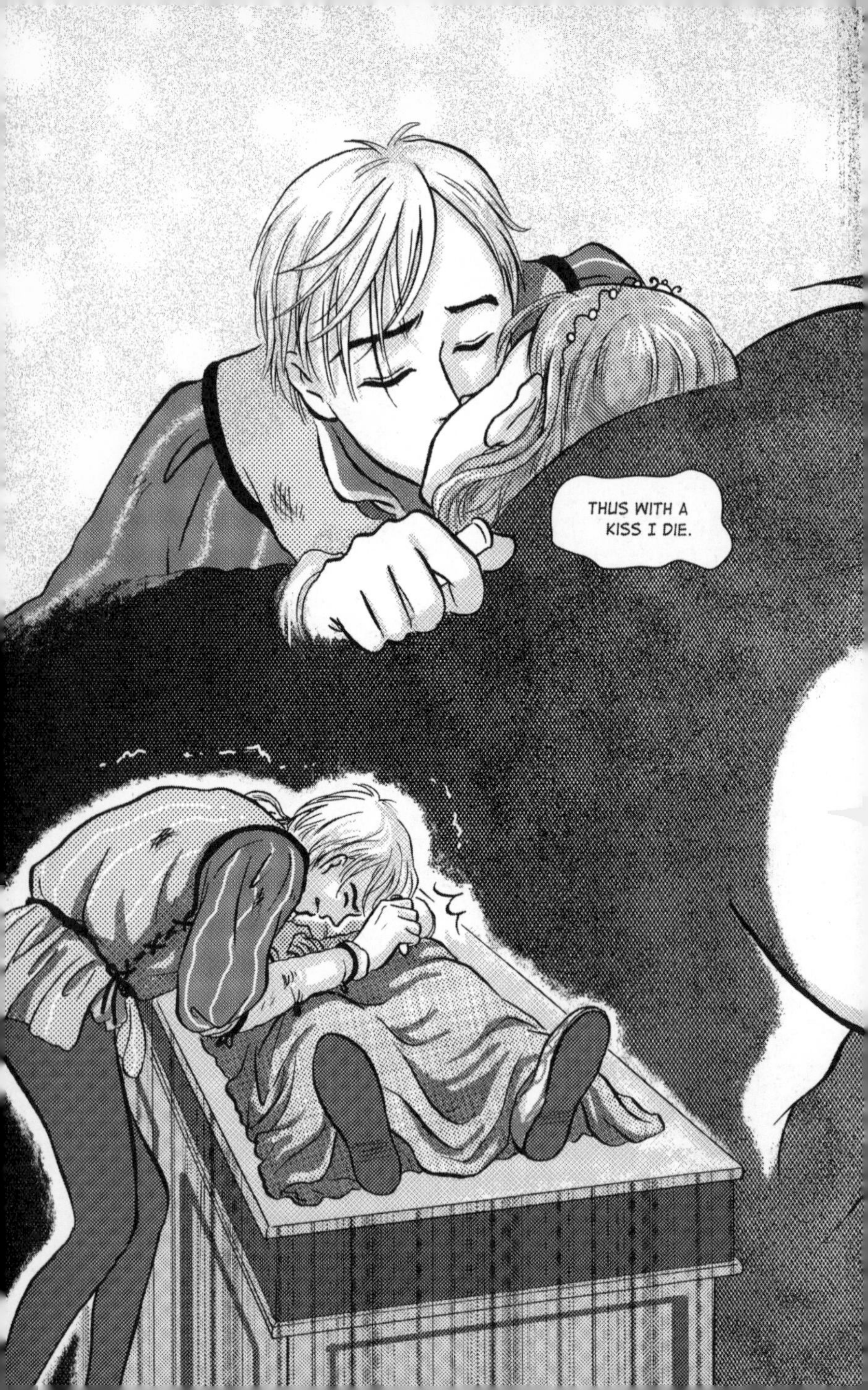
THUS WITH A KISS I DIE.

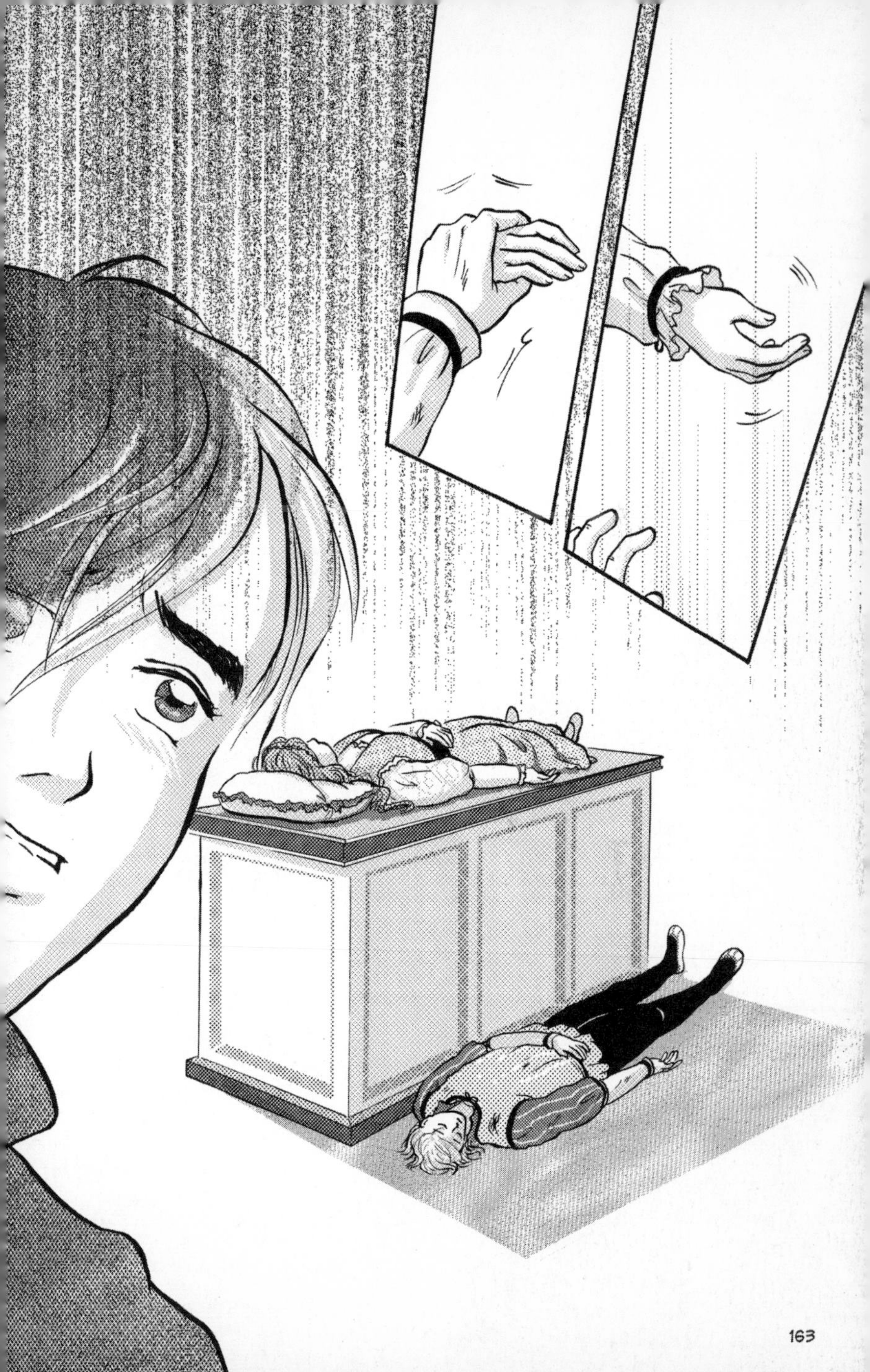

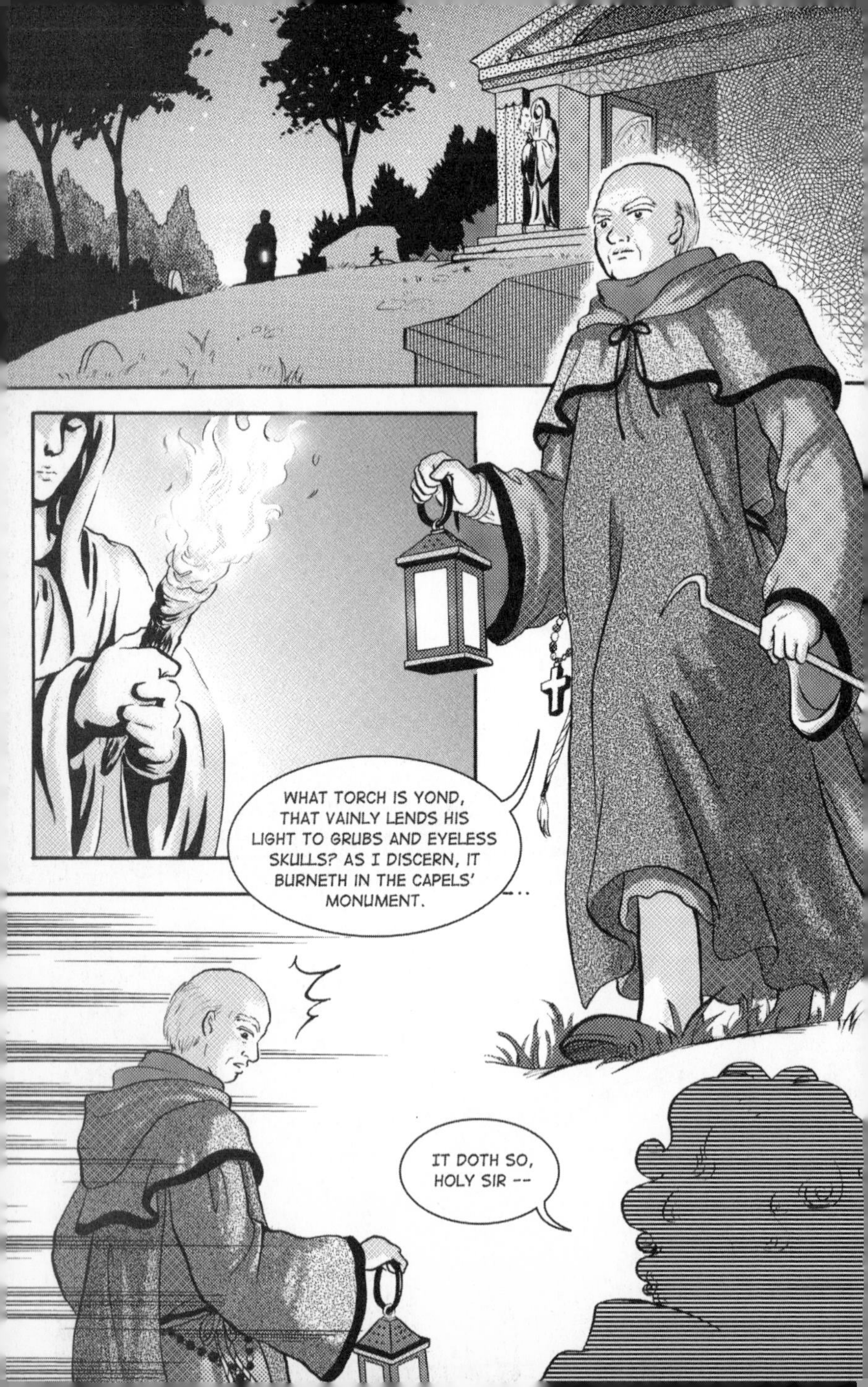
WHAT TORCH IS YOND, THAT VAINLY LENDS HIS LIGHT TO GRUBS AND EYELESS SKULLS? AS I DISCERN, IT BURNETH IN THE CAPELS' MONUMENT.
IT DOTH SO, HOLY SIR --

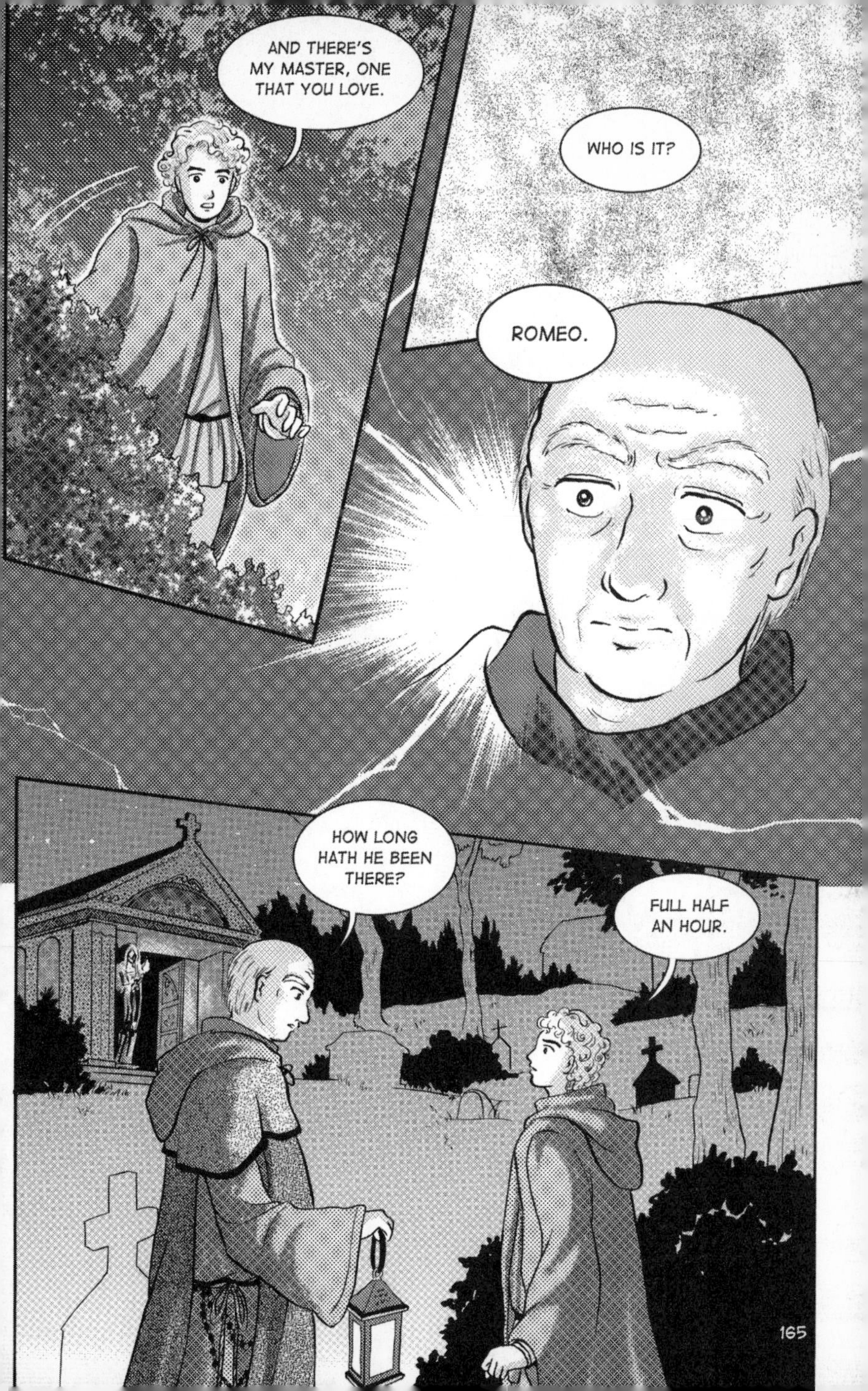
AND THERE'S MY MASTER, ONE THAT YOU LOVE.
WHO IS IT?
ROMEO.
HOW LONG HATH HE BEEN THERE?
FULL HALF AN HOUR.

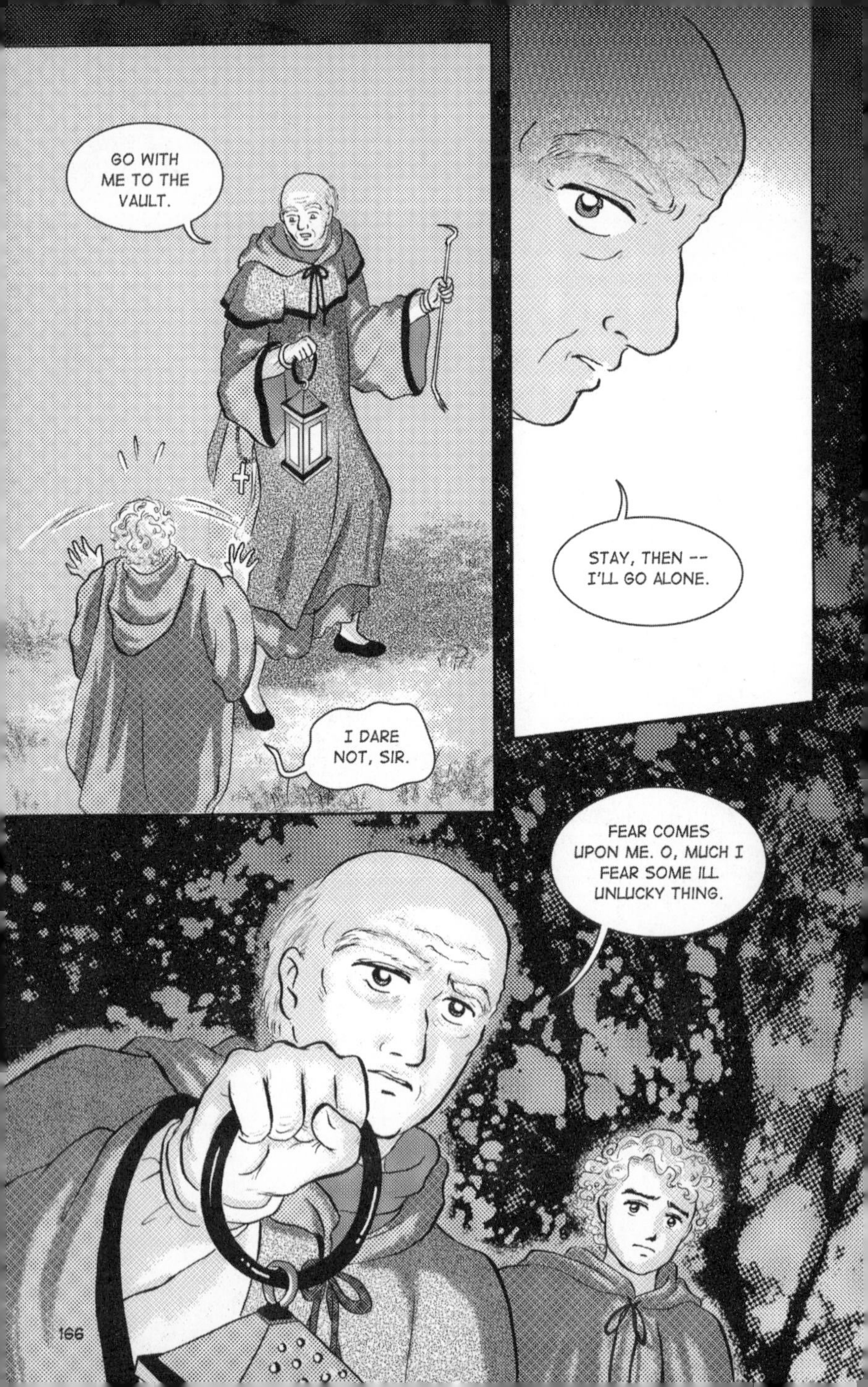
GO WITH ME TO THE VAULT.
STAY, THEN -- I'LL GO ALONE.
I DARE NOT, SIR.
FEAR COMES UPON ME. O, MUCH I FEAR SOME ILL UNLUCKY THING.

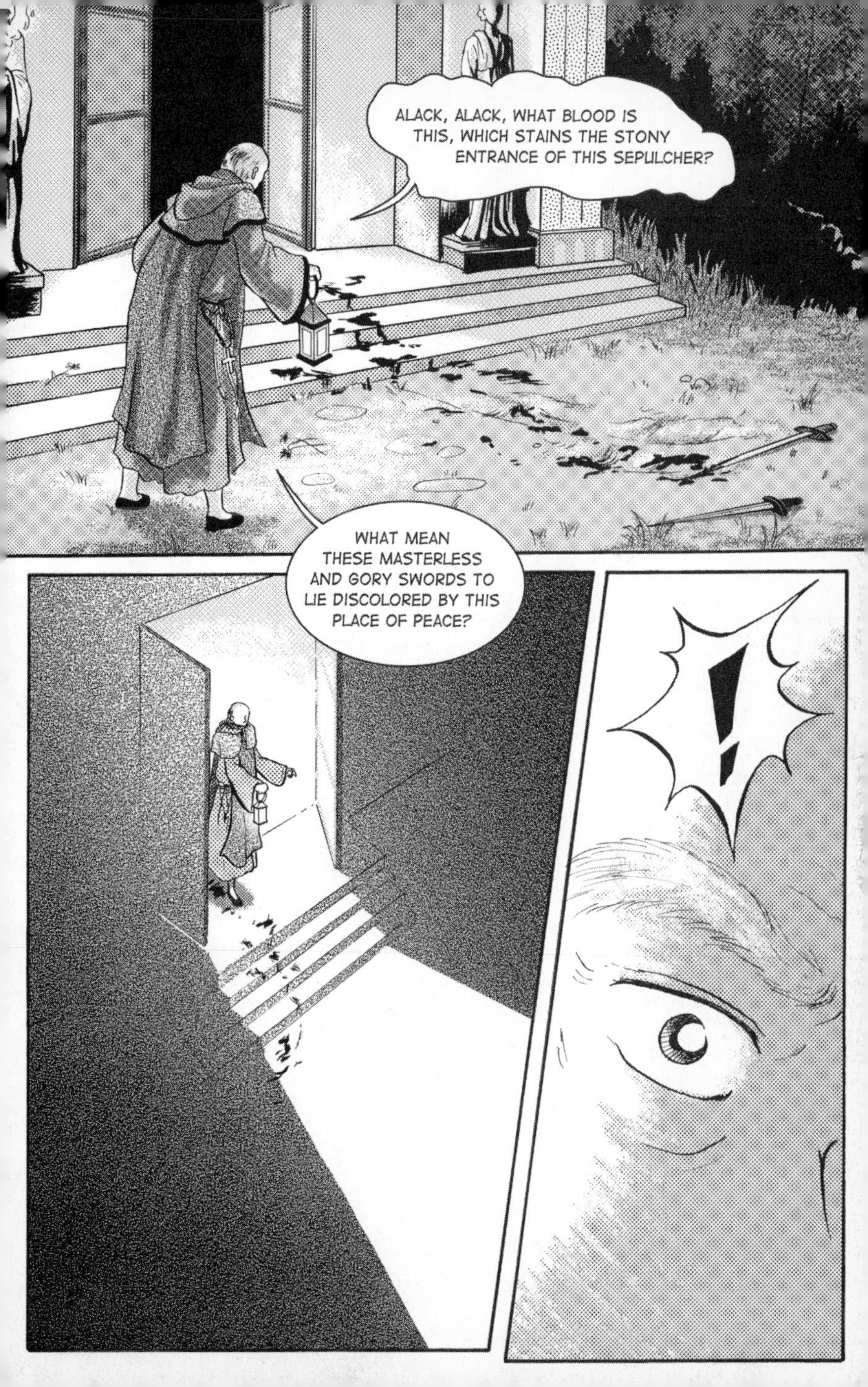
ALACK, ALACK, WHAT BLOOD IS THIS, WHICH STAINS THE STONY ENTRANCE OF THIS SEPULCHER?
WHAT MEAN THESE MASTERLESS AND GORY SWORDS TO LIE DISCOLORED BY THIS PLACE OF PEACE?
!

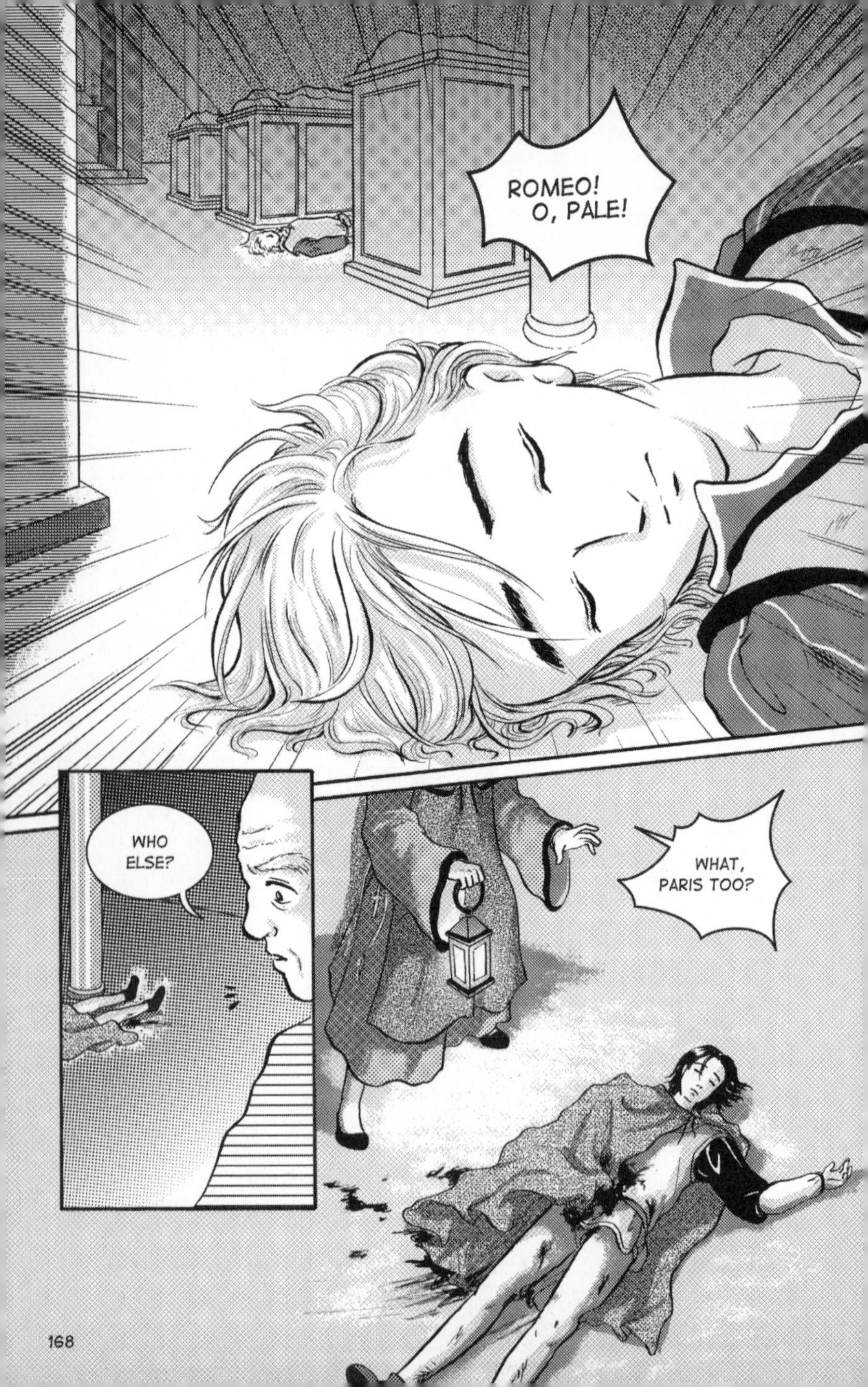
ROMEO! O, PALE!
WHO ELSE?
WHAT, PARIS TOO?

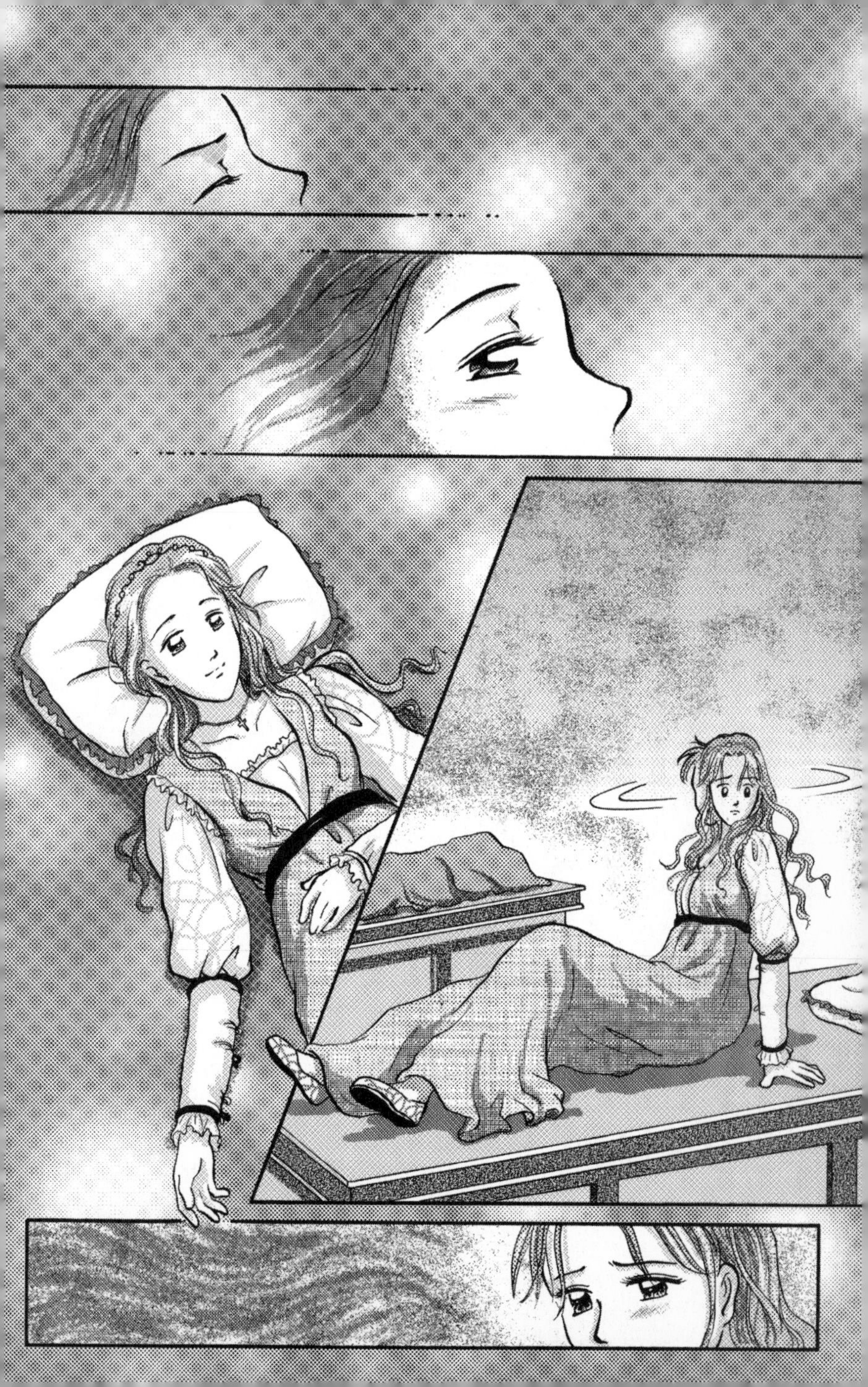

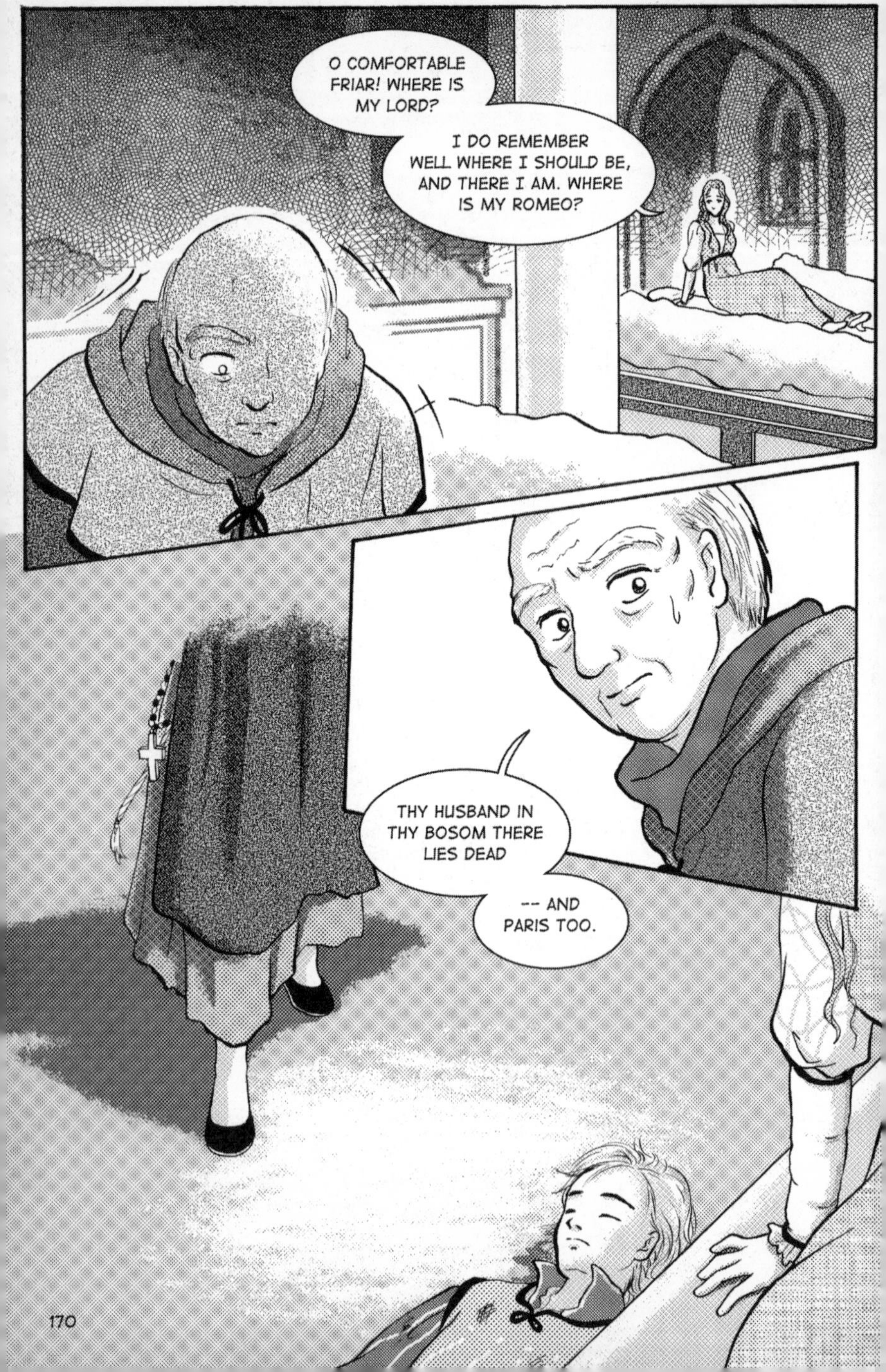
O COMFORTABLE FRIAR! WHERE IS MY LORD?
I DO REMEMBER WELL WHERE I SHOULD BE, AND THERE I AM. WHERE IS MY ROMEO?
THY HUSBAND IN THY BOSOM THERE LIES DEAD
-- AND PARIS TOO.

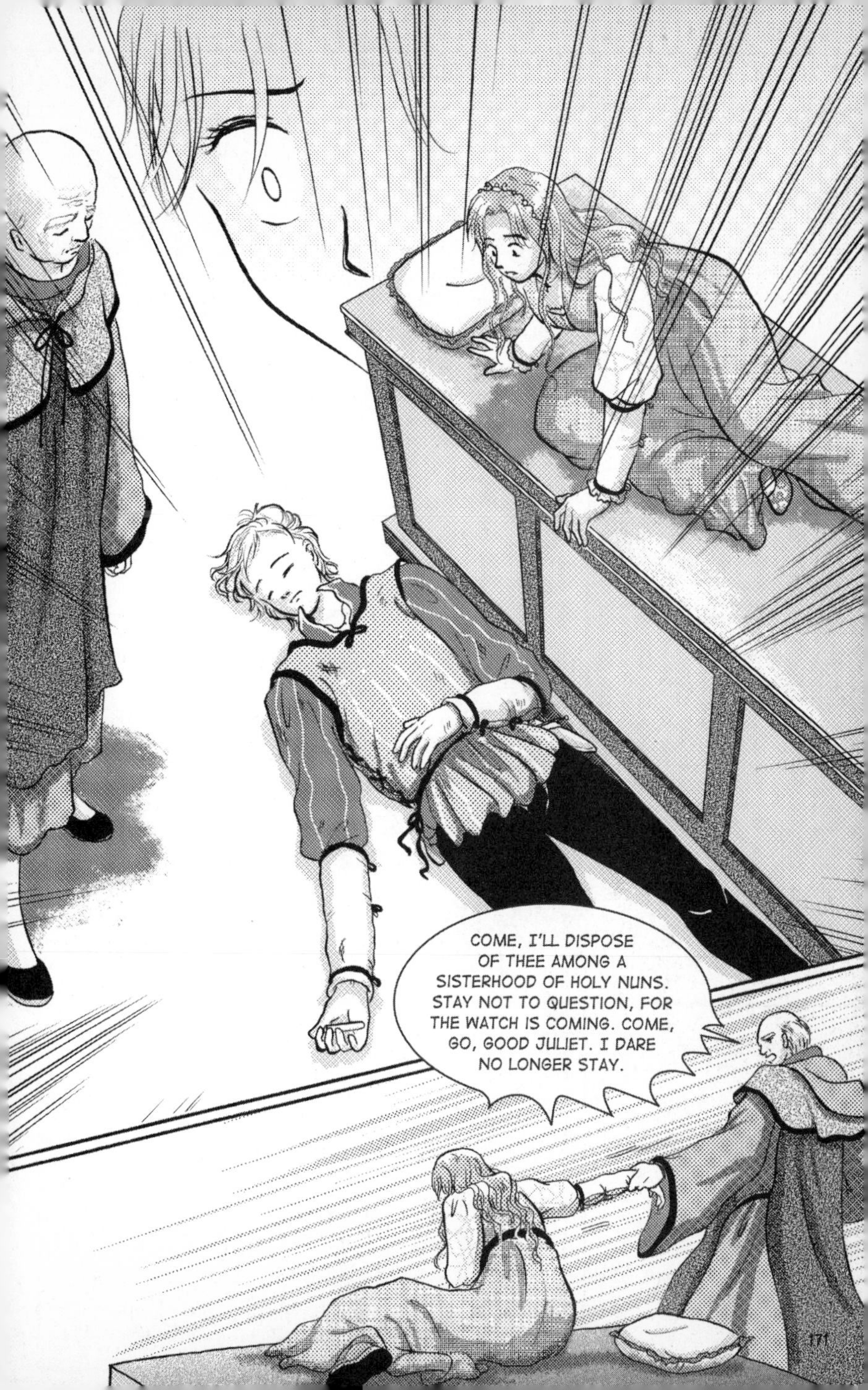
COME, I'LL DISPOSE OF THEE AMONG A SISTERHOOD OF HOLY NUNS. STAY NOT TO QUESTION, FOR THE WATCH IS COMING. COME, GO, GOOD JULIET. I DARE NO LONGER STAY.

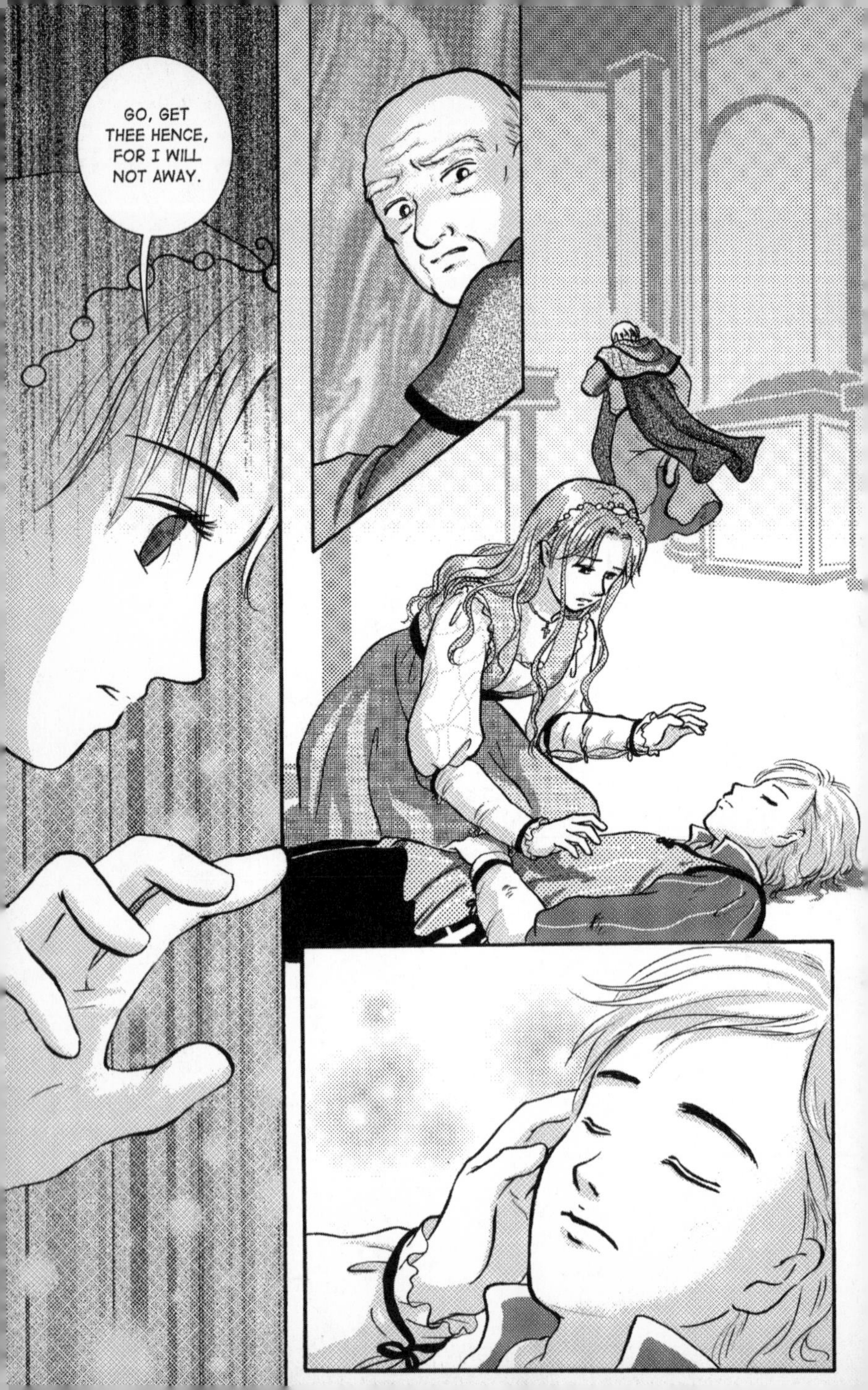
GO, GET THEE HENCE, FOR I WILL NOT AWAY.

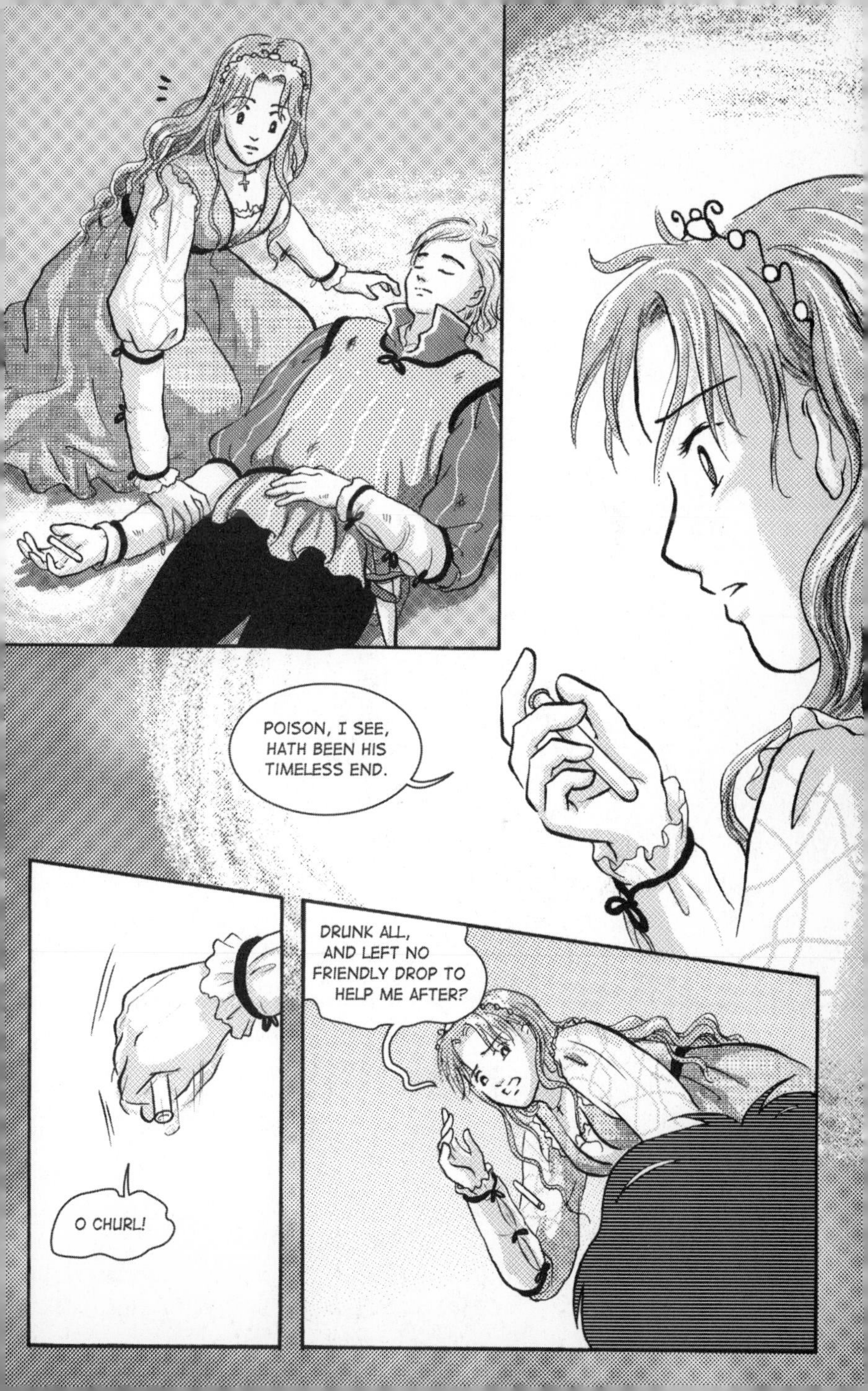
POISON, I SEE, HATH BEEN HIS TIMELESS END.
O CHURL!
DRUNK ALL, AND LEFT NO FRIENDLY DROP TO HELP ME AFTER?

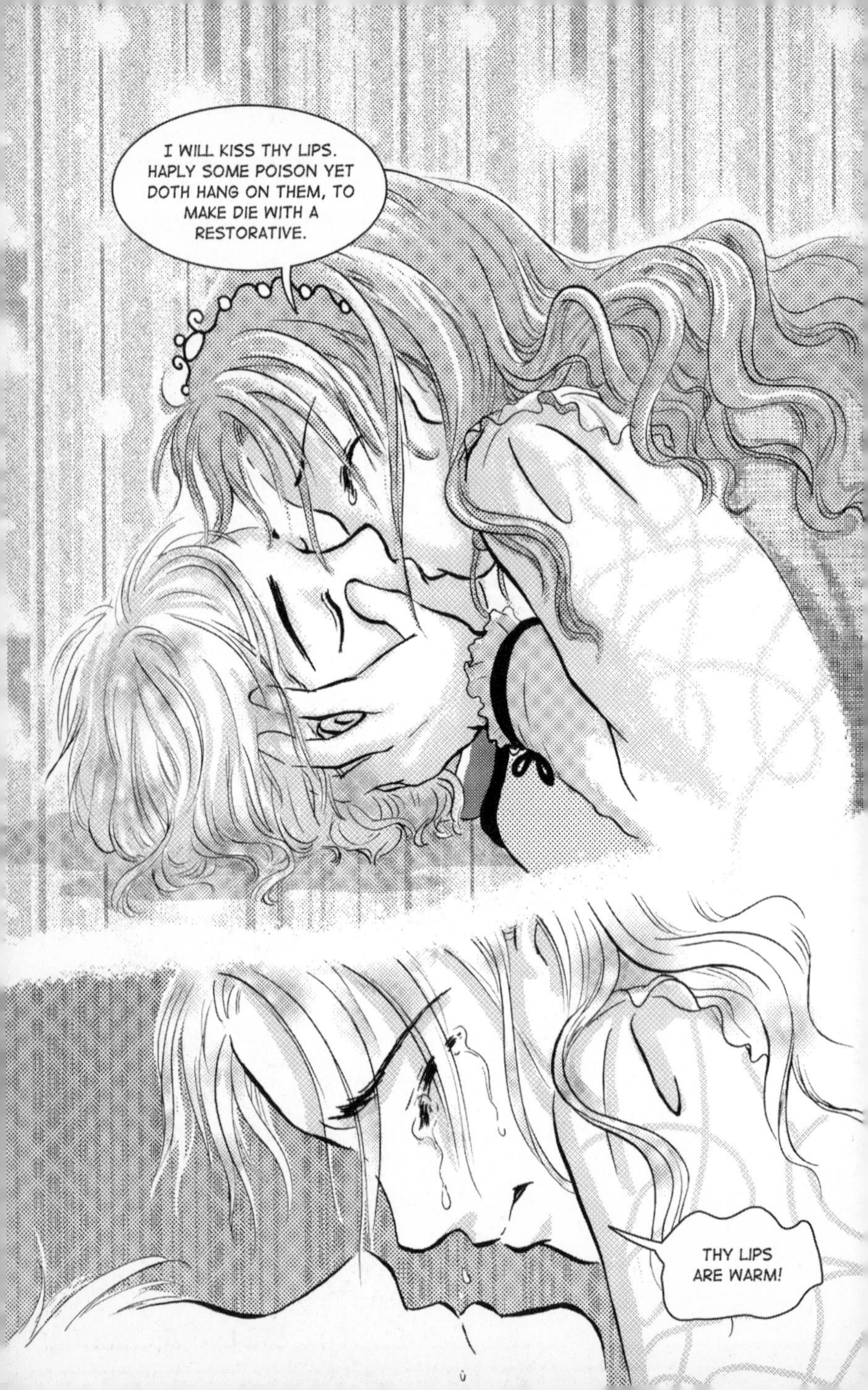
I WILL KISS THY LIPS. HAPLY SOME POISON YET DOTH HANG ON THEM, TO MAKE DIE WITH A RESTORATIVE.
THY LIPS ARE WARM!

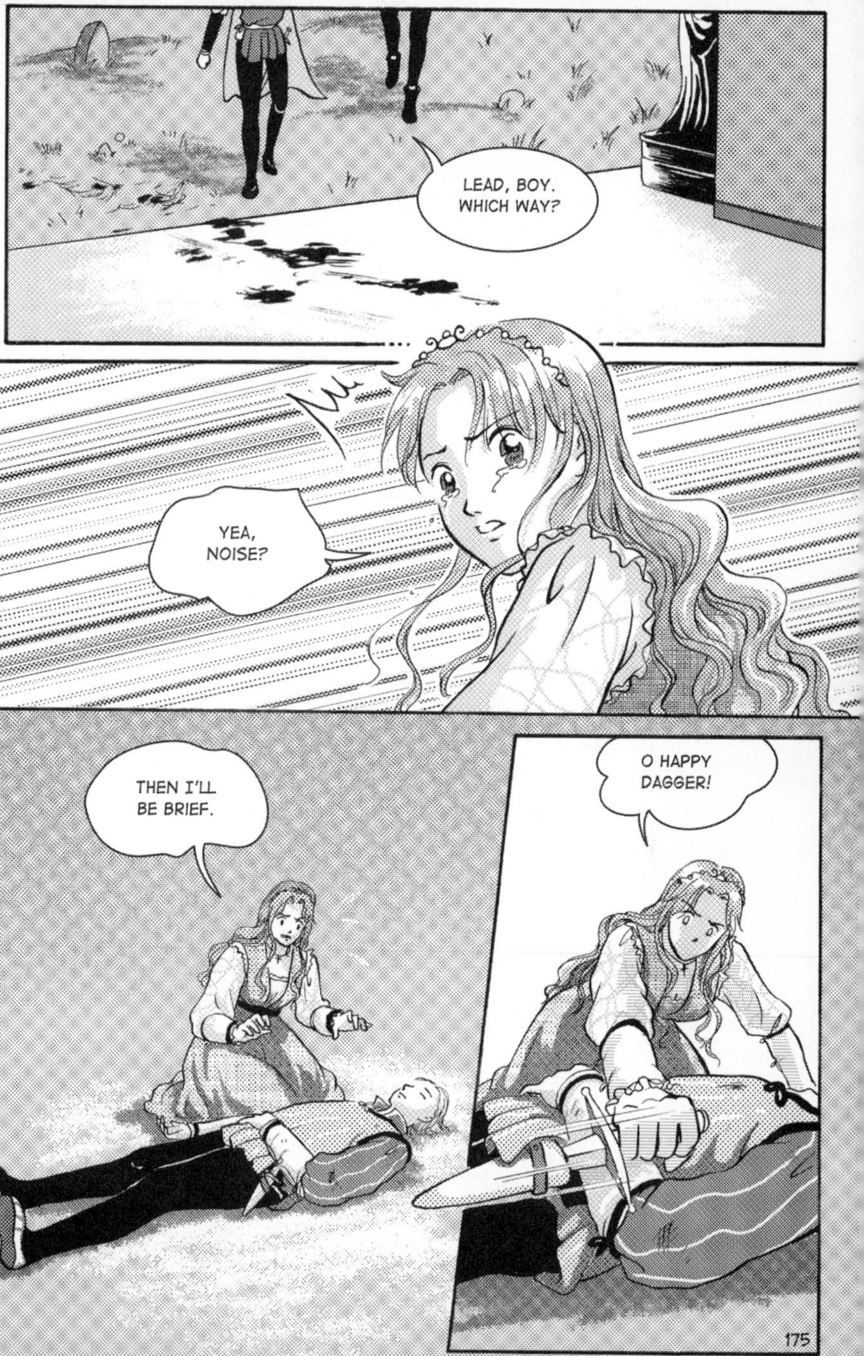
LEAD, BOY. WHICH WAY?
...
YEA, NOISE?
THEN I'LL BE BRIEF.
O HAPPY DAGGER!

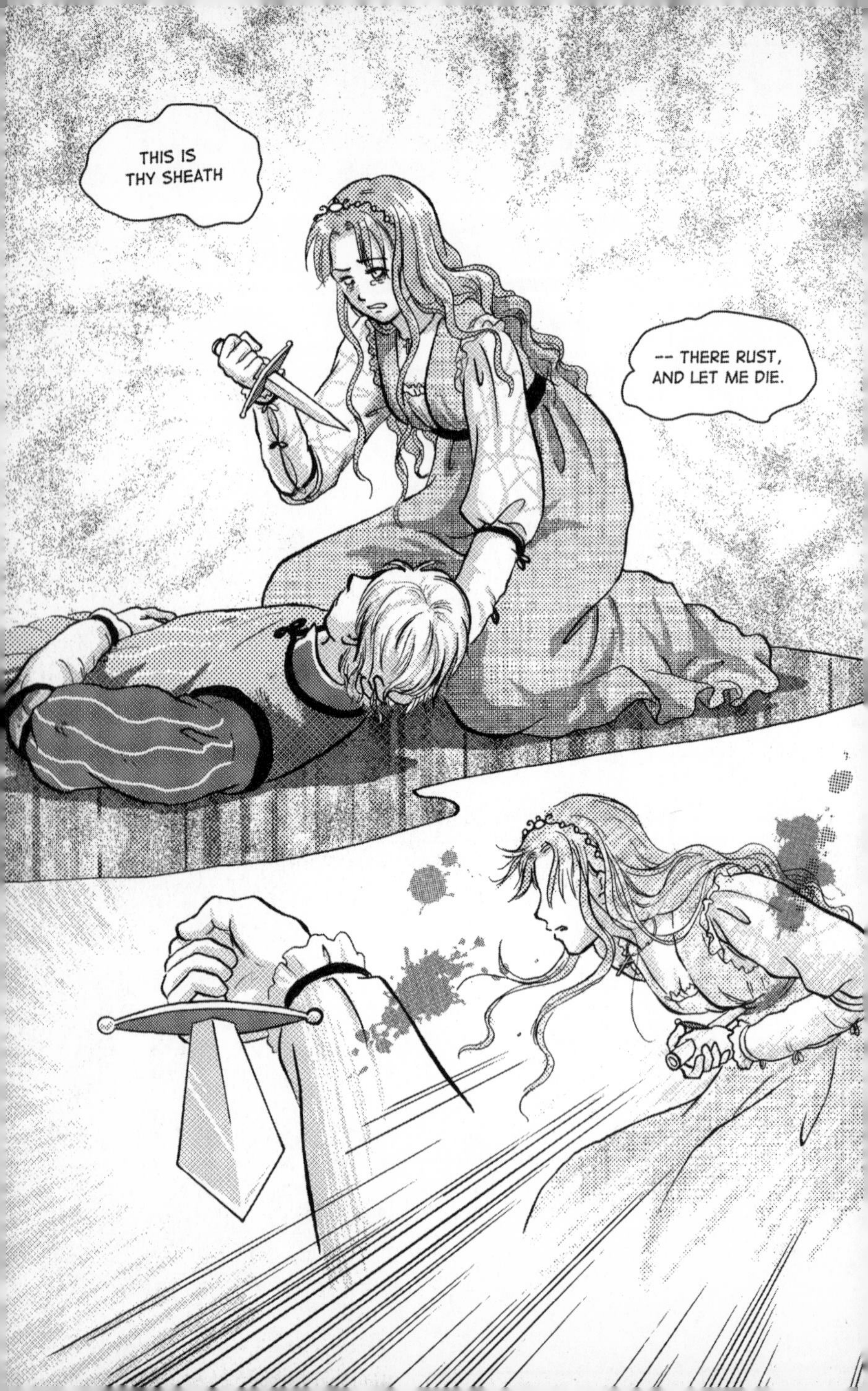
THIS IS THY SHEATH
-- THERE RUST, AND LET ME DIE.

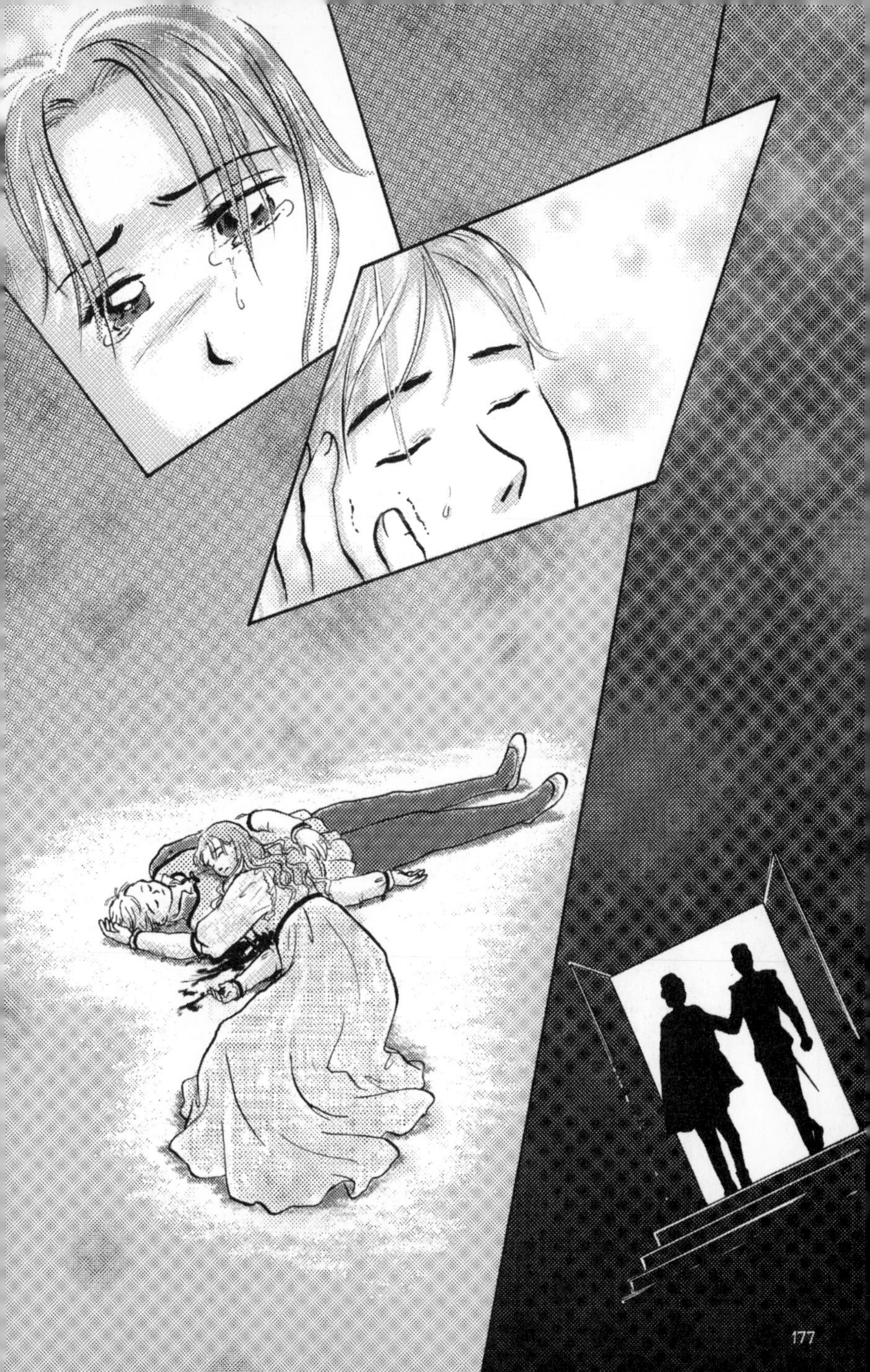

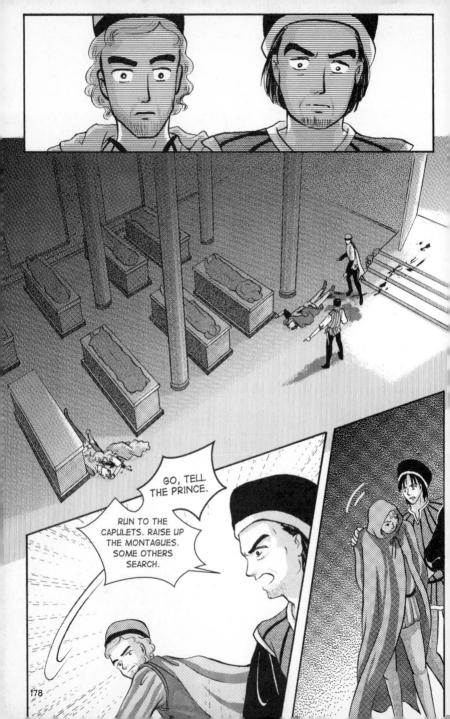

GO, TELL THE PRINCE.

RUN TO THE CAPULETS. RAISE UP THE MONTAGUES. SOME OTHERS SEARCH.

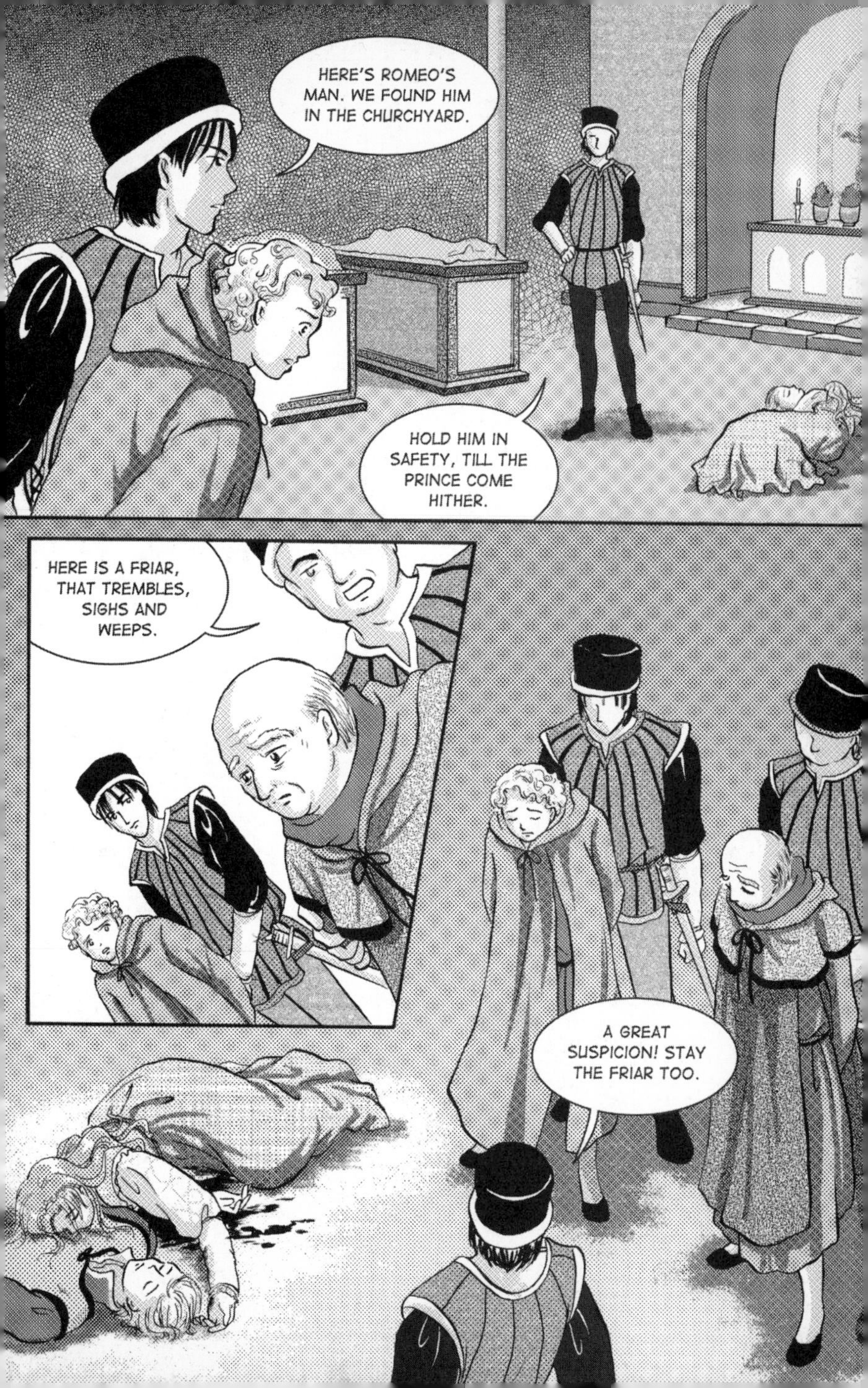
HERE'S ROMEO'S MAN. WE FOUND HIM IN THE CHURCHYARD.
HOLD HIM IN SAFETY, TILL THE PRINCE COME HITHER.
HERE IS A FRIAR, THAT TREMBLES, SIGHS AND WEEPS.
A GREAT SUSPICION! STAY THE FRIAR TOO.

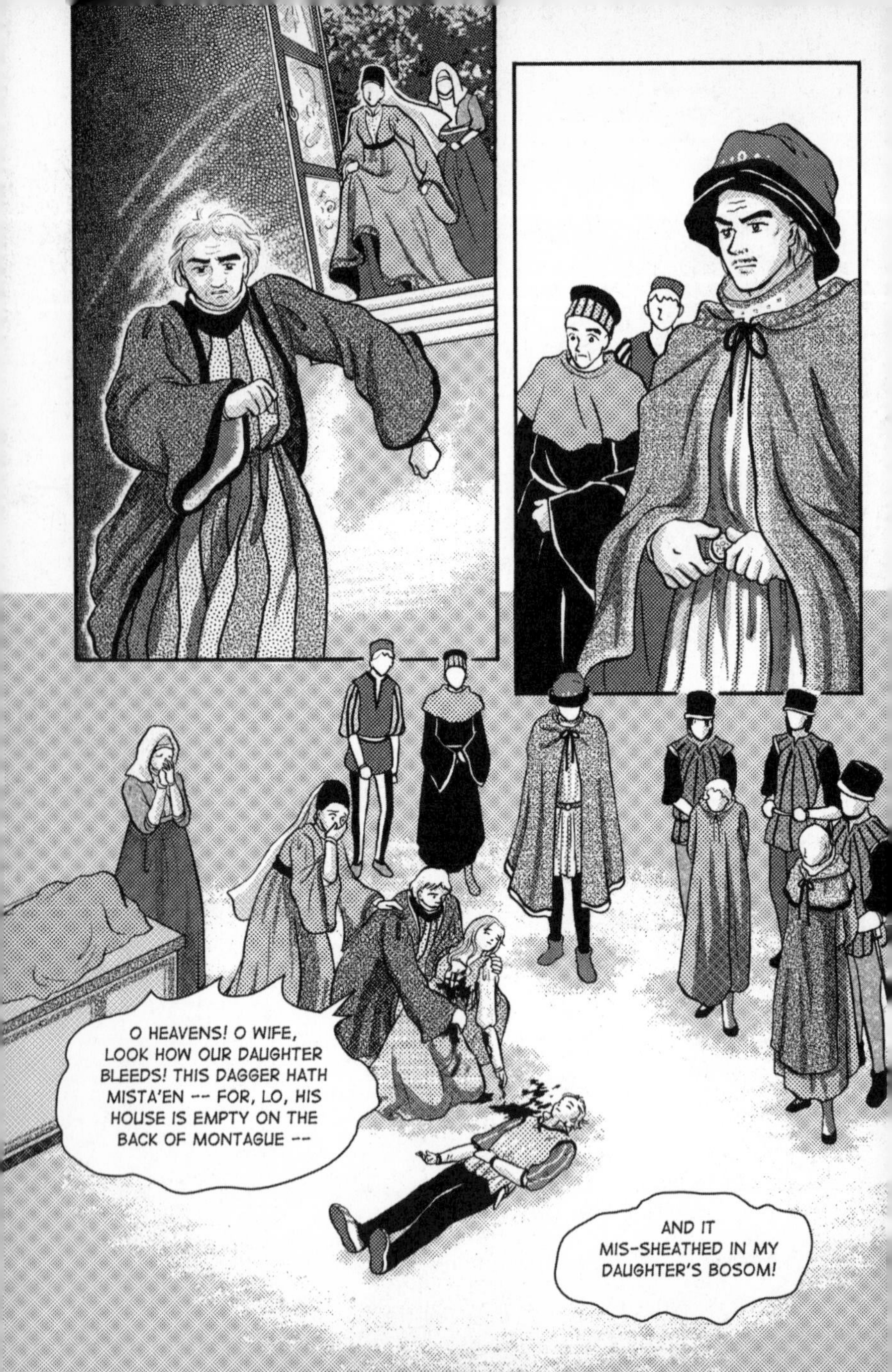
O HEAVENS! O WIFE, LOOK HOW OUR DAUGHTER BLEEDS! THIS DAGGER HATH MISTA'EN -- FOR, LO, HIS HOUSE IS EMPTY ON THE BACK OF MONTAGUE --
AND IT MIS-SHEATHED IN MY DAUGHTER'S BOSOM!

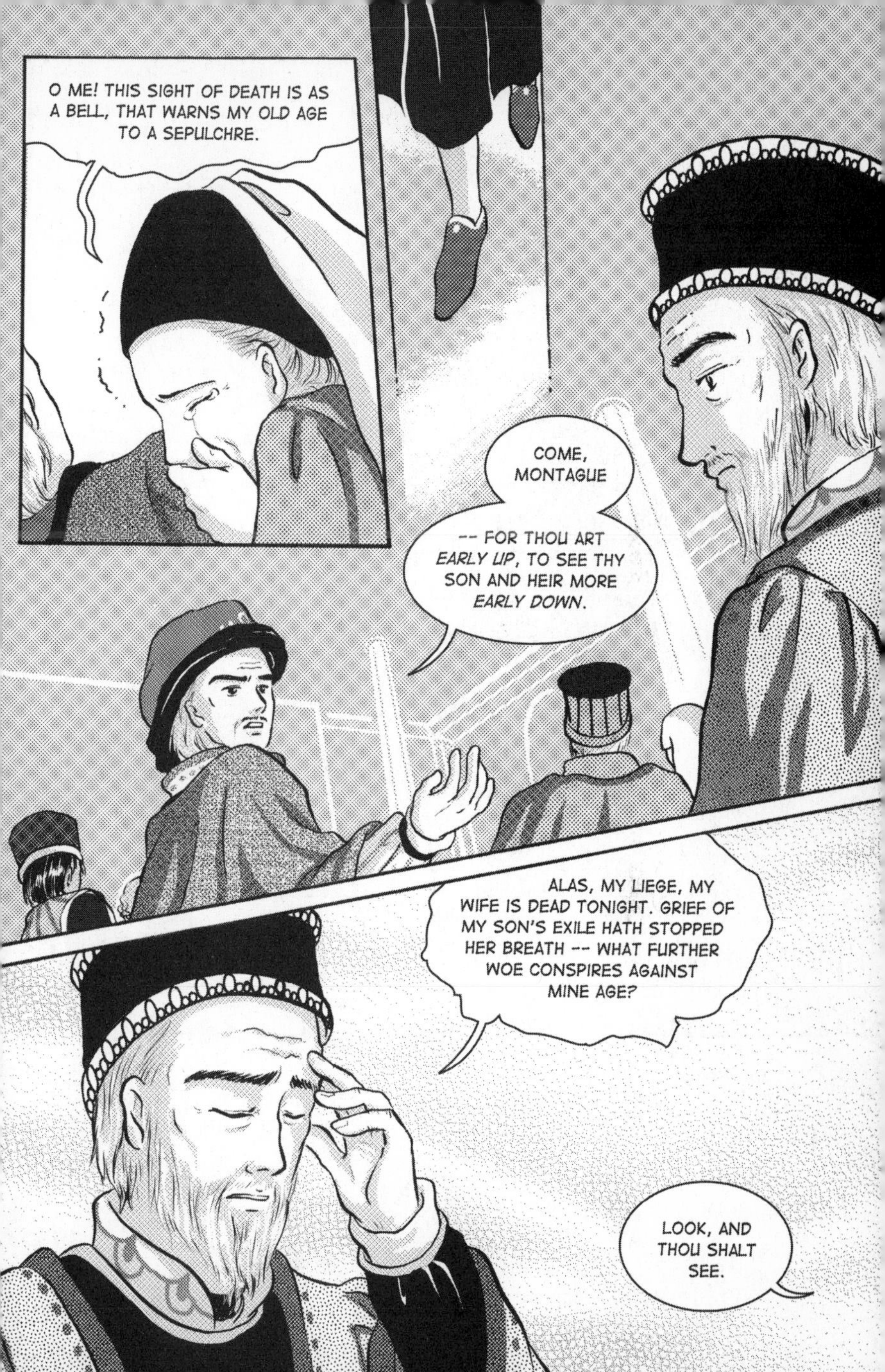
O ME! THIS SIGHT OF DEATH IS AS A BELL, THAT WARNS MY OLD AGE TO A SEPULCHRE.
COME, MONTAGUE
-- FOR THOU ART *EARLY UP*, TO SEE THY SON AND HEIR MORE *EARLY DOWN*.
ALAS, MY LIEGE, MY WIFE IS DEAD TONIGHT. GRIEF OF MY SON'S EXILE HATH STOPPED HER BREATH -- WHAT FURTHER WOE CONSPIRES AGAINST MINE AGE?
LOOK, AND THOU SHALT SEE.

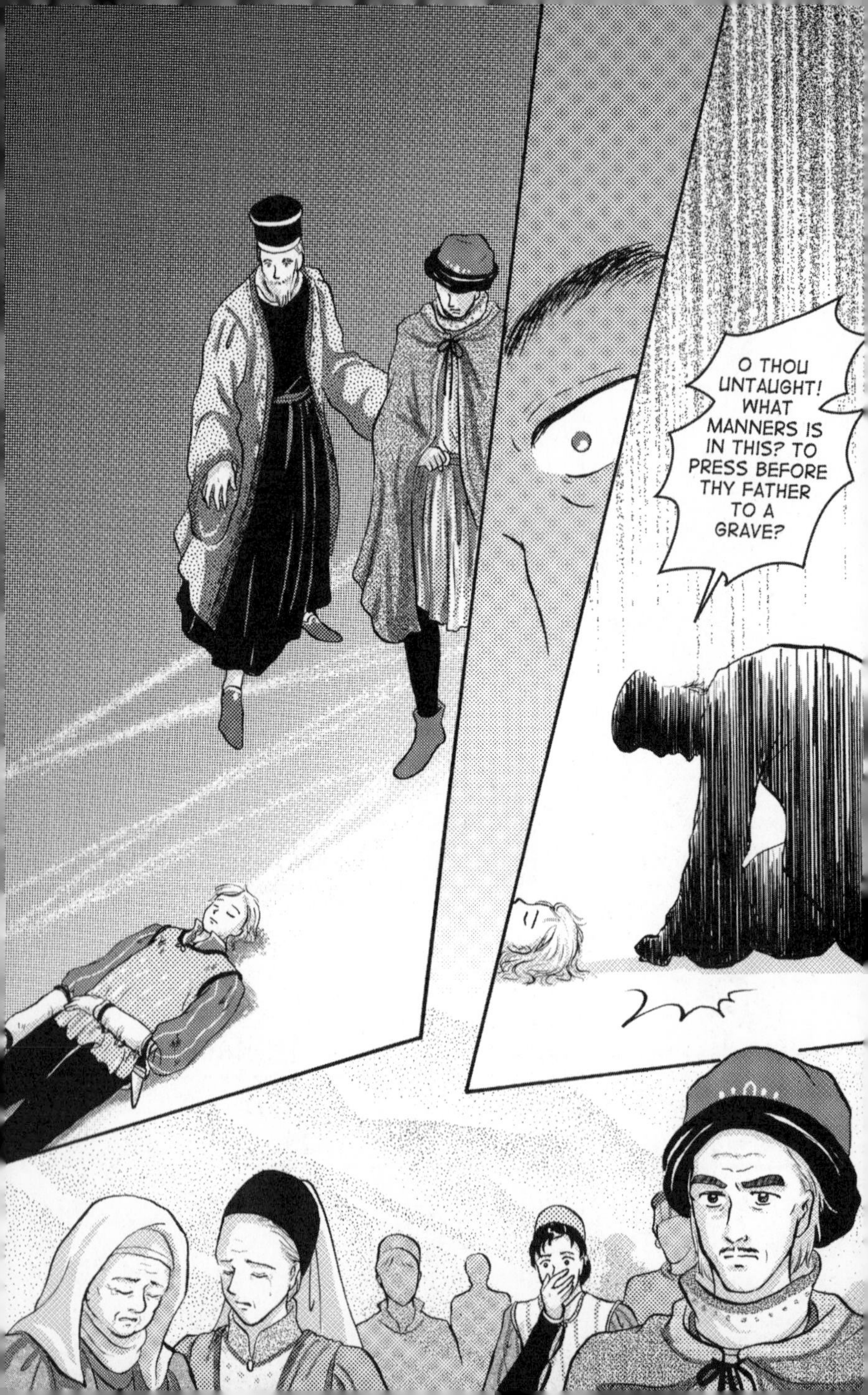
O THOU UNTAUGHT! WHAT MANNERS IS IN THIS? TO PRESS BEFORE THY FATHER TO A GRAVE?

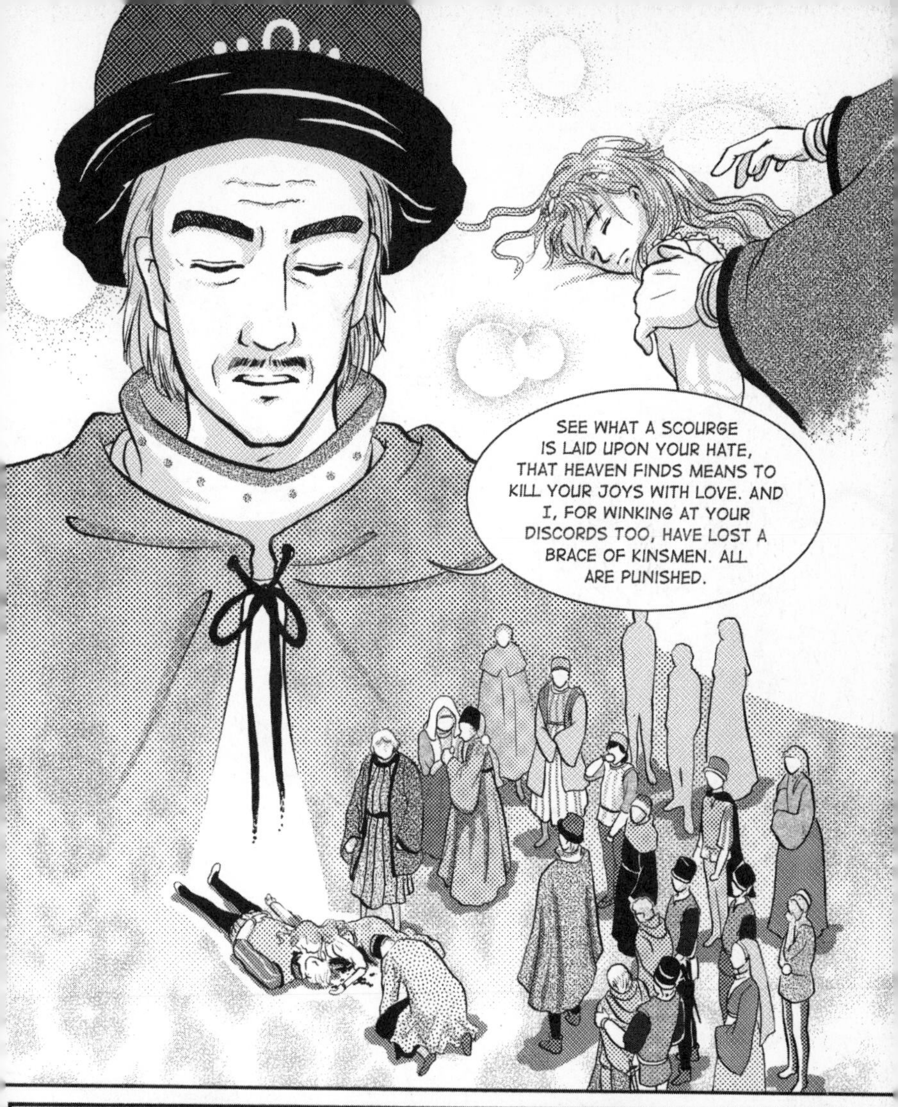
SEE WHAT A SCOURGE IS LAID UPON YOUR HATE, THAT HEAVEN FINDS MEANS TO KILL YOUR JOYS WITH LOVE. AND I, FOR WINKING AT YOUR DISCORDS TOO, HAVE LOST A BRACE OF KINSMEN. ALL ARE PUNISHED.

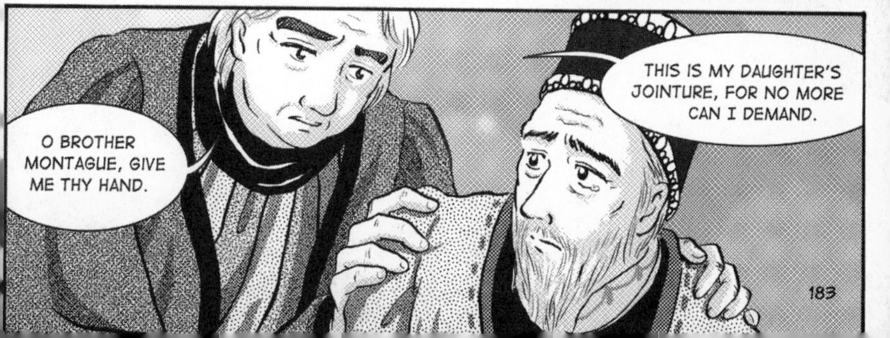
O BROTHER MONTAGUE, GIVE ME THY HAND.
THIS IS MY DAUGHTER'S JOINTURE, FOR NO MORE CAN I DEMAND.

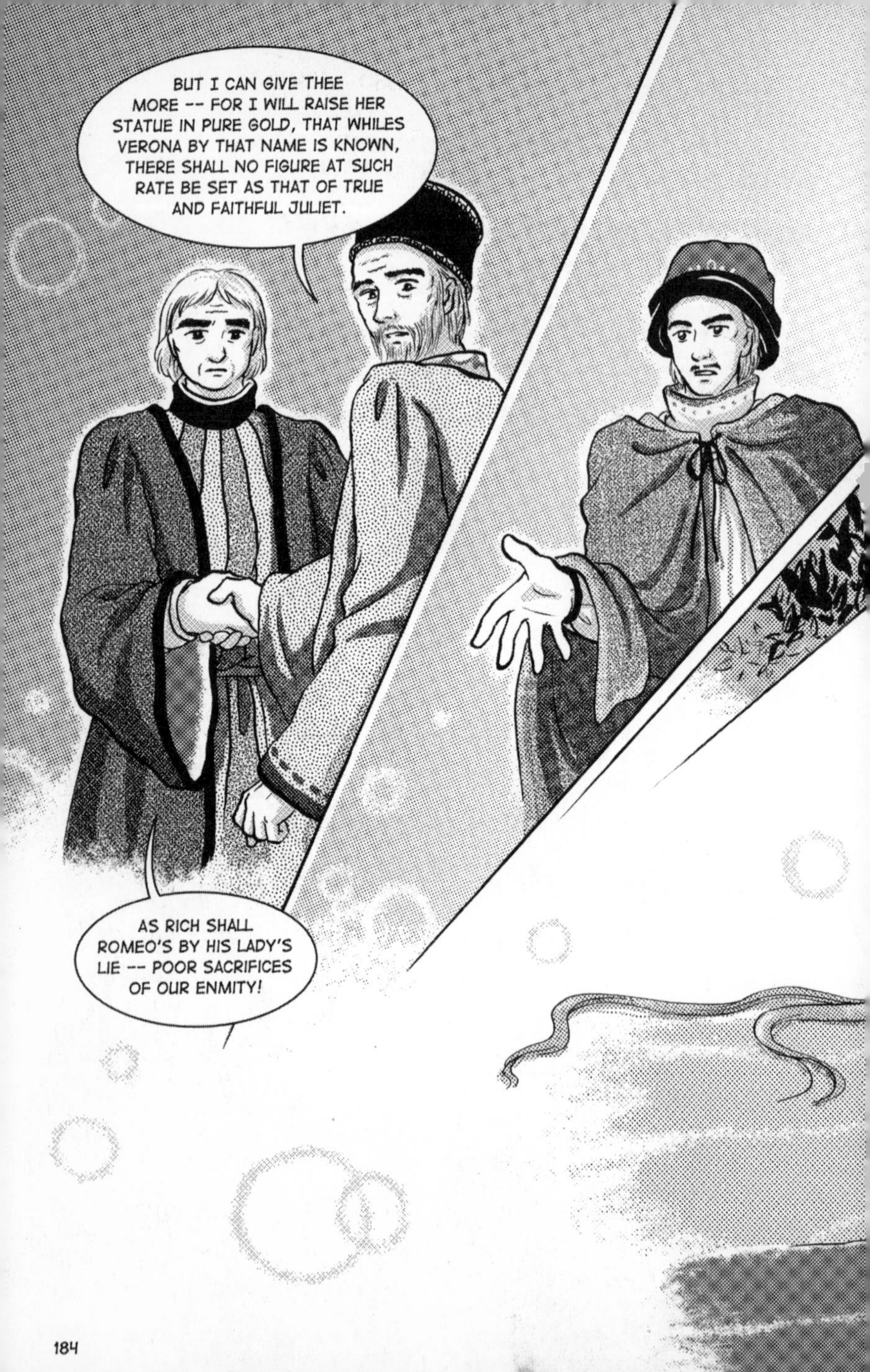
BUT I CAN GIVE THEE MORE -- FOR I WILL RAISE HER STATUE IN PURE GOLD, THAT WHILES VERONA BY THAT NAME IS KNOWN, THERE SHALL NO FIGURE AT SUCH RATE BE SET AS THAT OF TRUE AND FAITHFUL JULIET.
AS RICH SHALL ROMEO'S BY HIS LADY'S LIE -- POOR SACRIFICES OF OUR ENMITY!

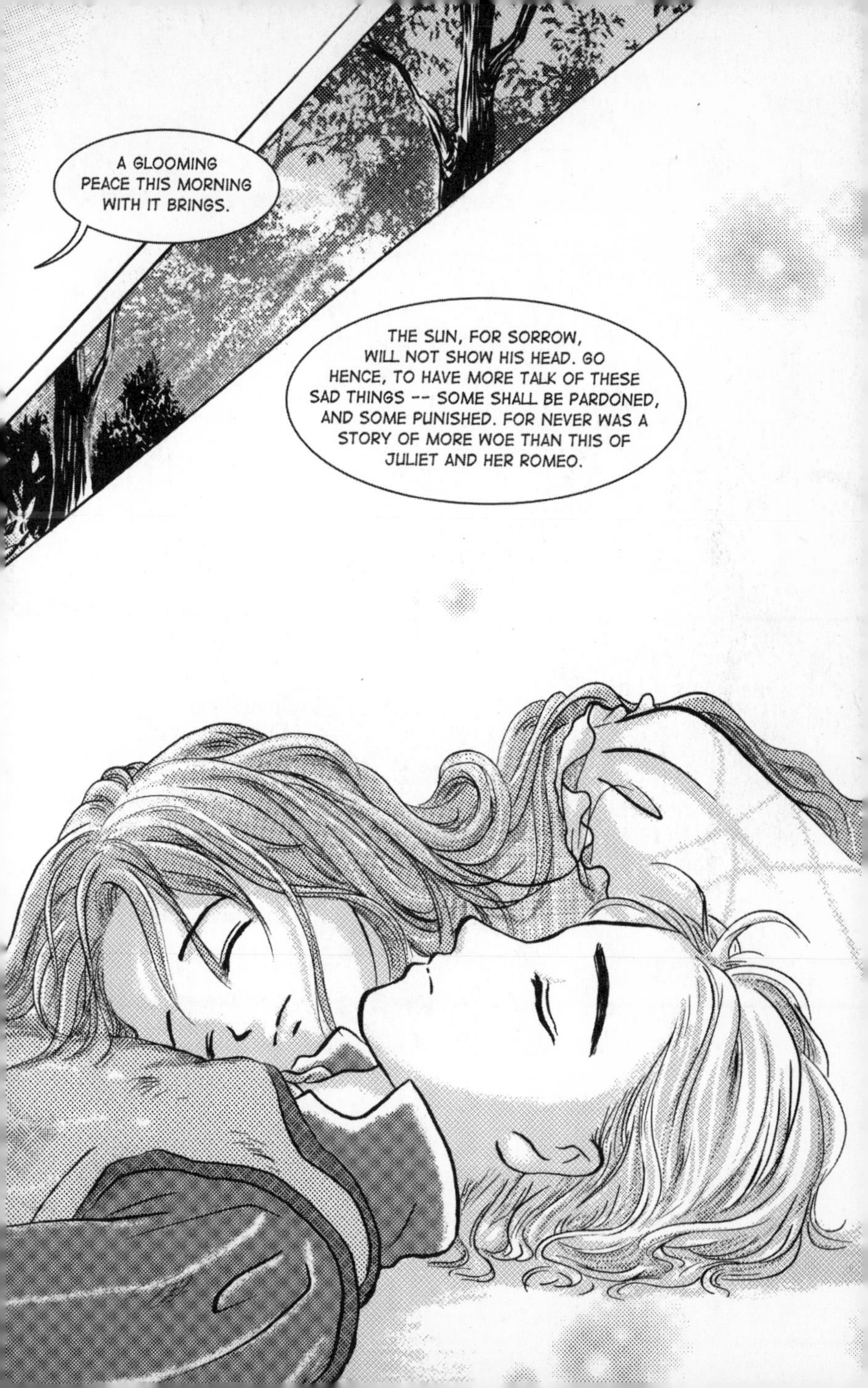
A GLOOMING PEACE THIS MORNING WITH IT BRINGS.
THE SUN, FOR SORROW, WILL NOT SHOW HIS HEAD. GO HENCE, TO HAVE MORE TALK OF THESE SAD THINGS -- SOME SHALL BE PARDONED, AND SOME PUNISHED. FOR NEVER WAS A STORY OF MORE WOE THAN THIS OF JULIET AND HER ROMEO.

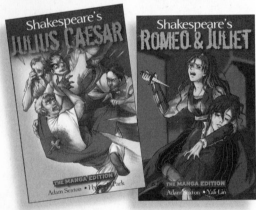